WATCH ME PLAY

PRINCETON STUDIES IN
CULTURE AND TECHNOLOGY

Princeton Studies in Culture and Technology

Tom Boellstorff and Bill Maurer, series editors

This series presents innovative work that extends classic ethnographic methods and questions into areas of pressing interest in technology and economics. It explores the varied ways new technologies combine with older technologies and cultural understandings to shape novel forms of subjectivity, embodiment, knowledge, place, and community. By doing so, the series demonstrates the relevance of anthropological inquiry to emerging forms of digital culture in the broadest sense.

Sounding the Limits of Life: Essays in the Anthropology of Biology and Beyond by Stefan Helmreich with contributions from Sophia Roosth and Michele Friedner

Digital Keywords: A Vocabulary of Information Society and Culture edited by Benjamin Peters

Democracy's Infrastructure: Techno-Politics and Protest after Apartheid by Antina von Schnitzler

Everyday Sectarianism in Urban Lebanon: Infrastructures, Public Services, and Power by Joanne Randa Nucho

Disruptive Fixation: School Reform and the Pitfalls of Techno-Idealism by Christo Sims

Biomedical Odysseys: Fetal Cell Experiments from Cyberspace to China by Priscilla Song

Watch Me Play: Twitch and the Rise of Game Live Streaming by T. L. Taylor

Watch Me Play

Twitch and the Rise of Game Live Streaming

T. L. Taylor

PRINCETON UNIVERSITY PRESS
PRINCETON AND OXFORD

Copyright © 2018 by Princeton University Press

Published by Princeton University Press
41 William Street, Princeton, New Jersey 08540
6 Oxford Street, Woodstock, Oxfordshire OX20 1TR

press.princeton.edu

All Rights Reserved

LCCN 2018946247
ISBN 978-0-691-16596-7
ISBN (pbk) 978-0-691-18355-8

British Library Cataloging-in-Publication Data is available

Editorial: Fred Appel and Thalia Leaf
Production Editorial: Natalie Baan
Jacket/Cover Design: Amanda Weiss
Production: Jacqueline Poirier
Publicity: Taylor Lord
Copyeditor: Cindy Milstein

This book has been composed in Adobe Text Pro and Gotham

Printed on acid-free paper. ∞

Printed in the United States of America

10 9 8 7 6 5 4 3 2 1

For Pop, through whom I found my love of television

CONTENTS

ACKNOWLEDGMENTS

Writing a book is, for me, a long process involving the curiosity and excitement of exploration during research followed by the tough marathon of synthesizing and externalizing years of work via writing. I am incredibly grateful to have had so many wonderful people to lean on during that cycle over the last six years of this project.

First and foremost, my profound thanks to the many folks working in live streaming who have been so generous with their time and insights. Your letting me interview you, shadow you at events, visit your homes, and examine this fascinating domain through your experiences has been irreplaceable. Special thanks to both Twitch and the Electronic Sports League, which were kind enough to open their organizational doors to me and provide glimpses to a side of this industry most of us rarely see. That so many people from each company were willing to explain their work, show me what they do, and discuss complex issues with me made this research possible. They have my deep appreciation.

Sincere thanks to Kendra Albert, Ian Condry, Megan Finn, Kishonna Gray, Dan Greene, Flourish Klink, Greg Lastowka, Claudia Lo, Kat Lo, Kaelan Coyle McDonough, Kate Miltner, Dylan Mulvin, Hector Postigo, Jesse Sell, Adrienne Shaw, Abe Stein, Jonathan Sterne, Nick Taylor, William Uricchio, Jing Wang, and Emma Witkowski for additional valuable input and conversations along the way. My appreciation to Morgan Romine, my co-conspirator at AnyKey, for sharing in the work we do, which often provided useful insights to this project. Thanks to Tom Boellstorff and Bill Mauer for bringing this project into their Culture and Technology series as well as for helpful input at crucial moments. Thanks to Princeton University Press's Fred Appel, Natalie Baan, Thalia Leaf, Cindy Milstein, and the manuscript's anonymous reviewers for valuable feedback and support.

I owe a special debt to the Social Media Collective at Microsoft Research New England, especially Nancy Baym, Tarleton Gillespie, and Mary Gray. I had an amazing experience being hosted there for a number of months, and the entire group was willing to read a draft of this manuscript and offer incredible feedback; it was both truly encouraging and insightful in pushing the work to the next level.

A special shout-out to Mary Gray, who in addition to supporting my visit to Microsoft, was my regular conversation and writing partner during this project; I couldn't have done it without ya! Your always-astute feedback, caring encouragement, and being just an amazing all-around friend helped keep me paddling.

Finally as always, my sincerest gratitude and affection to Micke, who despite hearing me say "never again!" after each book, continues to support and cheer me on in ways large and small. I'm truly lucky to have you in my life.

WATCH ME PLAY

1

Broadcasting Ourselves

In May 2012, I was sitting on my sofa browsing the internet when I stumbled on a website showing a live feed of a *StarCraft 2* computer game tournament taking place in Paris. In esports competitions, professional players compete in a formal tournament setting for prize money. Having done research and written a book on esports, I was familiar with game broadcasting attempts over the years, but this production particularly caught my eye. The event was taking place at the beautiful Le Grand Rex concert hall, and camera shots of an energetic, cheering audience of over two thousand people were interspersed with live feeds of the game competition. The strange world of *StarCraft*, populated and fought over by human Terrans, otherworldy Protoss, and creepy insectoid Zergs, shared screen time with the faces of the players, commentators, and audience that filled the large theater. Yet there was also another set of spectators—ones solely participating online. Along with thousands of others around the world, I was watching this match in real time over the internet. On our screens, alongside the video piping out from Paris, a chat stream (an old-school Internet Relay Chat [IRC] channel) flowed by with hundreds of people talking to each other about the event, and cheering through text and emoticons.

As someone who has not only studied gaming but also has roots in internet studies, virtual environments, and synchronous computer-mediated communication, my research ears perked up. What caught my attention was not only the spectatorship; it was also the forms of communication and presence among broadcasters and audience, both on-site at the venue and distributed throughout the network. I was intrigued by the experience as a *media event*. This show was being broadcast to a huge global audience, and as I came to learn over the course of that night, was being talked about in a variety of other online spaces such as Twitter. I had my television on in the background, but soon turned the volume down. This game "channel" being broadcast on my laptop captured my full attention. It was immediately clear to me that I needed to explore this space more.

That feeling—that I was not watching alone but instead alongside thousands of others in real time—was powerful. It was a familiar, resonant experience for me. I've long loved television, especially live content, and even as a kid I felt its pull. I remember getting a small black-and-white television in my bedroom as a preteen, and staying up late to watch *Saturday Night Live* and tap into an adult world I didn't have access to at that age. Breaking news frequently had the effect of helping me feel an immediacy of connection with a larger world. My father always either had on the evening news or a sports broadcast, and our family typically had the TV on from late afternoon through to bedtime. Beyond live shows, we constantly had on cartoons, sitcoms, and procedurals, and rather than going to the theater, watched most movies through it. The TV was an object our family shared and gathered around. We kept it on constantly. Much like Ron Lembo's (2000) account of "continuous television use" (including his personal reflections on how TV was situated in his own working-class home), my personal and social experience of television has ranged from the mundane to meaningful.[1] Sometimes it held my full attention, while at other moments it was simply background noise, offering a welcome ambient presence.[2] Television was not only a presence in my family's life; it connected me to the outside world, entertained and informed me, offered material for conversations with others, gave me broader cultural waypoints, and sometimes just kept me company.

This relationship with television is not, of course, unique to me. Scholars over the years have documented the profound role it can have in our lives—from politics, ideology, and mythmaking to socialization—structuring our domestic lives and mundanely offering its presence.[3] Unlike some television scholars, I never undertook this object of my affection and attention as a site of research. It simply *was*. But that night, watching the game live stream and audience engaged alongside me online, I paused. Though I have remained a television viewer my entire life, like many I also came to spend a lot of time online and in gaming spaces. This broadcast seemed to weave together all these threads at once: it was an interesting collision of the televisual, computer games, the internet, and computer-mediated communication. Its vibrancy as a live media product, both like TV and yet very much something else, was captivating.

Within esports—formalized competitive computer gaming—there has long been a quest to see gaming make the shift to television, despite many bumpy attempts over the years. The hope has been that if it could get into broadcast, not only would its legitimacy be signaled, but the audience for it could grow significantly. In my prior analysis of that industry, I briefly discussed the use of streaming media to broadcast competitive play, and remarked on how "social cam" websites like Justin.tv and Ustream were being utilized by gamers (Taylor 2012). These sites were typically hosting people simply streaming their everyday lives via webcams, offering amateur talk shows or even mundane "puppycam" channels where viewers could watch litters of sleeping newborn dogs. Yet some gamers were also gravitating to these sites, pushing their personal computers to crank out live video of their play to whoever wanted to tune in and watch. Though they didn't easily fit in the model of expected use of the sites, they were there pressing it for their own purposes.

Things have since changed quickly in the world of live streaming. Twitch, a broadcast platform dedicated to gaming that spun off from the social cam site Justin.tv in June 2011, has in a handful of years dramatically reshaped the landscape.[4] By 2017, the site boasted 2.2-plus million unique broadcasters per month with 17,000-plus members in the Twitch Partner Program and 110,000 "creators" in the Affiliates Program—content producers that receive revenue from their streams—and about 10 million daily active users (Twitch 2017b, 2017c). It hosts a wide variety of games from various genres. Major esports tournaments will, typically over the course of a weekend, reach millions of viewers. Variety streamers, those broadcasters who play a range of games, can pull in thousands of viewers per session. Though a thin slice of broadcasters get the lion's share of the audience and smaller channels often only host a handful of viewers, browsing the site you can find hundreds of channels at any time of the day.[5] Though most major televised sports events still trump esports live streaming in terms of audience size, and specific numbers for any single session should be taken with some caution, the overall growth of live streaming as a medium for new forms of broadcast and game content is indisputable.

Twitch is certainly not alone in helping build esports; other platform companies such as YouTube or Facebook, organizations like the Electronic Sports League (ESL), DreamHack, PGL, and Major League Gaming (MLG), and game developers such as Riot, Valve, and Blizzard have all tossed their hat into the live streaming ring by producing and/or distributing broadcast content. A generation of game consoles, the PS4 and Xbox One, both launched in 2013–14 with functionality to support broadcasting your play through live streaming. And traditional media companies such as Turner have gotten into the mix via the ELEAGUE tournament, which appears on both traditional cable and Twitch. Hours and hours of gaming content are now produced and consumed every day, 24-7, via live broadcast over the internet.

Though speaking about "waves" in any domain risks obscuring the threads of continuity or earlier experiments that never caught on, it can be helpful in broad strokes to describe esports this way, especially for those who may not know much about gaming. The first wave (the 1970s and 1980s) was anchored in arcades and around home console machines where the local dominated. The second wave (the 1990s through 2010) leveraged the power of the internet for multiplayer connections and a more global formulation of the competitive space. That period also witnessed the power of networking as a means to jump-start an esports *industry*—one that largely had its eye on traditional sports as its model. The third wave (starting around 2010) has at its core the growth of live streaming that takes the power of networking we saw earlier and powerfully combines it with the televisual. It is during this period that esports has become not just a sports product but a *media entertainment* outlet as well.

Live streaming offers professional esports players and teams opportunities to build their audience, brand, and incomes, while streaming their practice sessions—often straight out of their bedrooms. Tournaments are leveraging the medium to expand the reach of competitive gaming by building global audiences largely based online (see figure 1.1). Being an esports fan suddenly became much easier with live streaming.

You no longer needed to download a game replay file, track down a video on demand (VOD) on YouTube and a niche site, or constantly search out tournament results after the event. Twitch hosted massive amounts of content, from practice time to tournaments. There you could also talk to fellow audience members, "follow" your favorite channels to receive notifications when broadcasters went live, and subscribe to channels for a monthly fee, which, among other "member perks," would remove ads from the stream. With Twitch's purchase by Amazon in 2014, "Prime" members eventually got additional benefits on the platform (such as free game content) if they linked their accounts.[6] Having previously tracked the second wave of esports, the emergence of game live streaming illuminated for me how profoundly

FIGURE 1.1. The International grand finals, 2014. Teams selecting their match characters. The lower-right corner below the image shows the number of people currently watching (213,391), total views of the channel (38,693,102), and number of people who have specially tagged the channel to follow. The right side of the screen is a live chat window.

a televisual experience combined with the power of network culture could transform a nascent industry.

As I began spending more time on the site, however, I realized there was a much bigger project lurking. The growth of game live streaming wasn't simply a story about esports but also about larger changes in game culture and sharing your play. While the competitive gaming activity on Twitch is tremendous, it's not just esports that is finding a home in live streaming. The medium has offered players of all kinds an opportunity to build audiences interested in observing, commenting, and playing alongside them. Live streaming was allowing gamers of all kinds to *transform their private play into public entertainment.* While sites like YouTube have long tapped into this desire with the ability to distribute game videos, live streaming upped the ante by offering broadcasters the opportunity to interact with their audiences in real time through a synchronous chat window. Audiences—and their interactions with broadcasters—were themselves becoming integrated into the show. Game live streaming has become a new form of *networked* broadcast.

These non-esports broadcasters, typically called "variety" streamers due to the range of game titles they play (from new AAA releases to old Nintendo console games to niche indie games), are an important part of the platform. Frequently utilizing a green screen so their own face appeared overlaid onto the game, they were playing all kinds of titles in real time for a growing audience. Alongside the game and camera window, there is a chat space filled with audience members engaging with the broadcaster and each other (see figure 1.2). Rather than the kind of cheering you'd see in the chat pane during esports events, talk in these channels ranged from conversation with the streamer and others about the game or just everyday life.

While computer games make up the lion's share of Twitch, over just a few years, channels have also sprung up covering nondigital gaming. Avid card gamers, such as those who play *Magic: The Gathering,* can be found practicing and competing. Old-school "tabletop" role-playing sessions are now being streamed, complete with innovations for visualizing player characters and dice rolls (see figure 1.3).[7]

Alongside these diverse and sometimes-experimental forms of broadcast play, Twitch has also become a place to share creative work (such as making cosplay costumes or art), cooking and "social eating" (where people simply broadcast eating a meal), and music (from practice sessions to full-scale concerts). And in a twist back to its Justin.tv roots, the platform introduced an "in real life" (IRL) broadcast category allowing people to stream their everyday lives.

FIGURE 1.2. MANvsGame broadcast, 2013.

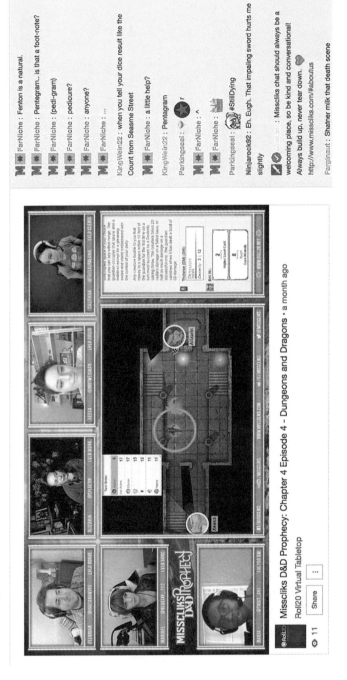

FarNiche : Fenton is a natural.

FarNiche : Pentegram.. is that a foot-note?

FarNiche : (pedi-gram)

FarNiche : pedicure?

FarNiche : anyone?

FarNiche : ...

KingWein22 : when you tell your dice result like the Count from Seasme Street

FarNiche : a little help?

KingWein22 : Pentagram

Parkingseal :

FarNiche : ^

FarNiche :

Parkingseal : #StillDying

Ninjarock92 : Eh. Eugh. That impaling sword hurts me slightly

[____] : Missicliks chat should always be a welcoming place, so be kind and conversational! Always build up, never tear down. 💜 http://www.misscliks.com/#aboutus

Farginaut : Shatner milk that death scene

Misscliks D&D Prophecy: Chapter 4 Episode 4 - Dungeons and Dragons • a month ago

Roll20 Virtual Tabletop

11   Share   ...

FIGURE 1.3. MissCliks D&D broadcast, 2017.

What began as a platform to support digital gaming has quickly expanded to accommodate people who want to produce a range of creative content for others. Some of these broadcasts have small audiences of friends and family who watch, and others draw thousands or even millions over the course of a weekend event. Across the platform, participants are creating new entertainment products that mix together gameplay, humor, commentary, and real-time interaction with fans and audiences. As with esports broadcasters, some variety streamers are working hard to convert their playtime to a professional job through advertising, sponsorships, donations, and other forms of monetization.

Though deeply innovative, all this creative activity is not taking place entirely outside existing media industries. Game companies, suddenly attuned to the potential of broadcast to get their products in front of gamers and build interest in their brands, are experimenting with live streaming as a form of marketing and promotion. From hosting launch events to developer chats, a number of companies are utilizing the space as a new form of PR and support. Some developers, such as Rami Ismail of the Dutch indie studio Vlambeer, have integrated the platform into their design process. In addition to live broadcasting his development sessions of the game *Nuclear Throne* twice a week (including real-time conversation and feedback with the audience), early builds (distributed via Valve's Steam platform) could be purchased through Twitch, and came with special chat emoticons and a subscription to the channel.[8] Game developers, such as the Massachusetts-based studio Proletariat, focused on making a title specifically *for* live streaming. That game, *Streamline*, allowed broadcasters to play in a game with their audience members, who also voted on new conditions that would instantly appear in the game to challenge everyone (such as the ground suddenly erupting in flames, thus requiring the players to jump onto platforms).

Underneath it all, technology companies—from core platform developers to third parties that build broadcasting tools—have been working to build and sustain infrastructures for video services as well as create economic models that allow them to survive. Tough engineering and network infrastructure challenges, video compression technology, and large-scale customer management systems are all being wrangled with and developed across a global context. The tremendous emergent activity occurring via live streaming is fundamentally engaged with sociotechnical artifacts built by both professional and amateur developers.

Amid the innovation and experimentation lurk a number of critical issues. Decisions about how these platforms and technologies will function is deeply interwoven with ideas about networked play, audiences, and the future of media writ large. As is the case with many user-generated content (UGC) platforms, advertising continues to be a prime model of monetization, but one that comes with its own set of persistent challenges—from ad-blocking software to ad inventories and concerns of oversaturation. On many UGC platforms, especially those that interweave original creative material with existing intellectual property, skirmishes continue to break out over ownership and regulation. The governance and management of these spaces as subcultures within a platform, hosting dynamic communities of practice, continues to pose vexing problems. And as is the case with a variety of internet and gaming communities, the tremendous creative energy driving innovation and new forms of culture is frequently in tension with existing legal or social frameworks that struggle to manage it. Though live streaming is transforming media production, distribution, and everyday practices, it continues to exist in legal and governance frameworks that are often deeply out of step with where the culture is headed.

Live streaming—from individuals broadcasting their gaming to the many people watching them—gives us a fascinating peek into when network and media culture collide with contemporary digital play as well as the future(s) of online producers and audiences. We are seeing the rise of a new form of *networked broadcasting*—one tied up with aspirations to transform otherwise-private play into public entertainment. But this emerging thread of game culture is also part of a larger change happening in media more broadly. From cord cutting to alternative paths of production and distribution, game live streaming is part of a larger transformation happening within the media industries.

Games Matter

In setting out to write this book, I felt the pull to make sure to anchor it in broader conversations happening outside game studies. From work on television to how the internet was affecting creative practice to sociotechnical systems, there is much to be leveraged back into understanding this slice of game culture. For many of us who came from traditional disciplinary training, this move is not unusual. We regularly, and fruitfully, look back to our home or other established disciplines to help guide us through the terrain of game culture, and hopefully that thread is evident throughout this book. But I want to make a brief call here for those various home disciplines to take games seriously as a site of valuable empirical data and knowledge creation, and see games as now a decidedly central part of our media, networked, and sociotechnical landscape.

Game live streaming intersects many contemporary issues not only around media transformations but also larger considerations of cultural production and everyday users. Understanding this space helps us see the whole better. Over almost two decades of watching game studies develop as an area of research, I've seen it wax and wane in the attention of scholars outside the domain. While researchers in a variety of spheres became attuned to massively multiplayer online games (such as *World of Warcraft*) or virtual worlds (like *Second Life)* in the mid-2000s, far fewer have kept sustained attention to what is happening in game culture. The responsibility of this certainly partly lay at the feet of game scholars who have not always done enough to continually connect their domain to wide-ranging scholarship and public interest. But scholars outside game studies who are not paying enough attention to this area of study also bear some responsibility for our current state of affairs. This is not just unfortunate; it has serious consequences for our broader collective research agenda of understanding not only socio-technical systems but how more traditional forms are changing too. Those who are interested in a critical analysis of platforms, emerging media, and civic engagement online can benefit from seeing how serious cultural matters are unfolding in what is otherwise thought of as leisure spaces.

Everyday life, filled with both work and leisure, is where people regularly navigate deeply political, culturally productive, sociotechnical systems. It is where politics comes at us sideways. While many are detached from what we might think of as serious civic engagement, all of us each and every day confront a range of critical issues in our domestic and work lives, among friends, colleagues, strangers, and family. Coming home and trying to tune out the "real world" by relaxing through various forms of leisure is a normal part of everyday life. Increasingly gaming has become one of those spaces. Players regularly encounter people from outside their own social worlds, and construct networks and online lives in concert with these systems. Yet games are now routinely tied to commercialized platforms, complex networks, and media infrastructures like never before. Companies, policies, and laws, addressing everything from intellectual property to standards of behavior, govern games. Users, owners, and systems co-constitute a space that in turn shapes experience. This means that those very moments when people are engaging in play remain some of the *most* politically infused spaces.

Much like sports or other forms of media, leisure is deeply tied to gender, race, and sexuality, social identity and community, normative models, and complex systems of regulation. What is often cordoned off as "simply leisure" or "fun" is actually deeply central as well as formative in all our civic and political lives. Certainly some game studies scholars have been guilty of reifying the division through the notion of the "magic circle" of play. Frankly it has caused more conceptual harm than good. This has been a position empirically challenged not only by sociological studies of digital gaming but also the longer trajectory of play studies rooted in anthropology.[9] What those early scholars found has only continued to be echoed in our current studies of digital gaming; our play and gaming is always inextricably linked to our everyday lives. Our identities, bodies, and social and political worlds are always tied up in it. In the same way that game scholars must pay attention to the context of play, those interested in what is frequently seen as the more "serious" side of our lives—the political or civic—can benefit from keeping an eye on leisure and gaming.

It is typical that in gaming and leisure spaces you can catch foreshadowing glimpses of critical issues that will arise in the mainstream years, or decades, down the line. Think about how, for example, early studies of text-based multiuser dungeons (some of the earliest virtual worlds) were tackling the relationship between code, governance, and forms of participation.[10] Game scholars have long wrangled with the interrelation between technology and social practice, how technological systems co-construct experience, including how forms of social control and order get embodied in systems.[11]

Early game researchers also explored what it meant to have online social networks via games, through which communication, presentations of self, forms of embodiment, and the circuits between off- and online life were connecting us to friends and strangers.[12] Though "social media" has become the dominant term of use to refer to our online experiences, early multiplayer worlds were some of the first to explore what it meant to live life online, and have our identities and social networks extended beyond the physical and geographic. Amid the riches of emergent culture in games, scholars studying gender, sexuality, and race in those spaces illuminated key nodes where sociotechnological systems intersected more troubling behavior. They helped us understand how communities, platforms, and games foster systems of inclusion and exclusion tied up with offline notions about self and identity.[13] They tackled how communities themselves policed borders, enforced particular forms of communication and behavior, and often harassed and excluded.[14]

Game studies work tackled the rise of player productions before UGC shot off as a term in both academia and industry. Research on how average gamers were creating content for other players—be it through game mods, videos, or web-based sites—offered an analysis of how typical configurations of producers and consumers were being disrupted.[15] These kinds of activities in turn helped push inquiries into the iterations between platform and formal design and actual use, where UGC or practices were picked back up by developers to refine official products.[16] Tied up with this has been a consideration of the growth of global commercialized platforms as prime nodes in people's lives—something anyone now concerned about Facebook or Twitter can appreciate.[17]

Game research has offered sustained and early explorations into what has come to be seen as some of our most important political and critical conversations. This has happened in large part because these issues are inherent within leisure and gaming; they are not separate from it. While some in game studies have tried to carve off the field as exceptional, this has been a mistake. There is much game scholars can learn from fields like sociology, anthropology, media studies, and science and technology studies (to name only a few). And likewise, there is a great amount that studying games can bring to those with an interest in the critical and political side of media, both old and new. Far too often, scholars have expressed to me that they are not "enough of a gamer" or are too intimidated by games to actually know what is happening in that research space. This is unfortunate; it's a missed opportunity for all of us to be connecting up our work across "object" lines so as to watch for resonances or gaps, moments where our data and arguments bolster each other's assertions, and places where they pose real challenges to it.

Our media lives are not cordoned off in discrete parts. One is not simply a television watcher, Twitter user, sports fan, or game player. Media and leisure practices take place *across multiple platforms and communities; they intersect and inform each other.* There is a circuit of practice, experience, and production at work. By default, any node is already entangled in the others. They are always multisited. Even if we hold a single object of analysis in frame (for example, my choice of Twitch as an anchor platform), we must be attuned to the *assemblage* that makes up our media lives in order to fully understand what is happening.

Play and gaming are deeply connected to the things that matter, and impact our lives. This means, ultimately, that gaming is a civic space, political domain, media sphere, and site of critical work, while simultaneously being a place of leisure, even rest and respite. Gaming cannot be set off to the side, a quirky outpost functioning as an academic novelty. It is a huge—indeed for many, the *most significant*—space where they engage directly in core cultural issues and debates. It shapes and deeply impacts mainstream conversations and culture. Games matter.

Historical Snapshots and Methods

When I first began this research project, I thought it'd be a one-off article, something to bring my work on esports, published as a book in 2012, up to date. It instead grew into this full-fledged case study of a particular live streaming site. But it is crucial to understand, as with many such projects, it is deeply situated in a particular historical moment. The fieldwork for this book primarily took place over the course of several years (2012–15) as early Twitch broadcasters were engaged in some of the first experimentations not only on the platform but also with live streaming more broadly. This was a time where esports organizations were taking so many nascent media practices from earlier periods and beginning to bring them to fruition. Variety streamers were working hard to carve out a set of creative practices, and in the case of so many I spoke with, aspiring to professionalize in ways that then were yet unimaginable. And my visits out to Twitch's San Francisco offices began when it was still a small upstart company, not yet owned by Amazon, and living decidedly on the outskirts of game and tech culture.

The platform as well as gaming and media more broadly continue to transform and change, often quicker than any of us can keep up. While throughout the book I've tried to provide waypoints to some of these changes, the bulk of the data and analysis here should be seen as closely tied to this early period of game live streaming, just after the launch of Twitch. Much of what I chronicle are practices first and foremost undertaken by early adopters: those individual gamers and organizations that actively sought out live broadcasting, and pushed the form in fascinating ways. Over the last few years in particular, I've had the privilege of meeting many new scholars, frequently in the thick of graduate work, who are sure to provide us rich accounts of what this space looks like as it becomes more firmly seated into game and media culture. My hope is that this account, bound by time and platform, serves as a useful historical case that offers conceptual interventions and provocations—ones that future readers will find of interest alongside more contemporary accounts of this emerging media form.

As with my prior projects, this research is deeply anchored in qualitative social science methods and multimodal techniques that range from interviews to archival work. Given the unique challenges I faced in my prior esports book with the research being spread across a large number of sites and domains, I decided fairly early on to go back to my methodological roots and primarily focus on a single platform: Twitch. I use it as a critical case— one that by digging deeply into it, allows for a rich specificity that speaks to broader contexts. This style is much more resonant with my ethnographic sensibility, and to be frank, given the heterogeneity on the platform itself, offered a valuable practical anchor to a phenomenon in deep transition.[18]

I've spent hundreds of hours watching live streams and capturing interesting moments, including the chat that accompanies a broadcast (typically through screenshots and notes). Sometimes these streams were one-off events, while other instances involved broadcasters I followed for a longer period of time, often subscribing to their channel. At the beginning of the project, I learned how to broadcast my own gameplay as a way of understanding the basic functionality of the site. Watching practices emerge, morph, change, and even die out on Twitch over several years has provided a fascinating opportunity. It has also given me an intriguing glimpse into not only the culture of the site as a whole—for instance, aesthetic or communicative conventions that arise and spread—but the diversity that exists among different channel subcultures as well.

Speaking about "live streaming on Twitch" is a useful way of holding a cluster of things together to try to understand a broader phenomenon, but also has analytic limits when one looks at the variety of practices and subcultures within given channels. I've long found Geoffrey Bowker and Susan Leigh Star's formulation of "boundary objects" incredibly useful in understanding gaming spaces, and the case of live streaming is no exception. They note that "boundary objects are those objects that both inhabit several communities of practice and satisfy the informational formational requirements of each of them. Boundary objects are thus both plastic enough to adapt to local needs and constraints of the several parties employing them, yet robust enough to maintain a common identity across sites" (Bowker and Star 1999, 297). This framework is powerful when you are trying to understand how a variety of actors—company representatives, individual users, and third-party commercial interests—all engage in their own specific ways, many times fundamentally in tension with one another, but somehow still live alongside each other day to day. The provisionally cohered heterogeneity of game live streaming is perhaps one of the most important aspects to understand. It allows us to think, both critically and methodologically, about platforms as spaces of continuity across a site that simultaneously holds vibrant subcultural worlds that co-construct the culture at micro levels.

The research for this book also involved data collection via online forums, following people and discussions on a range of internet venues, and cataloging journalistic stories from both print and net-based media. One of the earliest lessons I learned in doing internet research is to go where the community leads. People rarely stay on one platform but instead use a variety of them to construct their overall online experience (Taylor 1999). This is also the case with live streaming, where participants leverage different outlets to assist their broadcasts as well as create and sustain communities. Internet users are savvy when it comes to cobbling together resources across sites to manage and enhance their online experience. My research in this project was likewise, by default, multisited and filled with "unexpected trajectories" (Marcus 1995, 98). While Twitch has formed the basis for the study, the work took me onto news sites, Reddit, Twitter, and Facebook. Like so many other internet-based communities before it, live streamers are avid catalogers and analysts of their own spaces and practices. Integrating these resources into the research has been crucial in understanding the ecology of streaming.

I've interviewed a range of game broadcasters (both via Skype and in person), from variety streamers who play lots of different games to professional esports players primarily focused on a single competitive gaming title. Because of my interest in how people navigate domains of "serious leisure"—putting in high investments, including time, money, and social networking—or seek to professionalize their gameplay and creative endeavors, I've concentrated primarily on broadcasters who have been striving to make streaming their full-time employment. I found people to interview through watching streams, attending events, and using the snowball method where people recommend others. I've done home visits to see setups and, on occasion, spoken with members of a streamer's family, both of which have offered additional insight into how this media work intersects with domestic lives. I've interviewed people who run moderation teams, create graphics packages or bot technology, or do other behind-the-scenes work assisting broadcasters. I've also hosted public panels where streamers talk about their work and convened private workshops in my capacity as director of research for AnyKey, an organization focused on fair and inclusive gaming.[19]

My fieldwork has extended to looking at how esports organizations are being impacted and developed in light of live streaming, and I've been fortunate to be able to talk to some that are leveraging the medium to broadcast large tournaments. Many of them have been in the business of esports for years, and have tremendous experience with the challenges of broadcast and spectatorship. Their insight into the transformations happening in the industry was valuable. In addition to a number of shorter visits "behind the scenes" to see esports media production in action, I got to spend several full weekends backstage at big tournament events watching technical, organizational, and production practices as well as talking to the professionals in the thick of work. Some of the most important wisdom I gained about the work of producing esports tournaments happened in these moments where I got to see media production unfold backstage. Being able to talk to people on the spot about how they were constructing and carrying out large events for global audiences offered tremendous insight. Having done research on some of these organizations for my prior book, I had the unique opportunity to see companies I was familiar with transition and integrate a new media form into their business. In many ways, these events provided me some of the most powerful glimpses into future media practices that weave together local events, global audiences, and internet distribution.

Beyond these focused offline opportunities, I got several chances to follow live streaming in broader public settings. I was able to attended the Penny Arcade Expo (PAX East) in Boston a number of times, thus giving me an opportunity to spend extended periods at the Twitch booth, meet and talk to a wide variety of broadcasters and fans, and situate streaming within a much larger game culture. I was also fortunate to attend the first three TwitchCons, the company's own convention dedicated to streamers. That event proved especially valuable in seeing how the organization itself was working to build its community, educate broadcasters, and support fans. In several instances at these various events, I moderated panels that dealt with live streaming, which in turn opened up many additional conversations with conference goers. Convention exhibition spaces also proved to be an opportunity to see and chat with companies—audio/video (A/V) manufacturers, software developers, and even service providers—vying for the attention of a nascent industry of small media producers.

Finally, while an important part of the story I tell here is the work that individual streamers and esports companies are doing to produce content, my research has also been keenly attuned to broader organizations and technology. The institutions and structures that facilitate these productions play a critical role in understanding this space. Platforms and the institutions that manage them construct powerful conditions as well as boundaries for user engagement. I visited ESL's Burbank, California, studio several times, including when it just opened and the technical infrastructure was still being laid out. I was also fortunate to be able to visit Twitch's offices in San Francisco a number of times over the years and get to see it grow as a company, adapting and iterating as its business did. I've spoken to employees and executives, who have offered great insight into their fast-changing world. While this book is not formally an organizational ethnography, I have been keenly aware of the significance that Twitch, both as a platform and company, has to any current analysis of live streaming. From technology to policy to marketing and economics, the organizational power of the company is a key part of this story.

Given the multisitedness of this project, there is no single answer for how I've handled issues around anonymization in this text. When it comes to individual participants, I have anonymized them, including those working at various organizations, when I am quoting from interviews or informal conversations. In instances where I am quoting streamers who were speaking on public panels or issuing public commentary on Twitter, I use their name and/or screen name (some prefer to keep their full name private for a variety of reasons that I discuss later in the book). I remain committed to the practice of anonymization because I see it as the best way of protecting those who are so generous with their time but control little of the outcome once they speak to a researcher. Even if they review drafts, which some of my respondents did, none of us involved can anticipate the consequences of publication and how readers will take up the material. For those who are building companies and livelihoods, particularly in precarious industries, utmost care must be taken, and I consider anonymization an important part of my ethical stance with this type of work.[20]

Organizational anonymization, however, offers additional challenges to projects such as this. Those of us who work in a case study mode often face how to attenuate the specificity of our sites for analytic necessity alongside protecting those who participate. As with individuals, we must balance our need to make larger arguments against the pull that naming people can have in a story. Because I have researched organizations in a domain with few competitors, and the specificity is actually important to the analysis, I am unable to anonymize the main platform of this inquiry, Twitch. Similarly, Turtle Entertainment and its ESL, which allowed me to observe work at major events, is difficult to anonymize. Its historical and organizational specificity within esports is crucial to this study, so I am unable to pseudonym it as an organization (though as with Twitch, individual interviewees are all anonymized). While I frequently double-checked facts with Twitch and ESL, or tested out arguments I was working on with a handful of especially helpful confidants, I did not provide the drafts of the work to either company to review ahead of publication. This was primarily driven by my wish to have scholarly autonomy. I am tremendously grateful to each for opening their doors to me, and I've done my best to treat that access with care and respectfulness, while upholding the integrity of the research and findings. It is also my hope that other organizations will, through this work, see the value of letting researchers in.

Structure of the Book

In the following I explore not only networked broadcasting across variety and esports domains but also various organizational and technological issues at play in this emerging space. I pay particular attention to regulatory and policy issues arising within game live streaming, from dress codes to intellectual property concerns. In many ways, the structure of the book is like an hourglass: I open with some large-scale considerations around media change, dive into the cases of variety and esports streaming, and then move back out for a consideration of how governance and regulatory frameworks are at work broadly.

Chapter 2, "Networked Broadcasting," opens with a look at changes happening with television production and broadcasting, and offers a historical framing of the rise of live streaming. I situate the development of game live streaming within broader trajectories of media production, internet culture and infrastructures, and gaming practices. I spend a bit of time talking about the networked audience as it is constituted via live streaming, exploring why people watch and how we might understand the work of audiences within this domain. I conclude with an overview of Twitch, a primary site gamers use to distribute their play to others.

In Chapter 3, "Home Studios," I explore individual live streamers who are in the midst of building a new genre out of their gaming. These broadcasters best exemplify the notion I present in the book of transforming private play into public entertainment. While spectating another person's play has always been present in game culture, the scale at which it is happening with live streaming as well as the broader media ecology and forms of monetization on which it is built all make these content producers a particularly important group to look at.

Typically based in home studios often located in a living room or bedroom, these streamers are developing new conventions for both game spectatorship and media broadcast. While most still hold day jobs, a number of them are pursuing full-time "professional" streaming, frequently supported by families or partners. These broadcasters navigate public and private spheres, weaving together their play with commentary, humor, and even pedagogical qualities. Given that Twitch supports synchronous chat running alongside the video, the broadcasters are also typically engaging with their audiences in real time—chatting with them, answering questions, responding to feedback, and over the course of months or years, getting to know and be known by them. Having a successful channel can also require attention to other forms of social media. Managing a presence on Facebook, Twitter, or even YouTube can become an important part of the overall ecology of building as well as maintaining an audience.[21] Finally, many live streamers have become incredibly adept at rapidly skilling up their video production skills and are typically "one-person shows." Eventually these live streamers become not only content producers but also brand and community managers. Yet amid all the creative production and exciting engagement with audiences, the harassment and "virtual gauntlets" that women, people of color, and lesbian, gay, bisexual, transgender, queer, intersex, and asexual (LGBTQIA) people (not mutually exclusive categories) face when wanting to occupy these spaces remains one of the most significant areas to explore. This chapter looks at the challenges to the space as a form of open, participatory media.

While thousands of channels dedicated to all types of games have sprung up over the last few years, esports has been uniquely transformed by the growth of live streaming. Chapter 4, "Esports Broadcasting," focuses on how the rise of networked broadcast has powerfully changed not only the everyday lives of esports players but organizations and tournaments. During the last decade, professional competitive gaming was intent on developing its spectatorship capacities to reach mass appeal and audiences. There have been a number of attempts to bring esports to broadcast television, usually with poor results. With the rise of platforms like Twitch, there has been a marked shift in how professionals in that scene approach the issue of spectatorship. Increasingly, the line they take is that they no longer need television—they have live streaming. Such statements are often framed as declarations of freedom from traditional media structures, an explicit turning away from what is sometimes seen as an out-of-touch sector. As esports organizations have often remarked in interviews over the last couple of years, they see their audience as primarily located online at computers and that is where they are going to reach them.

Whether it is the longtime esports player using the technology to broadcast to their fans or tournaments reaching millions of viewers over the course of a weekend, many of those invested in competitive gaming are using these platforms to continue to build a *sports/media* business. From the broadcast of mundane practice time to high-end spectacles, live streaming is being used to grow esports. As a fairly new media space, it is offering a fascinating set of experiments where broadcasters sort out new genre conventions (from the use of cameras and overlays), attempt to monetize audiences, and develop new enterprises around this emerging media form. Professional gamers and organizations are engaging in media work like never before, and this chapter tells the story of how a form of labor as play meets broadcast head-on.

Whereas just a few years ago it was unclear how niche an activity this slice of gaming and its fandom would be, live streaming has been a boon to building audiences for esports, and the content is coming directly from individual players, leagues, and increasingly game developers themselves. Live streaming has proven to be a profound promotional tool for titles, and developers are taking notice. Average gamers not only become engaged with formal high-end competitive play, but it animates their own leisure choices. Audiences not only watch, for example, *League of Legends* tournaments; they play the game, buy characters that the pros use, and refine their own playful strategies.

This media growth has been energetically developed not only by solo broadcasters in their living rooms but also by large organizations with a worldwide reach. In just the space of a few years it has transformed gaming. Yet there remain key critical issues lurking in this new form of media production and broadcast. In chapter 5, "Regulating the Networked Broadcasting Frontier," I examine how the tremendous creative energy and experiments discussed in the prior chapters contend with intervening organizations, regulations, and law. I discuss what I term the "regulatory assemblage" and in this chapter, move out to a macro consideration of forms of governance operating on the platform at several layers, from the social to the algorithmic.

I explore how various forms of community management function in game live streaming. This ranges from more positive inflections via grassroots channel moderators to the ways audiences enact social order, including destructively though things like distributed denial of service (DDOS) attacks or outright harassment and hostility toward broadcasters. I also discuss how nonhuman actors, such as bots, come to do management work and increasingly form a crucial part of the sociotechnical space that makes up live streaming.

Beyond community management, I explore how policy and law are involved in the governance of game live streaming. I analyze how various codes of conduct on the platform have enacted structures of governance, at times with serious pushback from members of the community. I discuss how policy gets embodied via sociotechnical artifacts of automated enforcement. As with YouTube, there are increasing forms of algorithmic regulation that monitor content and take often-contested action against particular channels.

Underpinning so much of what we see in these generative UGC spaces are laws that profoundly affect how live streaming is being handled by users and platform developers alike. With intellectual property claims and disputes, much is still in flux regarding ownership and rights in this space. Live streaming activities remain fraught with issues around how we understand *transformative* creative productions within a commercialized media sphere. What is perhaps most critical in examining how this media space is being governed right now is that conventions, norms, and precedents are being set for a form of broadcasting likely to grow.

Ultimately this book asks what happens when people begin to *transform private play into public entertainment* and an emerging media form of *networked broadcasting* arises. The threads of sharing play and spectatorship are at the roots of digital gaming, but live streaming weaves them into the flow of this particular moment of media and internet culture. In chapter 6, "Live Streaming as Media," I reflect broadly on the growth of game live streaming and potential media futures. I discuss the ways that marketing and commercialization increasingly shape how channels are framed along with the implications for live streaming as a form of creative cultural practice. I explore moments when Twitch finds itself host to more mainstream endeavors as it grows as a media entity in its own right, sitting alongside traditional outlets. I conclude with reflections on how the platform has, in some ways, turned back to its earliest roots with the inclusion of creative, music, and even IRL forms of broadcasting. Though this book focuses on game live streaming in particular, it hopefully participates in broader critical conversations we continue to have around technology, culture, and media.

2

Networked Broadcasting

Game live streaming is an excellent example of the ways multiple cultural trajectories collide and iterate. It evokes structures and modalities associated with television, but it also fits within broader cultures of gaming and spectatorship, UGC, and telecommunications. It is an emerging form of networked broadcasting. It is entertainment that has typically routed around traditional media production and distribution outlets, tapped into gaming fandom, harnessed the evocative power of otherwise-mundane webcams, and piggybacked on—as well as created—net culture and computer-mediated communication. To some it may seem like game live streaming came out of left field. It is, however, tied to a longer historical trajectory of television and internet broadcasting, yet simultaneously deeply rooted in our contemporary moment, which is filled with online media services, maker/DIY movements, online life, and creative cultural production from all sectors of society.

Television: Artifact, Experience, and Transitions

Media scholar William Uricchio's fascinating accounts of television help us understand how tied up game live streaming is with historical imaginations of what "TV" could be. As he notes, there has always been an "interpretive flexibility" to television, and one path early developers pursued related to liveness and interactivity. He shows, for example, that as early as 1883, French illustrator Albert Robida described a televisual apparatus that blended broadcasting with one-on-one communication, and could sit in both domestic and public spaces. This interest in facilitating "live extension, interaction, virtual presence, and communication" is woven throughout the history of television across a number of inventors and developers (Uricchio 2008, 291).[1]

Central to this particular project has been a focus on "technologies of simultaneity" that not only were in the service of communication but also national identity and state. Though the national project is not as resonant with game broadcasting, we can see how liveness works to bond people together, and create a shared set of experiences and identities around which they cohere. Whether it is in smaller streaming communities or large transnational audiences for esports, the liveness of game channels has proven a powerful, affective device. As I'll discuss in later chapters, broadcasters regularly speak of the power of simultaneity in the productions.[2] This ranged from the ability to engage in real time with the audience to harnessing liveness for sports broadcasts. The history that scholars like Uricchio present underscores how this approach has a long televisual history, and one that is tied up with deeper cultural and political formulations.

It's also helpful to situate networked broadcasting by contextualizing it within transformations happening across traditional media more broadly and within television in particular. There are at least several threads within television studies that I've found especially fruitful to pull from to help illuminate game live streaming: television "after" TV, changes in production/distribution/consumption, the postnetwork era, and niche programming.[3]

As Uricchio (2004, 165) observes in the collection *Television after TV*, "From its start, television has been a transient and unstable medium, as much for the speed of its technological change as for the process of its cultural transformation, for its ephemeral present, for its mundane everydayness." The tremendous shifts we've seen in just the last several years signal that we need always be attuned to this ongoing "transition" and the shortsightedness of conflating any particular historical instantiation of "TV" to "television" as a whole. This resonates with media studies scholar Sheila Murphy's (2011, 5) point that television is as much a "cultural imagination" as anything, "more a set of connected ideas, beliefs, and technologies than it is any one thing that can be reduced to the home electronics device with a screen." Shifting our understanding of television from both the network era model (think of the big three of ABC, NBC, and CBS) and material box in the living room toward broader transformations of the *televisual* across a variety of devices and protocols helps us situate game live streaming in a larger media context.

Seeing television as *always* in transition assists us in understanding some of the biggest shifts involving its intersection with digital technology along with alternative financing, production, and distribution models. The growth of the digital distribution of traditional content—such as Major League Baseball's use of a streaming service and dedicated "app" that lives on everything from tablets to phones to game consoles, HBO's popular Now service that bypasses cable subscriptions entirely, or Hulu's streaming service for network television and more—all suggest the ways traditional media organizations have leveraged the internet. More pointedly, though, has been the rise of services like Netflix and Amazon that have distributed acclaimed series like *House of Cards* or *Orange Is the New Black*, which are solely available through online services. These shifts have captured both audience and critics attention. The rise of nontraditional paths to production and distribution have highlighted how serialized and televisual content can thrive on systems not linked to airwaves or bundled cable TV packages.

The growth of the net has caught the attention of both scholars and the industry who have tried to make sense of the changes taking place. Some have championed "second screen" experiences whereby television viewers augment their viewing with their cell phones, laptops, or tablets. Marketers' enthusiasm for "engagement" metrics, often anchored around "social TV," which is seen as the integration of simultaneous social media practices while viewing, has expanded what gets conceived as media use.[4] And in much the same way scholars paid attention to how the introduction of the remote control reshaped home use, I suspect more will explore the ways computational technologies infused themselves into everyday audience experience.

Combined with the growing number of "cord cutters" or "cord nevers"—those viewers who forego traditional cable TV packages and make do with online resources (authorized or pirated)—we quickly get an image dramatically different from television's classic "network era" in which we all gathered around a box in the living room to watch shows on fixed schedules via a limited selection of channels. Television scholars have argued it is a mistake to equate "television" with that simple image tied to a particular historical moment.[5] Our current context is one in which traditional media organizations and the home TV sit alongside a myriad of devices we get content on as well as alternate production and distribution paths.

Televisual experiences are now significantly made up of a range of technologies we wouldn't call a TV, via services that are distant cousins of ABC, NBC, and CBS, bypassing the airwaves or massive cable packages, and are increasingly tied to our online practices and lives. We still have watercooler conversations about traditional cable/television shows, but we might also talk to groups of friends (perhaps even just online) about videos originating from home recording studios.[6] This is one of the most interesting aspects of our current media space: it interweaves traditional production and aesthetics with emerging genres and forms that are frequently created by fans, amateurs, or less mainstream media companies. Viewers consume content across this range. They may watch highly produced shows like HBO's *Westworld* while also seeking out amateur YouTube videos or game streams on Twitch. Cycling across devices, from a large-screen home TV to an iPad or PS4, is not unusual. Live game streaming just becomes one more node in the mix.[7]

These trends are tied to powerful changes in media production and distribution. Television studies scholar Amanda Lotz notes the economic shifts in television production, especially practices that challenged labor structures through using "runaway productions," which moved crews from union-based Hollywood to places like Canada that offered cost cutting measures. These shifts operated in tandem with new distribution channels—ones that also disrupted traditional revenue models. As she argues, "Changes in distribution shifted production economics enough to allow audiences that were too small or specific to be commercially viable for broadcast or cable to be able to support niche content through some of the new distribution methods, particularly those featuring transactional financial models" (Lotz 2014, 137). Attention to smaller audience segments certainly thrives on platforms like YouTube and Twitch, where viewers can track down content on both large games and quirky small titles that only a handful of people may avidly follow. The simultaneous growth of "reality television" and other content that does not require extensive writing, directing, and acting talent became a perfect breeding ground for the growth of UGC and low-cost game live streaming.[8]

This overall decline of major TV networks, rise in nontraditional production and distribution, and growth of niche outlets and programming characterize much of our current US television landscape. The emergence of game live streaming sits fairly easily within the historical trajectory of television writ large. Media studies scholar Lisa Parks (2004, 134) uses the term "post broadcasting" not to "refer to a revolutionary moment in the digital age but rather to explore how the historical practices associated with over-the-air, cable, and satellite television have been combined with computer technologies to reconfigure the meanings and practices of television." Lotz (2014, 8) calls this the "post-network era" (beginning around the early 2000s)—a time when "changes in the competitive norms and operation of the industry become too pronounced for many of the old practices to be preserved; different industrial practices are becoming dominant and replacing those of the previous eras." Game live streaming operates as a form of media production and distribution within these larger industrial transformations, and is a deep expression of them.

In addition to this shifting landscape of production, broadcast, and consumption, there is the long history of attempting to leverage interactivity in various ways. Children's television and shows with various forms of game content have been particularly creative in trying to find ways to bring audiences in through interaction. Quirky systems like the *Winky Dink* (launched in 1953), which provided children crayons and a transparent sheet to overlay on the TV screen so they could directly draw on it as a means of interacting with special content, are probably some of the earliest experiments in trying to get viewers to work with programmed material. More contemporary shows like *Blue's Clues* or *Dora the Explorer* formally structure themselves around a model of audience participation where they attempt to engage children in visceral, embodied ways by asking them to answer queries that the show's characters make. Though audience participation doesn't actually change the content, they are all examples of pushes to blur the boundary between program and viewer.

Other shows sought to encourage interaction such that audience input would actually change the content. The *TV Powwww* format (launched in 1978) had viewers use their telephones to call in and verbally issue a command (shouting "pow!" to fire on a target) that was then carried out in a real-time broadcast video game. The 1980s' BBC show *What's Your Story* utilized a phone-in choose-your-own-adventure model that allowed the audience to shape how the narrative unfolded. The 1980s' Canadian production *Captain Power*, picking up on the same technique as *Winky Dink* in merging content and equipment, offered a special toy for engagement. Children who had purchased the "Powerjet XT-7 Phoenix" (a light gun akin to the NES Zapper) were able to "fire" at the TV and carry out live battles. As the system warned, "The TV show will fire back. It *will* fire back. Score, or be hit. Do you understand?" (Toal 2012). Finally, shows such as *Big Brother* or competitions like *Eurovision* that rely on direct viewer engagement through voting systems also point to ways producers have sought to draw audiences into how content actually unfolds.

I leverage these threads of scholarship and examples when I use the term networked broadcast. Game live streaming—rooted in globally distributed user-content creators utilizing third-party platforms, involving social interaction as a core component of the broadcast, and embedded as well as amplified across a variety of sites—exemplifies the notion of a network. Game live streaming is, as I will show throughout this book, an assemblage of actors, technologies, and practices. It is a form that plays with the boundary lines between audience and producer. Content is co-constructed *through* the network and via the transformative work of play. This network of connections and content, all within a broadcast frame, articulates where game live streaming sits. Media studies scholar John Caldwell (2004, 45) argues that understanding the current moment in which digital technologies intersect television requires paying "as much attention to the communities and cultures of production" as to "either political economy or ideologically driven screen form."

Thinking of game live streaming as a new form of networked broadcast also speaks to a long-standing concern among some scholars who have seen TV as an overly individualized, personalized, and privatized microspace of viewership. While these tendencies are possible, and may even come to eventually dominate game live streaming, at its infancy they are not the core orientation. Game live streamers are deeply embedded in social networks and communities of practice. The platform has been rooted in communication between broadcaster and audience members, or audience members with each other. And though viewers can surf across a variety of niche channels in this space, they do so within a larger platform milieu—one that sees itself as both a "Twitch family" and a host to numerous smaller subcommunities. The network—figured in production, distribution, and consumption—is a central metaphor and actual anchor for game live streaming. Combined with the transformative properties of play, it is a vibrant space of new media development that builds on the history of television.

Internet Broadcasting

I would be remiss if I only looked at game live streaming through the lens of television or transformations in that space. In Murphy's (2011, 88) book *How Television Invented New Media*, she prompts us to ask, "How is new media not just television all over again?" She wants to make sure we don't overlook the televisual in the lineage of "new media," and it is certainly the case that live streamers have their eye on TV conventions and pull from them at times. Her historical look at television's influence on gaming (and new media broadly) anticipates what we see in game live streaming, and her book is incredibly valuable in situating a range of digital media within a longer television history.[9]

While she is working her analysis from the direction of understanding how television provided a foundation for what we often black box as new media, I find the question generative in the reverse direction as well, primarily analyzing with an eye *toward* internet and game culture. Though the internet is increasingly used to distribute traditional media content, Murphy's question can be productively turned to allow us to weave in early net histories around cam culture, UGC on sites like YouTube, and the rich legacy of multiplayer gaming and spectatorship to understand the growth of internet broadcasting. Game live streaming, while resonating with television and the televisual, also has a lineage that is a motley mix of several other domains rooted in specific technologies and cultures of the internet.[10]

CAM CULTURE

As someone who used old modem-based bulletin board systems and watched the variety of enthusiastic experiments that bubbled up on the net in the 1990s, I immediately thought of early internet cam culture when I first saw live streaming. The dream of videophones and telecommunication where you can talk and see people has long held sway in the popular imagination. What was striking in the mid-1990s is how viable it became for everyday users. We perhaps take this for granted now given programs like Skype or the small cameras that come preinstalled on everything from laptops to tablets to phones, but only a couple decades ago people were starting to play with live video feeds.

Using low-resolution black-and-white cameras, people began to connect with each other in real time over the internet, most notably through a free program developed in 1992 called CU-SeeMe (see figure 2.1).[11] While early initiatives were often based in education or science (the National Aeronautics and Space Administration being a notable early adopter), many of the connections that were getting made were simply opportunities to meet people and socialize.

Some, including myself, used programs like CU-SeeMe to augment their social connections in a variety of online spaces (see figure 2.2). For those who spent time solely with text, the camera offered an exciting new arena of play. As the early instruction book *Internet TV with CU-SeeMe* put it, "Computer-based videoconferencing is startling. It redefines your relationship with your computer and, more importantly, how you communicate

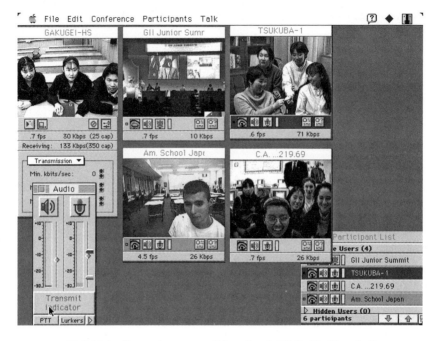

FIGURE 2.1. Global Schoolhouse classrooms collaborating via CU-SeeMe. Photo by Yvonne Marie Andres, Creative Commons Attribution 3.0 License.

electronically with other people around the world" (Sattler 1995, 2). Even in these early moments of using web cameras to connect with others online, people were sensing the power they had to shift otherwise-instrumental encounters to more relational ones. Using the technology to talk to each other and connect, frequently across distances, became a central part of these early explorations.

Internet users experimented with how to visually connect to one another and create shared spaces mediated through cameras. Media studies scholar Ken Hillis (2009, 9), in his rich study of online life, conveys the immense affective power of webcam usage, writing that "at times these encounters induce feelings of absence and 'wish you were here,' yet mostly they have the opposite effect: everyone feels that they are somewhat in each other's presence." This sense of presence at a distance, that you are somehow together with others via video, is a powerful hook in our shared network experiences. As cameras became less expensive and broadband access more widespread, technologies evolved that allowed inexpensive forms of telepresence.

The late 1990s and early 2000s were a tremendous moment of exploration for those looking to develop broader broadcasting possibilities, in

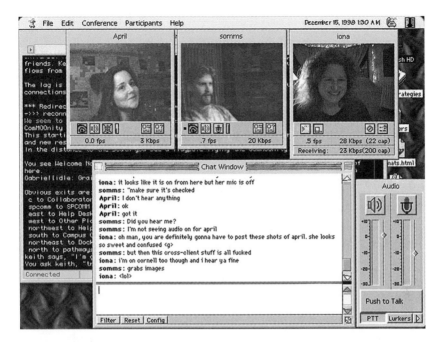

FIGURE 2.2. Multiwindow internet session from 1998 showing the author with friends simultaneously together in a text-based virtual world in the background and CU-SeeMe in the foreground.

particular though continual live streams of their everyday lives. Sometimes these involved sexual activity, but often they were simply mundane feeds allowing viewers to peek in and, notably, chat with the broadcaster.[12] One of the earliest examinations of this phenomena was internet researcher Theresa Senft's (2008) chronicling of the rise of the 1990s' "cam girls": women who would live broadcast often out of their house 24-7 to viewers who stopped by their website.[13] Though all too often these early net forays were written off as simply exhibitionism, Senft presents a much more nuanced analysis of the ways that "immediacy and intimacy" were created in these spaces between broadcasters and audience. Both Hillis and Senft highlight these links, the flow of conversations, getting to know and be known (even if within a frame of performance), and the disruption of an easy story of voyeurism. Understanding viewers as connected to the broadcaster (sometimes invoked through the metaphor of "family"), the emphasis on being "responsive," and the affective nature of cam work is key to this early moment of interest broadcasting, and harkens to similar moves we see within game live streaming.[14]

Senft's insight into not only the culture and aesthetics of camming but also the material and economic aspects provides a useful foundation for thinking about what we see on platforms like Twitch. Her notion of microcelebrity—described as "a new style of online performance that involves people 'amping up' their popularity over the Web using technologies like video, blogs and social networking sites" (Senft 2008, 25)—plays a powerful role among professional live streamers. Though she argues that both traditional and new forms of celebrity require one must "brand or die," Senft distinguishes microcelebrity as dependent on "connection to one's audience, rather than an enforced separation from them" (26). Fame on these platforms is one tied up with the affective and relational work broadcasters undertake.[15]

From these earliest moments of experimentation, the interaction between the person on camera and the watching audience was central. As the documentary *We Live in Public* (2009) recounts in its telling of some of the earliest experiments with online streaming, the audience being able to "chime in" has always been central to internet broadcasting. The film notes that whether it was in the broadcasts of early internet shows on the groundbreaking 1998 Pseudo.com network, which mirrored traditional television in having scheduled shows around various topics, or its founder and early cam adoptee Josh Harris's wired-up house that broadcast 24-7, a sidebar text window hosting the audience chatting away in real time was always part of the way these ventures mixed the televisual and internet culture.[16]

Though these early forms of cam broadcast certainly fit neatly within a story of the rise of reality TV, the distribution paths and synchronous communication between audience members with the broadcaster and each other are distinctive to the internet. Early cam culture highlights how average internet users in the 1990s were taking up various technologies, and mobilizing them to their own social and interactive ends. The power of televisually connecting in real time with others, navigating a space of communication *and* performance simultaneously, and revealing otherwise-mundane but evocative daily life to others are lines that connect these older video experiments to current game live streaming.

UGC, YOUTUBE, AND LABOR

While camming as interactive social space remained fairly niche in the 1990s, a second thread of internet culture played a notable role in the growth of live streaming: the rise of UGC.[17] The creative works of people well outside traditional industry production has been central to new media development in the last several decades. Players making "mods" (modifications) to alter their games or create content for them, fans producing videos or stories to augment or celebrate media properties, artists producing mash-ups, or extensive databases and catalogs created by users to facilitate the activities of others are all examples of UGC, and have become a strong component of internet culture. Audiences have been active in taking up this content.

Over the last decade, the creative activity of everyday users on YouTube and other sites has been tracked by a number of scholars, detailing a circuit that flows from user-producers to other audience members across a corporate platform.[18] For example, YouTube's 2017 statistics note it had "over a billion users—almost a third of all people on the Internet—and every day, people watch hundreds of millions of hours of YouTube videos and generate billions of views." Although traditional creative industries such as music or film production companies now supply significant content to the platform, its roots and the bulk of its material have historically come from users. Videos on the site range from independent musicians distributing their songs to silly pranks and stunts. Gaming-focused videos have grown in popularity. As it has come to be identified as a site of value, YouTube has also been monetized and regulated.

The site regularly serves as an exemplar of what is termed "participatory culture." Media scholar Henry Jenkins (2006a) describes our current moment as one in which fans are active producers and consumers of all kinds of material generated not by major media entities but instead by each other. Rather than simply passively consuming content produced by large companies, a notion of participatory culture is meant to evoke a sense that average people are generating all sorts of stuff and engaging meaningfully with it—and each other.[19] Digital media researcher Axel Bruns (2006, 2) has proposed the term "produsers" to describe those who undertake "the collaborative and continuous building and extending of existing content in pursuit of further improvement." This collaboration can take place not only between fans and commercial content but within communities too. Sometimes that content is wholly new, while at other times it remixes and repurposes existing properties, from books to songs to movies to games. Ultimately this perspective on cultural production is one that focuses on the mix of top-down and bottom-up creative practices across not only corporations but also individuals and communities—ones often rooted in fandom.

Internet and media scholars Jean Burgess and Joshua Green (2009, 25) leverage the concept of "vernacular creativity": "the wide range of everyday creative practices (from scrapbooking to family photography to the storytelling that forms part of casual chat) practiced outside the cultural value systems of either high culture or commercial creative practice"—to understand what we see, for example, on YouTube.[20] One of the strengths of Burgess and Green's approach to understanding the circuits of production and consumption is their emphasis on seeing not only the creation of videos but also the sharing and discussion of them as a form of *social* networking. This approach is incredibly important for analyzing game live streaming, and as I will discuss throughout the book, the networking and relational aspects are central for understanding not only the creators on the platform but those who are in the audience too.

They also resist any move to claim such activity as "either trivial or quaintly authentic," and instead want us to see how it "occupies central stage in discussions of the media industries and their future in the context of digital culture" (ibid., 13). Their focus on "consumer-citizens" is, as we'll see, particularly resonant for understanding game live streaming. While they rightfully argue that that simplistic dichotomies between professional and amateur, or commercial or noncommercial, is not analytically helpful, we can reflect on how the labor on these platforms is situated *within* contemporary capitalism. The platforms on which UGC frequently live are typically commercial entities in and of themselves, or are supported by advertising and thus tie them to such systems.

Going back to theorist Tizania Terranova's (2000, 34) foundational piece in which she asked us to consider the ways that the "cultural and technical work" of the internet is "a pervasive feature of the postindustrial economy" is a useful continued provocation for looking at platforms like YouTube and Twitch. Terranova, in tackling a framework for understanding a digital economy, asserted that we should not avoid thinking of labor, even if it doesn't look like the typical wage labor we are used to. Instead, she asks us to consider immaterial, often-free labor as central to how new media works. As she puts it, "Free labor is the moment where this knowledgeable consumption of culture is translated into productive activities that are pleasurably embraced and at the same time often shamelessly exploited" (ibid., 37). This approach helps us recognize the range of contributions made to platforms—from the production of YouTube videos to status updates on our favorite social media—as a form of labor that often taps into powerful affective, even relational modes. While the question of exploitation is one both theorists and users themselves wrestle with, at a foundational level this immaterial labor that unpins so much of our current digital life is a crucial part of understanding live streaming.

In many ways, this book extends the conversation about labor and the digital economy by situating the activities of the live streamers I chronicle here as undertaking new forms of media industry work. Production and distribution are salient categories that broadcasters themselves take up and articulate. For variety streamers, vernacular creativity sits alongside of and gets worked through traditional industry logics, while simultaneously pushing back on and at times transforming them. And for esports companies, live streaming is deeply located within unfolding shifts in sports/media industries. Game live streaming continues a conversation about labor in the digital economy, but also extends it by situating it within a media industry frame tied up with varying forms of practice and compensation.

Indeed this double side of YouTube has, for gamers, long been the norm as it became an important venue for remix and original work as well as amateur and commercialized activity. The platform offered gamers some of their first opportunities to not only engage in creative labor but also attempt to monetize it. "Machinima"—video productions that use game engines to create their content—found an ideal home on the platform so much so that it inspired the creation of the multichannel network (MCN) structure: a collection of many individual broadcasters banded together as a collective. Commentaries, tutorials, and general game entertainment shows have also taken off over the last several years. Due to the possibilities for compensation through the platform's advertising system, some content creators have been able to make a living from their UGC. Launched in 2007 as the YouTube Partner Program, approved content providers get a cut of the revenue from the commercials that run on their channels alongside their own original productions. Though in April 2017 the monetization model shifted the threshold for partners to start making money (at the time of this writing, you must now have ten thousand lifetime views on your channel), the program was groundbreaking for the way it sought to wed UGC and commercialization.

In her study of one group of content producers, the Yogscast, game studies researcher Esther MacCallum-Stewart provides insight into the rise of an expert team of media producers via their deep fandom. She traces the growth of podcasts and webcasts (typically recorded videos) within gaming, and shows how these casters "are not only spokespeople for the gaming community at large but they are also a powerful force in both spreading information and advertising various aspects of games and gaming" (MacCallum-Stewart 2014, 83). Tracing their economic success, she notes that their work is not limited to simply information dissemination.

MacCallum-Stewart considers their own status as celebrities, and leveraging the work of authors like Matt Hills (2002), positions these broadcasters as "big name fans"—a group that has gained notoriety, yet at its core retains a fannish identity and is deeply dependent on other gamer fans for its success. This border identity and the extensive work these content producers do (including community engagement) are similar in many ways to the live streamers in this book. Although the broadcasters I have studied produce a slightly different kind of content and raise unique issues with their live interactions with their audiences, the themes around fandom and communities are resonant with those MacCallum-Stewart identifies.

As she describes in her case study of the Yogscast, what began as fan activity grew into a business. Game studies scholar Hector Postigo (2016) has done important research investigating forms of gamer productions that are monetized, including "converting play into YouTube money." Of particular value in Postigo's work is his look at how the technology of YouTube is a critical component of the UGC system. Focusing on the affordances of the platform, he explores how everything from the uploading system to the ability for viewers to comment and rate work transforms "making gameplay" into "making game pay." His analysis is particularly helpful in both revealing the nature of this form of UCG and pushing against simple dichotomies of exploitation/freedom or work/play when trying to understand YouTuber's content production. As he argues, "Under these conditions, one should *not* conceptualize play and production as distinct. Rather, the creative and the productive processes are melded in the context of *making gameplay*, and play and production are unified processes" (9). In many ways, this is indeed the dream that YouTube sought to make real in its formulation of how the system would work, and Postigo insightfully reveals not only the labor of these gamers but also how the platform facilitates the commercialization of their creative output.

As live streaming has developed, more users from YouTube have begun to broadcast on sites like Twitch, and at the same time, content has cycled out from the live streaming space back onto YouTube as a host for VOD shows. Many of the themes around content production along with the relations between games, producers, and the fans of each can be seen first arising on YouTube. Some of the earliest experiments with UGC monetization and the development of sustainable economic models for producers began there. It, and the integration of UGC into gaming broadly, is a key node in tracing out a history of game live streaming.

Multiplayer Gaming and Spectatorship

Into this mix of inexpensive video telecommunications and the rise of UGC, we must now fold in the long robust history of multiplayer gaming and pleasures of spectatorship. From the earliest days of digital gaming, people gathered together to share their play, cooperate, and compete. Arcades were an important site of multiplayer gaming, and fostered not only competition but also spectating one another's play as you waited your turn or admired a skilled player at the controls.[21]

As home consoles rose in popularity (and arcades faded), people found themselves seated next to each other on floors and sofas playing together, often still having to hand off controllers. Game consoles brought digital play into the home, and as such, it became a part of domestic leisure practices and contexts. Sharing devices, controllers, and cartridges with families and friends alike extended the notion of multiplayer gaming beyond the constraints of the game itself to the social milieu in which play is located.

The growth of the personal computer as a device for play also fostered multiplayer experiences. In the beginning, this mostly ranged from once again taking turns at a machine to sharing games on disks. Eventually hooking machines up together into local area networks (LANs) and jumping into shared digital space to game together in real time became a significant development (especially around competitive gaming and early esports).

With the rise of the internet, the ability to play with those not in your immediate geographic area grew. No longer needing to be physically present together (bodies *or* machines), networked gaming online quickly took off starting in the mid-1990s. Massively multiplayer online games, team-based first-person shooters, or one-on-one strategy games all came to be hugely popular. With the growth of mobile gaming, one more node was added to the story in which the everyday experience of digital play is now deeply, even mundanely situated in a multiplayer context often mediated through a network.

Woven throughout all these variations on multiplayer gaming is the experience of spectating play. Whether waiting for a turn at an arcade machine, having a console controller passed over, or watching a heated online battle continue after your character has "died," spectating has been a part of gaming since the beginning. Even with single-player titles, watching another person move through the game can be compelling and entertaining. At times spectators even share labor with the primary player, as in the case of offering tips or helping map out the game space. Game scholar James Newman (2002, 409) has described these forms of engagement as having a notable role in play, arguing that though the spectator may not have their hands on the controller, "they nonetheless demonstrate a level of interest and experiential engagement with the game that, while mediated through the primary player, exceeds that of the bystander or observer." Spectating has its own set of pleasures and forms of affective experience. It can itself be a form of ludic engagement and has long played an important role in gaming.

It is into this mix of television transformations, internet culture, and multiplayer experiences that game live streaming arises. These are long interweaving trajectories across both traditional and new media. Game live streaming points to the ways that the televisual is worked over by internet and game culture. It can also be a tremendous "canary in the coal mine" for our broader critical considerations. It can give us a glimpse of cutting-edge media activities and cultural shifts. Live streaming intersects with conversations happening in internet culture around user-created content, monetization, and forms of governance. It dovetails with broader analyses of media, especially around alternate production and distribution mechanisms. At the same moment that services like Netflix or Amazon are shaking up traditional television production, distribution, and consumption, game live streaming is at the critical juncture of a new broadcast landscape. Gamers are creating media products for other players. They are doing so not via traditional television but rather through online sites and with techniques resonant with online life and gaming. Tracing out the growth of live streaming from its early roots that intersect the televisual, internet culture, UGC, and gaming, we find a domain that offers insight into the entwining of our network and media lives. It reveals an era of networked broadcast.

The Networked Audience

The notion of the network will figure into the story that follows in a variety of ways: via the assemblage of technologies and actors that make live streaming possible, through the use of the internet for distribution and participation, the construction of a media experience across multiple platforms and sites, and the complex connections and interrelations between broadcasters and audiences. Before diving more deeply into the cases of variety and esports streaming that is the focus of this book, it's worth saying a few words about live streaming viewers—the networked audience.

Media scholar Alice Marwick (2013, 213) also uses this term in her work on celebrity and social media to highlight the connected nature of the viewers, especially around the practices of "lifestreaming." As we've seen, live streaming is situated in a much longer history of television, the internet, UGC, and games. While it has resonance with other forms of media engagement, from traditional broadcast to recorded gameplay through videos on YouTube, the forms of engagement and work these online audiences undertake should be understood in their own specificity. Though I will discuss them in more detail as I concentrate on specific cases in the remainder of the book, a few broader strokes are worth laying down to help situate audiences.

WHY WE WATCH

While my fieldwork has not focused on audience members, over years of work in this domain I've come to have a better sense of why people tune into game live streaming. Simply put, there is no single reason. David Morley (1992, 139) noted that "'watching television' cannot be assumed to be a one-dimensional activity of equivalent meaning or significance at all times for all who perform it," and it is much the same for game live streams. Watching them happens in a variety of contexts, and depending on the game, viewers, broadcasters, and fellow audience members can tap into different pleasures.

There are six clear motivations for why people watch game live streams: aspirational, educational, inspirational, entertainment, community, and ambience.[22] These may wax and wane in any given viewing session, they are not singular, an audience member may approach different broadcasts for different reasons, and they are not determined by the content of the broadcast itself but instead tied to the context and disposition of the viewer. These six are a snapshot of what viewership currently looks like, and I anticipate audience motivations will shift and develop as the medium does.

> *Aspirational*: The aspirational mode is an orientation centered on wanting to be a better gamer, although it can be diffuse in its focus and is often an early entry point for many viewers when they find out about game videos. A viewer may aspire to be more skilled, hold greater game expertise, or display virtuosity. They may also aspire to be a popular, beloved public figure like their favorite streamer. While the aspirational at times weaves in with the educational or inspirational modes I will discuss next, it frequently

operates at a more affective level as a motivating feeling as well as embodied sense of desire and hope.

Educational: Aspirational forms often become educational motivations. One thread that connects some live streams to recorded game video on YouTube is the learning opportunity. This mode involves an audience member using the broadcast to investigate something about the game—perhaps to help decide if they want to buy it or gain insight into specific techniques for how to play. Within the educational frame, broadcasters may provide everything from how-tos to nuanced critique about a game based on knowledge related to a genre, for example. Viewers may also glean subtler tips and tricks from watching someone play, even if that is not the intended orientation of the broadcaster. Like the aspirational orientation, this mode is often a gateway to game videos, and live streaming in particular.

Inspirational: Another major driver in viewing is tied to fandom. People may find themselves looking up information on their favorite game, series, or even genre, and discover a pleasure in watching another person playing something they are passionate about. This mode tends to spur or trigger deep engagement in the viewer as they connect their own experience with that of the broadcaster's. It may tap into an aesthetic experience too, of simply appreciating the play they are watching. The audience member may feel things viscerally, prompting a remembrance of their own play. Usually it even inspires them to go play or replay the game being watched. For some it also spurs a desire to stream the game they are fans of, moving them from spectator to producer.

Entertainment: One of the most powerful motivators for watching live streams is the pleasure of being entertained. Often this is through humor and the performance on-screen by a sharp-witted fellow gamer. It can also be through the experience of discovery alongside the streamer, where you as the viewer "travel along" with them as they play the game or experience the emotionality of the game through their play. In live streaming, adept broadcasters are good at drawing the audience into the experience as well. They will ask questions, offer advice, and not only play the game but also "play to" the camera for the audience's benefit. The entertainment frame can be reminiscent of sitting alongside a friend on the sofa while they are playing or it can tap into the feeling of watching an accomplished performer, as on television.

Community: Woven throughout many of these other motivations can be a desire to have a feeling of community or a social experience. For many, live streaming becomes a place in which their fandom for a game is embodied in the caster, and as a member of an audience, is transformed into a collective experience. Viewers may enjoy connecting to other audience members through the live chat, which sits off to the side of the broadcaster's stream. There they can talk with other viewers or the broadcaster about the game or their lives, or make idle chitchat. It is common to hear longtime viewers remark on how they originally started watching primarily for the streamer yet ultimately became a part of the larger community on the channel. As I will discuss more in later chapters, broadcasters often work hard to foster this sense of social engagement and connection, and it can form a powerful tie between viewer and channel. On larger esports channels, the community motivation can morph into the pleasures of participating in a large anonymous collective. Much like sitting in a sports stadium and hearing the cheers of the rest of the crowd or participating in a "wave," joining in a live stream can anchor an individual to a broader group experience.

Ambience: A final category is one longtime viewers often know well, but that can surprise those who aren't familiar with live streaming. Time and again I've spoken to people who keep streams on all day as a kind of comforting background noise and movement. In these moments, play becomes transformed from discrete instrumental action or entertainment to a more mundane yet still-engaging quality of everyday life. I think of this as ambient sociality, where the broadcast becomes a fixture in one's space. The presence—of the game moving in the background, the broadcaster's image or voice, or even the audience visualized by the chat window—taps into a desire to be connected to something outside one's immediate surroundings at a deep sensory level. Much like people have done with television or music over the years, live streams can become a background ambience to everyday life.[23]

While the remainder of this book will focus on those on or behind the camera, it is important to get at least this small glimpse into the draw of watching live streams. The pleasures of being an online audience member are multiple, overlapping, and can vary even within a single viewer. They evolve and morph over time in tandem with the development of the medium along with the viewer's own experiences and contexts. Sometimes, as with ambient sociality, they are akin to what we have experienced in traditional television, while at other times, as in the educational mode, they speak to something distinctive in gaming. Overall, they reveal that the audience side of the equation is just as complex and nuanced as the production side, and well worth continued attention, especially by media scholars who might investigate this new form of cultural participation.

TALKING BACK

As I note above, connections with the broadcaster and other viewers can be a powerful draw to game live streaming. One of the most distinctive features of the form at this point is how central an online synchronous chat window for the audience to participate has become. On Twitch, text conversation occurs in a window off to the right side of the screen.[24] While originally built on IRC, it has now evolved into a specialized hybrid, though it continues to integrate with chat bots (small pieces of software that monitor the conversation, and do various forms of moderation or info sharing) and still lets you issue traditional IRC commands like "/me action." The chat window is also a key place where broadcasters can keep tabs on who is coming and going from their channel, see what their audience is saying, and catch questions that they then generally answer audibly via a microphone.

Chat is where you see mass crowd behavior too, for both good and ill. Researcher Drew Harry, who received his PhD from MIT's Media Lab and went on to lead the science team at Twitch, did fascinating work exploring potential systems for live streamed crowd experience (2012). He was the first person to explain to me how a fast-scrolling chat window, filled with text that wasn't conversational but full of excited exclamations, repetitive emoticons, and memes, could be seen as akin to the cheering one would find in a sports stadium. This form of communication, dubbed "crowdspeak" by Colin Ford and colleagues (2017, 859), while appearing on the surface as "chaotic, meaningless, or cryptic," actually has "'practices of coherence' that make massive chats legible, meaningful, and compelling to participants." Though there remains much to be done to better facilitate communication in live streaming spaces, many viewers have eagerly taken up the chat component of broadcasts.[25]

From my first interviews with Twitch developers and executives as well as streamers themselves, I was told over and over how central chat is to Twitch.

The platform's annual year in review stats typically includes the number of chat messages that flow through the system. In 2016, for example, there were 14.2 billion chat message sent (Frietas 2016). While YouTube content creators and their audiences use the comments field on a video's page to communicate asynchronously, what happens in Twitch chat is something quite different. It is a space of real-time dynamic exchange not just between broadcaster and audience but the audience members with each other too. Chat can also include references to things having nothing to do with gaming or Twitch that weave their way into an otherwise-specialized subculture. This component of live streams taps into language around "engagement" that social media marketers often use superficially.[26] It is part of a longer trajectory of interaction that spectators, fans, and audiences have always had with media objects. Contrary to the rhetoric of the passive viewer, many studies have shown over the years the creative, active ways audiences take up content. Live streaming chat continues this thread, and as users frequently do, iterates it.

While conversation and symbolic communication (in the form of emoticons and memes) makes up the majority of Twitch chat, it has also been used for gameplay. Twitch Plays Pokémon (TPP) was the first breakthrough that took the chat functionality of the site and, letting users actually input game commands via it, facilitated collective play (see figure 2.3). As you can probably imagine, thousands of people simultaneously inputting actions led to

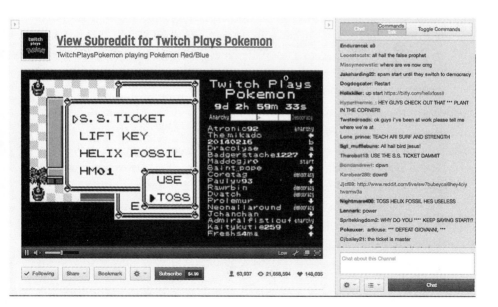

FIGURE 2.3. Twitch Plays Pokémon screenshot, 2014.

FIGURE 2.4. "First date." xkcd comic by Randall Munroe, Creative Commons Attribution Non-Commercial 2.5 License. https://xkcd.com/1333/.

often-humorous, sometimes-frustrating repetitions like endlessly attempting to use an unusable item or accidentally "releasing" Pokémon monsters into the wild. Player-spectators engaged in lively, if at times comic, debates about whether to use a voting system to tally inputs, thus trying to act cooperatively to make intentional game choices (dubbed "democracy") or surrender to the serendipities of chaos that emerge when thousands of people try to play a game at once—known in the TPP community as "anarchy." Players took up these positions with humor and frequently real intensity of purpose; your approach became a kind of playful philosophical declaration that itself was battled out via a metacommand system. The chat window evolved to accommodate a flood of commands while retaining discussion (via a commands/text toggle to help people follow it all).

TPP also produced an entire subset of fan engagement including stories and complicated mythologies, T-shirts, and memes, and eventually even leaked out into a broader popular culture (see figure 2.4).

Indeed, the first time my friends and colleagues started to talk to me about live streaming was as a result of hearing about TPP in major news publications. The idea of utilizing chat for gameplay purposes, and harnessing the engagement of the audience, is now a genre in and of itself that has been used for a variety of games on the platform.

AUDIENCE WORK

There is something generative about the way that TPP pushes a reflection on the nature of audiences to the fore. The very idea of "watching" can conjure up an image of a passive, individualized, even isolated spectator.

Yet this is something contemporary media studies has long problematized, well before we began collectively inputting game commands as we watched live streams. Media scholars Sut Jhally and Bill Livant (1986, 125), situating audiences within a media economy, argue that understanding "watching as work" addresses the concrete "value creating process" that audiences are engaged in as well as helps us think more broadly about viewership. Though their account is primarily focused on a critical materialist conceptualization of audiences, it does speak to the low-level affective ways audiences are always entangled in value production within the media industries. A model of viewing where people are always engaging with content, decoding what they watch, and making meaning of it within their specific contexts has been fundamental to contemporary media theories for decades now (Hall 1980). This engagement is deeply situated in personal and social conditions; understanding it as such disrupts the rhetoric that viewers are simply isolated passive receivers of a given media message. Whether it is via material arrangements and domestic conditions or identities and culture, we are always *working with* the media in our lives refracted through our specific contexts.

As I discussed earlier, theories of participatory culture have been central to understanding contemporary media and internet life. An important part of that intervention was highlighting the "once invisible work of media spectatorship" (Jenkins 2006b, 135). Though some examples in this domain focus on concrete transformations and interventions that audiences make to media they engage with (from remixing and republishing content to facilitating bottom-up funding campaigns), the approach illustrates the fundamental status of audiences as active. Theories of participatory culture build on a much longer history within cultural studies that understands the active engagements we all make with culture, even when commercialized.

This mode sets up for us a richer understanding of viewership reflected in the diversity of motivations, contexts, and uses of spectating live streams. From learning to be a better competitor to talking to people on a channel, live streaming audiences are regularly engaged and often social. Streaming communities will also frequently expand the sphere of interaction with other platforms or creative activities, such as forming groups in games or producing fan art. While some audience members may use a broadcast for a kind of ambient presence, this too can speak to an intentional form of engagement. Even lurking, quietly taking inspiration, or simply following a favorite broadcaster by clicking on a button all point to ways in which audiences actively navigate, experience, and are working with content.

These practices embody broader media trends where audiences are not simply consuming content but are also part of a circuit of production *through* their engagement. Aside from ways they are enlisted into productions by their very presence (something I explore more in later chapters), their own gaming becomes linked up with the experiences of spectatorship. Viewing others playing games can animate a desire to play, or play in particular ways (for instance, adopting the techniques and strategies of pro gamers). It can be an affective experience, pulling you in and kindling a ludic stance. It can be visceral and embodied; you can find yourself leaning forward, at attention.

Amid understanding spectatorship in these ways, we need to keep an eye on how the laboring audience is constructed and deployed within broader industrial shifts. That turn is crucial to not painting an overly celebratory or liberatory narrative about the active audience. Media scholar Jonathan Sterne (2012) wisely cautions about how "interactivity" and attention is leveraged into "market value," arguing, "When people's participation becomes someone else's business—and here I mean business in the market-share and moneymaking sense of the term—the social goods that are supposed to come with it can be compromised." Internet scholar Kyle Jarrett (2008b) likewise prompts us to critically reflect on the ways that interactivity becomes bound up with a notion of the neoliberal subject via systems that push us to always produce, always consume.

It is certainly the case that game live streaming is built on the commodification of a range of labor, and its audience work neatly dovetails with how the media industries have been realigning their production and economic models to deal with the internet. Enlisting participation for the purposes of monetization is in the DNA of not only Facebook and Twitter but Twitch as well. Traditional media has long chased after a dream of interactive audiences—valuable ones that can be captured and sold to advertisers—and the growth of new metrics and participatory fan communities online has been tantalizing to those in the business of selling audiences.[27] A significant part of the rhetorical framework around Twitch is, indeed, a focus on the breadth and measurability of its engagement—a particularly enticing rubric for advertisers.

Game studies scholar Nick Taylor's research on esports and the process of "audiencing" brings this conversation directly into the terrain of this book by looking at how esports audiences have developed from a space where the line between player and spectator was quite blurry to a more formalized boundary akin to traditional broadcast frames. Drawing on work by Jack Bratich (2005) and Shawn Shimpach (2008), he argues for understanding esports and live streaming audiences within a framework that recognizes the "extent to which our participation in contemporary media forms is circumscribed" (2016, 304). His examples of how esports audiences at events are positioned in ways that serve to enhance media productions or amplify the affective side of tournaments (for example, in building "hype") are instructive for helping us think about the ways these emerging audiences are woven back into productions in fairly constrained ways.[28]

So how to thread this needle? How should we understand the active work of live streaming audiences within a distinctly commercialized sphere of new media development? Rather than shy away from arguments about the commodification of audiences and the labor they engage in, or write off that engagement as simple exploitation or hollow participation, we need to understand how audiences are often knowing participants in the construction of new media forms, even ones for sale. Live streaming audiences are not dupes, though they may not always fully wrangle with the extent to which their engagement is a market commodity or the long-term costs.

In large esports broadcast events, there are absolutely moments when we might turn a critical eye to the ways that tournaments facilitate the production of an audience for broadcast and commercial purposes. The cameras that turn back on spectators show them wearing team jerseys or game hats, and play up the mass of the crowd. The handing out of "thunder sticks" and white poster board for signs—all of which let audiences create visually compelling, booming, and often-flashing cheers—are prime fodder for the camera. And yet at the same time we have to balance such accounts with the genuine passion, fandom, and authenticity of expression at work in the space. Esports audiences are often knowingly and meaningfully engaged as fans happy to support their scene, including the commercial entities involved. They regularly acknowledge the tension and are often highly attuned to coarse cash grabs.

And in variety streams where audience members are frequently deeply supportive of and connected to a broadcaster, understanding this balance requires even more care. Though both broadcaster and audience member are certainly "at work" in some way (as I'll detail more later), and contributing to the financial health of the platform—including even just as data points, statistics that fill up business PowerPoint decks and press releases—they are usually knowing, intentional, and still striving for meaningful creativity and connection. Even as the platform leverages the affective pull of live streaming, we would be remiss to write it off as simply about exploitation.

Media is ultimately *co-constituted* through spectators, producers, and texts, and seeing it as relational is key. Jenkins has called for "refusing to see media consumers as either totally autonomous from nor totally vulnerable to the culture industries." As he maintains, "It would be naive to assume that powerful conglomerates will not protect their own interests as they enter this new media marketplace, but at the same time, audiences are gaining greater power and autonomy as they enter into the new knowledge culture. The interactive audience is more than a marketing concept and less than 'semiotic democracy'" (Jenkins 2006b, 136). His encouragement to document these circuits is an inspiration for the work here. While in the following I will speak more directly to issues around labor, precariousness, and affective economies as well as critically reflect on how engagement is regulated, the analysis is anchored in a model that sees audience engagement and co-creation as central to the story, and my frame is one in which commercial platforms like Twitch occupy complex, often-ambivalent positions within the broader circuit of production and sit alongside often-knowing, meaningful, user engagement.

Building a Platform

PAX East, while not the original flagship convention that takes place in Seattle, is a tremendous weekend event. Tens of thousands of people come to the Boston Convention Center to celebrate, discuss, and play analogue and digital games as well as participate in fan and celebrity panels, hyped-up developer sponsored demos, and amazing cosplay (costumes based around characters). Given that I was living just across the river in Cambridge, Massachusetts, it was easy enough to pop over, so in 2013 I attended my first PAX and had a chance to check out the Twitch booth.

Descending the escalator to the large exhibition hall can be an overwhelming experience. Lots of noise, lights, booths, and crowds fill the space. I knew enough to scan while I had a bird's-eye view and spotted the Twitch booth off to the right, lit in its ubiquitous "Twitch Purple" hue. Its space that year featured a broadcast area with sofas for interviews and gaming with various personalities, a small demo area that focused primarily on *Smite* (a multiplayer game it was hosting a tournament for), some standing room, and several large screens to watch the ongoing broadcast. While not the largest booth there, it still took up a good chunk of floor space, and you could sense the company was figuring out how to showcase itself at an event otherwise dedicated to game developers and fan merchandise.

When I returned to the convention in 2014, it was clear that more was being done to make the booth a place to watch the broadcasts that were being piped out worldwide as well as hang around and mingle with others.

Large screens were hung around the booth, drawing crowds to watch both the live on-site performers and the production that was being broadcast online (see figure 2.5a). This was no small detail. Twitch had secured a deal with ReedPOP, the event services company that produces the PAX expos, to be the exclusive streaming partner for the event. This meant that the company would not only be featuring content each day as in the prior year (hosting streamers and developers, for example). It was now the site to go to for PAX East coverage if you weren't able to attend but wanted to keep up with the event. The booth was also the location for the Capcom Pro Tour fighting game competition and the TeSPA Collegiate Hearthstone Open (see figure 2.5b).

Although the competitions definitely caught my eye, the thing I noticed most that year was that the booth became a hub where people congregated to meet others who used the platform. Name tags were available for everyone to note their Twitch username on. One popular streamer described his PAX experience this way:

> It was more of a networking situation for me, and a time to meet with some of the personalities or some of the friends I've made, other streamers, and to be able to meet my viewers. I hang out and get to know these people. There was crazy happenstance meetings that we couldn't plan. Just being around the convention I ran into people that have led to other relationships that are opening up doors for me. It's just being around and being part of the community. And when I say community, now I'm talking about a much broader community, which is the Twitch community.

Being at the booth became an important part of the convention work and fun for many streamers. Broadcasters were meeting Twitch staff and each other—often face-to-face for the first time—and just as important, fans were swinging by to catch glimpses of their favorite personalities. Some of those streamers held a microcelebrity status; though likely not recognized outside the convention hall, inside they were experiencing their reach for the first time as people approached them to introduce themselves, say how much they loved their stream, and get a photo with them. Others got an additional notoriety bump as Twitch invited them onto the stage to help host sponsored game sessions.

As I hung around that booth for the weekend, I saw the beginnings of a fan culture emerge not around a game but instead around *broadcasters*. While the concept of cultural intermediaries—a class of professionals who promote the consumption of symbolic goods and services—can at times be

FIGURES 2.5A AND 2.5B. Audiences hanging out at the Twitch booth and watching fighting game competitions, PAX East, 2014.

resonant in understanding game live streaming, it also doesn't fully capture things.[29] Media scholars Sean Nixon and Paul du Gay (2002, 498) argue that the often-implied denigration of intermediaries or overly simplistic conservatism assumed in the concept (that they merely act as promoting given cultural artifacts) might cause us to overlook the more complex interplay of production and consumption, creative action, and the "interdependence and relations of reciprocal effect between cultural and economic practices." These broadcasters were not only doing the work of bringing games to audiences but also had themselves become valued creative producers. They didn't simply promote games, though that is a frequently implied part of a broadcast, but were doing something more as well. Game scholar Austin Walker (2014, 438) describes this expansive work of broadcasters as one in which "new communities grow around these streamers which sometimes offer an alternative to consumption-oriented 'gamer culture,' which work to bring attention to social and political concerns, and which highlight the work of independent and underrepresented developers, organizations, and groups." Seeing them at PAX East, in the mix of game culture broadly, and interacting with each other and their fans, it became clear that they were "talent" who were transforming play. They were also helping build a budding industry that was (and is still) trying to situate itself within a larger game and media ecology.

Over time, this theme was picked up and integrated in earnest into the design of the booth. A dedicated area was constructed for streamers to meet their fans and give autographs. Special trading cards and various other swag were made for the broadcasters to hand out (see figures 2.6a, 2.6b, and 2.6c).

A large internal VIP and meeting area also became part of the booth, where Twitch employees, partnered streamers, and assorted visitors could mingle. By 2016, the Twitch booth at PAX East had become the largest on the show floor and a huge hub of activity. Its presence and growth at the convention mirrored its overall development. In just a few years, Twitch had gone from a small site that offered gamers a way to experiment with sharing their play with strangers to a prime anchor in game culture; it became a place where taste and gameplay were shaped, and where gamers and their spectator fans rose in prominence alongside the titles they played.

It's important, however, to not overlook the real challenges associated with such rapid growth. Live streaming platforms have faced tremendous technical, operational, and economic issues. It is no small feat to build out worldwide infrastructure, navigate how to monetize it, and manage all the people participating, creating, and sustaining a live streaming platform with

FIGURES 2.6A, 2.6B, AND 2.6C. Meet and greet, VIP area, and broadcaster novelty card at Twitch booth, PAX East, 2015.

millions of simultaneous users. This is a crucial part of the story, not just for live streaming, but UGC platforms broadly. It is easy to focus on creative individuals—perhaps you remember *Time* naming "You" the 2006 person of the year for all the content "we" were producing online—and bypass exploring how technological development, organizational structures, or financial systems are central to online life.

In the following, I focus on Twitch itself as an organization and platform as well as an actor that serves as one node in a larger process of cultural co-creation. Game live streaming is only possible via a complex assemblage of technologies, networks, economic models, and governance processes. All these aspects are important to telling the broader story that connects up with individual and organizational practices in the chapters to come. While I'll be weaving these threads throughout the rest of the book, in the remainder of this chapter I present a bit of history about the company, tracing its beginning as a niche live streaming site to one of the major figures in not only the gaming but also the media industry.

ORIGINS

Twitch's roots are fundamentally in the cam culture I described previously. Its origins spring from predecessor Justin.tv, a website dedicated to allowing people to broadcast anything and everything. Launched March 19, 2007, by roommates Justin Kan, Emmett Shear, Michael Seibel, and Kyle Vogt, the platform was geared to "lifecasting," which essentially meant providing a website for people to pipe out their live video to others.[30] As Shear described their intent in a *Fast Company* article, "We were going to enable this new form of reality TV based on streaming people's lives 24/7, and that was going to be the business. We were going to be reality-TV moguls" (quoted in Rice 2012). With an initial investment of $50,000 by Paul Graham of Y Combinator, and less than a year later $2 million from Alsop-Louie Partners, the platform offered people the opportunity to broadcast whatever they liked (ibid.).[31] Kan himself wore a camera and streamed everything from coding sessions to sleeping, and "proclaimed what his new mission would be: 'democratizing live video'" (quoted in ibid.). Though he ultimately found the prospect of constantly streaming his life untenable, the site drew in others who wanted to provide content.

Kan's ambition was very much in sync with the cultural moment. Facebook launched just a few years earlier in 2004, then YouTube in 2005,

Twitter in 2006, and both Tumblr and the iPhone came out in 2007. This was, without a doubt, an intense period where everyday life was being interwoven with network culture, where people were producing content for each other whether it was routine updates on their daily life or special videos. And it was no longer fringe as in the old cam days; lots of internet platforms were experimenting with giving people ways to share pretty much whatever they wanted, however they wanted.

Despite the ways that mundane life was becoming visible more and more online, Justin.tv didn't seem to be sustaining content producers and audiences at the hoped-for level. As with many such platforms, the costs were supposed to be defrayed through ad revenue. Yet such a model required advertisers to relinquish a fair amount of control over what their brands would be embedded next to. As journalist Andrew Rice (2012) notes, "Even when the site was thriving, advertisers were wary of the unpredictability of live user-generated video. So were potential investors and buyers for the company." The potential volatility of allowing users to create all the content for a site is an important challenge that platforms have had to navigate and manage. Alongside this was Kan's own ambivalence, having grown both weary of constantly streaming himself and "struggl[ing] to find anything worth watching" on the platform (quoted in ibid.).

There are slightly varying ways the story of the shift of focus to gaming that propelled Twitch to emerge is told. I was fortunate to be able to interview Shear, Twitch's CEO, in 2013, and he spoke compellingly about how, when it came to Justin.tv, the gaming channels on the site were the ones that really caught his attention. Shear regularly speaks about his own gaming roots in interviews, and during our conversation he made a point that deeply resonated with my own thinking: there is an important historical continuum at work in live streaming. He observed,

> The way I think about [it] is I spent three-quarters of my childhood watching video games as a spectator. In fact, almost every boy my age and most of the girls did this, because if you think about it, we had one console, the person playing the game, and when they died, the next person took a turn. So there were probably three or four of us at any given time sitting there, and you're only playing a quarter of the time . . . and so in that way Twitch is not really all that new.

As he went on to explain, what we were seeing through live streaming was simply a "recapitulation" of these connections. The figure of an isolated gamer playing alone in their home was "the new weird thing," not this

(Shear 2013). Live streaming was an extension of the sofa space so many were familiar with.

This connection between being a gamer and seeing the power of the platform was something I heard often in my years visiting Twitch and speaking to people who worked there. Identifying as a gamer and remembering earlier moments of spectating play were consistent threads in what motivated the people building the site early on. This is not unusual in game-focused companies, where being an active gamer, even of the specific titles of the developer you are employed by, is a common part of one's professional identity.[32] Much development in that space comes directly from imagining yourself as the user, from projecting your experiences, pleasures, desires, and values onto the technology. Early Twitch innovation was deeply tied to executives and developers who were also identifying as gamers.

There is, however, a second significant thread in Twitch's development story: the powerful role of media piracy. Since its inception, the internet has facilitated free and sometimes-illegal access to media. Music distribution and early skirmishes around software like Napster helped set the tone that traditional media companies have taken decade after decade: regulation, enforcement, and technological interventions via digital rights management when possible.[33] With the growth of peer-to-peer distribution networks as well as broadband access, the ability to share larger and larger files such as movies and television shows also grew. It should not be surprising, then, that live streaming afforded yet another new path for media content distribution, including piracy.

Justin.tv, along with a number of other sites such as Stickam and Ustream, became a platform where people could rebroadcast live events, particularly sports. Everything from the National Football League (NFL) and Major League Baseball (MLB) to Ultimate Fighting Championship (UFC) games could be found online in real time. Exclusive broadcast deals (frequently via pay cable channels), blackout zones, and stringent licensing has contributed heavily to sports fans seeking out pirated channels to get games—often ones that they might not otherwise have access to. In an early piece analyzing sports rebroadcasting online, Bruns (2009, 2) described how Justin.tv users addressed a lack of media access through "following a 'gift economy' logic: they rebroadcast what sporting events are readily available to them on their local TV channels, and in turn profit by being able to watch the sporting events rebroadcast by fellow users from elsewhere in the world." The tensions between global online media and local regulations come into sharp relief via these platforms. Communication researchers Burroughs and Rugg note that despite the global frame that television typically circulates within, broadcast rights and regulations tend to still be done on a nation-by-nation basis, and fans regularly leverage a range of technologies (from live streaming to virtual private networks) to get around geofencing (virtual perimeters that regulate access to content by geographic location). They ask us to think about it as a tactical challenge to "the 'proper' strategies of mass consumer and television culture" (Burroughs and Rugg 2014, 370).[34]

This practice, unsurprisingly, did not go unnoticed; media companies and lawmakers got involved. The British Premier League had threatened Justin.tv, and a boxing company had sued Ustream previously (Roettgers 2009). In 2009, a House Judiciary hearing titled "Piracy of Live Sports Broadcasting over the Internet" was held to investigate the situation. Witnesses were called from the MLB, the UFC, ESPN, the University of Pennsylvania Law School, and Justin.tv. Seibel, CEO of Justin.tv at the time, testified before the committee, offering a story of the platform's place in the emerging networked world as well as its position on the content there. He began by noting that

> Justin.tv is, first and foremost, a technology company. We provide a platform that empowers people to create and share live video online. Our platform is the modern equivalent of the town square, but instead of standing on a soapbox to be heard by a few passers-by, a Justin.tv user can broadcast his or her message to the world. Our vision is to make live video part of the everyday Internet experience in the same way that Flickr, The Huffington Post, and YouTube have brought online images, news and video clips into the mainstream. In the near future, your cell phone, your gaming console, and your video camera will all be able to broadcast to the Internet using Justin.tv. Furthermore, users will be able to build businesses on Justin.tv by creating pay-per-view and subscription live videos. In a time of traditional media consolidation, Justin.tv is providing an important alternative platform for the distribution and monetization of live video content. (Seibel 2009)

He went on to argue that the platform was "content agnostic," and "as with many technologies created to advance the public good, Justin.tv's technology can also sometimes be used by individuals to violate the rights of third parties. Such abusive actions do not mean that the underlying technology is responsible for the bad actor" (ibid.). Linking to the Digital Millennium Copyright Act's (DMCA) "Safe Habor" provision (17 U.S.C. § 512), which seeks to protect service providers from legal liability because of content their users might circulate, he then noted that while it is impossible for the platform to monitor all the users' broadcasts due to the sheer amount of content on the site, it responds quickly to rights holder claims. He underscored that it made its policy clear in its terms of service, utilized banning (including internet protocol [IP] bans at times), worked with media networks, and was implementing "fingerprinting" technology that would automatically detect and proactively remove infringing material.

This stance was not enough to protect it from a lawsuit, however, and in 2011, Zuffa LLC, the company that owned the UFC, turned its attention not only to individual streamers but also Justin.tv itself. In its own announcement of the suit, the UFC (2011) said it initiated the action due to the "repeated and ongoing failure to meaningfully address the rampant and illegal uploading of video of live Pay-Per-View [PPV] UFC events by members and users of the Justin.tv website." As one article reported, there was serious money at stake via dozens of events and "an estimated $350 million in PPV revenue" (MMAJunkie Staff 2011). Claiming that the platform not only turned a "blind eye" to the pirating but "has actually induced its users to commit copyright infringement" as well, the UFC (2011) was making a fairly strong accusation.

It was a somewhat-complicated case, with the UFC pivoting to attack the issue through both trademark claims and a "stealing cable" approach (Thomas 2012).[35] Justin.tv fought back, primarily leveraging the safe harbor aspect of the DMCA that seeks to protect platforms owners who are trying to act as neutral conduits while still responding to content infringement when notified (ibid.). In 2012, the court partially dismissed the claims, most significantly noting that third-party sites are not liable for user's uploaded content and that a great many other tech companies (including Google, Apple, Dropbox, etc.) would be swept up in liability if the Communications Act were interpreted otherwise. Though other parts of the case went forward, by April 2012, Justin.tv and the UFC settled their lawsuit—the terms of which were not disclosed (Davis 2012).

Navigating this thicket is no small issue for platform operators. Part of the trick lay in balancing responsive enforcement of claims against overpolicing and extensive curation, which can end up undermining platform neutrality claims that providers usually utilize (not to mention curtailing UGC). One analyst remarked on this delicate balance, saying, "One problem with tightening up on copyrighted content is the flip side of the DMCA. If you actively patrol new uploads, you're no longer seen as a blind ISP, and could be held liable for copyright infringement. Letting a copyrighted upload through the cracks now becomes your responsibility, not the uploader's" (Gannes

2009). As media and technology scholar Tarleton Gillespie (2018, 35) puts it, "These competing impulses, between allowing intermediaries to stay out of the way and encouraging them to intervene, continue to shape the way we think about the role and responsibility of all Internet intermediaries, and has extended to how we regulate social media platforms." UGC sites have to carefully balance acting quickly on infringement claims while simultaneously not appearing to take on the burden of vetting all content lest they become fully responsible curators.

While in discussions with Twitch executives I never encountered this angle as an animating origin story, a *Fast Company* profile on Kan argued that "piracy did not appear incidental to the growth of Justin.tv," and that "after four years of twists and turns, the Justin.tv guys knew a couple of things: Their business was stagnant, and people loved to watch streams of live games. What if they could find a sport that didn't belong to anyone, one that would actually appreciate their attention?" (quoted in Rice 2012). While Kan and Graham were initially dubious about a gaming focus, Shear highlighted the value of game streams versus the more open-ended social cams: "It's advertiser friendly. . . . When you have a webcam, anything can happen. Gaming is much more controlled" (ibid.). On the heels of piracy concerns, the perceived controllability—and thus maybe legal safety—of gaming perhaps had some benefits.

Despite the imagined constraints of gaming, however, broadcasters continue to innovate in ways far beyond simply piping out gameplay. What we see on Twitch is a much messier mix of game plus creative user engagement. And it is also not at all the case that gaming dodges any issues about who owns things. The digital playing fields of gaming have an abundance of latent and sometimes rising scuffles over ownership (something I'll discuss in more detail throughout this book). We've also seen a number of ways that UGC within gaming can be rife with racism, sexism, and homophobia—all things that a number of advertisers (and indeed some game developers themselves) would not like their brand to appear alongside of. Although Twitch clearly captured an audience that previous social cam sites hadn't, it is in no way immune from the tensions that arise around platforms, creative user activity, and governance.

ENGINEERING AND CURATION

Part of what is instructive about the story of early piracy on Justin.tv is that it highlights the ways that platforms often have to navigate a complex relationship with UGC and expectations.[36] Sites like Twitch thrive or die through the active contributions of the user base, and creating an infrastructure to support that activity—and eventually regulate it—is key. I was struck during my first visits to Twitch in talking to various employees how much engineering played a central role organizationally. Producing a platform that can sustain massive amounts of video data flowing in and being piped out across multiple devices around the world is a huge undertaking. Doing engineering work to make live streaming both distributable and affordable was crucial to the success of the platform. It is also in engineering work that we see how a platform imagines its users and itself. It points to the interaction modes that a site values.

Justin.tv had worked hard on this, managing to build software that "had brought the cost of delivering an hour of video down to half a penny, cheap enough to serve constant video to a mass audience as an ad-supported business" (Rice 2012).[37] This engineering focus had migrated over to Twitch and became clear to me as I spoke to people working on the technical side of the platform. Video systems and servers, authentication systems, networks and load balancing, and many other components make the site possible. Engineering was historically situated across operations, video, and site teams, with the eventual inclusion of a platform team as cell phones and other non-PC avenues for watching arose. While the system has had important components drawn from other technical domains (transcoding, for example), as one engineer put it, "At the end of the day it's like, this is our video system and it acts differently than anything else." Different kinds of engineering projects have expressed this specificity.

In the earliest of my visits, the desire for a software development kit (SDK), particularly focused on allowing game developers to integrate a Twitch broadcast function into the game itself, was seen as high priority. SDKs are essentially sets of tools that allow for application development that works in conjunction with a platform. Given one of the biggest hurdles to broadcasting is all the software and hardware a user has to get to work on their specific machine, it's no surprise that the company thought a lot in those early days about making the process easier. At one point this was envisioned as helping game developers integrate the ability to connect up and broadcast from within the game itself. It's unclear how many game developers actively took up this functionality, and ultimately Twitch announced that the overall improvements to third-party broadcasting software led them to leave that technical focus to others; their SDK support was scaled back in 2014. While game consoles have built-in broadcast functionality, PC users still have to work with non-Twitch software (often subscription based) to carry out broadcasts.

By contrast, the company has been especially active in the last several years developing its application programming interface (API). The Twitch API is just one component in the platform framing itself as extendable by third-party developers. Facilitating those initiatives broadly is in part done via a portion of the website dedicated to developers who are building a variety of add-on functionality. From chat tools, graphical overlays, and interactive modes, Twitch seeks to encourage third-party developers to innovate on and extend its basic structure.[38] Perhaps one of the biggest pushes starting around 2016 has been tapping into the creativity of game and third-party developers, and supporting or integrating their creations back into the formal platform. Donation systems, dynamic graphical overlays, and leveraging interaction for actual gameplay have long originated from users and third parties and are now formally supported by the company. These developments tend to be rhetorically promoted as feeding into engagement, retention, audience growth, and community—and sales.

The move to a broader set of functionalities and tools also circled back to hooking in game developers. Rather than simply funneling them to an SDK, the platform has sought to enfranchise them in other ways. In 2015, longtime game industry professional Kathy Astromoff was hired on as vice president of developer success and was quoted as saying, "Reshaping the way game developers engage with their communities in the age of social video is going to break down a lot of barriers in our industry" (quoted in Weber 2015). From supporting "stream-first" games (titles built with streaming in mind), developer integration into Twitch (for instance, via loot box drops or other special items), or outreach sessions at events like the Game Developers Conference, there has been an expansive push to educate and bring game developers to the platform. With its purchase by Amazon, Twitch is also increasingly linking up to the infrastructures and tools provided by that that company.

This move from focused SDK development to the vision of Twitch as an *extendable platform* supporting a wide variety of technical innovations and experiments is, I'd argue, echoing the underpinning logic we see on the production side: the site is only truly animated by the creative activities of users and third parties, and can only survive with the buy-in of game developers. Twitch has made a savvy move to formalize that productive technical activity, now integrating it too into the very brand and activities of the platform. As Astromoff tweeted on October 23, 2017, after the announcement of yet another developer tool (Extensions), "When we say Twitch Extensions are 'live apps for live streams,' #gamedevs should read this as '@Twitch is building an App Store.'" Much like Twitch is able to monetize the creative broadcast productions of users, finding ways to align and harness the technical creativity of third parties as well as having game developers see Twitch as a central part of their product, it is now a part of its overall framework.

These developments point to the ways that the engineering side of the company has long had to work with the dynamic nature of the platform. As one engineer put it, "Scaling is hard. Even once you know how big you want to get, it's a matter of finding the bottlenecks, and sometimes they're apparent, but you want to figure out what the bottleneck is going to be before." Twitch has had to contend with not just building a robust video delivery system but also one that could grow amid unpredictability. Despite increased efforts to build sharing and communication between the company and third parties, it can be an ongoing challenge on a platform where users are constantly experimenting. At TwitchCon 2016, John Rizzo, a senior software engineer at Twitch, presented a postmortem of the company's system in the wake of TPP. His description was lighthearted yet reflective on how the platform was barely able to keep up with what was happening on it. The experiment was being pushed in ways no one anticipated, and rather than shut it down, the engineers worked around the clock to keep the site up and running despite sometimes-bumpy reverberations across the entire system.

While TPP is a more extreme example of engineering being pushed by user practices, gamers in particular are perceived as bringing high expectations to the service. One engineer spoke about this in terms of video resolution, saying, "One thing that was super interesting transitioning from Justin.tv to Twitch is that gamers care a lot more about quality. They make a lot more demands on like 'I want a higher bit rate stream.'" He went on to note, though, what he felt was a tension:

> This is like, maybe not entirely the company line, but I'm trying to make it the company line, is that like one of the things that we did with the transcodes: we gave them numbers. And it's like this is 360p. This is 720p. And then people were like "Well, I want to be 1080p." . . . I'm really worried about it because I feel like there's this, especially in the gamer community, it's like "I got the fastest hard drive" or "the fastest video cards so I can do this," and like, numbers matter. I feel like we've incentivized some of our partners to push the limits in what their system can do. So they're actually like trying to sell this product like "We have 1080p, 60 frames per second," and it's coming at the expense of their

audience because if like there's low room for margin, they're pushing more and more.

One of the ways he tried to navigate this tension was by mitigating technical risk as much as possible. As he put it, "At the end of the day, you will generate content, and the best thing we can do is educate and give our broadcasters the tools to make the best decisions, and like, we want to stop them from shooting themselves in their foot." Yet he also felt there were limits to what he could actually do, asserting that he could never make a "padded room padded enough," and "my path to this is let's just give them as much feedback as possible to help them make good decisions and educate."

This conversation was particularly interesting given it was a member of the engineering team and not, for example, community support staff. One of the most important things to understand about engineering is that while it is a technical pursuit, it always involves imagined (and sometimes real) users and stakeholders, and subsequent ideas about what they want and need. Engineers, especially team leads, regularly think about "users" even if they don't articulate considerations in ways that a researcher might. This is especially true for a site like Twitch where so many employees are constantly on it, even themselves streaming at times. But this can become tricky organizational territory when you also have departments whose sole focus is on sales or user relationships. These teams are directly engaging with broadcasters and companies, trying to make deals and sell the product, or support those already using it. So while an engineering team may have ideas about technical expectations, capacities, and limits, often, especially in sales, there are greater and greater pushes on the platform to help boost user numbers, close lucrative deals, or foster general hype about the service.

Over the years that I have been visiting Twitch and talking to various employees, I have been struck by how the roots in engineering have increasingly come to sit alongside significant development in sales, content production, community management, and data science/analytics. Setting up and managing the fundamental infrastructure and technical processes for live streaming operates alongside departments whose job it is to facilitate user-generated and in-house content, sell the platform to corporate clients, deepen the use of data and analytics, and generally foster a vibe that situates Twitch as an energetic part of internet and game culture.

One of the most challenging organizational growth points can be in the internal push and pull that can come from these branches, and finding ways to align or smooth processes. This is not unique to Twitch; many sites—from

YouTube to Facebook to Twitter—balance similar teams. Platforms that launched as a basic system for users to distribute creative works to others frequently come to grow and formalize, organizationally, the cultivation and curation of content. They create larger and often-specialized sales teams. They build departments focused on mining data on the site for additional "insights" that can be fed back into the system. For Twitch, this has meant the growth and maintenance of partnership and affiliate programs, allocation of coveted "front-page" slots on the main landing page that highlight particular channels, and sales teams centered on specialized products. In 2015, the company launched a "science" team focused on research. It has also increasingly gotten in the business of producing or curating content itself for the site—from esports to rebroadcasts of PBS shows such as Bob Ross's *Joy of Painting*, or shows that highlight up-and-coming broadcasters.

This is important because it points to the ways that Twitch, as with many social media companies, is not just about providing a basic technical service (acting as a neutral platform) but is also in the content production business. At times this involves the facilitation and curated promotion of UGC, while at others it is managing original in-house productions or working with outside companies. It can also offer structures, in the form of both human labor and technical systems, to moderate content. As Gillespie (2018, 46) argues in his analysis of social media sites, they resist simplistic dichotomization, and are "distinctly neither conduit nor content, not only network or only media, but a hybrid that has not been anticipated by information law or public debates." As I hope to demonstrate throughout this book, Twitch can often be seen as straddling a line between platform and media company. Understanding its work involves exploring not only technical infrastructures and choices but the content on the site and its governance as well. It is, fundamentally, a sociotechnical organization and artifact.

GROWTH

As I've studied game live streaming, and Twitch in particular, I've regularly joked to my various informants, "Please, no more new developments! I need to finish the book!" This wasn't an unfamiliar feeling. I felt it acutely as I was researching esports in the 2000s and eventually made the rather arbitrary decision to call that case closed (enough) to write it up. Twitch has been much the same. When I started visiting the company in 2013, it was staffed by under two hundred people working on a product that was still fairly in the margins of not only gaming but also media more broadly. In 2014, its

US network traffic at peak times ranked fourth overall—only surpassed by Netflix, Google, and Apple (Fitzgerald and Wakabayashi 2014). Amazon purchased Twitch that same year for $970 million. At the time of this writing, the company had grown to over a thousand employees and had expanded its offices several times.

Twitch has continued to cultivate the range of content that it hosts, now well beyond gaming. It offers a music subdirectory facilitating people who broadcast themselves creating music as well as live streams of a number of high-profile electronic music shows and DJs such as the Ultra Music Festival and Steve Aoki. While some in the community were unhappy with non-gaming content coming to the platform, the company has continued to expand what it allows. It has repeatedly demonstrated an interest in broadcasts that focus on performance and production, and as a result, a "creative" subdirectory now showcases people live streaming everything from cosplay to drawing. Categories for "cooking" and "social eating" have also been introduced. Such broadcasts seem to take early webcam culture impulses and hone them into more process-oriented activities, of which gaming was simply the first example.

Twitch also extended its reach into esports. Shortly after being bought by Amazon, it purchased—for an undisclosed amount—Good Game Agency, an esports organization created by Alex Garfield, who owned several esports teams at the time. The agency represented teams Evil Geniuses and the Alliance (both Garfield properties). Though Twitch went on to close the Good Game Agency within a couple years, it was a clear signal of its serious esports interest. It has partnered with former competitors (such as NGE, formerly Hitbox) and sought to build its own esports tournaments via the Rocket League Championship Series. Despite competition from established esports producers as well as other platforms such as YouTube and Facebook that have been actively building out their own esports distribution portfolios, Twitch has been instrumental during this period of esports media growth.

In perhaps the most interesting twist in its trajectory, in 2016 it began offering an "in real life" (IRL) category that encouraged broadcasters to "share your thoughts, opinions, and everyday life." As many noted, this was in some ways akin to its Justin.tv roots. Whereas just a few years earlier Twitch had actively prohibited people from using the platform for anything other than gaming, the IRL category legitimized the inclusion of all the other parts of broadcasters lives as fodder for content. Dovetailing with explicit support for mobile broadcasting, the IRL category dictates that interactivity is central yet it is expansive in its formulation of what can be broadcast. As the FAQ puts it, "Maybe you like working out and can make it interactive. You just read a great book and want to discuss it. Or maybe you have very strong opinions about the season finale of your favorite show. That kinda thing. Vlogs of your trips into the outside world, such as an amusement park, an event (TwitchCon!), or even the grocery store" (Twitch 2017a). Twitch seems to have made perhaps-pragmatic peace with its own roots by offering its broadcasters a platform for everyday, non-gaming life.

This growth has not gone unnoticed by mainstream media observers and cultural commentators. News outlets like the *New York Times* and *Wall Street Journal* have covered what is happening on Twitch, at times with the bemused glance of a media sector aware *something* is happening, but still not quite sure what. In November 2017, the *New Yorker* published a feature primarily focused on a talent management company that handled a number of prominent streamers (Clark 2017). It was a compelling tale, highlighting the growing industry building around all that UGC. In many ways, what follows here is a deeper dive into some of the nooks and crannies of that story, albeit without quite the glossy sheen of prosperity. What I present in the chapters that follow are of game live streaming before the talent managers arrived, of the handful of years after the platform launched when aspirational gamers and esports organizations experimented with transforming a media landscape through play.

3

Home Studios

TRANSFORMING PRIVATE PLAY
INTO PUBLIC ENTERTAINMENT

Late one February night around 2:00 a.m., I found myself heading down a Florida interstate to visit a popular broadcaster at his home to see him do his live stream in person. We'd previously spoken on Skype, and I had watched a bunch of his broadcasts, but I was interested in getting a peek into what it looked like from the other end of the screen. Despite being a night owl, I was already getting tired and couldn't quite imagine the prospect of rallying to go live to thousands of viewers at this time of day. But this was his usual broadcast slot, intentionally chosen to skim off North American audiences from other streamers who were wrapping up their shows and snag Australian viewers just starting their evening. Fortunately, I had the easy job; my plan was to sit off to the side and just watch. As I pulled into the driveway, I admit being surprised and impressed. I hadn't known quite what to expect, especially given the financial insecurity so many streamers endure. Yet this was a suburban middle-class home you'd see in any number of cities around the country: two stories with a little lawn out front, surrounded by others that looked a lot like it. The street was quiet at this time of night, and the house was dark. As I rang the bell, I worried for a moment that I was either at the wrong place or about to wake people.

But he answered, saying he'd just gotten up from a nap. The house was silent as the rest of his family—wife, baby, and brother who lived with them—still slept. The open-plan living room and attached kitchen were arranged much like you'd expect of a young family—with baby things, TV/DVD setup, and mail along with assorted other stuff cluttering the counter. He offered me coffee, but in a bit of grogginess put a cider pod in the machine by mistake. I didn't want to be any hassle (always the tricky bit of research as you descend into someone's work or home) so said no problem while he gave me a quick tour of the downstairs. Perhaps sensing that I was taking it all in, he spoke about how amazed he was that they got to live in this house, how lucky he was to have the viewers he did, and how he never thought that this could be his life. Having previously spoken with him while he and his family were living with relatives, I knew there was immediacy to this feeling and his gratitude felt genuine.

We made our way upstairs to the room dedicated to his broadcasts, and he quickly fired off a tweet giving his followers a heads-up that he'd be live soon. His setup wasn't anything fancy, just a generic black desk with a couple monitors, a few chairs, a lamp, assorted boxes, and gear here and there. His computer and monitors were already up and running as he sat down and began a ramp-up process. He started by looking at the Twitch front page, seeing viewer counts, assessing audiences, scanning the games and streamers that were on, and estimating when they were likely to sign off. Even before he began streaming, there were seven hundred people already on his channel hanging out in chat waiting for him. He decided to do a quick straw poll of the audience for them to pick what he should play. This involved using a third-party website to create a quick survey and pasting it multiple times to the chat. About twenty votes in, he settled on a game and sent out a "going live" message to Twitter. It was now approaching 3:30 a.m., and while the rest of the house was still asleep he began his broadcast. Although we'd been speaking in fairly quiet tones up until that point, with the start of the show, the vibe shifted and I saw him transition into his entertaining persona.

Over the next five or so hours, I watched him play through a few different games and keep an audience of four thousand entertained. Most strikingly, I saw the high degree of behind-the-scenes work happening. In interviews with streamers I'd heard about all the things they juggle while live, but seeing it in person was impressive. One of his screens showed his game, while the second monitor displayed a large chat window, his broadcasting software (which included a graphical trigger system for automatic messages that would pop up in the broadcast), and a window showing details about who was subscribing, donating, and following. The channel's chat window was a central part of the production, and he was constantly keeping his eye on the conversation, issuing hellos, thanks, and responses. Viewers reminded him a few times about donations he'd missed acknowledging, and he apologized each time, promising to catch up with the backlog. Amid all the humor and sometimes-raunchy jokes, his heartfelt thanks to his viewers came through. At one point, perhaps because someone spotted me in the background, he waved me into the frame to say hi. I did so quickly and then tried to scoot my chair back to the side. I definitely didn't have what it takes to stay on camera.

Eventually his brother popped his head into the room to check in about something. The rest of the house was waking up. He started wrapping up the broadcast. I noticed during the session that he hadn't run any ads and only now at the end showed a few. He took a look at who was currently streaming and picked a few fellow broadcasters to suggest that his viewers switch over to watch, instigating a friendly "raid." Once he turned off the broadcast, he showed me all the other tools in the background that he uses to monitor his productions. While he didn't need to directly call on them during the session, he pointed out the Skype window where all his moderators were gathered to coordinate their handling chat. Finally, he tallied up the results of evening's session: over fifty new subscribers, over eight hundred new followers, and over $500 in donations.

We headed downstairs to say hello to his family, now all woken up and starting their day. I'd met his wife before so we hugged and chitchatted, but it was the first time I'd seen his new baby. She was happy and reached out for her dad when she spotted him. He took her and bounced her around with morning hellos. The rest of his day would be a mix of helping with childcare, errands, and all the prep and postproduction work that streamers are constantly doing. I said my goodbyes, and as I pulled away from the quiet suburb to make my way back to the hotel for some sleep, I couldn't help but think about how in average homes around the world these quirky one-person studios were appearing and broadcasting out content to millions of viewers every day.

This chapter explores these individual live streamers who are transforming their private play into public entertainment. In particular, I focus on those aspiring to create a new professional identity in this space. Whether they are "variety" broadcasters who play many different game titles, or esports players sharing hours and hours of practice of a single game, streamers are not only developing conventions for game spectatorship as they broadcast but are also constructing a new form of work. While many variety streamers still hold day jobs, a number of them are pursuing full-time professional live streaming, often supported by family or partners. Esports competitors increasingly supplement tournament income and broaden their sponsorship opportunities via live streaming. Despite working with differing kinds of games and genre conventions, both types of streamers are typically based in home studios (frequently located in their living room or bedroom) and navigate the labor of producing one's play for spectatorship. It is usually an economically precarious, if personally fulfilling, path.

Given that Twitch supports synchronous chat running alongside the video, broadcasters are typically engaging with their audiences—saying hello, answering questions, responding to feedback, and over the course of months or years, getting to know them and be known by them. As one longtime streamer put it to me, Twitch allows him to say to his audience, "Welcome to my channel. Now you're a part of the experience." This social and emotional labor extends beyond the bounds of the broadcast platform; having a successful channel also often requires attention to other forms of social media. Managing a presence on Facebook, Twitter, and even YouTube and gaming platforms like Steam can become an important part of building and maintaining an audience. Live streamers are not only content producers but brand and community managers too.

Aside from this "front-stage" labor, live streamers frequently find themselves having to skill up into agile one-person production studios. Whereas traditional media production involves a division of labor spanning a number of skilled technical and creative professionals—from camera operators and audio experts to writers and producers—live streamers regularly take on all these roles themselves, especially when they start out. While broadcasting, they are not only producing all the creative content but also tend to be simultaneously managing all the technical components to make the production happen. Live streaming, particularly when undertaken with professional aspirations, becomes the work of play.

Trajectories of Engagement

Perhaps one of the most important things I learned early on when talking to live streamers is that there was no single reason why they broadcast their play. All had a deep core passion for gaming, but there were a range of reasons animating those who turned on a camera and started broadcasting. Oftentimes what initially got them to try out streaming evolved into something more. Motivations for starting streaming and keeping with it, especially over many years, differ among broadcasters and can change as one develops their profile. What may have begun as a fun thing to do after work at night, a hobby, can develop into a full-fledged creative endeavor with professional aspirations. I will discuss these in more depth throughout the chapter, but a brief description of how people get into streaming and some of the work involved is helpful in setting the stage for what follows.

> *Social connections*: Some simply start streaming from a desire to share their play with a small group of friends. Many times these streamers wanted to find new ways to build social connections with friends and strangers. The central pleasure was in being connected through broadcasting to others who love gaming. Many professional streamers begin this way, derive joy from it, and find they have a knack for it.

> *Transforming the play experience*: Others speak of how broadcasting play can become a means of amplifying the experience through a public performance. Esports competitors would sometimes tell me that broadcasting offered a form of public motivation and accountability. Variety streamers would note that introducing spectators into the mix made gaming more enjoyable. In both cases, broadcasting was a mechanism that changed the experience of play in a way the streamer enjoyed.

> *Creativity and performance*: Some streamers are excited by the creative or production aspects of broadcasting. They are drawn to the expressive aspects of live streaming and enjoy being an entertainer. Broadcasting their play became a new performative outlet, not dissimilar from theater and acting. Some found the more formal or technical challenges such as setting up a good system, creating overlays, or building the "set" an engaging experience in media production.

> *Professional aspirations*: Quite a few of the streamers I spoke to were attracted to live streaming to economically support their love of gaming, especially in the face of otherwise dire job prospects. One described struggling with traditional work, saying, "I had been meandering from one dead-end retail soul-sucking job to another and I was just trying to think what am I going to do with my life. These jobs are literally killing me." For these people, live streaming offers a space of meaningful and fulfilling work, unlike what they experienced in more traditional jobs.

Professional expectations: Finally, especially in the case of esports streamers, broadcasting has not only become an important part of how they make money but may often be required of them as well. Increasingly, esports teams are including live streaming expectations as part of the work that players must undertake and are putting it into contracts. In the same way that individual streamers can use broadcasting to solidify their brand (and revenue), teams have come to see it as a crucial part of their overall presence, particularly if they are luring sponsors with promises of getting their products in front of audiences daily.

While the motivations vary, for most individual streamers there is a common practical trajectory in terms of actually learning to set up a stream and broadcast.[1] While some utilize built-in game console functionality (for instance, PlayStation 4 has a "share" button that you push to broadcast), at the time of my research most people began by trying it out on their computer. This is not a trivial matter, though, since it requires downloading and setting up a third-party piece of software that pipes out to Twitch what is happening on the streamer's computer.

This step typically necessitates some basic research by searching online, visiting an official Twitch help page, or asking other streamers and viewers. Subreddits like /r/Twitch have become a valuable hub for aspiring streamers to share all kinds of information, from camera setups to tips on interacting with audiences. One streamer described how he began playing with broadcasting software:

> People usually don't just decide they want to jump on and start streaming like every day, or streaming a specific series or something. What usually happens is kind of like Photoshop or like how you learn anything that you do on computer as you start off with an application: you download the application because you think it's cool, your friends have it or you have seen someone else use it, and you start to play with it, you get comfortable with it, and then you actually start using it regularly and you try to build something from that.

If a streamer finds themselves getting hooked on the practice, they will often begin investing in equipment, adding in a microphone or camera. One woman I spoke with portrayed this transition in the following way: "When I first started, I was very, very nervous. I didn't want to add my microphone. I didn't want to add my webcam. I just wanted to let people watch me play the game." This initial hesitation is not unusual, especially for women or people of color, who might face additional barriers of harassment (something I'll discuss in more detail later), and streamers often spoke to me about the ongoing development of their broadcast as they become more invested in it. Ramping up the complexity of a production is not simply a design or technical choice but rather one that involves social and psychological considerations. As streamers develop their performance and voice as a broadcaster, they will frequently enlist new layers of design and technology.

Camera and microphone upgrades are common entry points when streamers build out their broadcasting setups. At the higher end, those who get more interested in the production quality side of things will often buy mixing boards and other professional A/V devices to handle numerous inputs and outputs. On the high end, this equipment can be so expensive that the broadcaster, like traditional production companies, will just rent gear for special events. For example, rather than buying four cameras that would cost $8,000 each and a TriCaster to manage a multicamera production for another $40,000, one broadcaster who occasionally does elaborate special shows will rent it all for $7,000 a week. Second (and third) monitors are not unusual, as are green screens to chroma key in other graphics.[2] For those fortunate enough to have the space, they may dedicate a special room to all this gear, creating an in-home studio. Others will simply set their production area in a corner of a living room or bedroom.

Aside from hardware components, as streamers become more experienced they will also typically start deploying software bots to help them moderate their channel. They will begin using graphical overlays and alert systems. They may also utilize third-party websites and software that help manage donations as well as giveaways. As a channel grows, a broadcaster may increasingly also find they need to draw more on others to help with the production. Moderation teams, often seeded with dedicated viewers, will get formed to help manage a channel's community and live chat. Contractors specializing in design may be hired to make graphical assets for not just shows but ancillary sites too.

Those who turn to making their live streaming a sustainable financial endeavor tend to implement scheduling and focused attention to building a quality stream with the hope of attaining partnership or affiliate status with Twitch, thus allowing them to tap into additional forms of monetization (such as ad revenue and subscriptions). As their practice grows, they may do more to experiment creatively, to connect up to larger networks of other live streamers by doing guest spots on other shows, sharing audiences, or joining a streaming community. If they are one of the fortunate few, they build a professional life as a broadcaster that supports them economically.

In what follows I will detail these various kernels in more depth, but it is key to keep in mind as we begin this chapter that individual streamers are not homogeneous in their motivations, and how they experience broadcasting may change over time. They take on a range of work, from social engagement with their audiences to performance and production. In this book, I specifically focus on those who also seek to build professional careers out of their broadcasting because they give us insight into a complex relationship between work and play as well as a form of creative yet precarious labor within a changing media landscape.

Layers of Production

As one can see from the brief description above, game live streaming can quickly become a serious production. The level of attention, labor, resources, and creativity that streamers put into their practice to take a game and make a product out of it that extends well beyond its formal properties is stunning. Accomplished broadcasters make compelling performances and productions that capture viewers and keep them entertained for hours. In just a handful of years, we've seen the practice develop from the simple broadcast of play to full-fledged "shows" with a range of genre conventions. The current state of top-level variety productions utilizes a range of technologies and practices. These live stream productions can be broken down into a number of layers:

Set design: While the game itself makes up a portion of the viewer's screen, accomplished streamers often use complex "sets" that involve additional audio, graphical overlays, green screening, cameras, triggered events (graphical/audio notifications of new followers, for example), chat bots, custom chat emoticons specific to the channel, and a customized channel page (see figure 3.1). It is worth noting that many of these components are produced not just by the live streamers themselves but also third-party graphics designers or programmers who have themselves sought to find a professional place in this new media sphere. The set of any given live stream is often constructed through the labor of a number of people, at times distributed globally.[3]

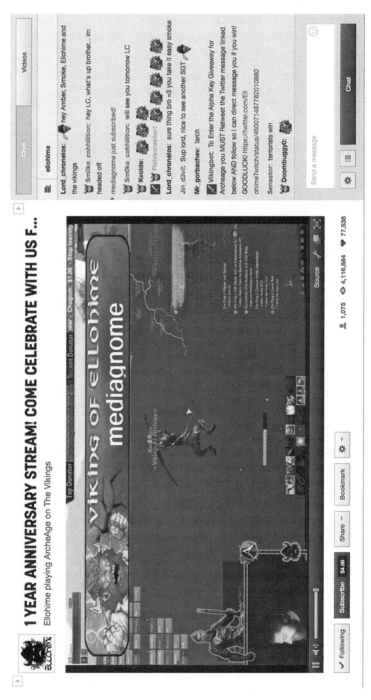

FIGURE 3.1. Ellohime broadcast with auto pop-up banner when the channel gets a new follower (dubbed a "Viking of Ellohime"), 2014.

Performance: Successful live streamers do not just silently broadcast their gameplay. Instead, they tend to mix together a "think-aloud" method similar to usability testing where the user speaks aloud their thought processes as they interact with a system and makes external that which would normally only be "in their head." This is typically accompanied with humor, frustration, and suspense. Streamers talk about this as trying to be entertaining or engaging. They frequently use physical expressions and gestures, at times theatrically, accentuated, or held for effect, to punctuate their communication (see figure 3.2). Esports broadcasters stand as an exception to this general rule where, for them, the very act of showing virtuoso play is itself a performance. These streamers usually do not speak much but rather perform and build audiences through their expertise. It is an entirely different genre that offers a variant on performance, though it shares some elements with variety streams.

Critique and evaluation: While a portion of the commenting that live streamers do is rooted in their moment-to-moment actions, analysis is also an important component of the work of play. Reflecting on mechanics, design, gameplay, "feel," and other aspects of the game itself can form a powerful part of the value of a stream. Astute streamers not only provide viewers with an entertaining performance of play but act as expert evaluators of systems too, conveying to their audience an independent analysis of the game as object.

Sociality: Live streaming performance is deeply interwoven with audience and community engagement. Core to this is the ongoing chat that takes place alongside and within the visual broadcast of the game and streamer. Viewers of the channel can talk not only to each other through text chat but the streamer as well. Accomplished streamers become adept at following this online conversation, keeping an eye on the chat window, talking to and engaging with their viewers, and all the while playing the game. This interaction can range from welcoming newcomers to responding to questions or soliciting feedback. In many instances, the audience becomes enlisted in the gameplay itself by giving input on choices within the game (see figure 3.3). These moments, especially in tense game scenarios, are particularly entertaining and regularly generate high audience engagement.

FIGURE 3.2. Futureman broadcast utilizing a green screen "set" that is part of the channel's theme, 2015.

FIGURE 3.3. SuushiSam broadcast with audience weighing in on what choice the broadcaster should make, 2012.

The social and community layers of a production routinely extend beyond the live streaming platform itself onto other social media sites such as Twitter and Facebook as well as other gaming platforms like Steam that allow for streamers to set up groups for their audiences. Streamers can also send private messages through the Twitch platform to communicate with their channel subscribers.

Material and digital infrastructure: While it is easy to forget about infrastructures when talking about internet platforms, it is crucial for understanding the complexity at work in live streaming. Beyond the technical components provided by Twitch (such as video codecs, storage, servers, transmission nodes, etc.), at the individual streamer level, a range of material and digital components make productions possible. This includes computers, A/V hardware (including mixing boards), furniture, and lighting (see figure 3.4). At the software level, it involves everything from graphics and A/V processing software to bot and notification/trigger systems to network functionality. Many people I interviewed talked about experimenting with and piecing together their systems. When looking at support communities for streamers (such as the Twitch subreddit), you will often find them analyzing A/V setups, preferred devices, and discussions of many behind-the-scenes details to facilitate quality

FIGURE 3.4. MANvsGame broadcasting room setup posted to Twitter, 2014.

broadcasts. The level of technicity—"particular kinds of attitudes, aptitudes, and skill, with technology" (Dovey and Kennedy 2006, 113)—involved in making more complex streams is key, and typically requires a tremendous amount of self-taught expertise and community-based learning.

Economic and commercial frameworks: The financial structures at work in accomplished live streams are also important to consider. Twitch offers select broadcasters (partners and affiliates) the opportunity to monetize streams in several ways, including channel subscriptions of which they get a cut, revenue from ads and game sales, and money from the platform's internal "Bits" donation system. Beyond these formal mechanisms, many streamers utilize third-party donation systems, sponsorship deals, and Amazon affiliate links.[4]

These various layers interact with and impact each other in meaningful ways. For example, in figure 3.5, while there is an economic framework being referenced (ads and subscriptions), the streamer also leverages a social as well as emotional valence with language of support, appreciation, and increasing chat functionality.[5] Likewise, software infrastructures like bots and notification systems or set designs (utilizing cameras or microphones) are deeply tied to producing particular forms of interaction and community engagement. Performative qualities are connected to wanting to create better content and communities, which for those monetizing their streams, draws

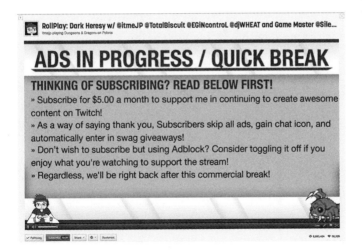

FIGURE 3.5. Itmejp channel interstitial, 2013.

and retains viewers. Live streaming is a rich illustration of the assemblage of play, whereby a variety of actors (human and nonhuman), infrastructures, institutions, and interrelations make play, performance, and work possible.

Producing a successful broadcast involves a great deal of cultivation.[6] Balancing the audience and forms of engagement with the content, deploying a complex array of material and infrastructural components, and managing a variety of relationships on- and offline (including economic ones) all become part of the work of streaming play. While it is easy to see a site like Twitch as just people gaming, looking closely at the components of successful broadcasts, with the creativity, labor, and systems that make them possible, pushes us to reckon with something much more. The game, as produced by the developer, while a critical part of an overall production, is only one layer. Peering more closely, we can spot the often-invisible nodes: the infrastructure of hardware, video codecs, network protocols, and software layers. And we can begin to see how forms of interaction, performativity, and social engagement flow through as well as across it all, shaping these networked broadcasts. The empirical and analytic limits of a framework that centers the game artifact becomes apparent. Digital play is constituted through assemblage, as is the work of broadcasting it.

Entertainment and Expertise

The formal components of a broadcast are matched in the sophistication that accomplished streamers bring to carrying out a show. Streaming is not simply playing a game, though that is certainly a key node, but also working with the play moment as a performative experience. As one of my interviewees who ran a daily broadcast put it,

> When I flip on the stream, I'm not just playing a video game. It's not like you're just sitting in your living room playing by yourself not talking to anybody. . . . It's not like that. I'm an entertainer. I'm performing. I'm trying to keep things relevant, trying to keep conversation cool. I'm trying to make sure that the vibe is right, that nobody's acting up in the chat. I'm trying to make sure that the gameplay is interesting, that I'm showing people things. I'm trying to make sure that I'm staying attentive to them.

For many variety streamers, a large part of what makes up the entertaining components of their play involves utilizing the speak-aloud method, enlisting humor, frustration, and performative action alongside interaction with viewers. The foundation of any basic stream tends to involve the broadcaster making external the range of internal processes that a gamer experiences when playing. They talk through actions or thoughts, typically giving the audience a glimpse into what might otherwise be hidden cognitive work. Indeed, new broadcasters are encouraged to "just keep talking" and rely on narrating their experience even if they have no viewers. At the base level, game live streaming is an exteriorization of an otherwise-unspoken ludic process.

Yet experienced streamers layer onto this an additional level of performance. Communicating with their audience in real time is a skill that grows as streamers not only gain more users but also refine their setups to allow them to more easily see the ongoing channel chat, and pull out key people or comments to interact with. This interaction may be focused on the game, such as asking for advice and strategies, or simply saying hello to fans and checking in with them. Amid this, streamers will also often "play up" a more performative interaction with both audience members and the game itself. Reactions, expressions, jokes, and even theatricality can form a critical part of successful live streams. Adept broadcasters engage in a kind of "crowd work" that involves not only the live audience but also the emerging experience of the game.[7] As such, they are incredibly flexible performers who, while frequently having set conventions (language, in-jokes, etc.), are deeply attuned to the audience.

Another slice of the entertainment aspect of variety streaming comes from audience members developing a sense of the streamer over time—their personality, life, quirks and style—across many different titles over months. One streamer I spoke with described how this side of the broadcast is important, saying, "They [the repeat audience] are here specifically to watch you and your mannerisms, and learn about your life and like what you got going on in this moment. That's what they are consuming; that's their content. That's their entertainment. You are the entertainment versus what you are streaming being the entertainment." This work is resonant with what Walker identifies the "active streaming posture" in which "streamers are able to develop a public identity connected to play style, on-air personality, comedic repertoire, their relationship with teammates or co-streamers, or even a style of critique." (Walker 2014, 439).[8] The distinctive qualities that specific streamers bring to their shows highlight the fact that it is not simply the game that is the draw to a broadcast.

This entertainment orientation is not separate from overall game expertise, however. While watching your favorite live streamer learn how to play a specific title can make for a compelling show, on the whole broadcasters tend to be adept, committed gamers. People who pursue professional live streaming come to it with a fundamental interest and passion for games. Unsurprisingly, as they continue to develop an identity as a professional broadcaster, this deep feel for games only grows, solidifying their public identity as a gamer, and at times, bolstering their profile for companies and developers that seek to leverage it for promotional activities.

Esports streamers trade on a different form of entertainment—one not based on humor or particularly theatrical performances but rather game expertise. Even though like variety streamers they run regular channels, have subscribers, and engage in broadcasting with a professional orientation, their audience draw originates in the desire of viewers to see an elite gamer practice. While variety streamers may not be expert in a particular title, or even aspire to be (failure, in fact, can be entertaining), esports streamers occupy a slightly different stance where the pursuit of virtuosity and expertise is key to both their performance and audience engagement.[9]

One of the most unique contributions of live streaming to the development of esports overall has been its ability to connect fans to top competitors. Watching your favorite esports player's live stream is a bit like what you might imagine it's like to watch your favorite baseball player practice for hours a day. Though mundane, it can also be riveting. Audiences get to view pro players practice their game, refine strategies, and reflect on their own play along with that of the competitors they encounter during a session. For those watching the stream, this can be a powerful learning tool, tapping into competitive aspirations or the hope to improve one's own play.

And while some esports streamers offer little commentary or engagement with their audience, others use the think-aloud method to make visible their processes, at times using communication with the audience to address their own limitations. As one streamer I spoke with observed, while there are better players than him, he uses interactivity to offset things: "I have a background in strategy so I can kind of explain the methodology behind decision making. So that's basically why I went into that route instead of just playing the game."

The ability to follow your favorite competitor in these ways is quite new. Rather than having to wait for tournaments to see a player, people can tune in to have a daily experience. One longtime esports competitor portrayed it this way:

> Your tournament victories [can] have so much dead space in between, but the streaming makes people feel part of your journey at a very

personal level. So instead of cheering for some idol, you're cheering for a friend. You're cheering for one of the people who you know very well. Sometimes I write something on Twitter and people say they've read it in my voice. So it's become very much a part of them, following my stream. For them then to see me succeed, if it happens in a tournament, would be like seeing a really good friend succeed. Even if I may not necessarily know them, for them it feels like I'm very close to them. It will feel very gratifying and satisfying for them.

This regular connection proves to be valuable on the business front as well, both for players who are able to keep their name out there between tournaments and sponsors who are happy that the pro is able to provide daily logo visibility rather than just at tournaments or special engagements. As one top player expressed in regard to live streaming being picked up by esports, "Almost every player pretty much uses it as a tool to interact with the community and pretty much market their name brand a little better." Another remarked that streaming has become a critical component of a longer career, pointing out that the actual life of tournament competition is finite: "You don't have enough deepness or longevity if for eight, nine, years you would try only to win. For very few people will this be a successful endeavor. So in the end, you need something that ties everything together. It can be video content you upload, it can be projects you participate in, or it can be streaming." And while not the norm, one tournament organizer told me that they had a player decide to drop out of a show match in which they would have received several hundred dollars so they could stream instead and make more money via ad revenue.

Of course, it is crucial to mention that watching an esports streamer is not a fully transparent window into their practice. Many pros will keep new tactics off the stream, practice on anonymous unstreamed accounts, and hide some important details of play. One pro described how he handles this, stating, "When I play on my own ID, and he [the competitor] knows it's me and we're both streaming it, I would rather not show how I'm gonna try and beat him the next time." This kind of gambit can end with him intentionally losing, which while having long-term competitive payoffs in a tournament, can produce some frustration in the moment. He continued:

> Then I read the chat, and people are like, "[You] lost to him!" and "He's so good!" and then I'm really annoyed but I can't show it because if I show that I'm annoyed or explain what I did, then the whole ploy would have failed. So there's a necessary step of deception to both my fans and

my rivals, and that's regrettable but since it's unavoidable I've accepted it and I've just tried to work with it, because the professional side is not just about how good you are but how good you are at deception. That's a part of it.

Another explained how he was able to benefit from some competitors not being as savvy about streaming their practice: "I've seen a lot of openness in terms of what people have streamed. I will also say that it's because of that openness that I was able to take advantage of another streamer because I got a lot of extra knowledge about what he was going to run and it did give me pretty significant advantage."[10] Balancing a professional esports identity, practice time, and audience engagement was something I heard regularly when talking to pros who were expanding into live streaming as a way to supplement as well as augment their competitive careers. Increasingly, it has become a way they not only leverage their expertise but also build economic models outside a more traditional team/circuit framework.

Affect and Connection

In trying to understand the work and experiences of live streamers, my eye continually caught the moments in broadcasts and on social media when they would not only express their joy or excitement but struggles, frustrations, and even weariness too. At times, these were deeply rooted in the experience of the body at play, at the screen, "onstage." This expression was not always spoken but rather conveyed in a variety of ways. I was most struck by this when one popular broadcaster tweeted the following image (see figure 3.6), captioning it as how he prepares for a cast.

While the image itself was powerful, the replies from his followers caught my attention. People responded with humor, concern, and encouragement, and shared other images that it made them think of. This moment of sharing, the circuit of connection it made, the depth and range of expressions it conjured, caused me to stop and think a bit more about the role that not only emotions and personal expressions play in streaming but also the range of experience, often inarticulable, that can produce unexpected connections between streamer and audience.

This vulnerability—both in terms of sharing your own experience and being open to hearing back from your viewers—is perhaps one of the most underdiscussed aspects of live streaming when it comes to popular coverage. Part of the rhythm of broadcasting, particularly for professional streamers or

FIGURE 3.6. "Dressing Up" by Kristian Nygård, www.optipess.com, September 28, 2012.

those aspiring to be, is having a regular, daily show. These frequently last for multiple hours, meaning that the streamers are on display for major chunks of time every week (including whatever social media presence they may maintain), and have to contend with normal ups and downs, often on camera. Popular streamer Adam Koebel (2016), speaking at a panel at Twitch-Con, hit on the complexity of this emotional work when he remarked,

> Some people run into a situation where their emotions become commodified, people will get upset on stream and it just becomes part of their thing. If that is [some]thing you find happening to you be careful with it, right? Find a space where you can be authentic with your own feelings that isn't necessarily on stream, even if you want to be emotionally open with your viewers. Because we all have to have something for ourselves, even if we're sharing a lot of ourselves.

Koebel's comment insightfully highlights the delicate balance that broadcasters face. While their work is performative and they spend huge chunks of time "on," it is also tied up with conventions of authenticity, connection, and immediacy in ways that can evoke powerful emotions as well as experiences with their viewers.

Because of the ways that streamers interact with their communities and fans across a range of media, it is not unusual to see them be frank at times about their own personal struggles, such as I described in the opening of this section. I have been struck over the years by the candor with which many streamers speak about issues like depression, personal or family troubles, or burnout. Sometimes these disclosures take place on stream, but just as often they come via other social media outlets. Subscribers to a channel can receive messages from the broadcaster directly, and this mode is used to sometimes convey more private, sensitive issues—a kind of middle ground communication space that only goes out to people who have signaled a next level of affiliation with the streamer. While there is frequently a sense that the show must go on (as one streamer put it, "There are definitely the days where I don't necessarily want to do my broadcast, but I have to sort of zip on that smiling face or whatever"), given the way that notions of authenticity and presenting some version of yourself currently dominate genre conventions, streamers regularly share not only their highs but their lows too.

While the expression of emotions is part of what we regularly see on streams, work on affect theory opens up the analytic space to consider encounters and movement, the body, interrelations, "passages of intensities," and an interest in the everyday or even mundane.[11] Though the domain of affect theory is multifaceted, contentious, and at times inscrutable, there is something there that speaks deeply to what we see in live streaming. It gives us a way to not only understand the emotional side of streaming but also much more. We are prompted to take seriously the experiential, performative, and visceral along with the interrelations and entanglements between broadcaster, audience, and technologies. Understanding game live streaming involves looking at the complexity of feeling and affect, embodiment, performance, relationality, and the everyday flows that make up the work as well as experience of both audience and broadcaster.

PERFORMATIVE PLAY

The entertainment stance that streamers frequently assume is deeply tied to a range of emotions and internal states as well as the flow experienced between player and audience. Enthusiasm, joy, anxiety, frustration, and even anger all become emotions to be conveyed and experienced together. Streaming is embodied work. As I noted earlier, being able to convey the often-inexpressible and visceral experiences that occur during play is a performative skill that accomplished streamers develop. They use evocative facial expressions, poses, gasps, or laughter to convey experience. While typically not as dramatic as some variety streamers, many esports players communicate tactical consideration or resignation though subtle gestures or expressions. A head held in both hands is widely understood as defeat, and an enthusiastic jump up and yelp at the end of a tense round is seen as victory. One streamer, in portraying the advice that he gives to new broadcasters, said, "I really hit hard on the idea of it being performance art. You are performing for an audience." As the broadcaster Ellohime (2015) recounted during a panel hosted at the MIT Game Lab on the subject of live streaming,

> People ask me all the time, "why do people watch you play video games?" And the answer is because people like how I experience, they like to watch me experience these games. And it's different for every single streamer. . . . We're all going to have a different experience walking through this together, and I think that makes it interesting as a form of entertainment. I think you don't get that in a lot of other forms of entertainment.

This focus on conveying experience is a fascinating one, tied up with performance, expression, and embodiment. Streamers work to convey the moment by moment of gameplay, externalize the internal, make visible visceral experiences, and render the affective legible to spectators.

Perhaps one of the most important things to understand in discussing the performative elements of streams is that it is not framed in contrast to authenticity. Ellohime (ibid.) continued:

> My girlfriend, I think she says it the best way. She says it's a version of you. Like, it's the more excited, more entertaining version of you. It's still you, and people see you. I wouldn't say I put on a persona. It's not like wrestling where I run out and I'm like "AUUGGH!" . . . I'm not going to get in front of you guys here [at the event] and be like "Hey, is everyone having a good day!? Ok cool let's play a video game!" You know, like the same kind of intensity that I give to my broadcast. That's what she says, it's a different version of you. It's more honed in on those skills that you feel is adequate for what you need to accomplish, which is entertaining this large group of people over the internet, playing video games.

Much of everyday life is performative, and live streaming merely picks up on that theme and amplifies it for entertainment purposes.

Perhaps unexpectedly, quite a few of the streamers I've spoken with over the years identify as fairly shy or introverted, and often surprise themselves as well as families and friends by gravitating toward broadcasting. Streamer J. P. McDaniel (2015) described his own family's reaction to his taking up broadcasting:

> Growing up I was kind of the quiet guy who was always in my room, they had no idea how I was going to make money when I grew up. And now they're like, "How did you . . . you don't even talk to us twice a

month, and yet you're broadcasting," and I'm always talking, I'm emotive, I guess, on screen. I guess a part of me is that talkative person on the screen, but as soon as it goes off I'm pretty, kind of keep everything to myself, I'm kind of a quiet person offstream.

He went on to note that "I think there's something that needs to be said about being in a room with the door shut and the camera on you, and you don't really think about how many people are actually watching you. You're just talking to the camera." Another esports streamer I spoke with said of himself, "I've usually always been an introverted person who just plays for himself. But now with streaming, it opened another layer, you could say, the interaction with other people and showing what you can do." Navigating your shyness by broadcasting and connecting socially this way was a theme I repeatedly heard.[12]

These performances, in expressing the player's internal state and experience, become an evocative tool linking the audience to the broadcaster. Finding a way to draw the viewer in and help them either directly experience a gameplay moment alongside you (such as when spectating a horror game) or vicariously (recalling your own memory of playing yourself) can be a powerful method of sustaining an audience amid a plethora of competing channels.

AUDIENCE, COMMUNITY, . . . FAMILY?

While at its heart live streaming is about broadcasting gameplay, a powerful component of the success of variety streams is linked to the relational. Engaging with the audience, feeling the vibe of the chat in conjunction with the game and your own experience, animates the channel. Perhaps one of the most fascinating, if perplexing, aspects of the labor of streaming is the way the mundane is amplified, tweaked, and transformed to draw an audience in and hold it. While "entertainment" is often a key component, the everyday feel of streaming can also play into performativity. For example, one streamer discussed how audience size and makeup shape a broadcast:

In the evenings, I'm much more willing to do more mundane activities such as crafting, running around, exploring, grinding certain aspects of a game or something. Much more mundane things. Because there's less people there [watching], I feel like I have to. . . . I guess it is that I have to entertain less. I don't have to be showing them like the craziest stuff. It's a nice social stream. I'm spending more time talking to the chat.

We're being more personal with each other. The game is there as kind of a backdrop for what we do.

Broadcasters work to create a shared sense of presence with the audience, drawing everyone into a feeling of togetherness. Sitting together on a channel with fellow viewers, watching a streamer live, and seeing a flow of chat alongside their video becomes a collective social experience.

Streamers I've spoken with over the years emphasize, almost more than any other element, how central chat and interaction with the audience is. This engagement is critical to understanding the space. A theorist Sara Ahmed (2004, 119) argues about affective economies, "Emotions *do things*, and they align individuals with communities—or bodily space with social space—through the very intensity of their attachments. Rather than seeing emotions as psychological dispositions, we need to consider how they work, in concrete and particular ways, to mediate the relationship between the psychic and the social, and between the individual and the collective." Successful live streamers recognize this dynamic. Building a thriving community— that transformation of a passing viewer into a regular audience member who is "in" on the subculture of the channel—is a key goal. For some this is more like building a large audience of enthusiastic or "hyped-up" spectators, and for others the tone is much more akin to a "family," and language gets used to help symbolize the connection not just between the broadcaster and individual but between community members as well.

Attention to the relational and affective is not unique to live streamers. Media scholar Nancy Baym, in her study of musicians, has analyzed the ways they navigate connecting to their audience and fans through social media. Baym (2012, 292) argues that "social media have made it all but impossible to practice celebrity with the aloof distance of yore." She observes, "When we ask musicians to be direct, unique, and personal with their audiences, we ask them to redefine a relationship that has been structured in particular ways for decades. We ask them to do more work, work that requires relational, communicative, self-presentational, entrepreneurial, and technological skills that music work had not previously demanded" (Baym 2018, 11). The musicians she interviewed often constructed complex relationships with their fans online, including ones of meaningful intimacy and forms of social support. She terms this engagement a form of relational labor, "the ongoing, interactive, affective, material, and cognitive work of communicating with people over time in order to create structures that can support continued work." Resisting a model that would frame the engagements between musicians and their fans as alienating, coercive, or hollow, Baym shows the ways that these relationships are woven through with professional labor. Rather than pitting the social and economic entanglements that creative artists have with audiences in opposition to authentic connection, she presents a more nuanced handling of the interactions between producers and audiences.[13]

This is deeply resonant with what we see among live streamers. How the broadcaster interacts with and builds connections to those watching them is a powerful component of the channel, and this is facilitated through the chat feature of the window, which allows audience members to communicate with the streamer and each other. Broadcasters will frequently keep an eye on who is on the channel via the chat window and call out hellos to regulars, sometimes asking them how their day is going or noting if they haven't seen them in a while. Language is often rooted in forms of care and attention.

Offering recognition of "follows" (when someone favorites a channel), donations, and subscriptions forms an important part of the work that broadcasters do to enfranchise their viewers. Streamers also use other platforms, such as Facebook and Twitter, to maintain additional communication paths to their fans. There they will post updates about broadcasts, things happening in their life, or the usual fare of social media like memes and funny GIFs.

The issue of connection and how broadcasters think about their audiences is something I regularly asked them about, exploring the language they used to describe the people who watched them. While esports players tended to mostly use the term "audience," nearly all variety streamers preferred other words such as "community" and, on occasion, "family."[14] Usually this orientation was incorporated into their aesthetics, performance, and language, where they would address their viewers with insider terms to denote membership in a special group. Making regulars feel that they were a part of a stream's community, that they were known and able to make use of special language or emotes to signal their affiliation, is something accomplished streamers spend a fair amount of energy on.

Though most of the broadcasters I spoke with (both esports and variety) acknowledged that there was a fan dynamic present in their relationship to the audience, they tended to shy away from this characterization, and I often sensed it left them uncomfortable. As one put it, "I tend to refer to people who watch my show as viewers. For some reason, I'm always careful not to use the word 'fan.' I don't know. I think I try not to buy in to the whole thing of it, like, 'My fans, they just adore me.'" Even though it would be easy to see this as a kind of false modesty or politeness about not touting one's celebrity, there is nuance at work in this position.[15]

While celebrity can be a powerful motivator, and certainly many streamers are indeed famous in a specialized domain, most still feel very much on the outskirts of mainstream entertainment and are aware of their own professional precariousness. They also frequently derive significant personal gratification and fulfillment from their work, and genuinely enjoy connecting with their viewers as more than distant admirers. The language of fandom can feel as if it short-circuits this. It often doesn't fully encapsulate the much more complicated and at times fraught relationship that broadcasters can have with those who watch them.

Many expressed that what shifts viewers from audience to something else, be it community or family, are gestures of reciprocity, familiarity, or intimacy. Given how much of streaming is a daily occurrence, often in a home, it is perhaps not surprising that broadcasters may share details about their lives. One discussed how he let his community know about his divorce and why it happened: "I explained it to them. We talked about it ahead of time. I let them know what was going on. I talk a lot about personal issues and that sort of thing on the stream. And again, it comes back to building a friendship instead of just a viewer base." Sharing was part of the kind of connection he wanted to create with the people who followed his stream. Streamers regularly spoke about how viewers themselves in turn would share personal information with them, often about their own struggles.

Another saw sharing as an important service to his viewers, some of whom were younger than him. He told me,

I even have a Tumblr account where I sometimes just word vomit my feelings and my anxieties and stuff. I thought for a while like I shouldn't do that, I shouldn't let them know that I have problems, that I struggle with things like anxieties. But I was like, that's a disservice, you know, because then they're going to think like I'm always on, I'm always this person. That's not true. If I let them know that, it's going to make them feel closer. And like a lot of them, the demographic is pretty much like teenagers, so they're going through hell right now, most of them, you know, and I've been through it so it's kind of nice to let them know, "Hey, you're not going to be fifteen forever." Things will still be tough, but at least you know you can drink beer or something. You get treated with a little more respect in the world and you're going to feel a little bit better.

Streamer AnneMunition described something similar during a Twitch-Con panel in 2016. She spoke of having been out as a lesbian since the age of thirteen, though it was typically not something she talked about much.

This was not because she wanted to hide it, but because she was "kind of a distant person naturally, and I just didn't think it was anyone's business." She recounted how this changed during the course of streaming:

> I don't know, it was about a year in when I started streaming, when I opened up about—I had a lot of people messaging me about the struggles that they deal with in their personal lives, dealing with depression and stuff, and so I posted this whole thing about my own struggles with depression in the past and dealing with it. I had a friend commit suicide and I had a cousin attempt suicide. . . . I kind of was open about dealing with this part of my life that was really sad, and how I got through it because I wanted to, hopefully, help someone. I had a lot of people respond to that very positively, saying, "Even if it doesn't fix the things in my life, at least I know there's someone out there who's like, has dealt with the same things, and has gotten through it." And at that point was when I was like, OK, I don't care if anyone knows that I'm gay, if I can use this to help somebody out there, I'm gonna be open about it, because it's important to them and not necessarily because it's important to me, because it's important to them. I had this opportunity to be open with people, and let them see somebody who has gone through all this and has come out on the other side, hopefully better. (quoted in Koebel 2016)

That so many variety streamers report this kind of experience speaks to the ways that their relationship with their audience is built and how they come to think about their connection with them. Most of their viewers are not there to learn how to play a specific game better but instead for the streamer *themselves*. The real or imagined authenticity of the streamer, even within a performative context, becomes a powerful affective anchor in fostering supportive communities along with building audience connection and loyalty.

For esports broadcasters, the balance is slightly different. It is not that the personality of the esports streamer is unimportant—in fact, their fans can usually identify things they like about the competitor beyond their skill—but rather that the focus is much more centered on the game. Esports streamers, while often noting the value of community and even at times sharing aspects of their lives, may not put themselves at the center. As one popular professional player phrased it,

> I had this really special feeling two days ago. I closed the stream, and there was this bunch of people that thanked me for streaming and I

thanked them for watching. But then I saw there were a bunch of people that were going out of their way thanking the moderators for keeping my chat a really pleasant place to be and interact. And sometimes I see them exchanging contacts and I see them go play together. Then I realize it's a little mini community, and every streamer has a mini community who watch them and who like each other because they're attracted to basically the same person.

Community for esports audiences is typically a mix of their own focus on playing a specific title, a passion for competitive gaming, and finding a specific esports broadcaster whose skill they admire. On variety channels, the personality of the broadcaster is so central to the content of the channel that they become the anchor. This isn't to say that variety stream audience members don't form independent ties as captured in the above quote but instead that the core mechanism centers on the streamer first and foremost.

Yet variety streamers sometimes aspire to have communities that sustain themselves even when they're not present, to have members connect with each other meaningfully or start producing culture independent of the streamer. For some broadcasters, engaging in relational activity serves to model behavior that they would like to see among their audience members. One streamer saw this kind of interaction as helping build a critical part of his stream, making it distinctive:

> The idea is that everybody who comes to my chat can recognize one another, and [it] becomes a community. So I interact with a lot of them. I talk to different people on the chat very frequently, and I lose games because of that. I mean, I'm not always focused on the game since I focus a lot on talking to people in chat. If people on the chat recognize one another, I think that it adds an anchor to my stream that other streams don't have.

The payoff for a broadcaster, both emotionally and professionally, can be powerful. McDaniel (2015) shared this experience of seeing such cohesion occur around his broadcasts:

> That's the weird thing, is when the community starts making things about your stream, where you didn't prompt them to. Wikis start popping up, or crazy fan art starts popping up for characters that we do on our show. And it's like, really, really talented stuff, and there was nothing to prompt them to do that. And I think that's kind of, a lot of people wonder like, when is the "when you've made it" as a streamer. And I think it's like,

when your community starts making you things, without you prompting them to do so.

Amid this generative fan engagement, variety streamers themselves continue to occupy a core central symbolic role; bringing their viewers *into* their community is key. Broadcasters utilize special terms for regulars, injokes, channel specific emoticons, and even customized graphics that react to viewer engagement (for example, pop-up notifications when someone donates money) to foster feelings of connection between themselves and audience members. These connections can be powerful, building emotional ties between channel participants and streamer. Broadcasters I've spoken with talk about making friends with their viewers, thinking of them as a quasi-family, and even inviting them to personal events like their wedding. They also speak of the ways that their community members convey to them how meaningful the connection to the channel can be. One said to me, "You should see some of the emails that I've gotten where people will just pour out pages of describing how my broadcast . . . where people say I just changed their whole lives around, like they were suicidal and they found my broadcast. And so again, going back to the community thing, yeah, it's very strong."

This kind of affective inflection has practical implications as well. Having large audiences brings its own set of issues, and online chats can pose challenges to a broadcaster. While it practically speaking becomes more difficult to keep up with and respond to chats during casts, more important, it can complicate the task of fostering a tone that the broadcaster wants. Many try to walk a fine line between allowing people to speak freely and wanting to make sure the space is welcoming for newcomers. In practice this means that most broadcasters end up confronting the challenge of community management and moderation. As one described their audience and the tone they want to set, "I like to say they're collectively a huge group of friends. You've got your strange ones and you've got your weird ones and you've got your happy ones. I like to say, 'We're all friends here, so let's be nice.'"

While new broadcasters are often able to manage their own channels, toggling between playing the game and engaging with the viewers, including deleting comments or timing people out if the broadcaster is unhappy with their behavior, streamers will usually start looking for "good community members" to help them as the chat grows. These individuals are given special moderation privileges for a channel, with the ability to delete comments, time people out, and in the best case, help set an overall tone for the chat.

As a channel grows, its moderation team frequently finds itself adopting third-party tools to help it communicate and coordinate internally. Many mod teams use applications like Skype, Slack, or Discord to facilitate behind-the-scenes discussions while they moderate a given channel.

Nearly all moderators I've encountered even at the professional tournament level are volunteers. These spaces, then, have a dual function: they help people feel special, and offer them a sense of having a more exclusive connection to the broadcaster they like. The ongoing work of moderators (something I'll discuss further in later chapters) can involve nuanced skilled engagement with communities to be in tune with the energy of the channel and pacing of the conversation and a sense of the back-and-forth rhythm for large-scale social environments. Though typically uncompensated, they do a tremendous amount of valuable labor in helping maintain live streams as functioning social and communicative spaces.

There is a circuit of affective labor that flows through fans, moderators, and broadcasters, with each in turn drawing from and supporting the other. Streamers regularly talk about the energy or buzz they get from a good session when the viewer interaction, gameplay, and their own experience gel. Moderators express their commitment to and fandom for a streamer by helping manage that flow of engagement coming from the audience. And audience members, not only through their viewing activities, but also via interactions off the channel on social media, provide a fundamental component on which the entire system relies.

AFFECTIVE ECONOMIES

This turn to befriending the audience or, more conservatively, tapping into their positive feelings about the channel is, of course, a component of the financial side of the system. Subscription requests framed as "Do you want to show your appreciation?" or thankfulness from the streamer when donations are made highlight how the emotional connections between producer and audience are an important part of the economic system on the platform. Streamers regularly effusively thank their subscribers and donors for their generosity, noting how lucky they are to be able to do this thing they love so much while still supporting themselves and their families. Moderators will often frame their volunteer labor in terms of wanting to help the streamer succeed, including making the work financially sustainable.

The economic side of the equation for professional streamers is often riddled with ambivalence, though. Some articulate that they don't want to feel like a "beggar" or find it running up against their own temperament, as the one who said, "I am someone who doesn't push [donations] too hard and is actually somewhat shy when it comes to asking for them." Others prefer to downplay the financial aspects of a stream, or delegate some of it to automated systems that notify when a donation or subscription comes in that the streamer then responds to.

Given it is a job that many gamers imagine they would love to have themselves, streaming can also include a stigma around discussing the difficulty of the financial or labor side. As one streamer noted, "There is no faster way to piss off my viewership than when I go 'streaming is hard.' There is no faster way to piss them off. What they see is a guy who sits down and plays a video game for a while, collects a bunch of money, and then, you know, rolls around on his bed in singles, I guess" (McDaniel 2015). Yet the challenges of managing the work of streaming, converting a passing viewer into a regular subscriber or donor, and building relationships with potential sponsors are ever present for professional streamers. And affective economies can be complex.

"Donation trains" (or "wars") are moments during a stream where a collective energy to keep donating to a streamer takes over and donations flood in one after another. They exist in large part due to the way financial contributions have come to be integrated into broadcasts. For those who have set up a donation system, when an individual contributes, it can trigger an automated event on stream. The name of the donor, the amount they gave, and occasionally a message will pop up on the screen for all to see. Donation trains happen when viewer after viewer gives money, often in increasing amounts, such that the notifications keep flooding in. They tend to be special events that can overwhelm the streamer; expressions of both amazement and gratitude tend to dominate in those moments. Viewers frequently want to get in on the action, enjoying being a part of a group event and the direct recognition they can get from the broadcaster. As one person (who is both a streamer and viewer) described it on the Twitch subreddit:

> Those donation wars are really kind of a hard thing to explain. ive done one with one of my fav streamers, bacon doughnut. some dude dropped like 500 bucks, so i dropped 1k in bitcoin, then the same guy upped me by like 500 more bucks. the rush that you get from doing it is different. there is a certain satisfaction you get that you just don't get from donating. its hard to explain, but i would say its somewhat similar to gambling,

except i *know* i am supporting a streamer i love. its endorphins, basically. and lemme tell ya, that ol slab of meat ya got up in that cranium *loves* itself some endorphins, to the point where logic and reason can become a very low priority. (Distortednet 2014)

When watching a donation train, you can certainly feel the energy of the crowd at work as both broadcaster and audience get excited by the expression of appreciation rendered in increasing amounts of money being offered. Pop-up notifications will keep appearing on the screen, often with an accompanying sound, which only heightens the experience. Sometimes an ongoing tally showing the largest amount, and the name of the donor, remains on screen during the broadcast. The financial base of the entire system is amplified and interwoven with an attention economy based in fandom.

At times, however, this excitement can leave the streamer feeling uneasy. In this same Reddit thread, people noted that the broadcaster in question had taken down his donation page and kept it down, despite his viewers asking that it be put back up. Some streamers feel it is unethical to benefit too much from what may be seen as irrational and spur-of-the-moment financial decisions on the part of viewers. They also regularly wrangle with "charge backs," when someone who has made a donation contacts their credit card company to dispute the charge and the money gets pulled back from the broadcaster. Donation trains are seen as a vulnerable form of support, and in a system were streamers often already feel financial precariousness, the volatility of donation trains is sometimes not perceived as worth it. While the economic side of broadcasting leverages people's care and enthusiasm for a streamer, there are moments where both viewers and streamer may feel this affective pull spin out of control.

HOLDING BACK

Over the years of talking to broadcasters and coming to understand the complexity of streaming, I've been drawn to trying to understand how it affects the experience of play for the broadcasters themselves. How, if at all, does streaming fold back on those producing it? How might it shape or affect their play, at times in unexpected ways? What do streamers get out of it, or have to deal with, in terms of emotion or experience? Depending on the genre of broadcast (variety or esports), and streamers' own temperaments and communities, this unfolds in different ways.

Perhaps one of the most interesting things I encountered when talking to variety streamers about the games they broadcast was when I asked them if there were titles they would "hold back" or keep for themselves. Over and over again I heard "yes!" and a deep affirmation that this was an important part of navigating sharing your play. The reasons ranged. Sometimes it was because they felt a title was inherently not entertaining enough or they couldn't quite figure out how to make it so. I was continually struck by the complexity with which accomplished broadcasters thought about whether a game would serve as a product they and the audience could *work over* within an entertainment frame. Given that the game itself is only one component of a successful stream, its ability to be transformed into a publicly performative artifact is crucial.

At other times streamers expressed a desire to withhold a game that they were particularly personally invested in, or wanted to experience in a more solitary or private way. For those titles, they wanted to have a space to play it in that removed the expectation that they would be entertaining. This can also be tied to a feeling of wanting to savor the experience. One streamer, speaking about a game they'd chosen to not broadcast, said, "I don't want to stream that out. That's for me. That's my personal experience." They went on to remark that because joking is one of the main ways they entertain audiences, they felt broadcasting this specific game would disrupt the play experience they wanted to have with it, saying, "I know that the story is going to draw me in." Another reflected similarly on the pull that a game's narrative can have, observing, "What's funny is I will sit and play a video game for six hours on my broadcast, and then when I get done, I will sit [with it] for a few more hours because playing that game with the viewing audience, it's such a stressful [experience], and for me, you really can't get involved in the story and things like that. That's why I tend to shy away from playing RPG-type games because I just can't get enveloped in that world, which for me, that's really everything."[16]

Each of these cases of holding back highlights how live streamers balance their own preferred experiences (personal and professional) and public performance. The setting, stance, and tone of variety streams often signal an intimacy or familiarity with the broadcaster. You see their bedroom or living room, you frequently watch them failing or even growing bored with a title, and you observe them interacting with an audience, perhaps even you. One can easily slip into thinking that what we watch on a channel is a direct, unproduced conduit of a streamer's experience. And yet for successful streamers, there is usually a considered stance about what they are broadcasting and how they are doing it. Some experiences they want to share with viewers while some games they may want to keep for themselves.[17]

Esports players also can also feel the effects of broadcasting—in their case, around streaming practice time to audiences. One, for example, described how valuable it was for him to have viewers as he played. He felt it helped his focus and upped the ante, pushing him to better perform than if he was alone. For some aspiring pros, having an audience can also act as an external form of accountability. They speak about it as making them commit to a goal (such as achieving a new rank) publicly. For single-player competitors, having a live streaming audience can in some ways fill in the gaps one may have by not having teammates to help with accountability and encouragement.

Others were more conflicted about streaming, often doing it out of a mix of contractual obligation or an abstract sense that it was simply what one should be doing now. Some felt that broadcasting their practice time converted it to entertainment more than they'd like. They felt a pressure to be engaging for the audience and not in a productive way. At times this could lead to an unwieldy mix of needing to engage in "real" practice outside broadcast times. It could cause them to feel a burden to be a "personality" in a way that was disconnected from what actually attracted them to esports, such as competition or a deep internal desire to always simply be better. It could also result in feeling pressured to behave in less natural ways, like censoring their own speech or reactions.

These experiences and feelings about live streaming, both satisfying and ambivalent, are a critical part of the broadcasting loop. They speak to how making one's gaming public can have ramifications for the player themselves, sometimes in unanticipated or unwanted ways. Streamers do not sit outside the system but instead often confront how what may seem trivial at first, public gameplay, can actually have profound effects on them.

Public and Private

Despite the tone of authenticity, affective engagement, and connection to the audience, broadcasters aren't just open books, exposing all aspects of their selves and lives; there is a delicate balance maintained between sharing and privacy. Given that so much of individual live streaming is done in people's homes day in and day out, usually in domestic spaces shared with others, I have been curious over the years to watch this negotiation between public and private. Some broadcasters stream from little makeshift studios where no other people enter the frame while on other channels you might see people they share the space with in the background, perhaps even popping on screen to wave a hello or answer a question. Streams also move between a sense of knowing the caster in a more personal way—from their full name to details of their private lives—to a more distanced stance where the main form of self-presentation is that of performer and mostly under an online moniker. As I watched and interviewed broadcasters over the years, I spoke to them about how they navigate this. Everyone I talked to had given it consideration, and made active decisions about what they were and weren't comfortable sharing.

EVERYDAY LIFE AND DOMESTIC SPACE

One of the most important things to understand about individual live streaming is that the home as studio shapes the form, content, and experience of broadcasts for both streamer and audience. Streaming has long been a way to invite a public into your private space, and the draw of seeing someone flip on a camera in their home and share their gameplay is powerful.[18] As a form, it straddles two pulls: the everyday mundanity of gaming that many viewers know firsthand and special status of peeking into someone else's experience in the most regular of settings.

At a basic level, the amount and configuration of space that a streamer has shapes the broadcast. It isn't that streaming from your home requires a huge amount of room but rather that the materiality present is always a factor in what can be done. For instance, being able to use a green screen, appropriate lighting, or have a desk that supports multiple monitors is contingent on not only enough space but also basics like furniture, including items comfortable enough to accommodate long stretches of broadcasting. The infrastructures can play an unseen role as well; internet connection speeds can influence stream quality, as can the computer that is a being used. Struggles with video production or being able to manage multiple programs at once can affect the broadcast. Gamers in places that lack good network access are often unable to participate in live streaming as producers and mostly stay within the audience.[19]

The materiality of the space can also have affective and relational qualities. For many streamers, being able to stream at home has not only been practically advantageous (no huge studio cost and scheduling convenience are both significant factors when streams normally last multiple hours) but often fits a temperamental preference too. As one streamer who broadcasts from a desk in his bedroom told me, "My bed is right here, and then my computer and my office area is on the side here. It's all one thing. I don't really think of it that much because I've always been kind of a homebody. I like my space. I'm OK sharing my space with thousands of people." For him, being able to bring others into where he felt most comfortable was the best of all possible worlds. Seeing such close quarter setups almost evokes a sense of a nest: a spot where a streamer can venture out over the network yet remain safely ensconced at home. For others who describe themselves as shy or introverted, such locations offer an interesting bridge between the comforts of home and a public endeavor. The domestic environment— surrounded by your things, items of affection or comfort, and your own fandom, often on display for the audience—provides a form of security and even safety to those who might otherwise find the idea of standing on a huge stage in front of thousands unthinkable.

The materialities of domestic space shape the content of streams and how broadcasters operate. One streamer, who started his broadcast in the living room of a family member's house where he and his partner lived at the time, said:

> I actually think that people enjoy that aspect of it. There are certain people out there that enjoy seeing the full picture up here. This is my grandma's house so my family stops by sometimes and they'll [his viewers] see like a train of them coming in. They'll be like, "What is happening over there?" My grandma walks outside to take the garbage out. They start to know my grandma. My grandma will occasionally come over here [to his setup] and say something.[20]

His girlfriend would similarly walk by sometimes, and the viewers would say to tell her hi. For him, letting the audience see into the everyday life of his home contributed to the tone of his stream; he told me, "I think it actually works really well with the community atmosphere." Another, who has long had a streaming setup in his home and whose child also often broadcasts (both with him and on their own), says, "It's a pretty normal thing in our household. Like I think more or less like I'm just happy that technology has finally caught up to kind of what we all like to do, and for me I see it as another way that I kind of spend time with my kid that's, you know, that piques both of our interest. And I don't know, I just see it as a really normal and kind of acceptable thing."

Others find it trickier to navigate sharing space with those who may not understand or want to be a part of a broadcast, even as background characters. As the streamer above whose whole family streams went on to note, "I have friends that just, they kind of get weirded out with the whole concept of streaming, you know. They just don't understand it. So that's probably when it feels the most awkward is when someone else is at the house and they don't maybe quite understand it." One esports streamer described being happy with a recent shift he'd made where he and his wife were now living in a home with others who were part of the scene and understood live streaming. He said, "Managing space has become easier since 100 percent of the residents here are into esports. It was different when I was living with my mom. She was understanding, but we had one out of the three floors available so it was very limited space." For others, the problem of sharing space stems from the challenges those negotiations pose for content production. Having to deal with noise from others or be self-conscious of one's presence can create problems for streamers who might feel impinged on. One broadcaster, who had actually rigged up a makeshift physical barrier around his computer, explained, "I do live with people, and that is a major sticking point and something that is constantly frustrating. I mean, it's only a problem because I'm streaming, but they're so distracting."

Sometimes rules, formal or informal, may develop as the use of the home for a public broadcast gets navigated. One streamer, who is fairly open with his audience about his private life, told me that the only rule in his home was, "If you're not wearing a bra, don't get in front of the camera. That's our biggest rule. I think it's the only rule that we really follow. Be appropriate when you walk past. Again, be cognizant that when you walk in this room, you're in front of the camera." Others manage the space by making sure doors are closed when they go live, utilizing a separate room, or using green screens to designate a stage area that people can walk behind to stay off camera.

PERSONAL INFORMATION . . . AND RARELY LOCATION

Though streamers often broadcast out of their homes and can regularly share deeply personal information about their lives, I found that some frequently drew other kinds of boundary lines. These tended to be tied to issues of offline identity and safety. Given the convention for streamers and gamers more broadly to let their online moniker be their calling card across lots of platforms, untangling what disclosure looks like online is not always straightforward. People may hide or downplay their legal names, but still share tremendous amounts of information about their personal lives. Or they may reveal their legal names or moniker, or even broadcast out of their homes, but still want to maintain some line of the personal that is not crossed with their audience.

Those who didn't share deeply about their personal lives tended to want to make some, if blurry, distinction between their online or esports identity and their offline one. One pro esports player who broadcasts daily utilized the third person to describe his stance:

> I'm not keeping anything super secret, but yeah, it's always the person of [his screen name] that's being discussed. So how did [screen name] come into existence, how did he grow through experiences? Yeah, sometimes I've gone very deep in some interviews, but it's still [screen name]. I never present myself as [offline name]. And I wish actually for [offline name] to not be the name people call me because first-name basis is something that I only really do either with sponsors because it's more professional or with people whom I first met through real life. And since my nickname is easy enough, there's no need to go to the first name.

This player's "real name" is actually widely known, and parts of his life are shared with his viewers. He broadcasts out of his home, and his wife regularly passes by on camera. Yet it is clear that there is a boundary line he does draw. The way he moves from first to third person when using his competitive moniker reminds me quite a bit of early work that I did talking to people about their relationships with avatars, where they had an adept way of shifting across how they wanted to present themselves as well as be known in the mix of on- and offline life (Taylor 1999). This is not an issue of the two domains being separate but instead of people understanding them as spaces unified by personal judgments and choices about what they want to disclose.

A nearly consistent theme I found across all streamers was the way that disclosing particular details about your offline identity was deemed a safety issue. A concern with "really dangerous or bad people" was one that came up regularly. This is not unfounded. The phenomenon of "swatting," whereby a streamer's local police department is called with a false hostage report at the streamer's address, has led to some truly dangerous instances of police entering streamers' homes looking for armed persons. These have been captured live on stream several times, and caused more than one streamer to think long and hard about disclosing any more than their region or city. The streamer I quoted above as having the one rule of "wear a bra if you are on camera" expressed concern about this, especially in relation to his partner, and felt a responsibility to make sure his family was safe despite his profession: "I try to make sure that my things are private, that my things are secure; my PayPal is secure, my email is secure, my game accounts are secure. That people aren't delving into our public lives and trying to stalk us. . . . I'd rather my name not get out there."

Interestingly, a significant part of his worry arose from his knowledge of how women in particular have experienced harassment and stalking; as his partner was a visible and known part of his life, he was acutely aware of this risk. He told me, "I think if I was on my own, I don't think I'd care so much." One of the women streamers I spoke with echoed how issues of safety influenced disclosures. She said, "I definitely have rules on what I'd like to share with people. I'm very limited on sharing my location just for my safety . . . Whenever I tweet something from Foursquare, I like to make sure that it's not my house or around my house." This tends to also mean that streamers, both men and women, do things like set up post office boxes for mail or deliveries, hide domain name registration addresses, and route voice communication through Skype, Discord, or services other than the telephone.

Yet many streamers are simultaneously aware of the delicate balancing act they do given the tone of authenticity and honesty they try to have with their audience. As one put it, "I am me 100 percent. Like when I get in front of the camera, I have no problem talking about my life and letting people into my life. A lot of people know I have a kid on the way. A lot of people know I live in [state's name]. I'm outside [a major city]. These are things that people know about me because I've shared that with them. But I keep it kind of not so specific."

This dynamic, perhaps sharing important life experiences and thoughts with people online, while maybe withholding things like your real name or where you live, is in fact not unique to live streaming but instead something that regularly occurs in online communities. It highlights the ways that tidy formal definitions of public and private rarely capture the complexity of how people navigate relationships with others online. Information science scholar Helen Nissenbaum (2010, 3) argues, "What people care most about is not simply *restricting* the flow of information but ensuring that it flows *appropriately*." Her emphasis is on "contextual integrity," which highlights privacy as a process undertaken by navigating, adjudicating, and balancing a number of concerns as well as conditions (rather than a priori universal frameworks). Although live streamers are not your typical internet users, the mode of nuanced disclosure is one that many can probably relate to if they've spent time in multiuser spaces, be they games or pseudonymous communication sites.

Viewer Expectations and Stereotypes

Live streaming audiences come to the platform with a range of experiences and expectations. They often select channels based on knowing something about the game being played or because of curiosity about the title. They may see large viewer numbers and want to check out what the crowd is up to. Longtime viewers who've sampled different types of content may find that they prefer particular genres of streaming—humorous ones, for example—and hit channels looking for that form of entertainment. Viewers may see a name or face that draws them in. Part of the power of live streaming is the immediacy of the broadcaster; you see them, hear their voice, and even usually get a glimpse of their home. Woven throughout this are the expectations that viewers bring to a broadcaster, ranging from the content of the show to who they imagine the streamer is in real life.

While most consider a microphone and camera pretty much a requirement for the platform at this point, their use does impact streamers differently. Women, LGBTQIA folks, and people of color regularly face harassment on the site, and choosing to broadcast, especially with a webcam and/or audio, is no small feat. As media scholar Kishonna Gray (2016, 366) notes in her study of Black gamers on the platform, "The mere presence of their marginalized bodies disrupts the norm of the space designated for privileged bodies. They participate as social agents that engage in a dynamic and ongoing process of producing and reshaping the discourse about what it means to be a true gamer." They can frequently feel the additional burden of being visible and a quasi role model. The risks and struggles they face are powerful, and often take a real toll. Race, gender, class, sexuality, and disability thus all come to play critical roles as viewers confront actual streamers, some of whom may be outside a viewer's social circle or everyday life. In this way, live streaming has components long heralded via television of connecting audiences to otherwise-unknown worlds and experiences. Unlike television, however, audiences immediately and directly engage with the person on the other side of their screen.

I've been fortunate to get to meet and talk to a variety of broadcasters over the years who are working hard to make a space for themselves on the platform in the face of a culture and audience for which they are typically invisible. The responses they receive range from enthusiasm or indifference to active opposition to their presence (I will discuss the issue of harassment further in chapters 4 and 5). While many have taken to heart the long-standing—and woefully insufficient—refrain of "grow a thicker skin," their work and strategies remain important to examine more closely. As a form of media, live streaming should aspire to open participation and inclusion. Creating content and sharing it with others has become a powerful part of everyday experience as well as social connection. Yet for many who are marginalized, it remains a space where meaningful participation, and creative expression are emotionally taxing, contentious, and sometimes dangerous.

STEREOTYPES

One of the challenges that streamers can face is balancing their own sense of self against the demands of audience (and market) expectations. Because of the way that live streaming can trade on notions of authenticity, viewers can also bring to streams an assumption of who the broadcaster is based on what they look like. These may not *actually* align to the streamer's identity, personality, or even desires for their content. Yet viewer expectations are oftentimes tangled up in stereotypes. Given that there is a transactional and economic aspect to the system, it can put streamers in tough or at least awkward situations. One Black streamer I spoke with illustrated one way that racial stereotyping regularly played out with his viewers:

> People tend to request like a lot of rap music on my stream, for example [laughing]. I'll play it if that means you stay. I'll play it [still laughing]. I mean, I like hip-hop and rap as much as the next guy, you know? Personally when I'm playing, that is not what I would stream to. But I got a lot of interesting comments like, "Yo, what is this music that you're listening to? Where's my Drake at?" [laughing]. I was like, I don't listen to any of that on my stream. I'm going to listen to like some instrumental stuff. I really like film scores, I really like classical music, so that's what I listen to because I feel like it really puts me into the zone when I'm playing. Once I have a couple of people on my stream, I will change it to hip-hop and rap because that is what people like when they are on my stream.

He talked about finding this expectation surprising as well as out of sync with his own preferences. Speaking of how he didn't experience his offline life as so constantly infused with questions about his identity, he remarked that "the internet is a very racially conscious environment, and being on the internet, it's interesting how much commentary and how much people talk about your race and stuff like that." He described having grown up amid a lot of racial diversity and so noticed when responses to him called out any distinctiveness. He spoke of the experience of playing an online game with someone who then visited his stream and realized that he was not who they expected. As he explained, he is routinely met with exclamations of "'Holy crap! You're Black!' That's like the first thing that they say, which is really interesting. I didn't know that it was all that special, but when you start looking at the kind of people who are actually streaming and creating content, a lot of them aren't African American."

His reflections reminded me that many times when I talked to streamers who are members of marginalized groups, they expressed felt gaps between their own sense of identity, personal histories, play preferences, and social lives and how viewers (or indeed the culture at large) saw and positioned them. While he went on to positively talk about how some people followed him because of "my unique contribution being my skin color," for many others this kind of dynamic is a regular source of resigned frustration.

Streamer DistractedElf, speaking on a panel at TwitchCon, discussed her disappointment with how some audience members had not been able to navigate her transition from male to female, visible through archived content she's produced over the years:

> So you can look back at my VoDs and be like, "Oh, that's very different. Yes, she sounds different, her hair is different, she's not even 'she' yet, hmm. Very interesting." And it's funny how, I've had an experience where in my chat recently, actually, where somebody said, "Oh, I really like your stream, I really like your content, it's super awesome, but then I went back and looked at your VoDs and now I feel weird looking at you." And I went, "Why? What has changed? Nothing! I am the same as when you looked at me the first time!" But it's weird how that context, I don't know, messes with some people. (quoted in Koebel 2016)

The sense that it was still her that the audience should be able to connect with is a theme that I've heard in various ways over the years from not just trans streamers but many others too. Broadcasters I've spoken with often talk about how they embrace the specificities of their identities (for example, a Black woman or gay man), yet also want audiences to connect with them *as* gamers and entertainers. Streamer AnneMunition remarked on that same panel,

> I'm more than just a gay woman. There's a lot more to me than just that. For me, it's always been about—especially with streaming—I've tried to

be this person who, if you enjoy that I'm playing video games, maybe I make you laugh, that's what's important. There's all this extra stuff that isn't that important, that's just part of who I am. So it's like, if I wanted to align myself with a community of people on Twitch, it's just, I want to be aligned with the people who are entertaining, rather than just "those gay people." (quoted in Koebel 2016)

Time and again I've heard people who are not white, heterosexual, or cis male streamers talk about the challenges that they face when they confront various stereotypes or expectations, whether it was about what kinds of games they were expected to enjoy or how they were expected to behave.[21] Often I've spoken to gamers of color who have had, for instance, to deal with people being surprised about their preference for role-playing games and generally being more of a "nerd" than stereotypes might suggest feasible. Women also continue to face stereotypes and pushback when they focus on competitive games and have professional aspirations—both positions that still disrupt more traditional stereotypes about who women are, and what they like or are good at. It is also not unusual to hear from LGBTQIA gamers about how they struggle with wanting to be a broadcaster "like any other," but the very fact of their sexuality, if publicly known, can make them a target or can put them in a position of having to constantly address it.[22]

VALUING DIFFERENCE

This feeling of not wanting to be hemmed in by stereotypes does not, however, mean that these streamers want to stake out a color-blind, gender-neutral, or heteronormative position. It is not about eschewing their lives, identities, bodies, and communities. Nor is it about hiding things that may mark them as different from some audience members. Frustrations with stereotypes are about constraints and real costs: from devaluing specific embodied identity and experience (including ensuing microaggressions or bruising harassment) to the marginalization of difference. Fortunately there has been growing attention to the importance of diverse bodies, identities, and cultures within gaming. Powerful initiatives like I Need Diverse Games, Feminist Frequency, Not Your Mama's Gamer, and many others have addressed not only the representational gaps within gaming but also the social impacts and costs to overly narrow conceptualizations of game culture.

Samantha Blackmon (2015), game studies scholar and cofounder of Not Your Mama's Gamer, reflecting on the importance of diversity within live streaming, argues that "we need to hear diverse perspectives and we need folks from diverse backgrounds to see themselves reflected in the communities that surround the media that they consume. In other words, we need to know what women, LGBTI folks, and minorities think about games too *and* folks from these communities (and folks in general) need to see themselves reflected in these communities." Another piece asserted that "black Twitch" actually offers spaces distinct from so much of what many find problematic on the platform. Columnist Andray Domise (2017) writes

> that [it] seems to stand out as an exception—a garden with walls tall enough to keep out the toxic elements, but doors wide enough to accommodate the folks you want at the cookout. While popular (and often white) streamers often let gross jokes, sexism, and other bigotry slide unaddressed—or worse, play along—for the benefit of building an audience, many Black streamers have made a concerted effort to keep their streams and chats as relaxed and friendly as possible.

Interventions like these, including podcasts like *Spawn on Me*, which focuses on gamers of color and regularly features live streamers, bring to the fore the value of difference. Diverse participation and its visibility is not simply a side issue within gaming but instead goes to the heart of both a fair and just society as well as what a participatory media culture should be.

It is, perhaps not surprisingly, common to hear many of these streamers talk about the work that they do to be visible, educate audiences, and give people a chance to learn and grow. While they typically shy away from the term "role model" and don't want to be pigeonholed as a "diversity advocate," they regularly enact tremendous labor to try to make the platform better for themselves and others. Although broadcasters often talk about not being there to fix big social issues but rather to just stream, recognizing the nuanced work they undertake in engaging with at times clueless, hurtful, and even harassing audience members is important. AnneMunition, for example, describes a real generosity when dealing with people on her channel who may not be used to the types of conversations happening there:

> Maybe this person just doesn't have any experience with anything that we're saying. Maybe they have literally no idea, and they're coming to you from this place of just complete not, like, ignorance in a malicious way, but they just don't know. So, taking that opportunity to explain that to them in a respectful way, versus just instantly shutting them down—I try and encourage everyone to have this conversation that's respectful and

not just about, like, "Well, you're wrong, and we're not going to explain why." (quoted in Koebel 2016)

Navigating this terrain is work, and streamers sometimes talk about developing their skills at handling this side of live audiences. DistractedElf has said that "there are a lot of people who come to my channel and don't have any idea what they're watching, so to speak, so I do a lot of that. A lot of education" (ibid.). Koebel, asking his TwitchCon panelists about this move, cut to the chase and observed, "So how do you develop those skills around knowing when someone's just being a shitlord, and when they're actually just curious?" Streamer UGRGaming answered, "Usually it starts with, 'Are you gay?' And I'm like, 'yes.' And then you wait for the next question, when you're waiting for the answer, and it's either, 'Oh, I didn't know' or 'Can you explain?' or it's, you know, f-word, f-this, blah blah blah. And it's like, okay, alright, you're out. Too late, too late. It's easier than ever now" (ibid.).

There are limits to this work, though, and regular streamers will usually have to decide just how much time and energy they want to put into this side of their engagement. UGRGaming's response shows that there is a balance most of these folks take to being open to educating people, and not wasting energy and time on them. As AnneMunition (ibid.) put it, like many in her position, she is clear about not overextending herself: "I feel like I'll spend a little time trying to educate people, so to speak, but I mean, if your parents failed you, it's not my job to fix you, you know? I'm not a teacher, I'm an entertainer."

SURVIVING AND THRIVING

These streamers demonstrate resilience and creativity in coming up with strategies to keep doing what they enjoy. In her book on race, gender, and Xbox Live, Gray investigates not only the representational problems at work in so many computer games but also the experiences of women and players of color in the multiplayer space. She paints a devastating picture of the racism and sexism that these players routinely face, highlighting the ways that intersectionality can position particular gamers such that "the combination of statuses one holds in society can create a multitude of discriminations and challenges." As she notes, "Interlocking oppression accounts for how awareness of race, class, gender (as well as other social locations) co-constitute one another in ways that cannot be separated in white supremacist capitalist patriarchy" (Gray 2014, 57, 58). Her astute assessment of the ways that sexism and racism are deeply woven through game culture is one we must all take to heart—and strive to change.

She goes on to describe the ways that women of color gamers have found to resist and speak back to an often-harassing, oppressive game culture. Drawing on digital activism literature, she identifies three branches of intervention that the women she studied took up: awareness/advocacy, organization/mobilization, and action/reaction. These women's responses to a hostile game environment range from forming their own smaller communities to play with, publicly promoting other women of color, or speaking out and pushing back on harassers when possible. Gray also shows the flexibility of the women she interviews to mobilize resources, particularly around technology, in order to challenge the racism and sexism they encounter as well as carve out communities of play that can thrive within an otherwise-hostile culture. Though she wisely cautions us to also be mindful of the continued need for broader structural transformation, she underscores the power of these tactical interventions, writing, "Because of the discrimination and exclusion that many women and people of color face, they have created their own spaces within virtual worlds. Given the relative ease in which spaces can be created, this presents oppressed groups the ability of being able to control and create positive content influencing our own images (granted they are fortunate and privileged enough to have access to technology and have the skills necessary to create)" (ibid., 76). The active speaking back and resistive engagement she portrays resonates with what I've seen among women, people of color, and LGBTQIA live streamers.

Broadcaster Chinemere "Chinny" Iwuanyanwu has spoken about the power of finding others like yourself, the support that comes through forming communities, and leveraging tools outside Twitch to do that. Herself a woman of color, she said on a TwitchCon panel on diversity,

> Women of color, that's a minority within a minority, so you know there's going to be problems there. But we're all out there and we're all here, and we just need to find better ways to connect, because if it's a toxic community out there, then our group will want to stay away from Twitch. We want to feel included. But if we find ways to connect, we will come together and grow our community. It's just [a] means of finding each other. (quoted in Vee et al. 2016)

From using Twitch itself to leveraging other programs (such as Discord or Steam), building communities has been a powerful method to find support and stay engaged.

Part of this is also enacted through supporting peer women, people of color, and LGBTQIA streamers. Hosting other's streams when you are "off the air," sending your audience over to another channel when you end your broadcast, or the creation of "communities" on Twitch (formal groupings of channels that users can create) or Discord have all become ways that broadcasters support each other. The use of Twitter, blogs, and podcasts are another way. In those venues, those who may not be reaching the front page of Twitch or getting much attention can be promoted to viewers who would love to watch their content but might not otherwise be exposed to them. As streamer Ryoga Vee (ibid.) put it, "We're huge. The number of us is growing every day. But for us to continue to be participants, we have to support each other. . . . And the trolls are always going to be there. Whatever measures Twitch puts in place, they're still going to find an avenue around it. But if we find ways to support the community, whether it's Facebook groups, whether it's Discord, we can find strength in numbers."

As I've previously mentioned, the role of moderation in maintaining a positive channel community is also huge, and it's certainly the case that many of these streamers make active use of these practices and tools. One player of color I spoke with talked about how he and his sister moderate each other's streams. Other broadcasters bring friends or exceptional community members onto their team. In a 2016 paper analyzing speech in live stream chats, researchers found distinct chat differences between the channels of men and women who were broadcasting. This was not a matter of the streamers themselves talking about different things but instead how their audiences communicated in and about the space. They noted that while the channels of male broadcasters tended to be overrepresented in terms of game-related speech, women's channels had a disproportionate amount of objectifying speech and warnings, signaling a high degree of having to constantly fend off problematic behaviors (Nakandala et al. 2016). This research echoes with what we have heard from women for a while now: there is a consistent onslaught of speech directed at them that has nothing to do with their gaming, and the work it takes to navigate and moderate it is nontrivial.

We also see how emoticons on the platform, small icon-size images (like emojis) meant to be fun in-group forms of shorthand and communication, can be deployed to ostracize, stigmatize, and harass broadcasters. Most notable is perhaps the use of the "trihard" emote, an expressive smiling image of the popular speed runner Mychal "trihex" Jefferson, who is a person of color. The picture, submitted in 2012 by one of Jefferson's viewers to Twitch for inclusion in its global emote category, has come to serve not only as an enthusiastic cheer but also a stand-in for calling out the race of a broadcaster or in lieu of a slur.[23] This repurposing of what was originally intended for entertainment and even celebration is especially egregious. Over the years, the trihard emote has been debated, with occasional calls for it to be removed from the platform entirely. Chinny astutely notes, though, that removing it sidesteps both its original intent and the larger stakes at work:

> I mean the trihard emote isn't meant to be a racist emote, it's not what it was created for, but people on the internet will look for any way to make something racist. Banning something like that emote would be the worst thing you could possibly do. . . . I mean look at the list of emotes we have on Twitch. Of course people are going to pick the trihard emote first. I mean how many black people are on emote faces on Twitch? So I think Twitch needs to see what they can do to make these emotes more diverse so trolls will have a harder time doing this. (quoted in Vee et al. 2016)

On a platform with so little diversity, ceding ground on one of the few emotes representing a person of color is a lousy option. And as Chinny emphasizes, it evades a more glaring issue: the overall lack of representation within these communication systems and persistent racism online.

The practice of flooding a channel with racist, sexist, or homophobic speech, emotes, or ASCII "art" works to stigmatize as well as police particular bodies and identities. It also attempts to constitute an alternate "center"—an erasure of the actual diversity at work in gaming.[24] Audiences will often leverage the functionality of the platform to enact boundary policing—one fueled by an emotional, angry, and anxious tenor. In turn, streamers are put in the position of not only doing the work of broadcasting but doing so within a context that requires them to be adept and creative resistors as well.

As with all broadcasters, there is real pride and relief when the community itself starts stepping up to help shape the tenor of the channel. Anne-Munition remarked on this, saying,

> I think both my mods and a lot of my regulars, subs, non-subs, anything, if they're there all the time, they know what I allow and won't allow, that kind of thing, and they definitely help groom my community. Because a lot of times, it's kind of nice because I'll sit back, and I'll see someone say something and in my mind I'm like, "Oh my God, here we go . . ." and I sit back and I just focus on the game, and I'll see my community handle

it without me having to address it, and that's really good. "Good job guys, you did it! I'm proud of you!" (quoted in Koebel 2016)

While the resilience and tactics these streamers deploy is impressive, it's crucial to acknowledge the additional practices that marginalized broadcasters do as labor—materially, socially, and emotionally—to remain on the platform.

WHEN ENOUGH IS ENOUGH

The fight to retain a sense of your own authentic identity, to even just participate and be present, in the face of a harassing audience takes a toll. As game scholar Emma Witkowski (forthcoming) remarks in her study of women in esports, they are "persistently derailed as authentic participants . . . via both personal and community attacks alongside of institutional positioning and dismissal . . . often leaving it to the individual players to tough it out and devise methods to self-protect in her positioning as a woman who plays." Many marginalized streamers decide, quite reasonably, that the costs are just too high to stay on a public stage. New broadcasters may, as Chinny put it, "look at their chat and see a racist mess going on, and they may find like 'I can't handle this, I need to stop'" (Vee et al. 2016). Vee, himself an experienced streamer, spoke about this dynamic, observing that he regularly sees other people of color take up broadcasting and build up a small community, but eventually stop due to the harassment. "When you feel like you're the only one out there," Vee (ibid.) explained, "you feel like you're a small fish in the sea and everyday they're coming at you, it weighs on you. Even me, I've got thick skin, but some days I wake up and I want to stream but I'm like 'I don't want to hear it today.' There's days I don't stream specifically for that reason."

Some reply to such frustrations by saying that everyone gets harassed online and in games, and expecting that women, people of color, and LGBTQIA streamers will be exempt is asking for special treatment. While some level of harassment does indeed happen to many on the platform, it is *disproportionately distributed* to broadcasters who are not white, hetero, or cis male. These streamers face consistent and focused attacks on their identities and bodies, not just comments about how or what they play. These attacks take a real toll, as already mentioned, and the exhaustion that comes from constantly confronting stereotype expectations and outright harassment makes walking away from broadcasting a completely understandable choice. As Not Your Mama's Gamer columnist Sarah Nixon (2015) points out, for women broadcasters "the very act of streaming can be a political decision, one that makes it difficult to see streaming for the rewarding and fun experience it really is." Harassment has the power to curtail participation, both for streamers and audience members (who themselves may not want to encounter the toxicity). At its worst, it drives people entirely off the platform.

The Business of Play

As perhaps is becoming apparent by discussing the layers of production along with the forms of less tangible but equally important relational, emotional, and affective labor, live streaming at any serious, even quasi-professional level is hard work. While we tend to think first and foremost about the playing that takes place on camera, there is much invisible labor happening before, during, and after a broadcast. Behind-the-scenes juggling, including coordinating with moderators, ensuring software is working, monitoring and engaging with social media, and even making sure that "people are kind of jiving to the music," are all occurring while the show is live. The work to produce a stream also doesn't end with the live components. One broadcaster notes that there is a tremendous amount of labor that gets done off-air, which only increases for streamers as they become popular:

> I mean every time I log off, I have anywhere from 30 to 150, even sometimes more than that, private messages that people send me that I need to go through. I've got to make sure that I'm keeping up with my YouTube, keeping up with my Twitter, checking my Steam group, making sure that I am prepared my next day of streaming, what game am I going to stream, why I'm going to stream it at that time and for what purpose, are the viewers going to like that. Planning, secretary, admin, administration work, keeping up with my website, making sure I'm following the posts on my website . . . keeping up with other streamers, making sure that I'm talking to developers, talking about contracts and sponsors. There's a lot of work that happens off stream. I would say for about every hour of stream time that you put in, I would say probably about half of that goes into work off stream when you get off.

As I indicated previously, live streamers currently act not only as content producers and performers but small business owners, designers, accountants, contract negotiators, agents, community managers, and technical staff as well. Aside from some notable exceptions, at the time of my research there was little division of labor at the "talent" node in the live streaming space, and broadcasters often run complex media properties with little to no help. Taking a closer look at this aspect of live streaming makes visible this crucial hidden labor.

ECONOMICS OF STREAMING

Getting paid for all that work, or at least attempting to, happens in a variety of ways. At a base level, the Twitch platform is organized around ad revenue, with commercials running on streams and the proceeds going to Twitch. This changes, however, if a streamer becomes an official Twitch partner or affiliate—an opaque process that is based on content, average concurrent viewership, and broadcast regularity.[25] Once admitted to one of these programs, the streamer gets a share of the ad revenue, which Twitch—though not disclosing figures—has publicly defined as an "industry-leading CPM."

Online ad revenue is not the most transparent of systems.[26] At the most fundamental level, there is the cost per *mille* (CPM), which is Latin for a thousand. This is the rate that an advertiser pays for a thousand impressions of their ad. The more important term and rate for streamers, however, is the effective CPM (eCPM) (the more precise, although less used term, is revenue per *mille*). This is the rate that someone *actually* earns for a given piece of content. The rate can also be structured along a "revenue share" or flat-rate model; revenue shares provide both platform and broadcaster a percentage based on whatever the ad sale was while flat rates operate via a fixed price (for example, five dollars per thousand views). At the time of my study, Twitch noted on its Partner Help page that it operated on a flat-rate model "based on feedback from the majority of Partners that they would prefer more stability in monthly revenue. This helps protect Partners from the CPM factor in seasonality."[27]

There are a range of variables that intervene between the CPM and eCPM. In a 2012 post on the popular esports website Team Liquid, Twitch chief operating officer Kevin Lin laid out a clear explanation of how online advertising works for platforms like it. He explained a third key term for broadcasters to understand—"fill rate"—which is "Ad Impressions [ads seen] divided by Ad Opportunities [ads available]. In an ideal world, everyone sells every single Ad Opportunity to someone. This would mean 100% fill-rate. In the real world, because there are other variables like country of viewer, time of day, number of ads seen by a unique viewer, etc. the Fill-rate is always less than 100%" (Lin 2012). This detail is critical because the *actual* payout to a broadcaster can vary widely based on audience regionality, the use of ad-blocking software, or how many other ads viewers may have seen online that day. For example, in general, a viewer coming from Russia will not net the same amount for ads as one from the United States. Also, interestingly, a viewer who consumes a lot of online video may be worth less in ad revenue. As Lin (2012) explained,

> If you as a viewer have been to other video sites or even other channels and see other video ads before arriving at a partner channel, then whatever ad you see on the current channel you're viewing will be lower in CPM value than the first ad you saw that day. Most big brands frequency cap video ads at 1 per 24 hrs, which means you should only see their ad once per day as a unique viewer. So as you see more video ads through the day, the value of the ad decreases.

Ad revenue also fluctuates over the course of a year due to seasonal variability. As a Twitch (2016c) Partner Help page stated, "Advertisers typically spend opportunistically to reach consumers when they are most likely to spend," and thus "start of summer, back to school, and of course the holiday season" are high points, as are big game launches.

While this may seem like an overwhelming amount of detail for a non-industry reader, it is an important part of the real economic challenges that broadcasters actually face. While it's easy for these platforms to be seen as offering incredible financial opportunities to content creators, the devil—and fragility of the system—is in the details. Indeed the complexity and even opacity of the advertising system may be lost on aspiring professional streamers. The system relies on a tremendous amount of data and situational complexity that broadcasters may or may not understand, much less even have access to.

Despite how central online advertising has been in the period since the web was opened up to commercial enterprise, there have been critics who warn that it is, essentially, a house built on sand. Ad-blocking software remains one of the strongest barriers to revenue from this source online. Once installed, it prevents many kinds of advertisements from appearing across all kinds of websites. From pop-up ads to embedded banners, ad-blocking software has a long history of being deployed by users to manage the commercialization of internet spaces. Starting around 2002 with Henrik Aasted Sørensen's original Adblock code, and now used by around two hundred million people worldwide across a variety of devices, ad-blocking software continues to grow in popularity (Scott 2015). As a sociotechnical actor, it has a lineage tying it to things like remote controls as well as the work that humans do to use those remotes to actually flip channels during a commercial.[28]

Ad-blocking software has historically had a profound impact on how people not only manage their experience of a live streamed channel but also discussions around the financial stability of streamers and viewers responsibility to support them. As a bit of software, ad-blocking browser extensions that were triggered in Twitch streams freed users from constantly doing the work of skipping around to other channels, and deciding each and every time if they want to support a stream by allowing a commercial to run. It often served to smooth out the viewing experience, though at a financial cost to streamers. Broadcasters regularly had to navigate around their viewer's use of ad-blocking software (recall figure 3.5). Communities themselves debate the legitimacy of blocking commercials, and frequently wrangled with complex ethical issues that traverse considerations of commercialization, culture, and what one "owes" creative producers.

In 2016, Twitch launched a new system, SureStream, which integrated commercials directly into a broadcast rather than overlaying them, thereby circumventing most attempts at ad blocking. Though in its public blog post announcing the new technology it said of ad blockers, "As a company we are agnostic when it comes to the use of this software. You are free to use it, or not, as you see fit," it is certainly clear that the actual infrastructure of the platform is not so neutral (Twitch 2016b). The rollout of the technology was also tied to a shift in the financial structure of the platform; Twitch would be taking over its own ad sales, thus bypassing third-party advertising systems.[29]

Analysts Tim Hwang and Adi Kamdar (2013, 2), reflecting in part on ad-blocking practices, have offered a theory of "peak advertising" (a la "peak oil") that posits "cracks are beginning to show in the very financial foundations of the web."[30] They identify four fatal trends in online advertising that pose real challenges to its efficacy: changing demographics, the ubiquity of ad blocking, "click fraud," and the growing density of advertising working to actually undermine it. In varying ways, each of these points touch the live streaming space and are in a continual dance with platform developers who race to mitigate them. Caught up in that dance as perhaps unwitting partners, however, are the broadcasters.

Hwang and Kamdar (ibid., 8) further suggest that standard web forms of banner and display advertising may need to be replaced by "less detectable forms of promotion"—that is, "content that is advertising but appears not to be."[31] These alternative forms of promotion are in fact part of the framework that Twitch now rests on. Live streaming pitched as a marketing tool has become one of the fundamental economic principles of the platform. This occurs through stories about how sales can be driven by spectatorship and deals that the platform makes with game developers. Twitch will at times facilitate its partners getting sponsored stream opportunities. It has also, as a result of its being purchased by Amazon, sought to reconfigure the platform itself such that a "buy-now" button will appear on channel pages, allowing audience members to purchase the game they are watching. Small freebies, in the form of in-game items for certain Twitch users, promote game ownership. While some of these forms of alternative promotional methods result in money to broadcasters, it is not a given.

One of the biggest upshots of this system—especially due to the early widespread use of ad-blocking software—is that streamers have turned to alternate funding paths to try to make ends meet. Relying on ad revenue alone is rarely enough. Partners and affiliates can take advantage of Twitch's internal subscription option. Viewers of a channel may choose to subscribe to the streamer by paying a monthly fee (at the time of this writing, $4.99), of which a percentage goes to Twitch and the remainder to the streamer (the baseline is a fifty-fifty split for partners, but can vary widely given a streamer's negotiating power). Or if the viewer is an Amazon Prime subscriber who has linked their Twitch account, they become Twitch Prime members and can dedicate one free subscription credit to a broadcaster each month.

Channel subscribers receive access to a special icon that appears next to their name in the chat, unique emoticons, and special messages from the streamer, and if the chat goes into "subscriber mode," they retain the ability to communicate on the channel. This method of revenue generation thus becomes entangled with how broadcasters cultivate their community and foster additional layers of in-group identification. The affective economies of live streaming become embodied in the structure of the platform. Fandom and connection are interlinked with monetization.

Partnerships can also open up opportunities to run T-shirt campaigns whereby a streamer has a shirt specially designed, and then utilizes Twitch, which outsources the production, to run a sale and collect proceeds. Twitch takes a flat fee (at the time of this writing, $2.50), and the profit margin varies based on how many shirts are sold. Not unlike how bands and comedians often turn to merchandise as an important revenue generator, broadcasters can offer audience members things to purchase to display their fandom and in turn financially support them.

Many streamers actively use donation systems, sponsorships, and occasionally Amazon affiliate links to generate additional income as well. Donation systems have proven tremendously popular and lucrative for many successful streamers, making up a significant part of their revenue. Streamlabs, one of the primary services that many broadcasters on both YouTube Live and Twitch use to manage their donation systems, reported processing $80 million in tips and donations for broadcasters in 2016 (Hicks 2017). This was an 84 percent increase from the $43 million it handled in 2015. Given that it only handles tips for 78 percent of the top twenty-five thousand Twitch streamers, the actual numbers are higher (Le 2017).[32]

Graphical elements overlaid onto the game denoting the name and amount of the highest contributor of the day as well as daily totals are common (see figure 3.7). Notification systems of when new donations are made—a pop-up image and/or sound—bring the activity into the core of the broadcast itself.

Donation systems have become a central structure through which streamers tie their performances of engagement with the audience to financial contributions. One streamer explained how he took lessons from the TPP phenomenon, which was a compelling example of how viewers can be actively involved in gameplay. He spoke of tapping into this by weaving together the performative and economic side of his broadcast:

> People want a different level of interaction. It's like they don't just want to watch. Interaction is huge with me, and I don't mean just me talking to my chat. That's one form of interaction. So it's like putting up a donation thing on my screen where people can see when they donate and it makes a sound. I'm sure you've seen that before. That is interaction. So think about this. Let's say I play a scary game and I put out a loud screaming sound for a dollar. If you donate a dollar, the sound is a scream sound. Now when somebody throws a dollar at me, not only am I making money to support what I do, but on top of that the users are actually altering the course of the stream based on their interaction. It's a way of interacting.

This approach highlights how streamers can be adept innovators, literally playing with more expansive definitions of interaction and engagement with their audience. It also shows how they see chat as only one component of the overall picture, and how they think about new ways to shape their content and bring audiences in, including ways that may motivate people to financially support their work. They are playing with, tweaking, and transforming the platform not just for entertainment but also for economic purposes.

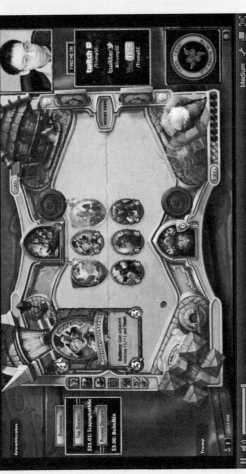

FIGURE 3.7. TrumpSC's broadcast with donation tally box on the left, 2014.

This is not new in online video and UGC. Creators are regularly looking to find opportunities to not only improve their productions but monetize them in ways that feel both authentic and viable. Donation systems on Twitch and their integration into the very content of the broadcast (be it the "inter-action" model proposed above or simply visualized in the graphics of the stream) represent an important case study in how the out-of-the-box design of a platform rarely addresses the full range of activities that users engage in.

This is a constant thread in game culture, where players regularly find that their preferences exceed that offered by the software or platform. Twitch, while supplying some mechanisms for revenue generation, can never fully anticipate either the aesthetic or economic practices of content producers who are seeking to go full time in the space. This is because as a creative activity, broadcasters are routinely shifting, adapting, and pushing the medium for new cultural production. Their aspirations and expectations may not fit with how the system is structured. Audiences, for their part, are always dynamically changing and adjusting expectations not only in relation to what broadcasters are doing but also to media practices well beyond the specific environment of Twitch.

For example, ads sometimes do not fit with the vibe that a streamer is going for, or how they prefer to carry out gameplay or interactions with the audience. As one broadcaster explained,

> I can make more money if I played more ads, but [my viewers are] taking care of me enough with donations. Why am I playing ads to these people? I can play games straight through and not have to interrupt this because that's my thing. I'm like, "Guys, when I come on here, I don't want to have to play ads to you all. I want to be able to show you straight gameplay." And they donate to the capacity where I don't feel like I need to play ads.

Early on broadcasters began finding ways, typically utilizing PayPal along with third-party software and sites, to get additional financial support from their viewers. Ancillary businesses emerged to specifically cater to live streaming donations. Popular sites like Streamtip or Twitch Alerts offered services to help track and manage donations. While the sites have been at baseline free, they do charge PayPal processing fees. Part of the draw of these tools also lay in the ways that they could be integrated into the overall performance of the channel.

Audience decisions about how much they want to pay, or "contribute," to content that they consume online is also continually in flux. Decisions can be tied to everything from their specific feelings of support for a particular streamer to their overall monthly media expenditures. For example, paying for HBO for a few months may throw off their ability to donate to a streamer or spend money on a game. Platforms such as Twitch are always having to contend with a multiplicity of factors—many of which they may not even fully understand—that go into why any given viewer might be willing turn off ad block, donate some money, or buy a T-shirt. Overall spending decisions on sites like Twitch are affected by a number of other areas people direct their money, from simply keeping up with their bills to other game, media, or leisure expenditures.

The platform does, however, try to stay on top and benefit from the new monetization paths that streamers are themselves creating. As is frequently the case with the cycle between user-generated modifications and formal developer uptake, Twitch launched its own system in 2016 to allow for donations, of which it takes a cut. "Bits" are purchased directly from Twitch at a launch rate of $1.40 for a hundred. Though the cut that streamers receive was not made public, at launch it was rumored to be around 70 percent (and as with subscription revenue rates, is likely to vary based on broadcaster negotiating power). Amounts are represented via different graphical icons and can be "tipped" directly on the platform to a streamer to "cheer" them. The donation is then visually represented in the chat via the graphic. The system mimics the public shows of support as third-party donation systems did and also assists streamers in bypassing PayPal, with which there have long been issues around charge backs.

Yet it has been met with mixed reviews. While Twitch rolled it out as a beta to some prominent streamers, there are those in the community—both streamers and viewers—who have criticized it. Among other issues, some decry it as a cash grab by the site, while others have expressed concerns about how it will be ethically integrated into tournament settings for the benefit of the competitors and talent.[33] Either way, it represents the company picking up on an emergent socioeconomic process—one that the content producers themselves developed and scaffolded from scratch—and formally integrating it into the system.

PLATFORM AND DEVELOPER DEPENDENCY

Twitch's Bits system is just the latest in the linkages between the financial opportunity of the streamer and the platform. On the one hand, the site relies on its users to constantly produce new and interesting content that will draw in viewers who will provide an audience for advertising and game exposure. There is no Twitch *without* the broadcasters. And yet at a daily level, the control and self-determination that streamers actually hold can feel fragile; they have cautiously noted the power differential actually at work in this emerging media system.

Gillespie (2018, 26) points to the power that platforms have on user activities, arguing that they structure "every aspect of the exchange":

> YouTube connects videomakers with viewers, but also sets the terms: the required technical standards, what counts as a commodity, what is measured as value, how long content is kept, and the depth and duration of the relationship. YouTube can offer established videomakers a share of the advertising revenue or not, and it gets to decide how much, to whom, and under what conditions.

While the system on Twitch thus far is not so totalizing, we must be cautious not to downplay how much users are reliant on developers.

Streamers regularly spoke about the gratitude they felt toward Twitch team members who helped them continue to "do what they love." This ranged from being seen by the company as talented and brought on as a partner—thereby giving them access to revenue possibilities—to brokering deals between them and game developers for paid promotional activities.[34] Top streamers as well as up-and-coming ones can be tapped for public engagements at events like PAX, or offered opportunities to work on early access or promotional gigs. As a platform, Twitch holds tremendous power to bolster someone's career. Beyond deal brokering, the site can give a streamer front-page visibility, showcasing them on the main launch page. Just as often, the informal processes of a high-profile Twitch employee tweeting out about a new favorite streamer helps generate buzz around a channel. Given the connection and reliance that broadcasters can feel with Twitch employees, it is perhaps not surprising that they frequently express a loyalty toward and love of the company, perhaps best captured by Twitch's own "bleed purple" (the company color) motto.[35]

Yet there are moments of unease or caution. Streamers have commented to me about the frustration of paying out of pocket to attend events to speak about the power of broadcasting on the platform while not being funded by the company to do so. These engagements were often terrific promotional opportunities for Twitch, but the streamers felt that their labor went undervalued. There is a fragile balance around broadcasters being considered independent business entities (contractors) with expenses for travel and professional development who nonetheless usually do not make a lot of money—certainly not enough to front for activities that benefit the platform as much as them. As one put it, "That was the greatest irony. Here

I was scraping up money, begging Twitch to help with this trip so that I could go speak on a panel about making it in broadcasting." This move to situate broadcasters as independent contractors is not, of course, unique to live streaming. Platforms that rely on this type of work, which is provided without salaries, benefits, or other intangibles that come from employment, is something we are seeing across the internet, from Uber to Amazon's own Mechanical Turk micro-work program. Broadcasters bear real costs, both materially and emotionally, via these labor models.

Twitch's own business interests can also sometimes bump up against those of individual streamers. I found this most pronounced when the company began giving a lot of attention, including front-page positions, to large concert and esports events. Variety streamers would at times remark on how esports was taking over the site or how high-profile non-gaming music streams, like DJ Aoki's, were being promoted. Competition for viewership is tight, especially for streamers still growing their audience, and while Twitch does support them, it also works to retain its position broadly as *the* live streaming platform. This can at times put the business interests of the individual streamer slightly at odds with that of the company. As Twitch itself has come to produce original content, or engage in partnerships to broadcast and promote particular events, it can at times feel to streamers as if they are competing against the very platform they rely on. Through such activities, we can start to see the shape of Twitch as a media entity in and of itself, and not simply a platform. It can thus at times sit uneasily along all the other media producers using its distribution infrastructure.

Streamers also place trust in the company to accurately pay them. I would query broadcasters I spoke with about auditing systems and transparency, asking if they felt they had a good way to keep on top of their own performance and revenue generation. I was regularly told that they rely on the company to accurately report to them. While broadcasters can use a variety of methods, both within the platform and via third-party tools, to track their numbers and performance, they regularly expressed that they didn't always feel they had complete knowledge, especially around the location of the audience, which affects ad revenue. As one observed, "There's this whole aspect where we have to kind of take Twitch at its word for the numbers that it shows us. A third-party sort of auditing system would be fantastic." Another described it this way:

> I do trust Twitch to an extent, not 100 percent of course, not with my life. It's still business, and I have been burned so I know that idealism and naivety doesn't really help. . . . I realize that even virtual analytics,

which seem to be very trustworthy, even that can be cheated. So really when you get down to the core of things, there's really almost no way to have a real auditing system except by reputation. Short of me seeing a person buy a T-shirt from a store and have visual evidence, I don't see how digitally, no matter how sophisticated the auditing system seems, it could be completely free of cheating. At some point you just have to accept it is in essence an honor system based on trust. Sometimes you gotta realize even if you are being cheated a little, your end of the bargain is still good enough [laughs].

More often than not this kind of pragmatism infused my conversations with streamers when it came to issues of trust and accountability with the company. While Twitch has continued to improve its behind-the-scenes dashboard for broadcasters, giving them more data around their channel's performance, the complexity of the systems has tended to mean content creators must rely on the platform's integrity.

Aside from this issue of auditing, stronger criticisms tended to be directed at game developers who were seen as not paying enough for the exposure that a top broadcaster could provide. Increasingly, live streams are being used not only for entertainment but also as preview opportunities for people considering whether to purchase a game. In the case of developers who work directly with Twitch infrastructure to build in special in-game giveaways, ownership is incentivized even further. Broadcasters therefore hold tremendous promotional power in the games market. Given the competition for viewers, having early access to games has proven to be important for broadcasters; they get content others might not have while developers get exposure. One broadcaster explained it as follows:

> There's such a symbiotic relationship developing between streamers and developers.... They're starting to realize what kind of influence we have in the sales of their game. So instead of coming to us and saying, "You're using our gameplay footage or whatever, give me a cut of your money," they're coming to us and saying, "Here's extra copies of the game. Give them out on your stream when you play my game." So we're playing the game. We're showing the game off to thousands of people. And then we're saying, "Hey, this company is so bad ass. They decided to come in here and they gave us five copies of the game to give out for free. Let's give them away right now!"

Still, the balance that such a system relies on is delicate. Early in a broadcaster's career, and indeed when sites like YouTube or Twitch were still relatively new, a beta key or preview might be enough compensation in and of itself. But for larger streamers, early access or free copies of a title may no longer feel sufficient. One streamer remarked:

> It's not as bad as it used to be because, especially like now, these developers and these publishers know that we are an integral part of their marketing strategy. Except they're not treating it the way they should yet. They kind of do this thing where they'll dangle free stuff in your face for promotions and stuff when, if this was Hollywood and you were, let's say, a shoe company, you wouldn't say, "Hey, Brad Pitt, we're going to give you three boxes of shoes, and you go on Twitter and say you like our shoes, or go to this event and show your face there." So right now they kind of treat it like, "Oh, these people are doing this as a hobby so they will take whatever we will give them." . . . It's just they are learning, and we have to be a little bit more stern like, "No, if I'm going to work with you, it's going to be a contract type of thing and there will be payment."

While the comparison with Brad Pitt may seem far-fetched, it's not entirely unreasonable. Popular YouTube stars have huge audiences, often made up of the younger people that advertisers seek out. Felix "PewDiePie" Kjellberg, for example, was named one of *Time*'s hundred most influential people in 2016 and is likely one of the few game content creators that average people have heard of. Before his awful behavior and ensuing scandals cut into his sponsorships and reach, he boasted forty-three million subscribers to his channel with an estimated earnings of $15 million (Berg 2016; Parker 2016). While Twitch live streamers have yet to make this kind of mainstream mark (or economic success), they are nonetheless increasingly important market actors. The sentiment that the streamer expressed above—that they deserve to be paid for their work—is not only reasonable but also acknowledges their growing role and influence in a larger media industry.

One of the more unfortunate but perhaps not surprising turns in this emerging labor and broadcast market has been the occurrence of both "payola" and staged gambling streams. Live streaming has encountered its own version of undisclosed endorsement deals, akin to those of the late 1950s' and early 1960s' radio scandals when stations and DJs did not tell the public that they were being paid to play particular records. Congressional investigations led to a revision of the Federal Communications Act, which "requires broadcasters to disclose to their listeners or viewers if matter has been aired in exchange for money, services or other valuable consideration."[36] In 2009, the Federal Trade Commission (FTC), spurred on by fashion blog practices, began formally going after undisclosed endorsements on websites and other new media. Over the years, it has continued to update its guidelines requiring online outlets to make sure "connections between an endorser and the company that are unclear or unexpected to a customer also must be disclosed, whether they have to do with a financial arrangement for a favorable endorsement, a position with the company, or stock ownership" (Federal Trade Commission 2000). While the blogging community had its own wake-up calls with these regulations a number of years ago, gaming has only just started to experience this legal pushback.

In 2014, the *Wall Street Journal* and a number of specialist gaming sites reported what appeared to be an undisclosed endorsement deal for Microsoft's new Xbox One console. Ian Sherr, a journalist covering the story, wrote that "reports began surfacing over the weekend that Microsoft and Machinima [a large publisher and MCN] had offered an additional $3 per 1,000 views if they included at least 30 seconds of footage from the new Xbox One video-game console in their YouTube videos, and mention it by name. People who signed up were asked to keep all matters relating to the agreement confidential. Bloggers swiftly began complaining about the effort, which was seen as potentially misleading YouTube viewers" (Sherr 2014). Microsoft ended the program and said that it was not aware of the specifics of Machinima's partner agreements, while Machinima stated that it was unsure why its usual policy of disclosure was not followed and promised to review the situation. This incident fueled continued speculation in the gaming community about how often these types of deals occurred and were never caught.[37] In 2016, Electronic Arts, a major game developer that had previously run afoul of FTC guidelines, announced it would be requiring any sponsored content on sites like Twitch to carry a designated hashtag and/or watermark.

Beyond what are commonly thought of as classic payola scandals, more recently issues have come to light around streamers not fully disclosing their ownership interests in sites that they promote during their broadcasts. Perhaps one of the fastest-growing trends in gaming has been the rise of gambling for in-game "skins," cosmetic modifications for items that are either purchased or randomly "dropped" in-game. The popular first-person shooter game *Counter-Strike Go* (*CSGO*) has become one of the biggest titles offering this kind of virtual item modification: weapons in the game can be visually altered. Esports journalist Callum Leslie (2016) explained how the system worked and its importance:

> These skins can then be sold on Steam, Valve's game marketplace, for Steam credit or sold on third party sites for real cash.[38] Skins can also be

gambled with on a myriad of sites, from casino-style chance games to sportsbook sites that take action on just about every level of competitive *Counter-Strike*. Many argue that this gambling culture around matches has served to boost viewership, particularly at those lower levels. It's controversial because these sites operate without regulation. They're not considered gambling sites under most current laws. That means minors and players in countries like the U.S., where traditional online gambling is illegal, can use these sites freely. It has long been considered a grey area.

It has proven to be a huge market.[39] An article in *Bloomberg* cited research claiming that "more than 3 million people wagered $2.3 billion worth of skins on the outcome of esports matches in 2015" alone and noted that "whenever CS:GO skins are sold, the game maker collects 15 percent of the money" (Brustein and Novy-Williams 2016). A number of prominent observers have commented on the correlation between the re-emergence of *Counter-Strike* as a popular title and growth of the gambling scene.

Live streaming and YouTube stepped into that mix. There were a number of popular streamers who broadcast or recorded themselves gambling on these sites, ultimately walking away with big "real money" payouts. Thousands watched these videos and saw firsthand the excitement as well as hype of *CSGO* gambling via websites like CSGO Diamonds, CSGO Lotto, and CSGO Lounge. Beginning in summer 2016, serious reports began to emerge that all was not as it appeared on these streams, and that several prominent gambling live streamers held undisclosed ownership or equity stakes in the sites, had been given advance notice of winning outcomes, or had been playing with "house money" and "creating entertainment" to generate traffic along with revenue for the site. The whole thing started to feel a lot like the quiz show scandals of the 1950s, although in this case actual people, including minors, gambled real money. The outrage about the lack of disclosure spurred videos, blog posts, and commentary across the internet.

Several lawsuits were filed, one against Valve, and eventually, cease-and-desist orders were issued to the sites and a new prohibition was created for this use of their application programming interface. Twitch, which regularly defers to game publisher rules of use, ended up issuing a statement in 2016 that *CSGO* skin gambling was no longer permitted on the site given Valve's own terms of service. In September 2017, the FTC settled charges against two content producers, Trevor "TmarTn" Martin and Thomas "Syndicate" Cassell, for their role in nondisclosure around *CSGO* gambling. While some of the gambling sites shut down, others continued to operate. A number of the most prominent offending broadcasters promised future transparency, though with Valve's prohibition on calling the API as well as growing concern from government regulators about its legality, it's unclear exactly what the long-term future of gambling streams is.[40]

MULTICHANNEL NETWORKS, AGENTS, AND LAWYERS

While it is hard to imagine that broadcasters who did not disclose their financial interests in the gambling sites were acting in good faith, it is perhaps easier to recognize that one of the challenges that beginning live streamers often face is a lack of business and legal savvy to navigate a web of financial systems, regulations, contracts, and multicompany agreements.[41] As the wife of one streamer put it when I was speaking to them about the business side of things, "We're just winging it because there's no blueprint. We don't have any idea what we're supposed to be paid or what contracts we should be signing. We don't know anything." Popular streamer Ellohime noted that this lack of business acumen, particularly acute in younger people who are streaming, can lead to some of the undervaluing that I described above. As he commented during an MIT panel,

> They don't understand their worth. . . . And so when somebody says "here's a free computer, just have this up for however many years and we'll just put it right here in the corner of your thing," and this and this and that, they're like, "I get a free computer!?" They're not thinking of the long-term here. . . . [L]ike any other legitimate business would go "ok, well that's a great offer, but here's what I was thinking" and boom boom boom lay it out. And I think as Twitch goes on and as these streamers grow, we'll see less and less problems with that. But I think right now, there's a big issue with people just not understanding how to be good businessmen. And the thing is it's not really their fault! They flipped on a stream to play video games! (Ellohime 2015)

Much like with live streaming, early YouTube developers found themselves having to learn to navigate unfamiliar contractual territory. These content producers were often under eighteen years old and without legal representation; the results were a number of shoddy deals over the years.

A key part of the early media structure on YouTube was the development and growth of MCNs: "third-party service providers that affiliate with multiple YouTube channels to offer services that may include audience development, content programming, creator collaborations, digital rights management, monetization, and/or sales" (Google 2018). MCNs, especially large ones like Machinima or Maker Studios, sought to offer individual content creators early paths to monetization (for a cut of the revenue in return) via scaling up alongside other content producers in the network. One of the most important things that MCNs offered was a form of IP protection for UGC. MCNs regularly signed licensing or rights with major IP holders, and in turn covered their network's producers under their legal umbrella. For new, frequently young content creators, joining an MCN could be a key step in building their brand, one that provided an umbrella of legal protection. MCNs were a significant form of organization on YouTube, and mainstream media and telecomm companies like Disney, DreamWorks Animation, Verizon, and Comcast eventually purchased the largest ones.

Yet over the years, more and more content producers became disillusioned with this model. Perhaps the most notable seed of discontent came from revelations that Machinima had included "in perpetuity" clauses in its contracts, essentially claiming the rights to its producers' content—or in some cases, labor—forever. As content-creator Ben "Braindeadly" Vacas remarked in a video that kicked off widespread attention to the issue, "I can't get out of it. They said I am with them for the rest of my life—that I am with them forever. If I'm locked down to Machinima for the rest of my life, and I've got no freedom, then I don't want to make videos anymore" (quoted in Stuart 2013). It didn't take much for analysts to compare the disputes to "the exploitative Hollywood studios of the 1930s and '40s: Both used the lure of fame and cash to convince naive talent to sign contracts that left them at a disadvantage" (ibid.). That underage producers signed these contracts made them even more egregious. Many videos were made and posted to YouTube decrying what was seen as an exploitative system.

One Twitch streamer I interviewed had been caught up in this contractual issue and had only recently extricated himself, with the help of legal counsel, from a lifetime Machinima contract. For him, Twitch represented a jump to a platform with more freedom. Though the protections that might be afforded through an MCN could be appealing to producers, most streamers I have spoken with over the years had heard enough horror stories that such a model was not compelling.[42] Despite the fact that MCNs had been a way that many navigated YouTube's intense copyright management system, the people I talked to viewed them with extreme caution. For many who had spent time producing material for YouTube under an MCN umbrella, the early years of live streaming presented a feeling of greater autonomy without a lot of constricting rules.

Perhaps what has been most interesting is seeing how Twitch streamers have formulated a twist on the classic MCN model by utilizing things like friendly channel raiding and hosting one another's content to build their own networks on the platform. Broadcasters at times band together to help audiences find what might otherwise be disparate small channel content. They may host each other's streams when they are not on or send their audiences to a companion channel when they are wrapping up a broadcast. These types of initiatives often involve community spaces via Discord channels and meetups at gaming conventions. They tap into the conversation and community aspects of audience members, offering opportunities for viewers to express their fandom and support beyond a single streamer.

There is, of course, an important business side to these initiatives. They can become known as the go-to place for a particular audience and allow streamers themselves to start operating as "talent" in the broader media industry framework. These kinds of grassroots enterprises increasingly find themselves sitting alongside management companies focused on live streamers and other related content producers. Though not at all the norm when I carried out my research, companies like Online Performers Group, which was featured in a 2017 *New Yorker* article on live streaming, are now brought on by broadcasters to help manage their business (Clark 2017).

Content producers on YouTube also have a history of being picked up by major entertainment industries. While at the Game Developers Conference in San Francisco one year, this became all too clear to me when I was contacted by an esports industry insider who had recently taken a position with the William Morris Agency | IME Group. When we met up, he told me about the work that he was doing on various new initiatives to bring esports content to broader audiences. Present at the meeting was one of his colleagues who represented YouTube talent, and I was amazed when I got the chance to thumb through a promotional booklet they had showcasing new media stars who could be hired for a range of activities. That people producing content online that brings in millions of viewers every day via online sites were being noticed by a traditional agency probably shouldn't have surprised me as much as it did. My time over the course of the last decade had been mostly spent with people on the fringes pushing hard to transform digital gaming into a larger media product. With the rise of both YouTube and Twitch, however, more traditional industries were finally taking notice, and stepping in to get a cut of the action. The era of networked broadcast was catching the attention of not just enthusiast audiences but big media players too.

FIGURE 1.1. The International grand finals, 2014. Teams selecting their match characters. The lower-right corner below the image shows the number of people currently watching (213,391), total views of the channel (38,693,102), and number of people who have specially tagged the channel to follow. The right side of the screen is a live chat window.

FIGURE 1.2. MANvsGame broadcast, 2013.

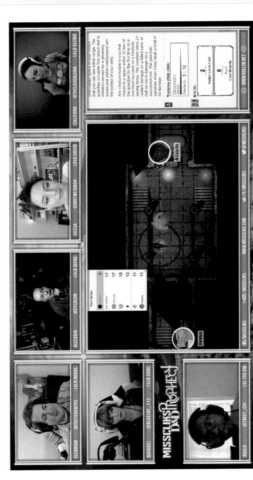

FarNiche : Fenton is a natural.

FarNiche : Pentegram... is that a foot-note?

FarNiche : (pedi-gram)

FarNiche : pedicure?

FarNiche : anyone?

FarNiche : ...

KingWein22 : when you tell your dice result like the
Count from Sesame Street

FarNiche : a little help?

KingWein22 : Pentagram

Parkingseal :

FarNiche : ^

FarNiche :

Parkingseal : #StillDying

Ninjarock92 : Eh. Eugh. That impaling sword hurts me
slightly

Moobot : Misscliks chat should always be a
welcoming place, so be kind and conversational!
Always build up, never tear down.
http://www.misscliks.com/#aboutus

Farginaut : Shatner milk that death scene

FIGURE 1.3. MissCliks D&D broadcast, 2017.

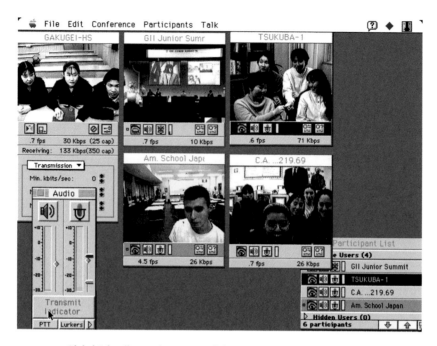

FIGURE 2.1. Global Schoolhouse classrooms collaborating via CU-SeeMe. Photo by Yvonne Marie Andres, Creative Commons Attribution 3.0 License.

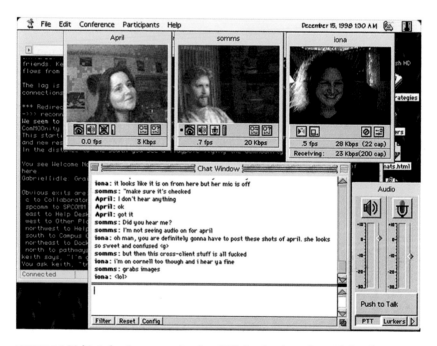

FIGURE 2.2. Multiwindow internet session from 1998 showing the author with friends simultaneously together in a text-based virtual world in the background and CU-SeeMe in the foreground.

FIGURE 2.3. Twitch Plays Pokémon screenshot, 2014.

FIGURE 2.4. "First date." XKCD comic by Randall Munroe, Creative Commons Attribution NonCommercial 2.5 License. https://xkcd.com/1333/.

FIGURES 2.5A AND 2.5B. Audiences hanging out at the Twitch booth and watching fighting game competitions, PAX East, 2014.

FIGURES 2.6A, 2.6B, AND 2.6C. Meet and greet, VIP area, and broadcaster novelty card at Twitch booth, PAX East, 2015.

FIGURE 3.1. Ellohime broadcast with auto pop-up banner when the channel gets a new follower (dubbed a "Viking of Ellohime"), 2014.

FIGURE 3.2. Futureman broadcast utilizing a green screen "set" that is part of the channel's theme, 2015.

2nd Episode of the Walking Dead with SuushiSam!

Following SuushiSam playing The Walking Dead on Internet Famous

SuushiSam | 👤 157 👁 687,522 ❤ 9,082

Hello and welcome to my stream! Please scroll down and read my 'about me' section because that will answer ALL your questions. Also, I run ads every 15 mins. Ads are a way of supporting my stream. So please disable adblock.

Connect to Share

Automatic Facebook Sharing ⑦ OFF

Heropietro: Give Food to the kids!

Iflashfrog: This game better give you the option to eat all of it

El_reaper98: give the kids food come on

Tyoske: awww yea chuweeze and krackaz

Letonr: lmao

The_human_sheep: i was gonna follow you on twitter but then i realised i was blocked

Pmnn: Breadsticks with cheese

Outsanity: was that an option to grab her ***?

Heropietro: Give Larry son food!!

Azmexican: grab dat ***]

Cakaluckyumyum: smack lilly with the jerky

Techgamer742: lol

The_human_sheep: don't give any to Duck, he's retarded

Azmexican: hey, some hammers are smart >=|

Cakaluckyumyum: hammers aka bag of rocks

El_reaper98: Give the kids food sam. don't be mean

Azmexican: those electric hammers are smart!

Cakaluckyumyum: ding dong

Heropietro: Be friend with Larry!

Vessman: WHAT YOU WORKIN ON SAM

Techgamer742: What u working on Doug? what u

FIGURE 3.3. SuushiSam broadcast with audience weighing in on what choice the broadcaster should make, 2012.

FIGURE 3.4. MANvsGame broadcasting room setup posted to Twitter, 2014.

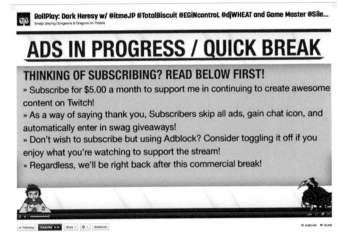

FIGURE 3.5. Itmejp channel interstitial, 2013.

FIGURE 3.6. "Dressing Up" by Kristian Nygård, September 28, 2012.

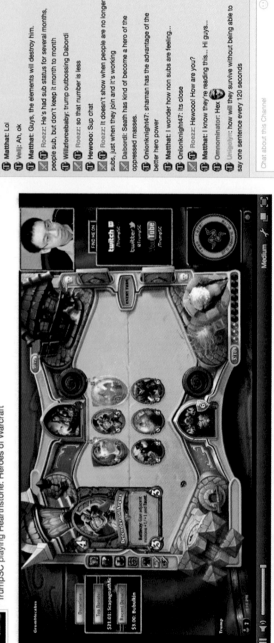

FIGURE 3.7. TrumpSC's broadcast with donation tally box on the left, 2014.

FIGURE 4.1. Backstage at Intel Extreme Masters, New York ComicCon, 2013.

FIGURE 4.2. Paul "Redeye" Chaloner at DreamHack Sweden, 2005.

FIGURES 4.3A AND 4.3B. Backstage at Intel Extreme Masters, showing multiple production stations and networking, San Jose, 2016.

FIGURE 4.4. In-game observer Phil "inFeZa" Bertino working backstage at Intel Extreme Masters, ComicCon, 2013.

FIGURE 4.5. *League of Legends* LCS Summer finals, TD Garden, Boston, 2017.

FIGURE 4.6. *Dota 2* International grand finals commentator desk, 2014.

FIGURE 5.1. Screenshot of the SpectateFaker channel in offline mode, 2015.

Alongside the growth of agency representation, lawyers have entered into the scene, especially around esports. As with YouTube content production, competitive gaming has long been filled with hopeful young people pretty much willing to take whatever is offered so they can pursue their dreams of professional play. Though professional teams have long offered contracts with varying degrees of requirements and benefits, with the introduction of live streaming, new forms of obligation and labor arise that pro players contend with. These players are increasingly expected to broadcast their practice time, often with sponsor brands on display. The contracts that competitive gamers are signing are thus not only tied to in-game tournament performance but also the overall profile of the player as a media producer and object. While retaining legal representation is still surprisingly rare for streamers and esports players, it is a growing component of the industry. At times these lawyers are also spinning up their own agency services, akin to what we see within the traditional sports space.

Passionate and Precarious Labor

As I hope to have shown through this discussion of the work of individual streamers, we are watching a new form of media labor arise on sites like Twitch. Whether it is the variety broadcaster who plays a range of different titles or an esports professional who streams part of their practice time, both are transforming otherwise private play into public entertainment. For most broadcasters, this comes out of their deep love for gaming along with their passion to do as much of it as they can and, especially in the case of variety streamers, derive joy from entertaining others.

While understanding their activities as deeply tied to the specifics of gaming or even media practices, I have also been struck by how much it resonates with the work of scholars who look at other forms of labor that have nothing to do with gaming. Beyond how we might link up live streamers to other forms of contract labor, as I noted above, we can consider how its affective, relational, and "always-on" qualities resonate with other kinds of technology work. Media and internet scholars Gina Neff (2012), Melissa Gregg (2011), and Baym (2018) all offer research that is particularly helpful in situating what we see happening among professional live streamers. Their study participants, like mine, occupy the complexities of workers in creative, knowledge, and innovation sectors. They each tap into the difficult work that these professionals do as well as the risks and precariousness they face.

Neff offers a glimpse into the risk navigation that dot-com era entrepreneurial workers, including creatives, were willing to take. As she notes, "People's desire and need to take economic risks stemmed from a *lack* of job security and an increase in employment flexibility—not the other way around (Neff 2012, 10). Though her use of the term "venture labor" is focused on "the investment of time, energy, human capital, and other personal resources ordinary employees make in the companies where they work," I find it resonant for live streamers (ibid., 16).

The broadcasters I've spoken to over the years occupy the betwixt and between category of being independent contractors yet deeply tied to a specific platform and culture that is not of their own making. They are frequently not simply framing their actions as investing in themselves but rather on the hope that Twitch and the media form more broadly will succeed. Their success is tied with the platform, and as such, they are dependent on it both practically and often emotionally. They also regularly expressed their dissatisfaction with either their former work life or what their prospects would be if they had to try to resume regular employment. The broadcasters' concern was not just around labor but personal happiness too, or more accurately, its loss if they stopped pursuing the creative work that they found in live streaming. Although they were usually clear about the precariousness, both financial and legal, on which this new professional identity was built, it remained a path they were willing to pursue despite hardship and risk. A sense of personal fulfillment, either through operating as a creative content producer or excelling at competitive play in esports, drove the choices they made to work outside more traditional paths.

Gregg's research on how the online lives of professionals, and ubiquity of computing, is reshaping work, home, and relationships speaks to what we see in live streaming as well. She describes what she terms the "presence bleed of contemporary office culture, where firm boundaries between personal and professional identities no longer apply" (Gregg 2011, 2). While she identifies this tendency for work to encroach on home life as something that white-collar professionals have long struggled with, Gregg links our contemporary version of it to online technologies and the growth of network life. She analyzes the ways that work often spreads out to overtake, practically, materially, and symbolically, what used to be designated as private time and domestic space. Gregg describes the ways that this process enacts itself as forms of emotional labor, intimate work, and reputational management with bosses and fellow employees. The "flexibility" and lack of boundaries between work and home form a compelling part of her story.

Live streamers regularly embrace many of the aspects that Gregg identifies in her research: relational work, blurred home/work lines, and a feeling of being nearly always on. Perhaps in part because these elements are so explicitly in broadcaster's minds as a component of their labor, contributing to the actual value of their work, they do not figure in as vexing aspects for the most part. The interactions with audiences, the fact that you share your personal life and/or space, and the ways that you construct a sense of community through your broadcasts can certainly cast a more positive light on things. Yet there are glimpses of the toll it can sometimes take—the weariness at daily performance or having to buffer against the fans whose emotions can be too much. The complex navigations around your own sense of self or wishes for privacy can be tough to sustain over years.

Finally, Baym's research on the relational work of musicians as they navigate social media use in a new economy also speaks to what we see among live streamers. Linking up to work on the gig economy, Baym (2018, 12) argues that musicians

> exemplify the individualized risks, responsibilities, and precariousness of contemporary work. Gig work is inherently unstable, and questions about where money will come from now and in the future cause anxiety. The threat of poverty is ever-present. This is the context in which forming and maintaining friend-like relationships in which you share your "authentic" self with audiences, online and off, comes to be seen as a potential means of maintaining a career.

Much like what game and labor scholars Mark Johnson and Jamie Woodcock (2017) have found in their discussions with streamers, many I spoke with framed it as something that they want to pursue as long as possible but concede that it is no sure bet. At the 2017 TwitchCon, I heard people wondering for the first time, and questioning company representatives, about retirement funds. They recognize that their own fate is tied to that of the platform, the willingness of developers and publishers to let them continue, and the overall robustness of this new form of media. Having a backup plan can weigh on their minds.

Of course, it is also the case that my conversations have primarily been with those who continue to work in live streaming and are still trying to carve out a professional identity within that frame. It may be that the best insight into the long-term costs of live streaming will be undertaken in five or ten years, after perhaps some of the current cohort of broadcasters leave the system or retire. Only then may we get a real sense of how the delicate balance between passion and precariousness in streaming life plays out.

4

Esports Broadcasting

DITCHING THE TV DREAM

The story of esports development is a complex one spanning multiple decades. It can be helpful to think about its trajectory as waves in which particular aspects come into focus and rise in salience. Such stories are, of course, always risky, potentially obscuring how earlier practices or forms of organization in the current moment can remain as tendrils, or making developments seem nearly predestined. They can also render invisible the ways that prior phases had innovations or experiments that were only later picked up in earnest. But with such caveats in mind, thinking with particular lenses can help refract and highlight important shifts. The history of competitive gaming's development up until now might be formulated as such:

> *First wave*: "Game" is the predominant frame in this moment. It is rooted in enthusiast and serious leisure communities. Amateur and pro-am orientations and competitions dominate.
>
> *Second wave*: "Sport" becomes the predominant frame. The rise of third-party organizations—sustained infrastructures of competition, formalization, and professionalism—takes over as a dominant rubric for not only players but also many ancillary actors involved in creating an industry.

Third wave: "Media entertainment" rises as the predominant frame. Serious attention is given to media production, audience, and entertainment. Infrastructures, both organizational and technical, become attuned to as well as configure themselves around media production and distribution. Tournaments are harnessed as media events with an emphasis on the visual and narrative.

Though we are currently seeing traditional sports organizations wake up and pay attention to esports, it would be a mistake to not situate that interest within a media entertainment frame. Sports are, as a number of scholars before me have noted, largely "media/sport" now.[1] In the following, I begin by exploring the transition between the second and third wave when DIY productions were developing esports as a media product, and then turn to the contemporary moment where creating ambitious productions that get broadcast to millions globally has become a prime focus for the industry.

Beyond Television

In 2013, I took the train down from Boston to New York City and attended my first ComicCon. Though the original and largest one takes place each year in San Diego, the New York event has been growing in size since first launching in 2006. I knew how big the Southern California one was, but was stunned when I arrived at the New York City venue before the doors opened and already found hundreds of people waiting to get in. Some were dressed in impressive and elaborate costumes from both comic-based franchises and games. These fans had clearly come out not only for the comics subculture but to tap into the growing number of talks and exhibits around gaming and other pop culture products as well.

I had reached out to some folks at Turtle Entertainment, the company that runs ESL, and told them that I would love to take a peek behind the scenes at one of the tournaments they'd be broadcasting. Turtle is one of the oldest esports organizations in the world and has run major tournaments since 2000. It had been incredibly helpful when I was doing research for my book on esports, and its story figured prominently in my research into that scene. If anyone was tackling the changes occurring within the industry as a result of live streaming, I figured it would be them. My plan was to spend the weekend backstage observing tournament production.

My contact met me at the VIP door and quickly handed me one of a number of exhibitor passes that he had hanging around his neck. This was a helpful gesture, as it allowed me access to the venue before and after show hours. Perhaps more important, it was a valued talisman to an ethnographer: an external signal that says, "Don't worry about me, I'm allowed to be here," while hanging around backstage. It was my first time meeting him, but he was friendly and immediately willing to answer questions as we made our way to the ESL area on the convention floor. Things were still in setup mode, and he explained all the prep that was happening. The show floor was close to opening, and staff members were putting the final touches on the stage as well as doing a quick dress rehearsal with the talent. I've been to many esports events over the years and have seen the setup, stages, and even behind-the-scenes work as the commentators prepped, but this event especially caught my eye once I saw backstage.

In a fairly compact area tucked behind the main stage, there was essentially a mini–television studio (see figure 4.1). My guide explained to me that the production team travel around the world producing events. All the gear I was seeing fit into reinforced travel boxes, and at each venue they set it up, tie it into the site's electric and internet infrastructure, and produce major events for broadcast. Over the course of the weekend, I watched a full-fledged crew in action—one complete with emerging professionalized spheres of expertise and divisions of labor. As I have continued to visit backstage productions at esports tournaments, these setups have only grown, and now occupy some of the most cutting-edge work happening not only in gaming but the broader media industries.

From nearly its start, esports has been intent on developing spectatorship capacities. Though the roots of the scene are based in grassroots communities, competitive gaming has long been closely tied to a variety of media practices.[2] In the earliest days of esports industry development there was a push toward establishing a presence on television that was often seen as a legitimizing move. As one longtime esports broadcaster put it, "I think we all wanted and felt that if we had TV, it would validate what we thought was real and we all compared to TV and appealed to TV sports." While he didn't feel esports needed television to be meaningful, he did see the media transition as important. In the early 2000s, I continually heard this sentiment from people working to build formalized competitive gaming. Frequently people cited the success that esports had found on television in South Korea along with the widespread broadcasts of gaming there, and used it as an almost-mythical waypoint guiding development. They were

FIGURE 4.1. Backstage at Intel Extreme Masters, New York ComicCon, 2013.

simultaneously convinced that the scene would find inevitable success and that a transition to television was part of that trajectory—one that would both build audiences and signal they had "made it."

There were various attempts to bring esports to broadcast television during that period, usually in the form of one-off novelty shows. But the one that captured the most attention was the well-funded Championship Gaming Series (CGS), which launched in 2007 as a partnership between DirectTV, British Sky Broadcasting, and Star TV.[3] The CGS brought in traditional sports media professionals (such as Emmy-award-winning producer Mike Burks, who had worked with outfits like the NFL, the National Basketball Association, and the National Hockey League), executives who had their eye on traditional sports advertising and markets, and some of the groundbreakers in the esports industry such as Paul Chaloner, Marcus Graham, and Craig Levine. The venture proceeded to buy up, franchise, and regionally brand already-existing North American players and teams.[4]

While much hope was placed in the CGS, it ultimately did not successfully navigate merging competitive computer gaming with television. Despite some longtime insiders doing hard behind-the-scenes work to help guide the executives in ways that preserved an authenticity while attending to the specificities of competition in a digital milieu, many missteps were made in the service of broadcast. Game choices, altered structures and rule sets (ones that did not correspond to grassroots preferences, built over years of tournament trial and error), uneasy links to regionalism, and an overall mismatch in tone and approach led to a surprisingly quick demise of the organization in 2008. With it, many existing North American esports structures collapsed; it took years for the scene to recover.

As one current production director who lived through this era put it, "All [these attempts] failed because they tried to take something that was really its own thing and were sticking a round object into the square hole. They had this model of what they're used to doing, which is old, old media, old broadcast, and they tried to apply it." The failure of the CGS acted as both a serious blow to those who aspired to grow esports and ultimately reignited a focus on the roots of the scene. The risk to the stability of an entire region and pro player base—in this case, North America—also became clear with the demise of the organization. Being on television began to be seen as costly, with a high risk that outweighed the benefits. One organizer, summing up an approach I regularly heard post-CGS, said, "What I always wanted was TV quality, and if it ends up on TV, great. But don't ever change our games again for TV." Another remarked, "Being on cable television is way too hard. It limits yourself to where you can even broadcast. It's expensive and it just didn't seem to be the way that esports was ever going to thrive. Other attempts had been done previously that failed epically. It's really hard to try to consolidate a game that should go forty minutes into a thirty-minute program. It just didn't work."

Amid the high-dollar experiments like the CGS, however, there continued to be grassroots media development by other esports professionals and fans. As I'll discuss a bit more later on, many people in competitive gaming continued to look for new technologies that might assist them with distributing their content. The rise of internet-based live streaming ended up bolstering a turn away from broadcast or cable television.

Players and organizations alike now regularly say that they see their audience as primarily located online, and that is where they are serving them. Whether it is the longtime esports player using live streaming to broadcast to their fans or leagues and tournaments reaching millions of viewers over the course of a weekend solely via the internet, many of those invested in competitive gaming are using these platforms to continue to build what is increasingly a sports-*media* business. From the broadcast of mundane practice time to high-end sports spectacles, live streaming is being used to grow competitive gaming. And it's working. While esports once held a place as a fairly niche segment of game culture, this shift to live streaming has been a boon to building audiences and bringing in even casual fans. Live streaming has been a powerful accelerant to the growth of esports, and broadcasts now routinely tout viewership numbers in the millions over just the course of a weekend tournament. Competitive matches are shown on channels at Twitch nearly all hours of the day and night. Fans, located around the world, would be hard pressed to not find something to tune into whenever they want.

One producer connected this trend to broader media shifts and what he sees as the cluelessness of mainstream media's continued attempt to capture this emerging market with existing paradigms:

> I think traditional broadcast television is going to slowly go away, and online streaming is going to be the future. Funny thing I always hear when mainstream news media cover esports, when they ask when do you think it's going to be on TV? And I always shake my head at that question because it doesn't need to be on TV. Yeah, it's one of those things where the mainstream news media think that if it gets on TV, it somehow becomes legitimized. It is legitimized already. It's big. It's a big industry. Having people want to watch it and interact with it rather than just sit down on their couch and watch it where it could be prerecorded or available in only these certain regions doesn't work for it. So I think traditional broadcast television is really going to go away and online streaming is going to be where it's at, video on demand, anything like that.

This was a sentiment that I repeatedly heard as I spoke to esports organizations, particularly during the earliest years of the streaming boom. They were not only looking at how the technology and platforms like Twitch were helping them reach audiences in ways that felt more "natural"; they regularly linked up that development with broader media transformations.

Unlike previous broadcast attempts, live streaming content is generally coming directly from individual players, leagues/esports organizations, and game developers themselves rather than filtered to, or through, preexisting traditional media structures. And while moves to align esports broadcasts with sports media tropes continue to grow, live streaming typically breaks standard conventions around run time or commercial breaks. The inclusion of synchronous communication elements via chat windows that run alongside produced content are also pushing models of audience engagement.

Although the individual competitive players who utilize live streaming to assist their own professional careers offer a fascinating case, as I discussed in the last chapter, it is in tournament broadcasting that live streaming has had the biggest impact on esports. If any one thing has happened to assuredly secure the notion of an esports "industry," it is the ability to now easily broadcast events online, globally, and to large audiences. The position one regularly hears now within esports is that they no longer *need* television. For many, live streaming has offered a declaration of freedom from traditional broadcast media.

And yet while television as an industry structure is no longer a driving goal in esports, it continues to hover as a *broadcasting frame* in a few ways. This is where disentangling television as a node of the media industry, hardware device, or set of televisual genre conventions becomes helpful. It is also where understanding the transition that television is making to "on-demand" modes becomes important. When esports broadcasters talk about ditching television, they don't always mean ditching those boxes in our living rooms, or even the aesthetics or "live" aspect of sports television. What they do mean is jettisoning an old network era model, and imagining a media future that understands the role of the internet, interactivity, and on-demand and context-driven viewing.

This is not a conundrum unique to esports. The media industry writ large is grappling with these shifts. Be it the rise of companies like Netflix or Amazon, cord cutting, over-the-top models, niche on-demand products, time shifting, "binge watching," or "social TV," the industry as a whole is facing profound changes in consumption practices. As a longtime tournament organizer remarked,

> Everything is on demand these days. Everything is moving away to the internet. I mean, you don't watch TV shows anymore by waiting until Sunday to turn on HBO or whatever. You go to play soccer on Sunday, and after the episode is released, whenever you're ready with your peanuts and Coca-Cola, you're watching. You're watching whenever you please. So that basically destroys the concept of television as we know it.

Though perhaps understating the power of a timed broadcast (many eagerly sat down for the latest *Game of Thrones* each Sunday night, for example), there is an insightful point in their statement about how much of our media consumption now rests on our own schedule and the explicit choices we make.

Esports broadcasters also understand that the current media landscape often involves users cycling across a variety of websites and devices, including their televisions. One describes it this way:

When I watch esports events, I'm at home watching on my sixty-inch TV. All I'm doing is pulling it up on my iPhone, and I have an Apple TV that you can just browse through them while you're watching and boom! I flick it up to the big screen TV. That's how I'm watching it. I'm watching it in my family room, or friends are over watching it with me, or my girlfriend is even watching it with me. . . . You're going to start being able to tap in a live stream there.

Others emphasize the ways that users are watching primarily at their computers because that is where they spend the majority of their time. As one prominent organizer put it to me, "There's no point in taking it [esports] to television because anyone that's already interested in it is online and watching it most likely. Or is playing the game and is online. It's like saying, 'Hey, we need to take this baseball game and play it inside of Times Square because there's more people walking around there, right?' It doesn't work that way. There's no point to force a gamer to walk away from his PC and watch it on television." Your own computer acts as a device to both play on and spectate others through.

These models of audience tend to firmly situate viewers within a demographic that has rejected broadcast television—a trend that indeed worries the larger media industry. As one producer observed,

To be honest with you, I feel like television, broadcast television, will do a disservice to esports. I'm actually pretty against it ever moving over to television as a platform. These guys from thirteen to thirty years old, they are consuming their content online. So the people who are into esports, the demographic that esports will always serve, even as it scales, will still all be thirteen- and thirty-year-old males. Let's just be honest, right. They're not going to like magically really just start going to broadcast television. So I feel like the internet is where it really needs to be, where it can reside, and it's where it's in the best interest of esports, because I don't think you can put esports in a broadcast television model and make it work.

There is, of course, an old dream of convergence—one in which digital and networked experiences become interwoven with more traditional forms of media and their technologies. But that is currently challenged on at least two fronts when it comes to game live streaming. Generally speaking, the TV as a display device continues to be hampered, whether technologically or owing to price point, by resolutions that simply aren't high enough to handle the level of visual detail one can easily see on a computer screen. Currently, game live streaming is also strongly defined by the interactive chat component of platforms like Twitch. This element is a part of the broadcast that doesn't translate well to TV. Most people simply aren't sitting at their televisions with a keyboard hooked up.

Still, the idea that the home television can be integrated into new production and consumption practices within esports is certainly part of a larger trend in how media industries are trying to understand the shifts that are occurring not only in their ecosystem but also within domestic spaces. Like television, esports is invested in the long-standing imaginary of display devices located throughout the home, seamlessly serving up a variety of content to a diverse household. Whether it is viewing on your personal PC (the current norm), cell phone, or console or streaming device hooked up to the television, both traditional and esports broadcasters are looking for ways to constantly provide programming at a moment when the equation of "TV" with broadcast network or cable television is eroding.

Esports broadcasting, though, is leveraging the power of live content to navigate the media future. The ethos of "do it live" and power of real-time broadcasting is one that I've heard over and over again from those who've been pushing media development in esports.[5] Even the producer I quoted above who spoke about how time shifting was destroying "the concept of television as we know it" tagged on a caveat: "except for major live events." Indeed, traditional television stakeholders hope to retain some power amid changing media trajectories via live events—often sports. While watching rebroadcasts of historic or "classic" matches is certainly part of the media landscape, the overall liveness of broadcast sports is considered by many analysts to be the levee against profound shifts in the industry. It is frequently held up as the saving financial anchor for traditional media.

In one regard, esports producers echo traditional media analysts in their assessment that sports will be one of the few content areas with a shot at surviving the disruptions that the industry faces. Yet the focus on liveness is, in the case of esports, simultaneously uncoupled from traditional subscription television models. While traditional broadcasters and cable operators look to live sports to stabilize unsettled financial structures, esports has become a media product offering many of the pleasures of consuming high-end competition native to internet-friendly devices and digital technology, boasting engaged and interactive audiences, and without costly subscription fees. Given that this has all happened on the back of a fairly new technology and within just a handful of years, a look at the roots of esports broadcasting can provide a useful balance to some of the more ahistorical narratives that circulate.

DIY Roots

Esports has always had a deep affinity with spectatorship and audiences. From the earliest days of LAN parties to contemporary tournaments where tens of thousands fill a stadium, competitive gaming has long been a space where the pleasures of playing with others and spectatorship find their home. These in-person events have had a symbiotic relationship with media technologies; they exist, rise, and thrive alongside emerging production and distribution systems. Even among competitive scenes that have deep roots in local communities and co-located play, finding ways to distribute matches has been important. As one longtime fighting game participant told me, "Before streaming, you go to the arcade and how did you get well known? You'd have to win and then people hear about you, or you travel to other arcades. It's almost like a dojo. You train at this arcade and you go to another arcade and you beat up their champion and you become notorious. [It was] all very word of mouth. When streaming came out, it was another way to get your name out, your scene out." Video and broadcast are not a secondary thread in the history of esports; amateur producers have long used media technologies to foster engagement among dedicated fans and bring new people in.

Even from my earliest days of my interviewing esports professionals, I consistently heard a belief in the inevitability that esports would grow. But as one producer put it, the road to that point was never certain: "None of us sat there and went, you know, one day a live streaming platform or the whole concept of live streaming is going to blow up. That will really push us to the next level. We knew the next level was there. We didn't know how we were going to get there." The indeterminacy meant that early innovators were constantly trying lots of different approaches, experimenting, and hacking together components to share tournaments. Scholars Sherry Turkle and Seymour Papert's (1990, 136) article tracing out "bricoleurs," those who "prefer negotiation and rearrangement of their materials" as well as "associations and interactions," who "have goals but set out to realize them in the spirit of a collaborative venture with the machine," resonates with what we see among esports broadcasters. The media history of competitive gaming is rooted in improvisers who pull together a variety of threads for both inspiration and practice.

While some leaned on their experience in traditional sports or media, most people I have spoken with over the years tend to frame their endeavors as ongoing experiments and DIY ventures where figuring out on the fly how to make things work led the way.[6] As one longtime industry insider who has done everything from marketing to directing noted, when confronted with new challenges, his approach was "this is something I didn't do before and if I don't do it, we're probably not going to do it. So I just have to figure out how to do it." This ethos has extended into the live streaming era, where esports professionals who cut their teeth on building that scene tackled the challenge of broadcasting to hundreds, then thousands, and then millions. The desire to be able to distribute content that they were passionate about was often challenged by technological constraints and capacities, skill and expertise, and economics.

TECHNICITY AND HACKING

Though there has long been A/V technology available out-of-the-box ready to use, those wanting to broadcast game live streams frequently struggled with it being either too expensive or not quite suited to gaming.[7] In much the same way that enthusiasts created tournament structures and found ways to sell their competitions to sponsors, technological challenges tended to be met with a "let's just make it work" attitude. Three particular production techniques are especially worth mentioning when tracing the history of esports media: video capture, replay files, and audio overlay.

People who pointed a camera at an arcade machine or TV to record high scores produced the earliest-recorded material. These tapes could then be sent to organizations like Twin Galaxies for review and ranking, or shared with other members of the scene, as was the case with the fighting game community's tradition of passing around tapes chronicling notable games.[8] One of the limitations to this system is that the recordings, unless physically duplicated or digitized, didn't support widespread spectatorship, and primarily served a niche group of competitive players and fans. While some dedicated participants learned how to digitize recordings and distribute them through software like Direct Connect (a file-sharing system) or websites like Shoryuken, for the most part sharing these videos posed a serious challenge.

As games expanded to personal computers that had the ability to save video directly from the machine, recording and sharing became more viable. Although still requiring hardware and software capable of capturing and processing the data, this shift toward pulling directly from the machine to produce digital recordings that could easily be copied was a key development. The proliferation of dedicated video distribution platforms such as YouTube allowed even nonenthusiasts easy access. Rather than having to know about an often-obscure fansite or exactly what you were looking for, YouTube increased access beyond the most dedicated fans and removed the costs of hosting content.

While video capture was, and remains, a critical component of spectatorship, some game developers addressed the desire to rewatch sessions *within* the system itself. Instead of mediating the game through another layer of technology (videotape recording), the advent of replay files took advantage of the fact that digital games are at a basic level simply bits of data rendered on the screen. One of the early ways that these developers accommodated the desire to review completed games was to offer the ability to save a play session as a file of game data—essentially digital notations about positionality and action. This file could be downloaded and launched within the game client to then "replay" the saved match for the viewer. A spectator could watch the game as it unfolded for the person who recorded it. These files were typically distributed through dedicated sites such as XSreality, Got Frag, HLTV, and GTV.org.[9] Scholar and archivist Henry Lowood (2011, 7) argues that these replays, which were often then edited into smaller movies (dubbed machinima), were not just technical interventions; rather, "learning about gameplay by viewing these movies depended upon the development of practices for spectatorship, witnessing, and certification. The result was the full utilization of this new game-based performance space." Each of these angles that Lowood identified in the earliest machinima without a doubt hold true for game spectating as we see it now within live streaming.

Lowood's three core components to sharing gameplay—code, capture, and compositing—were mirrored in early approaches to spectating technology. Replay files and recorded video allowed players and developers to share their gaming across time as well as space. Audio overlays to commentate on and narrate games were also widely produced. Yet all these methods posed challenges and carried limitations. Though a tremendous technical feature, replay files require the viewer to not only own the game they wanted to watch but know where to find the file and how to run it. These built-in limitations created a hurdle for how widespread viewership could be. And while recording gameplay video directly from the computer was a big improvement from pointing a camera at a screen, it was often still cumbersome. Many players didn't have hardware good enough to run processing software and games at the same time, while others lacked the software along with the know-how to edit files and then distribute them.

As Lowood notes, players and producers were experimenting not only with what was possible but also what *could be*, frequently via cobbling together a variety of technologies. This dynamic mix of technologies interwoven together, emerging practices of fandom, and a new form of professionalization hit a pivotal moment with the advent of voice commentary. Alongside the development of replay files and consumer-level video capture hardware and software, the rise of digital media players and distribution systems had a tremendous impact. Two early pieces of software, Winamp and SHOUTcast, both developed by Nullsoft (which was later purchased by AOL), played central roles in the production and digital distribution of esports content.

Before the days when it was possible to widely use video to broadcast and commentate on esports events, voice was a key augmentation method. Paul "Redeye" Chaloner (2015) humorously observes in his book *Talking Esports* that "back when I started streaming (in 1834 or thereabouts), we didn't have video streams—we relied solely on Winamp and shoutcast [*sic*] software to broadcast matches and tournaments. In fact, in 2005 I streamed an entire DreamHack *Quake 4* tournament live from the venue via audio!" (see figure 4.2).[10]

I first met Chaloner at that event and was instantly convinced of the importance of commentating work. While the setting was a far cry from the polished and large-scale productions we now see, even then I was captivated by the skill that he demonstrated in making the competition come alive for those listening. That he was doing it all via audio was both familiar in that it reminded me of when my father would listen to baseball on the radio and odd given how much advanced technology—from computers to networks— was the bedrock of this emerging sports scene.

With people using players like Winamp to listen to digital media in the late 1990s, however, an infrastructure was in place to transmit all kinds of audio to and from PCs. The broadcasting side of the equation was developed via the SHOUTcast program, which allowed people to distribute content through media players such as Winamp. Although SHOUTcast was primarily used to get "internet radio stations" up and running, gamers quickly found a way to harness the program for their own purposes. For example, one longtime esports broadcaster described his first uses of combining audio and video to assist his team as he was transitioning away from competing himself

FIGURE 4.2. Paul "Redeye" Chaloner at DreamHack Sweden, 2005.

One of the things that I used to do for my team is that I would watch their demos and I'd watch the replays of their games, and I would record an audio file for them over it. And so I would watch the game [and say], "OK guys. I'm going to talk about your game and I'm going to try to explain to you guys what I felt you did wrong, where I feel we need to improve." And so I was really using it as almost like a coaching technique.

The jump from doing this to providing commentary for a broader audience was clear.

Chaloner, Marcus "djWHEAT" Graham, Stuart "Tosspot" Saw, Trevor "gfmidway" Schmidt, Scott "SirScoots" Smith, and others grew this early form of esports broadcasting, developing important outlets such as djWHEAT.tv, GotFrag, Radio ITG, and Team Sportscast Network, which produced and distributed live audio, and later video. Content ranged from commentary on tournaments to weekly shows focused on gaming and esports.[11] As Graham (2011) wrote in a Reddit thread unpacking some of the early history, "Up until early 2010, djWHEAT.tv still broadcast via 'Shoutcast' and usually had about 400–500 people who would listen just via the audio."[12] Combined with software like GamersTV, which Graham recalls allowed players to log in to a *Quake 3* server and spectate any game they wanted live, broadcasters and viewers were cobbling together ways to produce and consume early esports content. The use of this tool was so impactful that the term "shoutcaster" lingers as a name for esports commentators.

These earliest forays into what Lowood would call "compositing"—in the case of esports, mixing audio commentary over gameplay—were critical threads in what would eventually develop into the contemporary live broadcasting we see today. The ability to watch, comment on, and interpret gameplay is a mode taken up not only by professional esports broadcasters but also casual variety streamers. Both become adept at occupying a dual position during the live broadcast: being at once in the moment of play and standing slightly outside it, reflecting, joking, and talking about it to their viewers. Though the current landscape of esports media production increasingly takes on familiar conventions, these earliest iterations remain a crucial waypoint in understanding more recent developments.

As production standards rose to include multicamera shots, voices, and graphics, early innovators often turned to traditional A/V products meant for different markets. One longtime professional in the space described utilizing whatever tech they could: "Little things like the basic ATEM switcher you can buy from Black Magic that a lot of churches and other public service things use have certain limitations, that's the way it is.[13] But if you're a nerd, you can get around these things. You can make hacks and macros and things that they don't tell you about. It's not an add-on you buy. So there's nerds that build computers; we have all these guys that are nerding out on capture cards." This sentiment was repeated over and over in my conversations with esports producers. Many of us in the audience have never paused to think about the unique challenges that come from broadcasting in-game visuals. As the producer I quote above went on to remark,

> The hardest thing to encode and show is a video game. It moves faster. Like [basic] encoding, [I just need a] shitty PC, shitty camera. But they encode *StarCraft* and all those armies and everything . . . so just the fact that we're broadcasting this kind of content pushes all that technology. So I might have to go "OK, I need to take this TriCaster, but I got to somehow use this replay system and how do I jack that in because I can't afford to buy this system." And everyone is doing that.

The reliance on personal computers augmented with third-party A/V gear often posed tremendous challenges for broadcasters. Software troubles and hacking solutions to solve problems were common. One recounted,

"We were doing all the broadcasts off our own personal computers. There would be one person who would be producing the entire thing off his home PC, and sometimes that was me, and I remember on our very first broadcast day, we built up all this hype from the community and we started, and my computer crashed." He went on to note that "we would build an intro video, but the codec wouldn't be compatible with the broadcast software and the whole thing would crash, or little things like that were just a total hassle to deal with that are just so trivial now, because XSplit or OBS [third-party software now widely used for live streaming] basically handles everything you need to do."

The impact of this has meant that the earliest broadcasters were doing a tremendous amount of skilling up to learn how to become media producers (not to mention network engineers), frequently utilizing cobbled-together systems with constant limitations. Though well versed in the games they were involved with, many of the people who were creating these broadcasts did not come with professional production skills but instead learned them along the way. While a few had some A/V experience from working with non-gaming events, such as large sales meetings or school productions, they were in the minority. Most were learning how to use these tools on the fly as needed, and as various tech emerged and became affordable.

This DIY attitude comes with a strong infusion of what game scholars Helen Kennedy and Jon Dovey (2006, 113) describe as technicity, "particular kinds of attitudes, aptitudes and skill, with technology." It isn't simply a matter of having specific skills but instead an orientation that gives you assurance that you can muck around in systems, tweak software, and push and pull machines to get them where you want them to go. This level of technicity is a central component to high-end competition, where players don't just pick up a game and play as given but rather are engaged with tweaking hardware and software where possible. I was struck when this theme emerged on the production side of the esports equation too. The technicity present within production became an incredibly powerful ground on which broadcasting innovations were built.

The uptake of the SHOUTcast module is a prime example of how esports broadcasters were often early adopters, constantly on the lookout for tech that would let them do what they wanted. As one put it, "I mean I think in some regard this world [esports] is pushing technology or using tools that traditional broadcasting uses in a very set way, and jackknifing it and doing stuff that it was never meant to do." Hearing them describe their early forays, what usually shines through is a passion for creating a media space and belief that somehow they would, through sheer persistence and dedication to using whatever was at hand, make it happen. One longtime shoutcaster said to me, "I didn't know how to broadcast over the internet. I just said to myself, 'I'm going to do this and I'm going to put effort into it,' so I learned about what new radio stations used. Is there any cheap equipment that I can buy to make it sound better? Oh, now we're doing video, how do we do that?"

While we may think about this stance as distinctly contemporary, it is connected to traditional sports broadcasting. Roone Arledge, the longtime ABC executive who is generally credited with how modern sports media looks and works on television, would probably have found early esports producers his kindred spirits. In a *Playboy* interview, he spoke about the origins of the instant replay—something that we now take for granted in sports broadcasting—saying, "I asked him [engineer Bob Trachinger] if it would be possible to replay something in slow motion so you could tell if a guy was safe or out or stepped out of bounds, and Trach immediately began sketching on the napkins. We talked and sketched and drank beer that whole afternoon and when we were finished, we had the plans for the first instant-replay device" (quoted in "Playboy Interview" 1976, 66). These "experiments" outside the eyes of executives are strikingly similar to what I've seen in esports media over the last few decades. While pornography is often cited as a driving innovator for media and network technologies, it is likely that any of us interested in the interrelation between cultural products and sociotechnical production should pay similar attention to what is happening in sports as well as computer games.

CONTENT AND AESTHETICS

While these early innovators were tweaking technology to serve their purposes, they were simultaneously engaged in thinking through content and aesthetics for their broadcasts. It was typically the case in the early days of esports that the person running the technical side of the show was the creative director as well. Just getting the game *out* was a huge challenge in itself, and creating shows that drew viewers in developed over time. Opening shots, narrative devices, action, and commentary eventually came to be a part of the esports media aesthetic, although balanced against a "playing field" fundamentally rooted in a digital space as well as beholden to a broader culture and community of esports enthusiasts.

Specific competitive communities within esports hailed different traditions such that there wasn't always one standard "esports aesthetic." Early on broadcasters drew from traditional sports, game culture, South Korean esports broadcasts, and even poker and lifestyle sports. Different games leveraged slightly varying conventions when it came to show productions. Within the early *StarCraft* broadcasting community, one producer said that their inspiration came from watching esports television that was coming out of South Korea: "All we were doing was watching Korea for Brood War. So that was 100 percent of our influence, watching what was going on in Korea. . . . Which is crazy for me now, but that's all we were watching and being inspired by was the stuff that was going on crazy in Korea, and trying to get whatever degree of the same feeling we could do ourselves . . . we were trying to do." A producer for a different league that often replicated the tone of North American sports spoke of using graphical elements and arrangements (lower-third graphics and a theme) to evoke traditional sports shows. And as a fighting game producer explained,

> There are some conventions that I feel that our fighting game broadcast needs to have to be successful. For one thing, I think the fighting game community has the most high energy in that fans and players get crazy, they jump up and down and stuff, so we call them "pop-offs." . . . That happens quite frequently in the fighting game community. Whereas you know in *StarCraft*, what happens when the guy wins, he goes to the other booth and shakes his hand. Here, people get hyped, they jump up and down, people rush the stage. That is very important to capture.

Early esports broadcasts, much like competitive gaming as a whole, were experimenting with a variety of ways to frame their content, drawing from both conventions that resonated within the specific community and media tropes more broadly.

Content was also deeply tied to the abilities and size of the production team. While there was an attitude of "let's just try it and make it work," one producer described the challenge of doing events with their two-man team. They faced having to balance keeping content flowing with low-level tournament chaos:

> You're trying to hunt this player down, just going to the [online game] lobby, and still trying to entertain the people on stream. And we weren't running commercials. It was like, again, static images with music playing to like buy you time. It was just rough because you look at what it takes now to run a proper live broadcast and twenty, thirty, forty people are sometimes involved to just make sure they nail it. It was rough. It was

rough. No doubt about it. In hindsight, it was rough. We tried to do exciting things like fly through the map and kind of talk about it. Sometimes we got in over our heads because from a production standpoint, it's like a two-man show. It's me and one other guy. So it was really difficult to dive too deep into making the broadcast look really sleek.

Content and aesthetics in these early days thus involved a mix of technology, inspirational sports/media waypoints, and the vibe and values happening within the local scene.

ECONOMICS AND LABOR

As I've spoken to producers over the years, the themes of hacking together technology and pushing it beyond its typical uses as well as constantly trying to innovate content remain steady. Since the early days, however, there's been a dramatic change in terms of economics and an increasingly specialized, professionalized division of labor. There was always a complicated mix of professional aspirations and what we might think of as serious leisure—activities in which significant time, money, resources, and overall identity investment occur—in early broadcasting.[14] This form of leisure is often the kernel that grows into increasing professionalization, where being a hobbyist or enthusiast becomes your day job (or at least you hope it does). One of the most important stories not just in esports broadcasting but also the scene writ large has been transformations from serious leisure to professionalized endeavors.

In the early days, there were several areas that frequently incurred high costs for production teams: equipment, travel, and bandwidth. As one longtime broadcaster put it, "The biggest issue is we were all spending for a dream we knew would become a reality but we never really thought how it would happen." For some, the financial outlay was just part of the package for trying to pursue what you wanted:

> It was just we were doing it because we love to do it, and since everybody in the community, at the time we organized it, we all knew each other. It's almost like the tight-knit family. "Can we stream your event? Yeah, sure. All right. Fly yourselves out, and OK, we'll get you a room," and that was it. It was more verbalized than anything, and we relied on I guess a sort of an old-boys network too because we'll just be like, "Hey, we go way back, can we stream your event?"

Others utilized any gear that they had access to, such as the student who made a weekly three-hour drive from his college to another city where the production equipment was located. Many of these people, who began their media careers as enthusiasts wanting to support the scene, came to see what they were doing as something that could be transformed into a job and professional identity.

Shifting to thinking about their media production work as something tied to professionalism was often prompted by economics. Early producers who kept at it and scaled up what they were creating would find the financial side becoming more pressing. As one portrayed it, "In the very beginning, it was more of we'd use these big events to showcase 'here's the production level that we can do,' and it was practice for us. And then I think it was probably around late 2010 was when I think a lot of the people in the community started saying, 'Look, we can't keep doing this for this amount of money, we're losing our own money spending money on our own gear. Please pay us.'"

Soon these relationships became formalized. As the same person explained, "We start[ed] to really learn about the business side of things like, 'Oh yeah, we can't really rely on people to say they'll pay us. Maybe we should make a contract.' We got burned by that a couple of times like, 'Yeah, we'll pay you,' and then nobody paid us. And like, we can't go to his house and break his legs. We had a contract. We could take him to court and stuff." Even with these structures, most continued to hold day jobs, and produce shows on their own time and dime. Others, even while holding a day job, saw these early ventures as investment opportunities.

While physical gear costs were a constant theme in my conversations with early producers, even more significant and consistently mentioned were data costs, software, and technical infrastructure. Unlike current platforms, which rely on advertising and thus don't charge users for the costs of streaming content, early broadcasters would typically buy bandwidth from server companies. This involved both estimating one's audience and being on the hook if your broadcast took off and pulled in more viewers than you budgeted for. As one explained, "Before Twitch.tv, we were doing our own broadcasting of our own tournament online. We set up a bunch of servers, and one of our programmers programmed a load balancer, and I think on our finals we had ten thousand people watching and we were doing all the bandwidth ourselves, and it was crazy! We would have to call the server company and buy more bandwidth and that sort of thing."

It was not unusual to hear stories of successful broadcasters both thrilled by their viewership but bracing for the anticipated bill from the server company. The sponsorship of streams still wasn't widespread, and as one person put it, "It was all funded out of pocket. So we were only just playing with the idea of getting sponsors to look at the stream. Our broadcast starts snowballing. We're like, 'Oh, my God. We have fifty people watching!' It's just every month it was like, 'Oh, we got a hundred. Five hundred. Oh shoot, two thousand people are watching! Five thousand!' So it just kept snowballing." These outfits also regularly faced issues around DDOS attacks and found themselves hustling to not only keep a show on schedule but also make sure it actually got out to an audience.

Some worked with companies that utilized slightly different setups, but those could pose challenges on the audience end. An early producer observed that

> you would make a deal with Akamai where you would pay them a little bit of money. You would use their peer-to-peer sharing client. But the problem was for you to watch an Octoshape stream [Akami's proprietary system], you had to download the client. And people were especially like, internet nerds, like, "I'm not putting this on my computer. What the hell is this? Malware or a Trojan?" It was a barrier of entry. You want to hit a button and it plays, right?

Issues on the client end were not constrained to these. While early producers typically pushed the tech to its limits, audiences didn't always themselves have the hardware or network to keep up. As one simply remarked, "Not everybody could watch our stream because not everybody had a good enough computer or connection."

As live streaming platforms such as Stickam or UStream started coming online—in 2005 and 2007, respectively—producers began exploring ways to use them to offset costs and broaden distribution. These were still met with frustration, though: "For a while we had zero options and then we had slightly shitty options." Another noted that "a few sites started to pop up—Ustream; Livestream was another big one—and I remember looking at them and telling our programmer, 'Hey, maybe we should do this,' but they actually had viewer caps on them at that point because the bandwidth was so expensive for them."

Recounting their annoyance at trying to explain the emerging esports media space to companies that were more focused on a model of live streaming rooted in "real-life" cams, one producer said, "We had these conversations [with] these guys at Ustream like, 'Yeah, you guys really should think about this demographic better. We are pushing your technology. Look at our viewership compared to some of this bullshit.' Paris Hilton on the front page or whatever this other stream shit is. Puppies and whatever. And they would never really, like, put us in the rotator. Never enhance it."

Justin.tv eventually became an important service in terms of handling bandwidth, network infrastructures, and ease of use for audiences. He continued, "And then, Justin.tv was doing roughly the same thing. But it was just all bullshit like live cam. It didn't have corporate clients, but we jumped on it because it was just as good at bandwidth. It was free. And then they went, 'Oh, shit. Look at how many people are gaming and streaming!' And obviously they took it so seriously they shifted their entire business model, renamed it, and closed the other one. What does that tell you, right?" Though esports production teams continue to pull together equipment whose primary use cases are decidedly *not* competitive computer gaming and frequently require their own network specialists on-site for events, the rise of third-party streaming platforms offered tremendous financial and infrastructure assistance to what was previously a grassroots as well as self-funded venture.

As we can see, there are deep interwoven threads between technology, content, and economics. They are interdependent with each other and co-construct what esports broadcast is. These productions extend the event space well beyond the digital gameplaying field itself, from audio commentating to progressing to having multiple cameras (in game, onstage, *and* pointed at the audience), graphics, commentary desks, and even narrative interstitials to entertain the audience between matches.

The technology works in constant conversation, however, with the creation of aesthetics and conventions for how esports should be presented as well as experienced by audiences. This includes ideas about what the preferred referent is (sports versus, for example, music concerts), notions about ideal and expert play, and models of who the audience is and how it consumes content. Amplifying, constraining, or subtly nudging it are the financial, infrastructural, and labor underpinnings. Promoters could have blue-sky ambitions, but without economic models or networks to make it happen, it would simply have remained a dream. Not unlike the instrumental mind-set that one utilizes when playing, esports media broadcasting itself became a puzzle early producers sought to crack.

Esports as Networked Media Event

Over and over again, interviewees told me about the profound shift that has occurred in esports with the growth of live streaming. While early large-scale tournaments like the World Cyber Games or World Series of Video Games were foundational in conceptualizing esports as spectacles or pushing media components, tournaments have been amplified by the ability to broadcast them live, globally, over the internet. The recording and distribution of competitions has always been a part of esports, but the current approach focuses on the creation of *media events*. Pairing live tournaments with streamed broadcast is now a huge component of esports. Doing so has become not simply an exercise in scaling up tournament production but also iterating processes to account for a range of media technologies, new aesthetic and genre convention, forms of audience (onsite and via the internet), and emerging business models.

TECHNOLOGIES AT WORK

Competitive gaming has only been possible via an assemblage of technologies, and this is just as true for the viewing practices that have come out of that space (Taylor 2009, 2012). Almost from the start, the desire to share experience and foster spectatorship took hold among gamers. As discussed, game developers began to experiment with building in spectator modes (allowing people to log in and watch the game as it unfolded). Early innovators (from gamers to tournament organizers) often pieced together expensive gear to pipe out the game "stream" for capture and distribution. At times a full broadcast was only produced after the fact, when recorded gameplay was then overplayed with voice commentating and distributed via a website. The goal of live broadcast with multiple cameras, rich visuals and commentary, and compelling production values has been something that producers have been working on for decades.

Backstage areas demonstrate the culmination of gaming interweaving itself with broader media production technologies (see figures 4.3a and 4.3b). The most basic nodes in esports, game and player, are extended and stretched; other technologies insert themselves into the dyad with the goal of bringing viewers into the experience. The system at this level adds a range of audio and video mixers, monitors, graphics packages, recording racks with hard drives, and cameras (both physical and digital). Headphones, microphones, walkie-talkies, keyboards, laptops and desktops, handwritten tags that notate the mixing boards and audio switch box, desks and less than ergonomic chairs, paper (and digital) scripts and schedules, and endless amounts of cables and cords link it all together.

As noted previously, large-scale production teams operate out of traveling road cases known as "fly packs" that gear is bundled up in, shipped off to the next international location, and set up to do a show all over again. As

FIGURES 4.3A AND 4.3B. Backstage at Intel Extreme Masters, showing multiple production stations and networking, San Jose, 2016.

one producer explained, "It's easy for load in, load out. It all travels together." When I asked him to speculate on what a sports broadcaster might think if they walked in and saw a large tournament setup, he replied,

> If they came in now, it is fairly close to TV-quality content being produced around esports. Pretty damn close. We're not in trucks yet, but we're pretending like we're in trucks, TV trucks. Years ago we were on shitty little tables with shitty little setups, so the director walks in [and] he goes, "Oh, we know what we're doing all about this. We got trucks and we're smarter than you about the game." They had trucks. [But] they didn't know how to shoot our game.

Although some broadcasts are now using production trucks (for example, ELEAGUE's Major series in Boston rolled out one of its standard rigs to the venue), it is still not the norm across the board. This has long been one of the fascinating tensions in esports broadcasts: while the setups and tech were frequently less sophisticated than traditional broadcasting, it was *esports* producers who knew how to tackle the specificities of computer game content and events. Some skills certainly transfer over from traditional broadcasts, such as, "The jib movements that these guys are doing at *StarCraft* stage are no different than the jib movements the guys are making the Beyonce videos or in an N.F.L. pregame show." Yet others remain deeply tied to the specific context of computer games, from in-game cameras to knowing how to effectively capture a visually explosive digital field of play because you understand what is actually happening in-game.

The development of specialized tournament heads-up displays (HUDs) is just one illustration of the ways that knowledge of the game becomes critical in helping render a playing field legible to fans. While those who don't follow a particular game may mostly focus on the center of the screen action filled with sniper fire, or lots of magical spells and action, for more astute viewers, all the additional information provided on-screen is important to "reading" the match. Esports producers rely on their knowledge of the specificities of the game that they are working with to create broadcast HUDs that will help audiences engage.

Consider, for instance, what it would look like if you sat down to watch a baseball game on television with someone who has never seen the sport before. You both would certainly be paying attention to the action in the center of the frame, where the camera would be directed to the pitcher, the hitter, and the ball as it flies across the field. But if you were a baseball fan and knew how to watch the broadcast more fully, you'd also be noticing the details on the screen that show how many balls, strikes, and outs there were. You would notice what inning the game was in, and if it was the top or bottom of it. You'd catch when a stat popped up helping you contextualize this particular pitcher/hitter matchup. It is the same for esports.

Broadcasts regularly tweak the HUDs of games to provide richer info to the spectator than what any individual player is seeing within the game at that moment. This can range from mini maps that reveal the location of all players to having the full team lineup visually represented on the screen with some information about them (name, weapon or class, amount of in-game money that they have, etc.) as well as a way to visualize when their character gets killed. HUDs are tremendously important not only to good gaming experiences but broadcasts too; they help the viewer make sense of an otherwise visually complex field of play. They provide vital information to help an audience synthesize what is happening overall, and for more expert fans, provide a hook for deeper engagement. They are also a space that can be branded with sponsor content such as logos.

Perhaps it's obvious from this example that given the level of detail on digital playing fields, broadcasters often have to contend with pushing their technology to handle better resolutions. Traditional sports broadcasting generally goes out at a lower resolution than esports. Gaming fans and those attuned to making a visually compelling broadcast will seek out much higher resolutions, and especially if watching on a computer screen (incredibly common), they will want at least 1080p. Esports events will frequently be creating and distributing content at resolution levels well beyond what is being used in traditional productions, and, in turn, can sometimes push media companies to upgrade their infrastructures and systems.

Overall, the level of production and gear in esports is creeping up to traditional media, and in some cases surpassing them. When I visited a new studio being built in Burbank, the engineer putting the technology together noted that he had pushed for that location so that they could be near all the broadcast suppliers. His background was in traditional media, and being in a location where they could easily buy and rent gear was a serious consideration when he gave feedback to the executives about where to set up shop. He noted, though, that it turned out that the media companies he usually dealt with didn't quite know what to do with his esports productions. He described trying to explain to his suppliers when he picked up mixing boards and other equipment what he was doing with gaming content. He said that they looked at him with confusion and shrugged, not understanding or doing much to help him fit their gear into his production system. Within months, with the help of a young "hacker" (who he proudly pointed out to me during a tour), he was working with traditional A/V gear in ways that had not been done before. Over time his suppliers had started to catch on and began using *his* setup to show off the features of their equipment to their regular clients.

While mixing boards and cameras are visible technology, the unseen infrastructure is just as, if not more so in the case of digital gaming, critically important. Communication networks—from an internet connection to cell phone service to the private audio channels that allow the production team to constantly be speaking to one another—form the backbone of esports being transformed into broadcast event. This is perhaps one of the most challenging aspects of doing research about online and gaming spaces. Much of what makes it up is simply not visible at a glance.[15] It is only after watching for a while that you really start to notice how often people are looking at their phones, talking into headsets while flipping a mixer switch, hunched over a laptop furiously dealing with a downed internet connection, or typing in commands to start a game in the private chat window.[16]

Invisible infrastructure, however, is regularly embodied and made material through the people in the space. On the second day of an event, I heard that there were some network hiccups (not unusual in esports), so I casually asked those backstage what was happening. It was at this point that someone pointed to a long Ethernet cable that went into the rafters and said, "See that? That's our internet connection." They walked me through how the connection was interfacing with firewalls, a virtual private network server, and their own proprietary system meant to foil DDOS attacks. Across that communication system, the data coming out from the event was being transmitted to various servers around the world and then picked up, localized (with custom graphics and language translation), and broadcast online in different regions. Various forms of A/V encoding were happening along the way, advertising servers were jumping in to add content, and metrics were being generated and collected. The network problems had, up until that point, been entirely unknown to me. My attention had been so focused on being physically present and observing backstage that what fell out of my view was the experience of the event unfolding within the infrastructure that made it possible.[17]

But these various communication networks form a critical component of esports productions. Digital playing fields are fundamentally networked spaces where players and individual instantiations of games are communicating with servers, and production systems are picking up feeds and working with them. That content then gets sent out worldwide across both satellite and terrestrial systems, and in turn, often goes through another round of reworking (localization, for example, or meshing with ad systems) before getting transmitted out to audiences. Esports broadcasts are multinodal artifacts that exist only through various networked assemblages.

PRODUCTION LABOR

As game live streaming has developed, the systems themselves have become more complex. Technologies get pushed and prodded to better work together. Much of the gear that game live streaming uses comes from traditional media production, and regularly has to be tweaked to do what is needed. Software is developed to facilitate game video production and distribution. Engineering steps in to create servers to handle loads. These operations and technologies require their own mix of human labor to make it work.

The rise of esports as a professionalized domain has meant that it has undergone transformations in its division of labor. While the earliest tournaments were players and maybe one or two organizers running the whole event, over the last decade and a half, various roles within tournament organizations have been broken down and covered by people with increasingly tailored skills—from team owners to event planners. This specialization is extending into the domain of media production. As one longtime producer speaking to me about how he got in on the ground floor of esports with no special training said, "There's no doubt in my mind that I just lucked out on the window of time that I was at a certain age, and we were at a certain place in the industry. And everything from here on out is very quickly getting professional."

Though you can still find smaller tournaments operating with amateur labor, larger-scale productions require more extensive teams including technical engineers, audio engineers, graphics/overlay specialists, camera operators, in-game observers, event producers or managers, technical and creative directors, stage managers, network administrators, ancillary content producers (photographers, interstitial video creators, etc.), hosts, analysts, commentators, and communications personnel handling press and social media.[18] This team is also typically working with contracted-out laborers who may handle things like lights, audio, or any other number of production details. Venue-specific teams (including unionized ones, most of which don't specialize in esports at all) take care of rigging, stage build-outs/teardowns, cabling, and general events labor.[19] The game developer themselves might want representation on or oversight of a production as well. Some of these roles mirror what you would find in a traditional live television broadcast while others are unique to competitive gaming.

One of the esports broadcast teams that I shadowed has refined who does what over the years, and their team now includes people with both esports and traditional media production backgrounds. One creative director explained how he and the technical director worked together on a production, and where some of the segmentation lay:

> We just have a great working relationship together because we've done so many shows and we've pissed each other off [laughs]. And we understand exactly where the boundaries are. . . . So how are we transitioning from one segment of the show to another? We will sit down together and figure that out, and sometimes we involve [the host] in that and we'll have a little powwow back and forth.

He went on to note that while he was charged with having an eye on the high-level creative issues, his counterpart focused on the technical implementation and handled communication with the various engineers on the team. He, by contrast, was the one who dealt with the clients, which were typically game developers or other organizations that hire the company out to produce their competitions and shows:

> I handle all of that relationship management on our end with their management people and creative people so that there's this barrier between the client and all of our technical guys. We have very strong rules that you do not talk to anybody on our team except for me or [the head].

This kind of division of labor and formalized lines of communication is something that I saw much less of in the earliest days of esports. While there were certainly particular roles that people occupied, and those who handled clients specifically, the scale of productions along with the money at stake has grown such that specialized skills and sticking to your own domain has become much more common. It is now not at all unusual to find production areas with formal directors, assistant directors, producers, technical directors, and an assortment of engineers who all work within more constrained spheres.

Other roles, such as the observers who operate an in-game camera that shows the audience varying player views during a match, speak to how new forms of labor are needed (see figure 4.4). Though akin to a traditional camera operator in that they are in the game and pointing a digital "camera" at particular locations on the game map that then gets broadcast out, their

FIGURE 4.4. In-game observer Phil "inFeZa" Bertino working backstage at Intel Extreme Masters, ComicCon, 2013.

role is unique to computer gaming and a fairly specialized skill set. Observers are expert enough at a given game to know how to parse the action, including anticipated moves, and shift around the digital playing field, providing a view of the action for the audience. They also work closely with the analysts who are supplying live commentary for the match.

One observer, Heather "sapphiRe" Garazzo (herself a former pro player), described the job as akin to an "in-game director" and distinguished her role, saying, "There's a main director who's telling people when to go in game, when to look at the team, the analyst's desk or the host. Then there's the in-game director, which is the observer. My job is to direct the action in the game. Essentially I'm a storyteller. I'm telling the story of a round or the match" (quoted in Stenhouse 2016). In talking to observers over the years, I've found that while they have an open communication channel to the director who can weigh in, the most experienced ones develop an independent feel for not just individual "shots" but, as Garazzo puts it, also have an eye on the larger "story" of the game that viewers should pay attention to. They give us a glimpse into a new form of labor that mixes several traditional media roles within the specificity of gaming.

Perhaps one of the most interesting shifts that I've found while talking to people in various roles over the years is that they come from a wide range of backgrounds—some with formal training in the domain that they are now working, and many others not. They also bring to the job a mix of referents for what it *should be*. Some lean on their experience in traditional media productions and talk about their job through that lens. Others are self-taught and root their training in their gaming passion. They sometimes see what they do as fairly unique and requiring a different mind-set. In much the same way that I saw early pro players and tournament organizers working through different models to make sense of what they were doing (typically using a "sports" framework to interpret their passions and activities), these folks are constructing meaningful ways of working and talking about their labor as not only esports but also media professionals.

As with other parts of emerging new media spheres, questions around compensation remain critical. Historically esports labor has been seeded from fandom roots, with those producing events receiving little compensation, and in fact often incurring debt along the way for their activities. The earlier periods of esports production were typically a form of a serious leisure where people spent not just time but also money to participate in an activity that they love. In conversations with them over the years, I've found that they are frequently acutely aware of balancing their hopes for a living wage against what they see as realism about the state of the industry. Some see foregoing a competitive salary as an "investment," imagining that their work in a nascent industry will eventually pay off when esports gets big. With growing professionalization, however, especially on the media side, this model has been shifting.

As major money has entered into esports, the status quo around "sweat equity" and other low/no-pay models has been met with more dissatisfaction. Previously private labor skirmishes have come to public attention. The hype around esports, where industry reports proclaim that there are millions of dollars of revenue to be made every year, has at times come to leave people even more acutely aware of the cut that they *aren't* getting. I previously discussed the ways that early producers have faced the economic challenges within esports. With live streaming, the powerful role that "talent" (including hosts, commentators, and analysts) have in making broadcasts successful has become apparent. This has meant that many of them now situate their work within an entertainment labor market where reaching massive audiences and being a celebrity in their own right should come with meaningful economic boosts. Chaloner (2015) outlined in an article overviewing talent pay that there is a range from "TV rates" at the highest end of the scale all the way down to low-end rates with online leagues or small organizations.

In 2016, popular commentator (and onetime team owner) Christopher "MonteCristo" Mykles issued a statement along with several other free-lancers that they would not be working at one of Riot's *League of Legends* competitions due to the failure "to arrive at an industry standard rate for our services." The group said that it had carried out research across a va-riety of caster contracts and found that Riot was offering 40 to 70 percent less than other productions. Mykles and his colleagues said that taking the contract could "damage our careers in the long term by accepting below-market rates," and that "by agreeing to a significantly lower wage we fear that we may contribute to the regression of standards for freelance cast-ers in the industry as a whole" (OGNCasters 2016). They had in fact been longtime commentators and analysts for the popular South Korean outlet OnGameNet, a media company that had been bringing esports to audiences for over a decade, so it is perhaps not surprising that of all the freelancers to push back on this issue, publicly no less, it would be them. The case caught a fair amount of attention, due to both the popularity of the game and the high production values that Riot had brought to its competitions.

While public opinion was split on the matter, it did make visible con-versations that had been going on behind the scenes for years. It crystal-lized the ways that the emerging broadcast side of esports was changing the labor landscape, and where growing audiences and revenue—be it hyped speculation or actual—were causing everyone along the chain of production to rethink their value. As with esports players, there continue to be new-comers who are willing to forego higher pay in hopes of getting a foot in the door or for whom the activity was more hobby than regular work to pay the bills. In an emerging industry without any unions or other regulatory mechanisms helping gate keep and maintain pay standards, the economic precariousness is real.

AFFECTIVE AESTHETICS

Nick Taylor (2016, 296), in his work around live esports audiences, notes the ways that spectatorship "becomes a crucial site of experimentation for an e-sports industry eager to sell the excitement of live competitive gaming events to a mass audience of online spectators." Beyond the actual matches of the tournament, the auxiliary content, stage and theatrical lighting, and cameras that capture the on-site audience currently make up a big part of

FIGURE 4.5. *League of Legends* LCS Summer finals, TD Garden, Boston, 2017.

broadcasts. Audience banners and signs, clapping and thunder sticks, rising to their feet to cheer, and other embodied performances of engagement and excitement all get leveraged back into the broadcast (see figure 4.5). As one director put it, "My saying is there's a difference between streaming and putting on a show. Everybody can stream, not everybody can put on the show."

There is, however, nuance in this sense of a "show" being created. Media producers must negotiate between building compelling content, retaining a sense of authenticity for hard-core fans, yet simultaneously harnessing and developing newcomers' enthusiasm for the games and competition. One director—who began in the early DIY days and now manages some of the biggest broadcasts around—highlighted what they felt can be compelling in even low-end live streaming: "You may not have any of the technical parts, but you've got the emotional experience for people, and that is often good enough." He explained that a large production "can be crystal clean, and you can hit every shot that you need to and every transition you need to, but you're like 'It's just . . . something is not there.' And it's sort of the passion, a lot of it is the passion of the crowd, but it's also sound and light and everything that's going on and creating something that is sort of this big cohesive package."

This focus on creating memorable, compelling events that pull in and capture the audience (both off- and online) is similar to the affective turn that individual live streamers make. Whether small or large, these productions are meant to be evocative. He continued:

> We want to create these legendary experiences, and I mean, the big thing for me is that, and I've been preaching this a little bit to my friends. I didn't even know if it was real until I went and Wikipedia-ed the other day for "emotional memory." I was trying to figure out for the longest time why do people remember these esports events that were fairly crappy production value, and it usually comes down to like there were these few epic moments, and people have really good memories for those and really terrible memories [meaning forgotten ones] if there was a two-hour delay. And then I went and studied it, and it's like a negative bias where people just don't remember negative things as well as they remember positive things. I was like, oh wow, well that's what we have to do right.

Even though he was particularly thinking about how to construct on-site live events, he was keenly attuned to their need to be broadcast in such a way that viewers were also drawn in. This sensibility echoes the work that traditional sports broadcasting has long done to bring a stadium experience to the home viewer. Sports media are broadly used to tap into and build fandom, and emotional resonance for viewers, to help them connect with a remote event and keep watching.

The structure of modern sports broadcasting is generally traced as arising from Arledge's shaping of North American sports media starting in the 1960s. Almost mythical in recounting now, he is said to have brought "unheard-of techniques [such] as the use of directional and remote microphones, the replacement of half-time shows with highlights and an analysis of the first two quarters, the use of hand-held and 'isolated' cameras, the use of a split screen and the filling of 'dead spots' during the game with prerecorded biographies and interviews" ("Playboy Interview" 1976, 63). These conventions are familiar to anyone who has watched sports *and* esports productions. Esports producers have long looked to how compelling emotional and even visceral content for viewers is created by traditional sports broadcasting. Indeed, these dominate both the look and feel of esports now. They have become a kind of orthodoxy within broadcasts.

Esports business developer Jesse Sell (2015) has noted the high level of "sports emulation" in how esports tournament broadcasts are structured,

FIGURE 4.6. *Dota 2* International grand finals commentator desk, 2014.

from stats and show rundown to aesthetics, wardrobe, style, and narrative frames (see figure 4.6). Game scholar Elizabeth Newbury (2017) has found similar patterns in some segments of esports such as *CSGO*.[20] Esports broadcasts are now regularly filled with story arcs and pivot points in the game that amplify tension and excitement.

Personal stories and trajectories as well as team and player rivalries figure into the framing of a game. Interviews, hype reels, and interstitials (often comedic) entertain audiences between matches. The early days where esports events were fortunate to have a commentator or two on hand regularly now have full-scale teams producing all kinds of material. Analysts and commentators outfitted in suits sit at sleek desks. Hosts manage onstage activities. Multiple cameras cover a range of shots, including on the in-person audience, especially between matches. The focus on showing passionate fandom to those watching is a huge part of the staging. Spectatorship is not only produced on site but also folded back into the broadcast to in turn bring an affective experience to home viewers.

At tournament venues, the spectating experience is also interwoven with various media practices, from small screens scattered throughout the environment, jumbotrons, and a myriad of cameras installed everywhere that capture both the game and spectators. Being on-site at the event is an experience tied up with media too. This is certainly the case within esports, where there can be significant chunks of dead time between matches or during technical breakdowns. Given that esports tournaments are often multi-day affairs, producers typically deal with having a live audience that needs entertainment during these times. While some events have experimented with live musical acts (perhaps akin to the Superbowl's famed half-time show), such attempts have been met with mixed results, especially from hard-core esports fans who feel it is a distraction.[21] In many ways, the live event experience at esports tournaments currently reflects a scene betwixt and between its roots in LAN parties, where people would have their own gaming to keep them entertained between competitions, and the conversion of a scene into a straightforward media-event spectacle.

MANAGING DIGITAL STADIUMS

While an important component to esports broadcasts has become the show on-site at a venue, another critical part of a stream is the chat happening within the platform, live alongside the content coming from the tournament. Unlike variety streamers with their more focused viewer interactions and socialization practices, a large remote audience poses serious challenges to channels that want to keep their chats intelligible or perhaps even positive. Though I'll discuss this issue further in the next chapter, it's worth saying a few words about managing this part of esports broadcasts. As one producer put it, "It gets extremely wild west. Like every time we have like one or two like specific teams, like some of the big-name teams on our stream, there have been times where chat gets so crazy, we just make it subscriber only."

But this level of moderation often doesn't get at the truly pernicious speech that happens in tournament channels, where harassment, racism, sexism, and various forms of hate speech are a sadly regular occurrence. Harassment on the platform is a major barrier not only to entry but retention too. Legal scholar Danielle Citron (2014) argues in her extensive treatment of online harassment that these are fundamentally civil rights issues that warrant serious attention, prevention strategies, and focused redress. If we understand live streaming as an increasingly significant sector of media, and thus cultural, development, this is a major ethical and business issue. It goes to the heart of full participation not only in media and gaming but also in popular culture writ large.

In one of the white papers published for AnyKey—an initiative to foster diversity and inclusion in esports that I codirect with Morgan Romine—we explored a persistent theme that occurred in our conversations with professional women players who live stream: the continual harassment and abuse they face. As one of them told us, they came to think that "being insulted is a regular part of the job" ("Workshop #1" 2015). For some, the toxicity became so great that they left live streaming and sometimes competition altogether. For those in the audience who witness these ongoing verbal assaults in streams, it can also be a powerful reminder of the boundary policing at work. You may come to feel quite sharply how that space is simply not "for you."

Unfortunately in the case of large esports productions, managing the community in event channels has been woefully under attended to. The focus of tournament organizers and broadcasters has thus far tended to be on the stage productions and competitions themselves. Online chat in live streamed broadcasts, where huge audiences are participating, is, if moderated at all, generally handled by bots, volunteers, and on rare occasions, a couple of paid staff members. Given that many of these tournaments have millions of viewers over the course of a weekend with just as many lines of chat streaming through, this is shocking.

While there have been many instances of harassment and hate speech taking place in esports streams over the years, one that brought the issue to greater public attention happened during a *Hearthstone* match at Dream-Hack Austin 2016. A large audience watched the final match between professional players Terrance "TerranceM" Miller and Keaton "Chakki" Gill as it was broadcast live via Twitch. Journalist Colin Campbell (2016a), covering the incident for Polygon, described how "during the Twitch livestream of his performance, and the interviews that followed, Miller, who is African-American, was the subject of a torrent of racist abuse on the stream's chat panel. The abuse included hateful language targeting African-Americans, as well as graphic descriptions and imagery. There was so much abuse that moderators were unable to keep up." Even though Miller himself did not witness the hate speech in real time, others, including his family, did. And he saw it all after the fact when he got a chance to watch the broadcast, where an archive of the chat played alongside the match.

There are many devastating common threads in Campbell's recounting here. The resigned predictability of this kind of hate speech in tournament broadcasts (he quotes Miller as saying, "I knew it would be bad, but I didn't think it would be that bad"), the hope that people just hide the chat, and the continued frustration at the lack of meaningful oversight within online spaces. Yet unlike so many other incidents of this type that have happened over the years, one important difference occurred this time: a moderator spoke up publicly and called the process as well as organization to account.

In a piece posted at the popular esports site Gosu Gamers, Carling "Toastthebadger" Filewich, a longtime *Hearthstone* community member and chat moderator for DreamHack Austin, offered a reflective accounting of what happened during the tournament, and revealed the gaps that currently exist in how most moderation and community management get handled. She specifically called out what many of us have long observed: far too often, chat is somehow not considered organizationally central to the broadcast and the responsibility of the organizers. She wrote, "Tournament organizers spend countless hours trying to get every little detail just right for their event. They take time to ensure they have the right casters, the right administrators, and the right production staff so that the final product presented on the broadcast is something they can be proud of. Very little, if any, consideration goes into what happens once the broadcast reaches the public" (Filewich 2016). She continued by astutely observing that the failure of DreamHack to properly moderate the channel is an all-too-common pattern, where many organizers simply do not put the time, labor, and I'd argue, money into actually building out robust community management. She asks,

> Why wouldn't you screen your moderators like you screen your casters? If you logged in at the right time over the weekend, you would have seen a moderator joining in on the racist spam and offering to unban anyone that had been permanently banned from the channel for horribly racist messages. Why was this person ever made moderator? Why were moderators with experience dealing with large chats only brought in after the racism became unmanageable? Tournament organizers should consider chat moderation an important part of the broadcast and plan ahead for it. (ibid.)

Her account painted a devastating portrait of a moderation team made up of volunteers, many of whom were working hard to keep the chat from running off the rails while others were actively undermining them. The lack of clear guidelines, training, and accountability is striking.[22]

It is also, sadly, unsurprising. When reading her recounting of the incident, I couldn't help but think about a long-standing pattern in both gaming and social media: the lack of meaningful community management. Over and over again, both game developers and platforms build tremendous communities—and capital—by having users constantly engaging with each other, producing content, and deeply building value by their presence and interactions. Yet at the same time, it is stunning how underprepared and undercommitted companies can be in terms of managing those communities. They want the value that all those people create, but on the cheap. From Twitter's ongoing foot-dragging on tools and processes to combat harassment to games that continue to be home to a consistently toxic culture, companies continue to want to bring people onto their platforms but neglect them once there. Far too often, corporate calculations focus on high daily active user counts while not investing in making these spaces sustainable. Not only are there real ethical issues with this approach; there are also actual long-term economic costs to this lack of attention. Harassing and toxic behavior has the concrete impact of pushing positive users off the platform, and keeping others from joining and participating.

Game developer Jessica Mulligan's (2003) book *Developing Online Games* called on the industry to take community management as a core aspect of production. The minute you put multiple players together, you need to realize that you are now also fostering community. Esports tournaments and broadcasts need to face a similar truth. It is one thing to live stream matches, but the moment you put in a communication method for people, you have to attend to them. Tournament organizers are responsible for that space in the same way that owners of sports stadiums are. They are not exempt from managing the behavior that happens within them. Intervening in bad behavior on the part of attendees is incumbent on those who run the venue, and online spaces are no different. Part of this is, I would argue, an ethical condition of providing public environments. Both competitors and those in attendance (even digitally) have a right to a safe, nonharassing experience. This includes not being subject to racist, sexist, and homophobic slurs while you try to play, live stream, or spectate a game.

Most traditional sports stadiums have attendee codes of conduct, and some even offer confidential texting so that you can contact help without drawing (perhaps-risky) attention to yourself. These codes, of course, do not fully prevent bad things from happening; there remains more to be done on building inclusive traditional sporting communities. But the presence of codes and methods of enforcement (visible staff, mechanisms to reach out for help, etc.) signal a fundamental understanding of *responsibility* from the organizers that what happens in the stadium is part of the experience that they are *accountable* for. Esports organizers need to come to recognize that their live streaming and chat spaces are part of a digital stadium that they must manage responsibly.

There is also an economic angle that, if nothing else, broadcasters (and game developers) should certainly care about. For those who are really thinking about long-term growth, understanding how your product is affected—both symbolically and practically—by the chat is critical. One organizer noted the impact of bad stream chat on potential sponsors, saying, "I don't want to see them scared away . . . You know you're doing a 'listen in' [popping into a stream to show a sponsor], and people are dropping racial slurs or using the f-bomb and stuff like that it takes away so much space and it only sets us back. Esports is still, although growing, too fragile to have any setbacks where people are publishing really bad stuff about it." Even just sticking to the main demographic that esports chases after (young men), it's important to realize that many of them *also* don't want to inhabit toxic spaces. It is woefully shortsighted to overlook the tremendous impact that unmoderated channels have on industry growth.

We can also think more expansively about audiences. In the case of traditional sports, women make up significant portions of both stadium and broadcast audiences. People of color and LGBTQIA folks are an always-present part of sports and gaming player bases, audiences, and leisure communities too.[23] If you are fostering, even through negligence, the construction of an online stadium where a large slice of the audience will not want to spend time, you are affecting your bottom line. Conversely, if you work to build spaces that accommodate diverse audiences and construct possibilities for fandom along with engagement—especially in the current esports climate—you are likely to be well ahead of your competitors.

BUSINESS MODELS

The economic side of esports has always been one of the most ever-changing and fraught aspects of the scene. Hype bubbles, shady promoters, and impatient investors have long disrupted stable growth. One of the upshots of this has meant that successful organizers have become adept at finding a variety of ways to pull in revenue, often extending their focus of running tournaments to game event media productions. Live streaming, in particular, has not only heightened some traditional outlets but also produced new ones. One streamer described to me the shift that has occurred, saying, "It's a big game changer for tournament organizers, because as opposed to actually renting out a streaming service, and paying big money for it, we actually now make money by creating good events. So that turned from 'Hey, we have to pay $20,000 to stream for three days,' around to 'Oh, we're *earning* $20,000 because we streamed for three days.'" This transformation—from producing and broadcasting an esports event on your own dime simply because you are an enthusiast to being able to actually make money from a production—has come through a variety of economic structures.

Revenue generation in esports is a motley mix of sources such as partnerships, licensing white label productions, sponsorships, in-game content, ad revenue, pay per view, event revenue, and crowdfunding. One person active in formulating tournament deals described it to me as different "buckets" and noted that how organizations tap into them varies not only from company to company but across titles as well. For some, the revenue mix will be made up more of white label productions and sponsors, while others will strongly utilize in-game content. Given that it is all still very much an industry in the making, new opportunities continue to present themselves (often in concert with platform development) even as others fall away. At the time of this research, the following were most important to understanding revenue in esports broadcasting.

Partnerships. As game developers/publishers have become more interested in leveraging the potential of broadcast competitions and game content, esports organizers have been able to step in and bring games to larger viewing audiences. Developers uninterested in or unable to carry out productions in-house will often reach out to an esports company that specializes in running tournaments and ask it to produce one for them, complete with a broadcast component. They will often issue a request for proposal (RFP) and have multiple companies bid on a project. An increasingly important part of organizer's operations are sales teams that work with and pitch to potential clients to create "partnership" deals in which, for a fee, they will produce an event around a specific title. Revenue from these productions is a critical part of a company's financial life. Indeed, one of the most interesting challenges that some of these organizations face is an energetic sales team making deals (commission being a driving factor), frequently beyond the current capacity of the production and event side of the company, pushing it to continue to expand aggressively.

Media licensing. Given the ways that traditional sports utilizes media licensing as a major revenue generator, it will perhaps be surprising to learn that third-party esports organizers have operated relatively free from burdensome licensing costs over the last several decades. Historically, organizers have not paid developers/publishers to use their games, and if they did, the amounts weren't large. In fact, the money has tended to flow in the *opposite* direction, with game developers and publishers actually paying third-party organizers to produce events. Prior to living streaming, esports productions were seen by developers/publishers along a continuum: a distraction from their core business of making games and not warranting their time to simply a good source of free marketing.

Organizers are now dealing with game companies paying more attention and wanting in on the action. For example, in 2016, Riot agreed to a $300 million deal with BAMTech, the venture spun off from Major League Baseball Advanced Media that pioneered the MLB's use of online streaming for games, for the right to distribute *League of Legends* matches. BAMTech's gambit was that it would monetize advertising (of which Riot would also get a portion). Blizzard's *Overwatch* league set several exclusivity deals in its launch year. Preseason matches went out on the MLG platform (Activision-Blizzard purchased MLG in 2016) while Twitch paid "at least $90M" for streaming rights to the regular *Overwatch* league season.

One of the critical things to keep in mind with media-licensing deals is that they may often tap into other "buckets" in the overall revenue mix, especially when a platform like Twitch is involved. Once you have bought the rights to a tournament's broadcast, tying it into other revenue-generating systems such as in-game content (discussed below) can mean that an otherwise-stunning number might be offset by unique forms of revenue sharing in the gaming space. As I will explore a bit more at the end of this chapter, it is possible that as future deals like these get made, they will transform and at times cut into the financial models that traditional esports organizers currently operate with. If game developers start exercising more sports-like terms in their licensing deals, it could pose challenges to both online platforms and third-party organizers.

White label products. Probably the least known outside the industry, but of growing importance in terms of media development, are esports companies taking on clients to produce and broadcast events. Unlike partnerships in which the organizer is still identified and a game title may even be integrated into one of its regular leagues, white label products typically have no explicit linking to the esports company. Game developers and others will hire outside teams (again typically using an RFP process) to handle their tournament or event, frequently from prep to media production to pack up. From the viewer's perspective, the entire operation appears to be run by the event or game developer, but behind the scenes another organization will handle all or part of the production. One notable example of a white label event has been BlizzCon, which has historically had multiple companies running both event broadcasting and tournament production. White label products transform esports tournament companies into *media* companies. White label contracts can involve a tremendous amount of prebroadcast work such as setting up brackets, scoping the event including with floor plans, producing the show, and having connections to the right talent (host and commentators) to bring in. As organizations develop their ability to do these productions, they are simultaneously figuring out where the sweet spot is in terms of costs and production. One noted, "I think one of the things we also learned early on is how little that little added boost of production value actually gets you in relation to viewers. If you double your time on a piece of content, you're not going to get double the viewers for it. So it's trying to find that, you know, nice balance." Because esports media production has grown to such a massive scale, often with deeply specialized labor, it is probably not surprising that some organizations have stepped in to augment their revenue this way.

Sponsorship. Esports has historically rested on endemic sponsors: those companies and brands that are seen as hitting the core "native" interests of the audience. In the case of esports, this has tended to mean that computers and peripherals have been the dominant sponsors in the space. Some of these, such as Intel, have been major financial supporters of large tournaments and a significant part of revenue generation for organizers for many years. With the growth of live streaming and larger audiences, more sponsors are seeing potential and getting into the mix. One producer who has been working in the field for almost two decades said of the shift, "It's like so suddenly all the practices that esports has put in in terms of getting these sponsors and getting these sponsors exposure are now sort of like super amplified because now all these companies that sponsor get all this additional exposure through live streaming." While still not quite reaching what we see in traditional sports or esports in South Korea, where a range of lifestyle brands play a role, there have been new non-endemic sponsors including soft drinks and insurance companies. Live streaming also offers increased opportunities for team sponsors to get their brands out there by having logos on jerseys, which are now getting prime screen time during tournaments.

In-game content or items. One of the newest sources of production revenue comes from the collision of two relatively recent developments: the fact that game developers are becoming much more involved in esports, and the ways that microtransactions have become a huge part of gaming overall. Games now regularly feature the ability for users to buy add-ons to the base product, from "skins" to cosmetically alter weapons or characters to new game modes. As game developers begin to make deals with production companies to handle their events, revenue generated from microtransactions has become a part of the potential overall revenue mix that broadcasters can receive. Some of the in-game content can be branded in conjunction with the tournament and offered up as special limited edition purchases while others will simply be regular items. Revenue is negotiated between developers and broadcasters. Other technical developments, such as account linking between Twitch and game publishers or the platform's extensions and API, facilitates offering viewers opportunities to get game items via their Twitch account and even tied to their watching particular content.

This is a form of production revenue unique to gaming, and highlights just one way that audiences are getting enlisted as both viewers and consumers. That formulation is certainly at the heart of traditional advertising, but in-game merchandise takes it to a whole new level. Traditional advertisers have long dreamed of systems to connect up and quantify viewership to consumer behavior. While it doesn't yet seem that Twitch has reconceptualized itself as fundamentally a platform on which raw data on user behavior is a prime source of revenue generation, in-game content purchasing as well as linking up to game and Amazon accounts may signal what's on the horizon. If the platform that you watch games on has detailed information about your viewing and spending habits, and can structure and monetize them to sell back to game companies and advertisers, one can certainly imagine a future in which Twitch is as much a consumer data company as a gaming one, with its revenue shifting accordingly.

Ad revenue. Despite platforms using advertising as their underlying financial structure, commercials have not yet formed a major part of revenue for most broadcasters. Though one team owner I spoke with referred to ad revenue as "a cherry on top," allowing both the team and pros to supplement their incomes, as noted in the discussion in the last chapter, there remain issues hindering this bucket. While major organizations can negotiate more favorable revenue-sharing agreements, deeper systemic problems still pose challenges to a traditional model of commercials in esports broadcasting. While ad-blocking software has largely been mitigated, producers express concerns about audience pushback, worried that triggering ads risks oversaturating the audience. One producer said, "I mean we're like any other broadcast. We have to pause to give praise to our sponsors and then we also have to run ads. It's always trying to find that balancing act of when is it too much ads." Regional rates for ads may mitigate against the revenue potential of otherwise-large audiences. For example, the lower CPMs traditionally paid for viewers in Russia can particularly affect esports given that a significant audience for games like *CSGO* is found there. Although a component of a diverse revenue package, online advertising more broadly faces serious hurdles, and live streaming is no exception.

Pay per view (PPV). Given the difficulties with advertising, one might expect subscription or PPV to have stepped in to fill some gaps. It is certainly a mechanism that has been utilized successfully by traditional sports. There have been a few attempts to build a PPV model in esports, most notably from MLG before Activision Blizzard purchased it. There was a fair amount of pushback from the community to this approach because many felt that they had already invested both time and money by being paying members of the website. The resistance also dovetailed with broader expectations of free content online. In an interview addressing MLG's move away from PPV, Sundance DiGiovanni (then CEO) told journalist Rod "Slasher" Breslau (2012),

> The goal was never to block the community from having access to the Arenas [a *StarCraft* tournament]; the goal was just to prove that there were business models and revenue lines that we can associate with the activity. Everybody makes assumptions that we've got unlimited funds to invest and we're milking as much money as possible, but if these activities are able to sustain themselves, we can do a lot. We don't see ourselves getting a million people to sign up for PPV, but we do see an opportunity to get advertisers and sponsors interested based on the audience size. I'm hoping that stuff we have planned for next year is even more open, free, and available for the audience again. Somebody has to pay. It's either us, advertisers, sponsors, or the community. I want the community to be the last line in defense in that equation.

MLG's transition event was sponsored by game development trade school Full Sail, and while it continued to experiment with revenue models, it dropped a PPV approach. As DiGiovanni remarked, "There's a fine line between creating a sustainable business and keeping the community happy and making sure those things are in direct connection with one another" (ibid.).

One of the few exceptions to the informal no-PPV rule in the world of gaming has been the annual BlizzCon fan convention focused on Blizzard's games. Though it had a partnership with DirectTV in 2008, it expanded in 2009 to include an online live stream and now reaches huge audiences.[24] The "virtual ticket" costs around $199, and the broadcast includes a live stream of developer panels, assorted events, and esports tournaments happening at the convention (as well as some in-game items). The esports component of the convention is usually also broadcast on a free live stream, and the 2017 online esports audience for the matches was reported to be more than eight hundred thousand worldwide.

Perhaps sensing some potential still to be leveraged in pay models, just as this book was being finalized Blizzard announced that viewers could, for $29.99 a season, access additional content for its popular *Overwatch* competitive league. Its Twitch "all-access" pass would give subscribers access to special in-game skins—unique Twitch emotes for use in the live chat—as well as the "*Overwatch* League Command Center." While some expressed disappointment that, despite the language, they couldn't control in-game match views, those with access would get additional camera angles to matches, behind-the-scenes shots, and assorted recorded content. As an added content package, it seemed to scattershot hit all the revenue buckets that organizations have been experimenting with. Whether or not it succeeds is yet to be seen.

Event revenue. Esports productions currently approach live events as a component of a media spectacle. Elaborate lights, staging, preproduced content, and even musical guests now make up part of the show. At its heart, it also relies on visually folding the audience into the broadcast, turning the cameras on the cheering crowd. Filling up sports stadiums and turning grand finals into weekend-long events has become the norm. These then get broadcast to viewers globally.

The size, scale, and polish of these tournaments have grown. While in the past events like the World Cyber Games drew decent-sized crowds, current tournaments operate at an even greater scale. The International, *Dota 2*'s premier season finale, held in Seattle's Key Arena, has had around seventeen thousand attendees for several years in a row. Tickets cost $99 for a six-day ticket. The *League of Legends* Championship finals in 2016, costing $47 to $71 for a daily ticket, gathered twenty thousand people in Los Angeles' Staples Center. ESL's 2017 Intel Extreme Masters event in Oakland, California, cost $34 for two days and garnered in-person attendance numbers as high as six thousand people daily. Being able to buy T-shirts or fan gear is a growing trend at these venues. Enthusiasts, keen to express their love of a team, game, or player this way, will spend money at venue pop-up shops (with revenue divided up among various stakeholders).

Live events are still very much a work in progress, and over the course of my research for this book, they did not yet make up a meaningful revenue generator for esports (indeed, they could at times lose money or barely break even). They are often held in sports arenas, which while creating a compelling visual spectacle for the camera, frequently carries a significant price tag and means lots of seats to fill. They can be incredibly uncomfortable for on-site participants given that events frequently run for a full weekend or more. They tend to be odd mixes of competition and expo, with game/PC demo stations located at various places throughout the venue. With the amount of down-time typically at esports events between matches along with the challenge of keeping tens of thousands of people entertained at an otherwise-sparse stadium, producers face a real challenge with big on-site events.

The mirroring of traditional sports spaces may prove to not be the best option for live audiences, despite producers being drawn to the visuals. In 2016, I attended the Boston Major, a *Dota 2* tournament produced by the Professional Gamers League that was held in the beautiful Wang Theater in Boston. The seats were comfortable, and the space offered a more intimate experience that both captured the fans' enthusiasm well and was much more audience friendly on-site. It was a welcome contrast to sitting in a massive sports arena. It will be fascinating to see if either the visuals that producers seem intent on chasing via large stadiums or revenue from them can be reconciled against the specific conditions of esports tournaments as generally multiday affairs that pose an endurance challenge for the audience.

Crowdfunding. Though the last handful of years have seen the rise of free-to-play models within gaming as well as the widespread growth of free UGC, this does not mean that gamers are unwilling to spend money on esports. Tournaments like the International have benefited tremendously from sales of Valve's Compendium and Battle Pass, digital packages that include everything from in-game items to a "wagering" system. The more that people buy, the more incentives are added for purchasers. For each sale, Valve gives a cut to the tournament prize pool (currently 25 percent). When this crowdfunded system began in 2013, Compendium sales contributed $2.8 million to the tournament pot. Just a year later, that figure had risen to $10.9 million, and it broke $23 million in 2017. It is critical to understand that the International is not just a major esports tournament but a major *media* event broadcast worldwide too. And rather than being a production primarily funded through commercials or ads, fandom is at the heart of its economics.

Tournaments like the International reveal the power of funding directly from gamers and fans who often want to express loyalty, support, and enthusiasm via their spending. For some, this means purchasing multiple copies.

This is yet another powerful way that games, and their formal competitions and broadcasts, get woven together with the passions, commitments, and affective work of fans. It is also an example of a circuit of engagement that feeds back on itself constantly; players get a game and play it avidly, their fandom is harnessed so that they not only purchase digital goods for themselves but those purchases also contribute to a growing player base and expanding media space (tournaments and broadcasts), which in turn fuel more energy back into the game, retaining players (and drawing new ones in), and the loop repeats.

While crowdfunding, both in gaming and out, has proven a powerful mechanism for consumers and supporters to directly bolster goods as well as activities that they are excited about, I have some pause about the extent to which a system can and should healthily rest on this model. One component of my concern lays in the ethics of monetizing fandom to this degree. Of course it is reasonable and indeed exciting to see fans be able to express their financial support for the things they love. There is without a doubt a particular sort of power, albeit narrow, in their ability to use their wallet to vote things up or down. And esports has historically rested on fans being incredibly dedicated in terms of giving money, time, and labor to sustaining the scene. This has been a way for enthusiasts to exert influence on how it operates—whether in terms of helping decide rule sets or tournament structures, bolstering particular games that they find valuable, or creating the overall culture. The power of fandom expressed economically is important, and should not simply be written off as exploitative or superficial. Compendium and Battle Pass purchases can be a way to show support not just for esports but for the pro players in that space too. Team and player loyalties, and the desire to help sustain them, can regularly be heard when people explain purchases. Purchasing can also help people feel that they are participating in the event in a way they might not otherwise.

Yet we would be remiss to not think about the ethics of monetization. While I would not want to pose a theory that imagines gamers are simply being duped—they are often insightful about the economics of fandom—I don't entirely want to let companies off the hook for the degree to which they trade on the affective engagements of their communities. Matt Demers, a writer who regularly covers esports, signals this issue a bit in his discussion of the Twitch Bits system, which allows people to cheer within chat via an in-system currency, of which Twitch takes a cut. He argues that "if Twitch is going to sell us something based on the altruism of fans wanting to support their community it is hard to ignore the elephant in the room of their cut, and how it clashes with the current standard of 'hit donation button, send money directly, they (or you choose to) deal with fees'" (Demers 2016). In much the same way that some variety streamers express concern about and will even shut down donation trains if they feel like they are getting out of control, organizations should think critically about the ways that they monetize fan emotions without full consideration of the labor involved. For instance, it is perhaps a bit imbalanced to give only a quarter of the proceeds of multimillion-dollar digital sales back to the actual professional gamers who are doing a significant amount of work engaging a broader community of players.

This ties into a second component of my concern, which is more structural in nature: Are these huge crowdfunded prize pools actually distorting or neglecting a competitive space that needs to sustain itself day in and day out? As esports reporter Ferguson Mitchell asserts in his analysis of *Dota 2*'s massive crowdfunded prize pool tied to the final, it actually undermined the long-term stability of the competitive community. He observes that "the scariest fact is simply how many teams build around the event," and this clustering (combined with a qualifier system) produces an all-or-nothing model in which only the topmost competitors have resources. Mitchell (2014a) maintains that in its current configuration, the "underclassmen"—those players not yet at the most elite level that make that final event—"are being trampled by an unrewarding and unforgiving format." Game scholar William Partin (2017) argues for the ways that the system has created "tremendous wealth disparity and income inequality among Dota 2 players." By contrast, the major fighting game tournament Evo announced that it would donate crowdfunded money that it received from the Twitch bit system (30 percent of the total that Twitch took in) directly to the players and casters to whom it was directed rather than pocketing it themselves as part of event revenue.

This experimentation with shifting prize pool generation directly to the consumers has extended to Valve also attempting to integrate crowdfunding mechanisms into how it pays show talent. Unlike the embrace of the Compendium and Battle Pass system by most of the player base, crowdfunding talent pay was met with pushback, most notably by some high-profile commentators. The International 2014 implemented a system that would allow people to get "signatures" attached to their digital goods for a fee—a percentage of which would go to the commentator. But some, such as James "2GD" Harding, expressed frustration that they weren't guaranteed any base pay to supplement this system.[25] For commentators such as Harding, who will often be on-site at an event from when the doors open to long into the night, and be on camera for tens of hours, this model was woefully inadequate. The issue, having been made public, was rectified, but for many it highlighted not only the limits of this model for funding events but also the lengths some companies will go to in order to offset their costs directly onto consumers.

Given the economic precariousness that so many pro players and talent face, these approaches strike me as unethical. The disparity between how much money major game developers are making off esports (whether through direct sales or indirectly as a form of PR) and what the actual professional players themselves make underscores worrying stratification in the industry. This argument could also be extended to talent like hosts, commentators, and even production teams. For decades now, people playing and working in the space have been willing to forego livable wages, not to mention long-term professional stability, due to their love of esports and commitment to wanting it to break through. Given the fast growth currently happening, more must be done to take care of the people working in the sector. Game companies profiting off esports have responsibility to contribute to the long-term economic health of players and other professionals in the scene, especially when revenue is built on a foundation of fandom.

Looking at the range of economic models currently being used in esports broadcasting, it is easy to see that it is a motley mix of approaches. Part of this originates from no one being entirely sure what will work over the long haul, while partly it is a result of the unstable division of labor and emerging forms of specialization among organizations. Third-party organizers who have been building the industry for nearly two decades are finding themselves with both more interest in what they do and new competition. Game developers and publishers, with few exceptions long relatively inactive in building the esports scene, are now often stepping into the mix. Platform developers are trying to stake their own claims in the space. Combined with profound shifts in media production and distribution more broadly, iterations, experiments, failures, and economic flux are likely to continue.

Constructing Audiences and Markets

An important thread woven throughout questions about revenue models are how audiences and markets are being imagined in the esports broadcasting world. In my conversations with people creating products and conceptualizing audiences, I see two consistent patterns. The first relates to advertising, and the second concerns internal models of who gamers are. There are always imagined audiences when companies are working out event details along with how it will be packaged, marketed, and sold. Even postevent "hype reels" are tied up with audience construction and deployed as sales devices for future events.

This pattern is not unique to esports (or live streaming more generally) but rather part of the way that content sits within a commercialized sphere. Media studies scholar Toby Miller (2010) notes that producers don't simply want to attract viewers but also want to "make audiences." Audiences are not a given empirical fact; they are actually constructed packagings—ways of describing, understanding, and bundling a mass of viewers. In the same way that individual stream communities articulate a vision of their audience, platforms, game developers/publishers, advertisers, sponsors, and any number of other economic actors build models of their audience. Those conceptualizations, in turn, get fed back into the system and work to (re)produce segmentation. Audience making is always ongoing work, but it is particularly important to consider now, at a time of tremendous growth in esports.

IMAGINED AUDIENCES AND ADVERTISING

When it comes to imagining audiences, the digital gaming industry continues to lag behind cultural trends and practices. Though developers have made strides in understanding that there are heterogeneous users for their products, much more still needs to be done. A major factor continues to be deep misunderstandings around how leisure and gender operate in people's daily lives. While cultural expectations around who plays games have changed quite a bit in the last fifteen years, esports is still playing catch up. Despite women's actual involvement and interest in competitive gaming, they continue to confront uphill battles to full participation. A rhetoric of meritocracy prevails amid serious ongoing structural and cultural barriers to entry as well as retention. Outdated ideas that women are not interested in direct competition, or more sociologically inflected issues around recruitment paths, the power of social networks, or outright harassment and sexism, are still prevalent.[26]

The belief that women are outside the core for esports has, unfortunately, also spread to audience construction and participation. Women are not seen as important stakeholders in terms of spectatorship, and by extension are sidelined from its economic underpinnings. Put simply, over and over again young men age eighteen to twenty-five are framed as *the* prized demographic for esports sponsors and advertisers; in turn, events and broadcasts are primarily constructed with them in mind.[27] They are "hailed" constantly in broadcasts in a variety of ways and become an imagined audience that ends up holding tremendous metainstitutional power.

Part of this stance comes from a longtime "truism" in advertising that sees young (white) men as valuable consumers unable to be reached via traditional paths. Advertisers are thus always on the watch for new ways to get their message out to this tough-to-reach market. Esports has, quite instrumentally, piggybacked on this panic by prominently building into its sales models the claim that it knows that market segment well and can reach it effectively. This is not by any stretch a hidden rhetoric. If you listen to any number of public interviews with high-profile esports executives and game developers with esports titles, this notion is clearly touted as a prime strength of their "product." This rhetoric about who the valued audience is represents a collision of survival pragmatism and ideologies of gender and race. Companies are desperate to find sponsors wherever they can and have not shied away from tapping into hackneyed verbiage.

Yet as we've seen in game studies research over the years, there is a gap between how industry actors conceive of their space and what is empirically evidenced. I certainly recall in the earliest days of massively multiplayer online game research how many of us had an abundance of data on the women playing as well as motivations that disrupted easy stories about "what women like," only to be consistently met with industry resistance. More often than not that pushback belied deeper assumptions about gender than actual user practices and experience. Indeed, if you had looked at qualitative work emerging early on in game studies, you would have clearly seen a cultural transformation in progress. Computer gaming was moving from an activity mostly taken up by young boys and men to a leisure activity also for women and across their life cycle.

Conversations in esports feel much the same. We see more and more women playing games like *League of Legends, Overwatch,* and other competitive titles, turning up to esports events, watching streams online, and developing fandom around games, players, and teams, only to be told by the industry that they are a negligible slice, anomalies, not the "core" demographic. Barriers to entry and retention are constantly reasserted despite women's expressed interest in competitive gaming. From the lack of hailing in stories, advertising, and visuals to outright harassment, women who try to enter esports in sustained ways face regular serious challenges.

Part of the ideological move within marketing and audience construction has been to render practices invisible, re-centering the imagined player. Given how much of the esports economy relies on sales—from advertising to deals with developers/publishers and other sponsors—there are huge incentives to construct a demographic profile of esports fans that can then be said to be captured and offered back to advertisers and sponsors. Traditional advertising, which fears it has lost the ability to reach young men, is now encountering esports companies (often in dire straits to stay afloat) confidently proclaiming that they have the prized demographic at the ready.

It's easy enough to see how this move starts out harmless. That demographic without a doubt makes up an important part of esports fandom, and it especially did in the earliest years. But the problems set in when it gets conceived of as the *unchanging and primary one*. As an empirical consideration mutates into an ideological one, other props (such as industry "reports" and repeated stereotypes) get raised to help perpetuate what has become an overly narrow understanding of the audience. As Miller (2010) illustrates with the example of the historic miscounting of Latino/a audiences, analytic errors can be rooted not only in poor methods but political, economic, and ideological frameworks too. Lotz (2014, 207) has also pointed out the ways that audience construction via measurement is tied up with advertising-supported media in particular as well as deployed as a way of "encouraging and discouraging various innovations during periods of industrial change."

The people esports sales teams are selling to—be they advertisers, sponsors, or game developers/publishers—often have audience models that tend toward a fairly conservative and outdated view of games as the domain of primarily young men. Pitching alternate productions and audience formulations simply doesn't get traction. The upshot is the continued same old story in which the imagined audience member is a young single man. This only helps reify that dominance of this demographic in everyone's minds. If you keep surrounding yourself with that model of participation, it's not surprising that you start thinking it *is* reality, which in turn limits how you might formulate more up-to-date possibilities. The cost of this decidedly unvirtuous circle has been several decades of inequitable access and participation opportunities for women and girls to digital playing fields, and that is now flowing over into audience construction.

As esports has risen in prominence as a media space with real economic stakes, a new actor has appeared on the scene: the analyst and their accompanying reports. This is not dissimilar from the massive industry around traditional media metrics and audience reporting. Usually replete with colorful graphics, and lots of hype and press releases, these reports have come to play a significant role in how the scene is developing. Unfortunately, retrograde ideas around gender and gaming regularly get bolstered by these quasi-research reports, which are not subject to peer review and utilize black boxed methodologies. They are often too expensive to be read and evaluated widely, so instead are used as "data" feeding back into the flawed cycle. Business developers, frequently with a model of use and audience already solidified in their minds, regularly turn to these reports not for meaningful research but instead to make cases for their own internal stakeholders.

The reliance on quantitative data in particular continues to produce profound misunderstandings of actual audiences, uptake, and use. Three major culprits are usually at work: surveys, algorithmically generated data and profiling, and "big data." It's important not just for researchers but also those in the industry who aren't analysts yet often rely on that work to understand the methodological limitations of each of these. So much of the industry in particular now claims to be "data driven," but stakeholders and executives often lack basic methodological social science training to evaluate the reports that they are utilizing. As Baym (2013) puts it in her excellent overview of measuring audiences and online metrics, "However magnificent it may seem to have so much data available and to be able to mobilize that material in different ways, the promises of big data are a mixture of real potential with uncritical faith in numbers and hype about what those numbers can explain."[28] With that in mind, let me say a couple words more about these methods.

Survey data can be tantalizing. They seem to offer big, confident, generalizable claims that are particularly easy to pull from for sales decks. With free online tools like SurveyMonkey or in-house "quick and dirty" surveys that are offered with some kind of token game perk for participation, it can seem almost dumb to *not* do a survey. But doing good survey work is hard and not cheap. Poorly worded questions and lousy sampling can be fatal blows to good data as well as subsequent analysis. And as television scholars noted decades ago, "watching television" is a more complex category than might appear at first glance, and quantitative measures often don't fully capture varying contexts along with nuanced behaviors and attitudes.[29] Morley argues, for example, that audience measurement has historically not been about quantifying viewing but instead simply capturing things such as if the TV is on. Such measurements have tended to assume that tuning into something indicates an affirmative desire to watch it (versus, say, a habit done when getting home from work). They have also been woefully unsociological in their orientation, imagining an individual actor making a singular choice versus social and contextual dependencies that shape what is on (Morley 1992).

Algorithmically generated data and profiling, and their companion of big data, represent the newest in the arsenal of "data-driven analytics" that are especially used in online spaces. They arise from an orientation that assumes most meaningful data can be automatically captured via platforms and various data sets (for example, frequent-buyer card tracking or purchasing data from credit card companies), and without needing sampling (there is no subset to consider when you think you have it all). There is often an unquestioning belief that all these data will offer clear patterns and trends. While profiling will often end up producing "personas" or types of users, big data will regularly be presented as if simply visualizing everything will offer obvious analysis and insights. I suspect most of us have encountered one of those evocative "network maps" at some point, with their threaded lines and words of varying font sizes seeming to indicate something meaningful. Or you've encountered demographic claims drawn from Google or an online analytics service.

This impulse is also not new, and it is tied to a much longer history within television audience measurement. Lotz does a good job showing how changes in distribution channels frequently upset traditional audience measurement techniques and how "engagement" has become a new currency in the postnetwork era. This chase after engagement, which is something more than simply watching but also includes demonstrating your participation as a viewer through things like sharing on social media, has become a rubric around which a number of platforms now offer metrics. Media critic Mark Andrejevic (2009c) discusses how the desire to track and quantify audiences, and thereby validate the efficacy of advertising, has grown with the use of various analytics.

There remain several serious and often-fatal challenges to these methods when trying to understand leisure, gaming, live streaming, and esports in particular. These data are produced with little consideration of multidevice use, shared accounts, non-signed-in use, everyday contexts, and how people *understand* and *give meaning* to their own actions. Usually sign-up processes do not actually collect data such as gender, much less data that can then be meaningfully linked across all behavior. Graphs that show big-bucket categories like "time watched" sidestep the fact that they actually can't capture watching; at best they can simply show how long something played on a screen. They can't capture the other people in the room who weren't signed in but were also watching and engaged. They can't count multiscreen or multitask context. Fundamentally, they capture only the coarsest of things, such as the number of calls made to the server to receive data.

Perhaps most pernicious, though, are the ways that big data and algorithmically generated systems are utilized in deeply conservative ways. I don't mean this in a political sense but rather a social scientific one. Such models often assume that you are a man or woman because you *do things identified as what men or women do*. This means, for example, that a woman who has leisure patterns or interests that "look like" a man's may, in fact, be miscategorized as a man according to the system. Data pulled from that system and sloppy analysis then feed back into lousy analytics that only reinforce stereotypes. Simply put, women who do "male" things look like just more men to the system (and vice versa). Only after a massive shift has occurred in the culture—typically one that bubbles up enough to redefine what a man or women can do without stigma—will this discrepancy get dealt with. In the meantime, counterexamples, innovators and trendsetters, and behaviors that simply don't fit dominant cultural models may be rendered invisible, irrelevant outliers, or wholly misunderstood.

One of the most significant problems with quantitative data in the domain of gender and leisure is that it is usually unable to capture fast-shifting changes in cultural patterns as well as preferences. And more often than not, these so-called data are captured in huge swaths with no rigorous interpretative work as a component of the analysis. While such approaches are meant to get at "actual behavior" and not claimed identities, in practice they lag too far behind what are really complex constellations of practices and how people understand themselves—engagements that shift far too quickly for quantitative models to usually account for. Some platforms have come to understand the ways that other variables may actually be more salient than gender. Netflix, dubbed by *Wired* as a "notoriously data-driven company," has, for instance, ditched gender as a variable in deciding which shows to invest in. Todd Yellin, Netflix's vice president of product innovation, has said, "There's a mountain of data that we have at our disposal.... That mountain is composed of two things. Garbage is 99 percent of that mountain. Gold is one percent.... Geography, age, and gender? We put that in the garbage heap" (quoted in Barrett 2016). While as a sociologist I would advocate for a bit more caution in a wholesale rejection of these variables, they must be carefully considered, weighted, and interpreted in specific domains and contexts. The problem lies in our often misattributing to gender what might otherwise be better understood through not just other variables but a specific intersection of them, of which gender may just be one.[30]

The issue of changing leisure patterns is tremendously important not only for researchers but also stakeholders who are keenly attuned to the rise and fall of markets. Capturing a known market or demographic is one thing; being ahead of your competitors can be a critical business advantage. Growth spots are frequently where people are at or want to be, but that haven't yet been saturated or leveraged by others. There are several noteworthy flavors of this: critical cultural moments and developing ones.

Big cultural shifts are usually unpredictable, although once upon us, can seem inevitable. Think, for example, about the mainstream changes that *World of Warcraft, Minecraft,* or *Pokemon Go* fostered. As someone who had previously done work on massively multilayer online games, I remember being amazed when this small slice of gaming became, for a time, a huge part of the popular culture with coverage reaching even mainstream outlets like the *New York Times. Minecraft* opened up UGC, as well as a practice of watching your favorite gamers on YouTube, to millions of kids. Most recently, *Pokemon Go* crystallized the powerful potential of alternate reality games—a genre that has existed in various forms for decades. All these practices and platforms previously existed before a particular title burst on the scene. All of them became mainstream cultural objects and activities that crossed gender lines, and became popular forms of leisure not strictly tied to any identity. They became transformational objects, bringing people into gaming but also shifting public conversations.

We've now seen within esports how the introduction of live streaming has opened up the audience for competitive gaming in significant ways. It has brought more mainstream attention in just a few years than decades of activity had. Time and again, I have heard from women (and, to be frank, men) about how they went from enjoying playing *League of Legends* or *Overwatch* with their friends or family to being amazed and excited about esports once they went to a Barcraft, their first live match, or even watched a tournament online. The rise and amplification of these massive events via live streaming—such as the International, Evo, League of Legends Championship Series, or Intel Extreme Masters—highlight how the long trajectory of a subculture can often burst through in unexpected, unanticipated ways. Models of audience, especially around gender, must be agile enough to handle these big cultural shifts.

EQUITY AND ETHICS

Beyond the unanticipated moments that shift behaviors, practices, and identities, there is the long game of cultural development. When conversations arise about the need to conduct surveys to see "how many women are actually into esports," I often ask how useful it would have been to query women fifty years ago about their interest in soccer or athletics more generally. If you had done that survey, you would have likely come away with a judgment of "nope, no big interest" and not pushed for any change. But that wouldn't have gotten you to an understanding of how audience and participation *develops*, and how to look for *potentials* and plant seeds for growth. This is not simply a market issue but also an ethical one.

In a US context, a profound social movement sustained through cultural and institutional interventions, including law and policy, has been fostering athleticism and sports participation among women and girls. The history of women in sports is unfortunately one in which many talented athletes were actively barred from competition, and just as devastatingly, women and girls were not even allowed the opportunity to engage in athleticism for fear it would cause them bodily harm or upset "feminine sensibilities." As recently as 1971, women were actively prohibited from, say, running in the Boston Marathon; dedicated athletes like Roberta "Bobbi" Gibbs and Katherine Switzer had to sneak onto the course or obfuscate their identity to participate. The prohibition against sports participation has long dovetailed with a desire to keep women out of public and democratic spheres. While there remain serious and deeply worrying regulations around gender and sports— witness, for example, the policing of bodies that the International Olympic Committee perpetuates with various "gender testing" or outright prohibition of women from certain sports as was the case in 2010 with women's ski jumping—tremendous progress has been made in the United States to bring women and girls into athletics, and by extension, the public sphere.

Early advocates ran "play days" where girls and women would try out sports in friendly, low-stakes environments. Various initiatives in communities and local institutions helped to seed ground for women's participation in physical play. A critical turn occurred though federal legislation in 1972, when the Title IX Act ensured that "no person in the United States shall, on the basis of sex, be excluded from participation in, be denied the benefits of, or be subjected to discrimination under any education program or activity receiving federal financial assistance" (TitleIX.info 2016). The law covers a range of domains from academic assessment to sexual harassment. It was also the lever through which sports was transformed.

An important part of what drove the adoption of Title IX and its continued defense has been the fundamental understanding that gender equity, even in leisure spaces, is a key human right, and fair access and support is central to a democratic society. While some tie the benefits of gender equity to increased leadership and teamwork skills, I want to make a much more basic case for why it matters. It's great if these arise as a side benefit, but sports, play, and games need not be in the service of instrumental aims. Access to leisure, and even its sometimes-professional transformation, is a human right. Being able to tap into a range of activities and subjectivities to develop as well as express our humanity and connection with others is due all. Even if it "serves no purpose," women and girls have just as much of a right to take pleasure in sports, competition, fandom, and spectatorship as anyone.[31]

As a *New York Times* article reviewing the law's forty-year impact states, "It's hard to exaggerate the far-reaching effect of Title IX on American society. The year before Title IX was enacted, there were about 310,000 girls and women in America playing high school and college sports; today, there are more than 3,373,000" ("Before and after Title IX" 2012). While there remains much to be done to support women's sports, the law has without a doubt opened up athletic participation to women and girls. Whether it is youth soccer teams, amateur marathons, any number of professional sports, or everyday exercise and just getting in those 10,000 steps, women's access to and desire for physical sporting activity has grown enormously.

Part of the power of Title IX was that it created a *legal framework that fostered structures* to support the exploration of activities one might not have otherwise known they would enjoy. As women and girls came to sports, it fostered legitimacy around their participating in not just physical activities but competition too. We are at a pivotal moment in esports where we must begin to take to heart not only the ethical call that legislation like Title IX prompts but also the larger imperative of equitable access as a fundamental human right. While this may sound hyperbolic to those who either continue to see esports as a strange niche of gaming or view leisure as frivolous, it does matter. The right to participate in esports—be it as a fan, player, or someone working in the industry—shouldn't be held to any lesser a standard than we do for traditional sports. If you would be aghast at the thought of the women and girls in your life being held back from engaging in physical activity and competition, you should stop to consider the trajectory that esports is on.

With live streaming, more and more game developers and esports companies are creating tournaments as well as grappling with whether they are going to import gender segregation from traditional sports. In my experience, many working in the space currently understand the power that esports has to upend retrograde formulations of skill and expertise, yet they often struggle with how to understand women's current marginalization in the scene, both as players and as potential audience. Faced with sponsors and advertisers who often turn to more traditional audience segmentation, even well-meaning insiders can end up reconstituting structures that they themselves take pause at. There are two critical threads to pick up in the face of this confusion—one around biological sex, and the other concerning sociocultural factors.

Esports industry professionals frequently remark on how digital game competition does not tap into physical differences. In this regard, they are hitting on the possibility of a truly radical disruption of traditional sports' long-standing problematic: the biology-as-destiny argument. Historically this model asserts that there is a fundamental reality situated around the "fact" that males and females are so physiologically different, the segmentation of athletics along these lines simply makes sense. Sometimes shorthanded as the "muscle gap," it is a framework for understanding human action along sex categorization and segregation. It underpins a notion that gender and sex is a simple binary. Esports participants often sense that this schema doesn't make sense within the space, though typically because they see esports as an activity that doesn't rely on traditional categories like strength. But this division of the world has been more broadly challenged by a number of scholars who have pointed out the ways that (sloppy) science gets deployed to reify this split and thus have contended that sex differences are regularly overstated.[32]

Sports scholars such as Mary Jo Kane have picked up on this critique and advocated for thinking about how a *continuum* is always at work within athletics—one that might help us fruitfully disrupt these reductionist models. She argues that a binary model is reproduced in a variety of ways, from rendering invisible women's participation in sports traditionally coded as male (such as rugby or ice hockey) to erasing the actual shaded gradation of physicality within and across sexes. Her example of marathons is a powerful one. She describes how we can literally see the "continuum of performance stretched out for miles along the road with women and men running simultaneously, interpreted randomly along the same course." Yet as she astutely notes, this visible complexity gets reduced down to men's and women's divisions, where "certain gender comparisons are highlighted while others are ignored altogether" (for instance, how women regularly beat men within the same race) (Kane 1995, 209). For Kane and others, there remains a fundamental ideological move in constructing sports as sex segregated, and one that erases the actual continuum along which athletic experience is inhabited.

As sports sociologists have long observed, however, it is gender, and not sex, that is a powerful category for understanding how athleticism functions in our society. By this I mean simply that it is not about the genitals one is born with but instead the gendered identity and body in a specific sociocultural context (woven through with race, class, sexuality, disability, religion, and nationality) that shapes athletic participation. And this is where the industry's intuitive understanding that a binary model doesn't hold real value might be fruitfully informed by thinking about equity in light of the social, cultural, and structural barriers to participation.

There are tremendous barriers to entry and retention for women in esports. Lack of access to competitive networks and informal learning, stigma and harassment, or even the lack of role models all highlight the social and structural factors along the way that often impede women's ability to advance in esports professionally. Scholars have also long pointed to the power of the media to render invisible or misrepresent women's engagement with sports. Sports media plays a powerful role in upholding the binary and segregation model. It offers limited coverage of women's sports despite audience interest (or potential), regularly focuses on women athletes sexuality or looks over skill and accomplishments, and constantly works to reproduce segregation and difference through visuals, language, and narrative framing.

As esports has become a media product, it too has become even more tied up in this reproduction of sports hegemony. While the scene has long grappled with its own varying forms of masculinity (geek and athletic) and how it has handled women, live streaming has upped the ante. Because of the reliance on traditional advertising and sponsorship within esports, hackneyed formulations of audience are increasingly coming into play. These have tended to be in terms of traditional audiences and market segmentation, which has, unfortunately, been consistently tied to chasing a young male market. Through its development as a media property, esports is formulating a public imagination of what it could and should be, who it is and isn't for, and who should and shouldn't be there. As we've seen from the history of traditional sports, an ethics of equity must be central to our understanding of this domain. Equitable access to and participation in esports—including being a spectator and valued audience member—is something not only game developers but also their allied media outlets must become attuned to.

FOSTERING NEW MARKETS AND AUDIENCES

Of course, many new companies, especially ones operating in niche areas or with tight margins, do not think about ethical imperatives or, even expansively, market development. They go for what they see as low-hanging fruit. In esports, this has meant "grab the guys we know for sure play our games and that advertisers want." I get it. Money is tight, labor is stretched thin, and things feel precarious. But it's also a head-scratcher when those same folks—ones who have ambitions to see massive shifts in sports and media driven by dreams where esports will rise to prominence, if not dominance—simultaneously do not carve out space in their business models to think about not just the future but, to put it coarsely, what money may be left on the table *right now*.

This attention to broader audiences is something that traditional sports have had to face after decades of serious neglect. A *Bloomberg* piece reported after a survey on football audiences that

> for the NFL to grow, it has to court women, its fastest-growing fan demographic. No matter how you measure it, female viewership has grown much faster than male viewership in the past several years. Conventional wisdom suggests that every man who could be a football fan already is. The NFL has squeezed everything it can from that segment of the population. There's still potential to convert more women into full-time fans, and that's where the league's revenue growth must come from. (Chemi 2014)[33]

Major sports leagues have, albeit with some missteps, begun to recognize that women make up an important part of their audience demographic and are starting to attend to them.[34] Reports place women as at least 30 percent of regular season audiences, and a 2015 Gallup poll showed 51 percent of women identifying as sports fans (Dosh 2016; Jones 2015). They are also engaging their fandom via fantasy sports and social media—both signals of what marketers call the coveted "engagement" metric.[35]

Beyond current attention to women in traditional sports, I would argue that there are other important financial angles that must be factored into how we understand audience value. Though they continue to struggle to attain wage parity, women do control a significant share of household spending and are a key economic actor. At a moment when young people in the United States are increasingly overburdened with student loan debt, and under- and unemployment across both genders continues to be a persistent issue, companies should tread carefully on writing off entire market segments.[36] In fact even when employed, men earn a lower median income than in the past (Thompson 2015).[37] When you look at the economic landscape now versus fifty years ago, it is clear that the old models that imagine high-earning white men as key consumers are woefully out of tune with current realities. Advertising models appear to be seriously behind actual practices, engagements, and, frankly, economics.

Rather than rely on outdated notions of an advertising industry behind the curve, I'd assert that developing the audience of women for esports is much easier than it was for bringing them into soccer or any other number of traditional sports where the very notion of physical engagement had to be evangelized. In the case of gaming, we have women already playing all kinds of titles and integrating it into their everyday leisure practices at growing rates. It's also the case that we now have decades of solid data to show how they are engaged players, and importantly, work that demonstrates that things often attributed to gender are actually about being new to gaming or a genre (Yee 2008). Women are also attendees at ComicCon, AnimeFest, PAX, and any number of fan gatherings, thus revealing their interest in participating in live events.

There has also been the evolution of a new generation of women for whom owning a laptop or PC that they game on, Nintendo DS, game console, or even iPad they use for games is simply normal. Devices themselves can be gendered, and as gaming technologies have become embedded in everyday gadgets, the possibility that women and girls take it up becomes all that much easier. Gendered leisure choices are not primarily driven by a deep essential psychological or biological orientation; there is a complex constellation of sociological and structural factors at work. As these shift, internal ideas about what might feel legitimate for a person to enjoy, what is reasonable for "someone like them" to do, also evolves.[38]

Finally, and crucially for esports, women and girls now have a history of engaging in sports and identifying as athletes, and have come to thrive in competitive spaces. Old-fashioned notions that women don't like competition (direct or otherwise), shy away from tough physical and mental challenges, and don't want to push themselves to be the best, to be a champion, simply no longer hold up. We now not only have the amazing history of groundbreakers like Billie Jean King or Switzer but several generations of women who have come after them as well, inspired by their accomplishments and pushing women's sports more. Athletes like Serena Williams, Abby Wambach, and even the young Mo'ne Davis are powerful figures. Alongside them all, we have the tremendous growth of women who are fans and spectators of sports of all kinds. It is not just that women and girls are playing but they also enjoy watching.

These are critical factors for esports and audience construction because they are about how forms of leisure come to be accepted as a part of gender identities, preferences, and possibilities that weren't before. It is stunning that an industry so willing to push the frontier with new ideas about what might count as sport would rely on outdated models of gender. Perhaps what is most ironic about esports' continued unwillingness to question its own assumptions about gender, audience, and participation is that traditional sports, a waypoint that it constantly uses, itself had to start wrangling with exactly these issues decades ago. Traditional sports—in part driven by a crisis in audience growth—has begun to face up to the reality that women are an important part of their space. Sometimes this is as players, but even more often it is as spectators. While some of us continue to press for interventions in esports and gender because we are motivated by the data we see along with the ethics of access to play, I continue to strongly encourage those stakeholders who may not feel a principled pull to recognize that the data are *also* in service of market expansion.

Growth, Competition, and Consolidation

The developments I've described in this chapter should signal that while companies, organizations, and players have greatly harnessed the potential presented by live streaming, significant challenges remain. Although the next chapter will focus on some of the regulatory issues arising within live streaming, in the remainder of this one I will take a closer look at how competition, licensing, and oversaturation are shaping the esports broadcasting space.

INTERINDUSTRY COMPETITION

In my conversations with producers over the years, I have often asked them at some point what worries them the most. One, hitting on something that I heard repeatedly, put it quite simply: "Competition in the space keeps me up at night. Trying to forward our company and make it a viable business keeps me up at night." While enthusiasts and third-party companies native to the scene, and often operating without outside influence, dominated esports broadcasting in the earlier years, they now face serious competition on a variety of fronts.

One of the most significant changes in the industry over the last several years has been the profound shift in developer interest and engagement in the space. The history of esports has been one in which the actual game developers (with a few exceptions like Blizzard) pretty much took a hands-off approach. With the advent of live streaming, a scene that was previously rooted in deep fan communities became accessible much more broadly, and as it began to garner larger and larger audiences, game developers in turn started to embrace esports. This has meant not only thinking about designing titles with suitable "esports elements" into their game but also seeing tournaments and broadcast opportunities of interest. Companies like Riot and its *League of Legends* title epitomize the absorption of previously third-party esports business activities—from tournament organization to media production—into a development studio. Riot runs its own worldwide league for its game, and handles event and media production in-house, utilizing crews with experience in traditional sports as well as gaming. Activision Blizzard, though it has a long history of working with third-party esports companies for its competitive gaming, purchased MLG in a move to own part of the vertical.

Such developments do not go unnoticed within esports broadcasting. As one producer put it to me, the vulnerability of the middle layer of the industry gets accentuated as game developers and publishers start saying, "Hey, we can do this in-house. We don't have to hire you." This extends to not only backstage production labor but also onstage talent that may have been nurtured outside a developer-driven system. A *Los Angeles Times* article on ESL briefly touched on this shift, writing,

> Industry experts fear that game makers could cripple ESL by bringing eSports [*sic*] projects in-house. ESL's hedge is dedicating 15 employees to developing fan bases for smaller, newer games. Executives also argue that publishers—or new entrants—would need a long time to match ESL's skills and efficiencies. ESL also is busy branching into related businesses. It's looking to spearhead drug testing, betting regulations, stat-keeping and other industrywide standards. (Dave 2016)

While these are certainly savvy moves, and ESL being purchased by the large media outlet MTG helps anchor it in a broader media ecology, as esports has become more interesting to developers and publishers, it is unsurprising that they would make moves to own that part of the industry when possible.

And while esports has certainly grown over the last few years, it is still an industry in which companies are competing for clients. While some of the biggest developers have turned toward in-house management of their scenes or to using traditional media production companies, developers and other organizations that want to run tournaments or leverage the enthusiasm for esports will still look to specialized third-party esports companies. Those companies then themselves rely on broadcasting platforms to provide distribution. But what happens when a distributor starts to make moves into the event and production space?

This is exactly what has occurred as Twitch has begun to build out its own esports team, which ends up at times competing with organizations like ESL.[39] Although tending to remain behind the scenes, this has been one of the most important industry collisions in this early period of live streaming growth. In the same way that third-party organizers have had to sort out where they could viably sit in the esports industry, platforms such as Twitch are constantly on the watch for emerging business opportunities beyond merely being a distribution platform. It holds a special, and in fact powerful, position in owning both the broadcast mechanism and possibilities for content production. While this is not unusual in traditional media spaces, it is unique within gaming. Though Twitch continues to primarily be a platform for broadcasting, it has extended its business into other domains, resulting in some skirmishes and tensions.

While companies such as ESL have a long history of being a key organization in producing esports content, it does not itself own a broadcast platform (though Modern Times Group [MTG], a big media company in Sweden that purchased a majority stake in it in 2015, does). This has meant that it has sought and indeed needed to maintain a good working relationship with Twitch as a core broadcast provider. It regularly partners with Twitch for events, but has also had to navigate competing via RFP bids and sales.[40]

Other companies, like MLG or the now-defunct broadcasting platform Azubu, faced their own unique challenges with the rise of Twitch. Each went head-to-head with it, trying to consolidate esports broadcasts on their respective platforms. Through exclusivity deals (sometimes with streamers, other times with teams and leagues) and attempting to provide better revenue sharing, both platforms tried to position themselves as *the* unique place for competitive gaming. For a brief moment it looked like, perhaps, there might be real broadcasting competition.

But constant issues around quality and audience sizes have plagued these attempts. Indeed, professional gamer and streamer Matthew "NaDeSHoT" Haag, who made the jump from Twitch to MLG's broadcasting service in 2013 (and encouraged many other of his fellow *Call of Duty* players to do so), reflected on the toll that this move took a year after saying, "Honestly, my biggest regret is leaving Twitch TV to go stream for another platform" (quoted in Hernandez 2015). He went on to note in a question-and-answer video how he saw the platform move as causing a serious disruption in the growth of the *Call of Duty* scene. The viewers, he observed, simply didn't follow.

I saw this dynamic play out firsthand one night in 2014 while watching another popular *Call of Duty* streamer, deathlyiam, broadcast his final night on Twitch. He, like many others, was moving to MLG. It wasn't an entirely voluntary move. He'd been caught between Twitch and MLG vying to own the esports broadcasting space for partnered streamers who would pull in big audience numbers, and was forced to choose between the platforms. Partnership contracts often contain exclusivity clauses, and Twitch was enforcing its version. As deathlyiam's bot explained in chat to viewers, "As of Monday I will no longer be partnered on Twitch due to a conflicting partnership on MLG. Since I livestream full-time, in order to compensate for the lack of revenue, I will solely be streaming on MLG. http://www.mlg.tv /deathlyiam." As a timer counted down and with nearly a thousand people watching, he got emotional, talking about his community along with his time on Twitch. With three minutes to go in his final Twitch broadcast, he went offscreen, put on a music video, and typed to his viewers, "I honestly love the shit out of you guys. Being forced to choose fucking sucked. I've never been happier of what I've accomplished." MLG.tv turned out to not be the "Twitch killer" some thought it might, and deathlyiam and NaDeSHoT as well as many others ended up back on the service. The platform remained committed to enforcing its exclusivity deals.

When Google launched its own competing site for live streaming in 2015, YouTube Gaming, a new wave of articles began discussing these clauses in contracts. Though it didn't start as a strong competitor, YouTube's dominance in hosting recording game video, and being the platform that innovated alternative modes of production and distribution, continues to make it a site with real potential to give Twitch a run for its money if it improves functionality and can get buy-in from creators who will help shape it. It has, like Facebook, brought on a former professional esports player, Ryan "Fwiz" Wyatt (who also did stints at MLG and Machinima), to serve as global head of gaming for the site.

Amid these forms of competition, I have been surprised by the frequency with which I heard professionals identify the ongoing work of amateurs and grassroots organizations as also posing a real risk. One side of this is tied to the number of people who really want to work in esports and will do so cheaply to get a foot in the door. As one producer told me, "There's always going to be a guy who could say, 'Hey, just fly me out to your event. I'll do it for free.'" This move has become as viable as it has given how accessible and affordable live stream platforms now are.

Professionals in the industry regularly reflected on how they are working to distinguish what they do from any amateur who sets up a camera and streams an event. Given a big part of what drives live streaming is its accessibility, there is an interesting tension at work between the draw of large spectacle events and everyday "bedroom" broadcasts that still pull in huge audiences. One producer described it this way:

> So for all the guys like the real big dogs on the playing field like MLG and DreamHack and ESL, we obviously distinguish ourselves through our production value. But our actual, the value proposition that we offer to your average esports fan is not hugely different. This is sort of a problem I've been discussing for a while; fundamentally we are all offering the same product. Say 80 percent of our show is in game. So OK, yeah, we have a different set of graphics. A kid at home who's very talented in Photoshop can make a great set of graphics. So for the live streamers, you can suddenly become Kripp or one of these guys from your bedroom, and pull in bigger numbers than something that might have cost a hundred thousand dollars in investment.

Esports companies work hard to prove their value to developers. As one producer put it, "Our product offering is not just we're going to showcase your event, but it's producing your event, you get high-quality production. So we learn to differentiate ourselves against the guy who will undercut us." Now, however, they are vulnerable because the lowered costs of broadcasting have allowed new competitors into the market—ones that, desperate to be a part what they see as an exciting esports industry, can now pitch at lower rates. As the above person noted, while 80 percent of an esports broadcast might be in game, it is critical for the more established companies to boost the remaining 20 percent if they are to survive.

TRADITIONAL AND SOCIAL MEDIA COMPETITION

One of the most interesting turns in esports and live streaming has been the way that both traditional media companies and non-game-focused platform developers have also entered the space. In July 2015, news officially broke that MTG had purchased a majority stake (74 percent for €78 million) in Turtle Entertainment GmbH, the holding company for ESL and its international subsidiaries. Though rumored since May, in a scene where speculation often travels across back-channeled Skype conversations, Slack and Discord channels, and specialist websites, the announcement still came as resounding news, and was covered and discussed widely within the community as well as in some mainstream media like *Forbes*.

Many of those who'd never heard of MTG before probably had some familiarity, at least among Europeans, with its media properties such as the extensive Viasat line of cable channels, TV3 network, or one of its radio stations. While MTG had a bit of experience in the esports world through its Viagame channel (which provided online esports content) and tournaments like the Viagame House Cup, most of the coverage specifically called out the importance of a *traditional* media company finally investing seriously in competitive gaming. As Leslie (2015a) described it in a news article, "Make no mistake, this is a huge deal for esports. It's one of the first times a traditional media organisation [*sic*] has made a major investment in esports. With MTG's experience and investment combining with ESL's reach and influence within the industry, this could be a very powerful partnership indeed."

Simultaneously, articles—in an almost-reassuring tone—mentioned that the founders and team that had built ESL would not be going anywhere, that this was an investment and not simply a takeover. Most pieces had substantial quotes from Ralf Reichert, CEO and founder, who tended to frame the deal in terms of the amplification and distribution that esports would get via MTG's extensive infrastructure. Despite my hearing over and over again in the field how people's attention was shifting *from* television, Turtle's press release underscored that partnering with a media company that owns television stations "allows us to reach an even wider audience and explore new opportunities. We will continue to work with our longstanding and awesome online partners but can now also explore avenues and channels which were previously difficult to get into" (quoted in Schiefer 2015).

MTG's interest in esports did not stop with its majority purchase of Turtle. In November 2015, it was announced (again after rumors) that MTG had purchased 100 percent of DreamHack (for SEK 244 million). Begun in 1994 as a hobbyist LAN party in Sweden, the event had since grown into a mega experience dubbed the "world's largest computer festival" and boasted a growing collection of esports tournaments.[41] No longer just tied to Sweden, DreamHack had started taking its show on the road and, combined with live streaming, had become an international media property. In contrast with the excitement that I sensed in conversation and coverage of the ESL purchase, the DreamHack sale seemed to tip the scales for many. It is one thing when an esports company gets recognized by a big-time media player and receives financial backing, but to many it is another thing entirely when that conglomerate buys up two major esports companies.

While MTG was purchasing esports organizations, other traditional entertainment companies like the William Morris Endeavor–International Management Group (WME/WME-IMG) worked on esports from alternate angles: player talent and media initiatives.[42] In January 2015, WME-IMG acquired Global eSports Management (cofounded in 2013 by Tobias Sherman and Min-Sik Ko), which represented players like Carlos "ocelote" Rodriguez and other talent such as commentator Mykles. Unlike the ESL and DreamHack sales, which the esports press primarily reported, Global eSports Management's acquisition extended to major entertainment industry news outlets like *Variety* and the *Hollywood Reporter*.

Although early reports framed the purchase in general terms (situating esports as a growing sector of entertainment), it was in September of that year that the big payoff news hit. It was announced that WME-IMG would be partnering with Turner Broadcasting to form a new series, ELEAGUE, which would be shown on TBS, a cable and satellite channel touted as reaching ninety million US homes (Spangler 2015). A *Variety* article noted that "the parties cut a deal with game publisher Valve to feature its 'Counter-Strike: Global Offensive'" (*CSGO*) game, and Valve hired Christina Alejandre, who had previously worked not only at Viacom but also within the game and esports industry, to be its vice president and general manager. Interestingly, Lenny Daniels, president of Turner Sports, was reported to have said of the possibility of partnering with an existing league that "'it just didn't make any sense' given the resources of each [Turner and WME/IMG] company" (quoted in ibid.).

Like many, I was curious to see how the first big sustained televised esports program since the failed CGS would fare.[43] While there have been some criticisms within the esports community along the way, the program has overall generated a lot of positive responses. I had noticed over the course of the first season that one longtime esports organizer was publicly praising the efforts. This surprised me a bit given how in other instances, they'd been fairly sharp in their judgment that being on television was not a goal for the industry anymore. I wondered how they reconciled this and reached out to them to follow up. They replied,

> My praise of ELEAGUE is genuine, for it really does make a good product out of the league, but the only thing that would make me excited over

the prospect of [our tournament] on television is the money we would get
from the broadcast rights that we could use to improve [the tournament].
Think of it this way. TBS has most of the content on Twitch, not on its
[cable] channel. If it so happens that a random person loves the content
on TBS, they will migrate to Twitch. And stay there. ELEAGUE is currently a tool to force some millennials to watch a Friday night broadcast
on TV, but at the same time it's a tool to funnel a TV audience onto
Twitch. There's one clear winner here. It's not TBS.

This was a fascinating way of thinking about the relationship between
traditional cable TV and live streaming. Indeed at the ELEAGUE CSGO
Major held in Boston in 2018, the online stream of the tournament broke
records by boasting of over one million concurrent viewers during the final
match while going *unbroadcast* on TBS. Whether or not this analysis bears
out in the long term, it does present a more complex model for how television might work—as a path of entry into *online* content. This is a decisive
upturning of how media flows have been generally conceived of thus far.

Not only traditional media were starting to get into the esports broadcasting game; so were social media platforms. In May 2016, Activision Blizzard
(which had acquired the majority of MLG's assets for a reported $46 million
in January of that year) and Facebook announced that they would begin live
broadcasting esports tournaments on the site. Starting with a *Call of Duty*
and *Dota 2* event at the X-Games Austin, and expanded into other titles, this
has become an interesting example of a social media platform getting in on
the growth of game broadcasting.

Notable to this venture have been people hired along the way on both
the Activision Blizzard and Facebook sides. In October 2015, Steve Bornstein, who had previously been president of ABC as well as CEO of both
ESPN and the NFL Network, was hired to head up Activision Blizzard's new
esports division. The same piece that reported this noted that Mike Sepso,
cofounder and vice president for MLG, was also hired for the team.[44] And
just a month after the Activision Blizzard / Facebook announcement, it was
reported that Facebook was hiring former *League of Legends* professional
gamer Stephen "Snoopeh" Ellis as a strategic partnerships manager.

Untangling which property was driving the partnership is tricky. Facebook pitching itself as a place where game developers should want to be
(and in turn making the platform even more valuable in users' lives) is one
important angle. As one article observed, "Using the massive reach of its
social network, Facebook and Ellis could lure in more game studios to

build integrations with Live that give Facebook content while promoting the studio's titles. When people watch an esports star playing a game, they want to buy it. Combined with the platform's biographical data, it could be a powerful place for game companies to advertise" (Constine 2016b). On the flip side, game developers have become keenly aware in the last few years of the economic power of esports fandom. Bornstein, reflecting on the thirteen billion hours that players dedicated to Blizzard games in 2014, commented that it "dwarfs the engagement that fans spend on all other sports," and added, "I believe eSports [sic] will rival the biggest traditional sports leagues in terms of future opportunities, and between advertising, ticket sales, licensing, sponsorships and merchandising, there are tremendous growth areas for this nascent industry" (quoted Spangler 2015).

Of course, bringing live streaming to Facebook is not just a simple matter of opening a video pipeline. As I've discussed throughout this book, thus far there has been much more to successful live stream productions than merely broadcasting game footage. One article captured this by writing, "Facebook will have to play catchup to Twitch, which has spent years honing its player-picture-in-game-footage-picture video streaming and its live chat. The dedicated interface, ad and subscription monetization options for video creators, and thriving community of gamers will be tough to match" (Constine 2016a). Esports viewers, having grown used to consuming content through Twitch, are coming to the experience with a set of expectations that any competitor platform will have to navigate and address.

Outside the esports domain, Facebook has had several powerful moments of live streaming, particularly around police abuse, thereby bumping the functionality into public consciousness. The reach of the platform is huge, and, as we've seen, it can provide powerful opportunities for video distribution. Whether it can be flexible enough to accommodate established tastes in the medium remains a crucial issue. Perhaps just as important to consider when thinking about Facebook entering into live streaming might be that the conventions we've seen arise on Twitch are, in fact, the anomalous moment— one tied to a history of a new, fairly open platform and a genre that had not yet stabilized. Aesthetics, forms of interaction, and other components are deeply linked to the architecture of a service, and whether or not they drive that choice, or will be driven by it, is yet to be seen. While the kind of innovation and experimentation that Twitch does such a good job supporting is critical to variety streaming, if esports goes more the way of traditional sports broadcasting, Facebook's ability to offer a pretty simple pipeline out to millions of users may be all that is really needed to upset the distribution balance.

LICENSING AND RIGHTS

Deeply interwoven into the rising competition issue is the role that licensing and rights are coming to play in the broadcast space. The earliest days of televised sports are again instructive here. While Arledge is regularly heralded for innovating production, less often remarked on is how central his ability to secure the right to broadcast was for modern sports. In this regard, he was, while highly respected, not especially beloved:

> The TV production of sports is a two-sided enterprise: physical production and the acquisition of rights. Arledge's gaudy genius for the former has been lavishly attested to by virtually everyone in the medium (his awards include 17 Emmys and the grand prize at the Cannes Film Festival), but his colleagues are somewhat less generous in their assessment of his performance at the conference table. "When it comes to acquiring rights" says a top executive at one of the other networks, "the man is totally unscrupulous. A jackal. He'd rip my heart out for a shot at the world series." A former associate claims that "beneath his Howdy Doody face lurks one of the most ruthless, opportunistic guys in the business." Arledge answers such criticism blandly. "If you don't have the rights, you can't do the show." (quoted in "Playboy Interview" 1976, 64)

Whereas Arledge had to negotiate with entities like the NFL, esports companies face game developers. Despite interesting skirmishes over the issue (which I'll discuss further in chapter 5), the game as an intellectual property remains the deciding rubric for understanding who controls the rights, licensing, and, increasingly, franchising around it.

As we move into a much more institutionalized form of esports media broadcasting, the fight over rights and exclusivity is growing. Whereas in the past game developers often just let people put on tournaments and distribute media for free or low cost, they have increasingly come to see their games as an asset to be leveraged, bargained with, and sold. This is not all that great a leap given how vigorously companies have long sought to protect their games as intellectual property, but it does represent a new node of ownership claims. And as game developers come to see their games as tied to broadcasting models as well as recognize the ways that leagues and teams can be deployed to build audiences *through* those broadcasts, their reach of ownership and governance has extended. As esports journalist Leonard Langenscheidt (2017) writes, "Publishers do profit from a stable scene and well-branded teams, as popular teams ultimately draw more fans and create rich storylines of rivalries and upsets. In light of this, publishers are understanding the value of franchised leagues and tournaments with regulated revenue splits and an established group of team owners." These are increasingly deeply connected to media broadcast.

Both Riot and Blizzard have been some of the most active in formally developing a model that interweaves media and league structures. From Blizzard offering franchise opportunities for *Overwatch* (with a rumored minimum price tag of $20 million per team) or Riot's close management of team ownership with its top-end Champions League, developers are increasingly coming to see the ways that these structures and media broadcast are tied together as well as worth attention and, increasingly, regulation. This has meant that both independent leagues and teams are facing entirely new terrain where domains that they were previously able to exist in without much developer input have become a business with increasing regulation and costs.[45]

Some team owners have been especially vocal about feeling caught in economic systems in which they are incurring the cost and facing the real risk while not financially benefiting equitably. In 2016, news broke that eighteen teams—including prominent ones such as Cloud9, Dignitas, CLG, Team Liquid, SoloMid, and Fnatic—had sent a joint letter to Riot detailing a number of concerns about the league that included both regulatory and economic issues (Nairn 2016). Financial matters dominated the leaked draft letter, and revenue sharing across a number of domains, from merchandise to digital items, was of key concern. Given the ways that promotional activities are deeply tied to audiences and visibility, the media context around esports is certainly at work implicitly in these sales. The handling of sponsorship and media revenue sharing was pushed off with both Riot and the owners agreeing that the issue wouldn't be pressed again until 2018.

This is perhaps a mistake given how fast media rights are being structured and staked out in esports, and how much they are getting valued at. Setting up a league or owning a team is no longer simply about competitive gaming but instead about creating a media product. A number of traditional sports teams and owners, including the Philadelphia 76ers, Manchester United, and Robert Kraft, owner of the New England Patriots, have expressed a newfound interest in esports. It will be intriguing to see if those coming from traditional sports bring with them some of the models and negotiation tactics we see there.

Of course, amid all these companies wrangling in the space are players who currently sit at the bottom of an increasingly industrialized model. While a handful of individual pros may fare well and gain some long-term stability, their precariousness is often not discussed publicly, and yet it is quite acute. Their churn rate combined with a general lack of legal representation along with, frequently, the desire to play at any cost sets players up to be on the lowest rung of the ladder in the future esports media economy. Player contracts increasingly detail requirements for broadcasting and indeed require signing over their rights to publicity. Few players, aside from those at the top of the "food chain" with negotiating power and/or excellent legal representation, are *meaningfully* given a stake in media rights and revenue.

OVERSATURATION GAME CHURN

Amid tremendous growth there remain persistent concerns by insiders about overly crowded tournament schedules causing even more broadcast competition. The ultimate life span of any game is also something that gets mulled over. While it appears that most fans have genre/title preferences, there nonetheless remains the potential for big scheduling problems. Imagine the NBA Finals and Super Bowl taking place on the same day; even if it may not be the exact same audience, the advertising collision alone would be impressive. We've yet to have that happen within esports, but as one producer cautioned, it's a real possibility:

> But also remember that, you know, it's not just *League of Legends*, it's also *StarCraft*, it's also games like *Call of Duty*. And at which point it's going to be a major clash like OK, we got both of these leagues doing an event the same weekend and it's going to boil down to a lot of factors, you know, prize money, loyalty. If it's a team sponsorship, they may send all their players to specifically one despite what their players think. But I think for now, the leagues, even like small tournaments, like small local tournaments and stuff, everyone's being very careful to try and not interfere.

While most organizers attempt to be watchful of these potential scheduling collisions, as the competition for audiences grows and more titles expand into offering formal tournaments, it will become more and more difficult.

Beyond scheduling are the ways that games are always at risk of losing player's interest. While some titles have had tremendous staying power, questions about their longevity and what new offering might come on the scene to sweep everyone's attention are always present. As one person put it, "The games could get stale. Nobody would want to watch [them] anymore." The current esports field offers a range of ways it can shake out. *CounterStrike* is a great example of a game that has supported nearly two decades of play. First released in 1999, it has undergone various iterations over the years and remains a popular competitive title. *League of Legends*, by contrast, quickly rose over a handful of years to become a prime illustration of a new title coming onto esports and taking it by storm. And *StarCraft*, a game that was a foundational esports title for many years, has faded substantially. The success of an esports game is deeply tied not only to its intrinsic properties with regard to skill and expertise thresholds but to the larger audience of players it thrives in. As gamers' tastes ebb and flow, so to do the fates of titles. And in a world filled with live streaming, this also quickly becomes a media broadcast issue. While there is a circuit that flows back and forth from everyday gaming to esports fandom, it is a fragile one. For companies, whether they are esports or traditional media, to invest millions of dollars in a broadcast future for any single game is a bold gambit.

5

Regulating the Networked Broadcasting Frontier

In early February 2015, stories started appearing about a Twitch channel named SpectateFaker being shut down by a DMCA claim originating from a competing esports live streaming site, Azubu. The channel had allowed Twitch viewers to watch the famous professional Korean *League of Legends* player Lee "Faker" Sang-hyeok's solo queue games whenever they were happening and without him initiating the stream (see figure 5.1). The channel wasn't a rebroadcast of anything from Azubu but instead leveraged the website OP.gg's ingenious use of the game's internal spectator mode. Utilizing a creative chain of technology, the SpectateFaker channel automatically launched whenever Faker was playing these types of games and broadcast directly to viewers via Twitch.

Azubu, which had entered into an exclusive broadcast agreement with the Korea Esports Association along with a number of Korean teams and players including Faker and his team SK Telecom T1 just six months prior, clearly got nervous. A clever fan utilizing a competing platform was now challenging that agreement, which Azubu had touted as "historic."

The Twitch channel owner who administered the broadcasts, a user going by the name StarLordLucian, posted on the *League of Legends* subreddit that he felt Azubu had made a "false claim" and he was going to fight it. He also sought advice, asking what he should do and if "there [was] anyone out there with 'Powers' like Azubu who could clear this up

OFFLINE

SPECTATE FAKER

This is an automated Livestream ready to go Live 24/7 for whenever Faker plays.

There are currently problems with OP.GG so a few games may be missed, but I'm working with the programmer of the stream to fix them ASAP

Follow to be notified for the next game! More info below the stream.

DISCLAIMER: This is not an official stream. This stream does not represent any players in the game or their likeness. This stream uses files in the public domain to spectate games. The content broadcasted on this stream is public domain which can be accessed by anyone on the website www.op.gg

FIGURE 5.1. Screenshot of the SpectateFaker channel in offline mode, 2015.

and get the channel back?" He noted that he was not making any money off the Twitch stream and was "running the stream 100% for fun" (Star-LordLucian 2015a). The thread reached over twelve hundred comments with people weighing in, including everything from asking for information about how the system worked to offering musings on intellectual property and ethics. That initial post was followed by nine updates from StarLordLucian as he began reaching out to Azubu, Riot, and Twitch to address the situation.

Over the course of the updates, you can see him trying to process the information that he is getting, especially the responses from Riot. The company initially emailed him to say, "If you are going to stream another player's games, it makes sense to reach out to that player first (in this case Faker) and get their permission. It's simply the right thing to do." While he at first expressed satisfaction with Riot's email answer, commenting that it was good to know its take on things, his next update reflected that he was unclear about what underlying principle was actually operating in its response. He felt that Riot didn't address head-on the DMCA claim or the intellectual property issues that were at stake, and instead focused more on how the player might feel not realizing that they were being broadcast (ibid.). In a fairly stunning move, amid it all, Mark "Tryndramere" Merrill (2015a), the president of Riot, posted a comment on the thread with a relatively biting reply:

You are rationalizing and trying to justify the fact that you have singled out a player against their will and broadcasting their games in a way that he can do nothing about. That reeks of harassment and bullying—Azubu vs Twitch is irrelevant in my view. If you can't see how this potentially harms Faker and/or anyone else in this situation, then that is more reinforcement that we need to take the appropriate action to protect players from this type of unique situation.

Merrill's response, strongly personal in tone and seemingly offside a principled consideration of a complex intellectual property issue, fueled even more heated debate in the forum as well as coverage on other esports and gaming sites.

StarLordLucian (2015a), having reflected on the discussion and replies, wrote, "I've thought over Riot's response and read some comments below and came to the conclusion their response really doesn't make sense. If you really should need permission to broadcast someone's game to 1000s of people, why don't the pro streamers like Doubelift, Bjergsen and the others require it for team mates in their game?" Given how many people (pros and amateurs alike) do, in fact, stream games that include other players without their permission, it was an astute question. The case as a whole ventured into terrain that esports and live streaming had long neglected to face directly. It also followed a pattern we've seen multiple times over the years where larger corporate entities issue DMCA claims and simply expect the user to stop whatever they were doing without pushback.

For over a week, none of the major corporate parties involved issued any formal statements, though Merrill did continue to tweet about the issue, invoking notions like "e-stalking" and how Riot wanted to protect players. The only exception was Faker's own team releasing a statement on its Facebook page:

Unfortunately, some of the fans have been re-broadcasting Faker's (and other SKT T1 players') games through the spectator mode, and this has negatively affected players' streaming business. Faker, a member of the SKT T1, also expressed discomfort over the current situation where his summoner name and videos of his games are being broadcasted with no consent. SKT T1 team and its players truly appreciate the fans' fantastic support and interest. However, we would like to politely request the re-broadcasting of our players' games without our consent to be stopped. (SK Telecom T1, 2015)

As I mentioned earlier, it is certainly understandable that a pro esports streamer would be troubled by practice time being streamed without their consent. It is reasonable for players to be concerned about their ability to improve on strategies without revealing new tactics prematurely, or to not have weaknesses in play systematically identified. One might also certainly imagine that the average player might prefer to have privacy while playing, and not be subject to constant or unpredictable surveillance by having their games streamed against their will. Even SK's team statement (despite its having organizational stakes in the matter) would suggest that it is indeed *the player* who has a final say over what happens to their games.

While Merrill and SK's public comments on the matter suggest that this was their underlying principle, Riot's actual legal guidelines (and likely SK's contractual relationship with its players) speaks to a much messier set of principles in operation. Riot's terms of use and "Legal Jibber Jabber" page (as Riot called it at the time) clearly stated that it was the sole owner of everything from game assets to chat logs as well as "methods of operation and gameplay." And within Korean esports, a fairly regulated industry, players regularly enter into contracts with teams and hand over a wide range of rights, including around broadcasting.

Even StarLordLucian himself didn't fundamentally offer a challenge to the corporate ownership of game performance. Doubling down on his project, he announced that he would continue the stream in the hopes of forcing Riot to address the core issue. He made a pointed argument on the subreddit:

> Faker does not have any rights over the game assets. I am streaming game assets—the spectator client, not anything Faker or Azubu owns. It's really that simple. I know some people will disagree with this and bring up ethics, but I think this whole issue is about a lot more than Faker. It's about Riot not enforcing their own legal terms of service. It's about a co-owner of Riot Games being completely out of touch with esports and the spectator mode. It's about a company (Azubu) issuing a false DMCA claim for content they didn't even own. These are issues that will affect the future of the game and the spectator mode. All of this needs to be debated for the future of League of Legends and esports. Right now nothing my stream does is illegal or against the League of Legends terms of service. Riot can always change their terms. And Riot *can* DMCA my stream at anytime, as they have the power to put any League related IP or Project to an end. (StarLordLucian 2015b)

For the next week, esports news outlets covered the story, and people debated the issue in online forums and via Twitter. Finally, on February 27, Riot published a statement from Merrill (2015b) titled "SpectateFaker: What We Learned and What We'll Do." The post recounted the incident, clarified its evaluation, and avoided claims of ill intent on the part of StarLord-Lucian. Riot's final judgment of the issue was that "we will intervene and shut down streams where we perceive that it's causing harm to individual players" (ibid.).

Of particular note was how it parsed the issue of interests and rights to the stream. Indeed, this was the animating point for most of the hundreds of messages on various Reddit discussion threads and Twitter conversations. Early in the piece Merrill (ibid.) reiterated the game's terms of use, clarifying that "players sign away rights of ownership to the gameplay content they create within the game," that "Azubu doesn't own the streaming content that Faker was producing," and that Riot had communicated this to the company. From this foundational point, he then shifted rhetorical gears to say that Riot was mostly concerned about protecting players' interests: "With any issue like this, our guiding philosophy is to protect the interests of players; in this case, things aren't so simple. There are two distinct player interests that are in conflict: the interests of the individual player (in this case Faker) with the interests of the thousands of players who enjoyed watching the Twitch streams of him playing via SpectateFaker (ibid.)." He described how Riot wanted to protect Faker and shut down the Twitch channel, while at the same time allowing other similar projects (such as SaltyTeemo, which broadcasts newbie games) to continue when it deemed no harm was being done. While Merrill and Riot in general tend to frame their actions in terms of "player interest," it would be naive to think that they don't also have their eye on ownership claims. Given Riot's audience growth and the resulting deals it was making (with outfits like BAMTech), it is apparent that it understood the value of asserting control over the game. At the same time, it has also had to navigate, at times unsuccessfully, a series of fraught public disputes with team owners.[1] While Riot emphasized player interest in its handling of the SpectateFaker case, it would be disingenuous to not situate it within a much larger media industries conversation.

One of the things that I find so compelling about this case is that it not only encapsulates so many of the most vexing aspects of regulation and live streaming right now but shows the kind of vernacular legal wrangling that everyday users undertake too. As they pick up technologies, often for the purposes of fandom, they can come head-to-head with thorny legal issues. It highlights how we are increasingly finding multiactor stakes at play in these spaces—from individuals to game developers/publishers to third-party organizations. We see the tricky line that developers frequently find themselves balancing on when trying to publicly navigate between wanting to be open to user innovation (or at least seem so) and wanting to retain foundational rights.

Over the years I've noticed how often the metaphor of the "Wild West" or "wild frontier" has come up in conversations and articles about live streaming. Aside from the grim subtext of these two phrases, there is certainly something that rings true about them. Live streaming is a fast-moving space, full of change and iteration. Practices, aesthetics, and genres evolve at a pace few can actually keep up with. User action frequently outpaces existing technology and tools. Just a handful of years ago, I doubt most people could have predicted things like TPP, broadcasting cosplay creation, or groups playing *Dungeons and Dragons* to an audience of thousands. The energetic, experimental, and inventive aspects of live streaming are indisputable.

But as the SpectateFaker incident shows, it's important to recognize that part of the work of culture, and cultural production, are entangled with forms of regulation. People are not unhindered actors freely exploring and developing; they confront and contend with various forms of ordering and control that tweak, push, pull, and inform their activities.[2] Gillespie (2018, 9) argues that "the fantasy of a truly 'open' platform is powerful, resonating with deep, utopian notions of community and democracy—but it is just that, a fantasy. There is no platform that does not impose rules, to some degree. Not to do so would simply be untenable." While live streaming has been energetically developed by not only solo broadcasters in their living rooms but also large organizations reaching audiences of millions worldwide, there remain critical issues around the regulation of this new form of networked broadcast. The tremendous work and creative energy examined in prior chapters contend with many intervening organizations, practices, and forms of governance and control.

Gillespie notes in his look at platforms that "in the context of these financial, cultural and regulatory demands, these firms are working not just politically but also discursively to frame their services and technologies." He argues that they "position themselves both to pursue current and future profits, to strike a regulatory sweet spot between legislative protections that benefit them and obligations that do not, and to lay out a cultural imaginary within which their service makes sense" (Gillespie 2010, 348). This means that while there are always important technical challenges and developments that these companies are engaged with, they are always also situated within the specificities of content distribution, which itself is subject to a wide range of legal, policy, and cultural forms of regulation and governance. While the emergent production of users and organizations alike has created amazing culture and content, we need to simultaneously keep an eye on the ways that it is not outside forms of social order and control, from the platforms that host it, the communities it lives in, or broader law and regulatory regimes.

In this chapter, I explore what I term the regulatory assemblage of networked broadcasting. Forms of governance and management operate at several layers, from the interpersonal to the algorithmic. This is not a unified system or one of shared values across all domains. Nodes often push and pull against others. The community, for instance, engages in its own forms of control, from the more positive inflections of user moderators in a channel to destructive forms such as DDOS attacks or outright harassment and hostility to a broadcaster. Law and institutional regulation become deeply implicated in how this space is adjudicating intellectual property disputes or policies around permissible subject matter. Much is still in flux around questions of ownership and appropriate content. And as with content on YouTube and other platforms, algorithmic regulation is on the rise with automated curation and monitoring. Technology is woven through all these domains, amplifying and extending the work of governance. Taken together, these varying actors and nodes mitigate otherwise-popular claims about any inherent openness of new platforms, instead highlighting how emergent practices are always embedded in complex systems of governance and regulation.

Community Management

Multiuser spaces, which include Twitch streams with their synchronous chat components, pose unique challenges given that people are engaging with each other online as well as frequently being deeply invested in the life of the channel and broadcaster. Creating these spaces requires responsibility and accountability to the communities being formed. Despite being left too often as an afterthought, or situated organizationally off to the side within game and social media companies, online community management—the governance of the environment and behavior of networked spaces—is one of the most important aspects of these sites. There is a multidecade history of volunteers stepping up and doing serious work in managing online communities, and companies are increasingly hiring community managers whose job it is to do the everyday work of engaging with users and mediating problems. While the term is now typically used to describe formal sets of policies and practices used by companies (and their representatives) to govern and handle the behavior of a platform/game/ services user base, I broaden it to include volunteers as well as informal behavior and interpersonal communication taken up by the community itself to self-govern. I will also discuss the more negative instantiations of group-driven regulation that occur. Threaded throughout all these are technologies that amplify and assist community management, governance, and policing.

MODERATORS

When thinking about how online communities are managed, moderators likely come to mind first. Their active, hands-on work has long been a key component of governance, social order, and control in network environments. Moderator teams tend to be volunteer organizations, though successful streamers have started to experiment with compensating high-level mods, and some of the larger esports organizations will have a couple of head mods who are paid. Equipped with special system privileges, these people are frontline monitors of behavior and speech. At the second TwitchCon, this theme was highlighted in a number of sessions where active moderation teams discussed the work that they were doing. Over and over again, they emphasized that chat is a reflection of a channel as well as a powerful part of the product, be it a variety stream or esports broadcast. Speakers encouraged broadcasters to begin thinking proactively about best practices for their mod teams and communities. They were also clear that good chats don't just happen by magic but instead are cultivated.

The work of moderation teams is important to understand in laying out the landscape of governance in live streaming. Game scholar Claudia Lo has distinguished between reactive and proactive models of moderation. The reactive model is likely the one most familiar to average users and mostly focuses on directly responding to negative behavior. In contrast, the proactive model seeks to foster good behavior but also undertakes "the technical work of developing, maintaining, and adapting both in-built and third-party tools for moderation would qualify as 'moderation work,' as would emotional and mental health work conducted by moderators for their communities and for each other" (Lo 2018, 11). The work of effective moderators and their teams is often much more expansive than normally thought.

They are tasked with monitoring the ongoing chat in a channel, and using a variety of manual and automated tools, they do things like answer questions, delete offending messages, and proactively build and sustain the culture of the channel. They may also at times assist the streamer in handling giveaways, donations, or other behind-the-scenes processes. Moderators are given an official system designation that allows them more control of the content in the chat, and beyond deleting messages, they can time people out (suspend them from chatting) or ban them from a channel altogether.[3] Moderators generally also have access to managing technology to assist in chat governance.

While part of the work of moderators is reacting to issues, another critical component is modeling the behavior that they want to see within the community. Helping to set the tone, socializing chat participants into the values of the space, and redirecting bad behavior to more positive engagement is part of the work that they do. The approach can vary from channel to channel, but it can involve anything from subtle jokes to explicit referencing of stream rules. Some moderators try to redirect negative conversation into chat games, such as cooperatively building a shape using ASCII characters together. Throughout the chat experience, from rules to emoticons to tone, socialization is a powerful component of moderating chats. Experienced streamers and moderators talk about how the ultimate success in their job is demonstrated when communities themselves take on the informal work of moderating. In those instances, community members speak up to correct bad behavior even before the official mods can.

Effective moderation teams are built and have intentionality. They aren't just formed by a streamer randomly giving mod rights to anyone who volunteers or a regular on the channel. Instead, they are cultivated groups of people who are chosen to explicitly take on the work and values of the broadcaster. Excellent teams regularly integrate application processes, training, mentoring, and trial periods. Some broadcasters have developed written guidelines to help bring some uniformity to practices and standards. A head mod or smaller group usually manages a team, thus creating additional layers of work and socialization. Successful moderation teams typically have some sustained back channel to coordinate, often utilizing third-party software such as Skype, Discord, or Slack to facilitate ongoing conversations in order to troubleshoot, iterate practices, and provide feedback to the broadcaster. In the case of large esports productions, requests for volunteers to staff an event or "emergency" calls for help frequently go out through them. Back-channel spaces are also used to build a sense of community and cohesion *within* the moderator group itself. This tightening of bonds, within the larger community and then within the subset of moderators, is a powerful component of managing the space. Building recognition, familiarity, and accountability between members—especially in environments with pseudonyms and transient audience populations—is no small feat, and the work that effective online community management teams do in live streaming is impressive.

HARASSMENT AND TOXIC TECHNIQUES

While the term "community management" tends to be reserved for a more positive view of handling user populations along with enforcing rules and norms, paying attention to the disruptive and disturbing forms of social control is equally important. Policing and social order can also be modalities in which harassment arises and a space takes a toxic turn. While this form of social control can have chaotic properties, we should understand the work it does to order, constrain, and regulate participation and behavior.

As I previously discussed, harassment is a common problem in game live streaming, and affects both variety and esports streams in devastating, powerful ways. Early work by internet scholars like Michelle White (2006) noted that online sites for spectatorship and performance enact forms of regulation and harassment as well, often around gender. Women, people of color, and LGBTQIA streamers—and at times even audience members—are especially subjected to a stream of cruelty that includes hate speech, incessant commentary on one's looks or behavior, visual abuse via unwanted imagery, and practices that disrupt the channel. These are not merely random acts but also an important component of boundary policing that gets taken up to signal, frequently in devastating ways, "you are not welcome here." Harassment can be deeply enmeshed with the policing boundaries of participation, forms of identity, and behavior. It is not simply something directed at an individual that incurs personal costs; it can also be a public act and form of socialization directed at witnesses and bystanders. It constructs values and seeks to set up norms for participation and speech. It signals what is permitted and even expected. Harassment is the flip side of the positive processes of community management.

Online harassment in game broadcasting can end up causing streamers to constrain or significantly alter their behaviors to mitigate risk and harm. This can include everything from not using a camera to building up large moderation teams to buffer attacks. It can also involve the substantial psychological work of "toughening up" or "growing a thick skin." Constant harassment, even at a low level, has become a way of producing a particular kind of subjectivity online where the expectation is "you shouldn't let it bother you." But this is not without costs, desired, or even possible, for everyone. Those who don't find this to be a viable position will often leave. Others will feel bad that they can't quite toughen up enough and still feel the effects of the harassment. As a form of boundary policing, it's a devastatingly effective technique.

One of the most dangerous forms of harassment, swatting (an acronym for "special weapons and tactics") actively disrupts the offline/online boundary and puts the victim in potential physical harm. Swatting incidents involve someone contacting law enforcement and falsely reporting a crime (such as a shooting or hostage situation) at the target's address. This leads police to show up at the victim's house anticipating an armed confrontation. These are extremely dangerous situations, and a number of high-profile incidents involving both YouTube and Twitch have brought visibility to the issue. For example, Jordan "Kootra" Mathewson was live streaming in 2014 when he was swatted, and the entire incident ended up being broadcast until the police noticed the ongoing camera feed.

Game studies scholar Alexander Champlin discusses how raids become "media objects" and that those who initiate them demonstrate "a dangerously blasé understanding of trends toward police militarization. These pranksters are participating in a game with stakes that appear game-like, but which have far more material consequences when we consider swatting in relation to broader tendencies in police deployment" (Champlin 2016, 4).[4] As shown by the horrific 2017 incident in which a Kansas man was killed when police responding to a swatting call ended up at the house of a neighbor, not the targeted gamer, such scenarios pose serious dangers.

Live streamers are aware of the risk of swatting, and some will contact their local police departments before any incidents to explain who they are and the potential risk. While most of the people I spoke with did not constantly worry about swatting, they all took precautions to make sure their home address was kept private. The use of post office boxes and being vague in conversations with audience members about where they lived (often talking about a region rather than a city) were common. Given how much variety streamers in particular utilize connection with their audiences, the threat that governs this boundary line is notable.

These forms of harassment not only affect the streamer but work back on the audience as well. They profoundly shape the tone of a channel, frequently setting up a cycle of amplification where other viewers chime in with further assaults. Harassing and abusive chat behavior can also be a powerful signal to any viewers who pop onto a channel about who the imagined audience is. It can telegraph who is welcome in that space, and who should "keep quiet" or leave. Rhetoric that someone should just "hide chat" if they don't like it is built on controlling boundaries of participation and inclusion.

SOCIOTECHNICAL ACTORS

Technologies are woven throughout both positive forms of community management as well as harassment. A variety of sociotechnical actors help govern (and at times disrupt) the space. For example, Twitch implemented an interesting system in which channels could elect to have users "agree" to rules that would pop up when they entered a channel. Its own internal research showed that the system did not meaningfully negatively impact participation, and indeed, there was a statistically significant reduction in time-outs and bans when a user agreed to the rules (Toner 2017). Paying attention to the nonhuman labor regulating live streaming is crucial to understanding how the system currently operates as a social milieu.

For example, bots, which are small bits of code that automate a variety of functions, have long been critical to managing online chat spaces.[5] At its base, Twitch chat was built around simple input/output communication system harkening back to IRC, a text-based multiuser technology from 1988. Users type in their messages, which then appear in the chat window to everyone else in the channel. They can also issue basic commands to get information. And unlike the original IRC protocol, which was rooted in ASCII text, special emoticons can be used (many of which are channel specific).

Twitch was actually quite clever in leveraging the power of IRC for its chat given not only that system's robustness but the amount of third-party development that had gone into it over the years. Special clients could be used to handle the text outside the Twitch user interface—an important function for moderators given the amount and speed of chat in large channels. IRC also had an extensive set of bots that could be used nearly right out of the gate. Bots not only can automate some processes but also "sit" in the channel and "listen in," providing useful information to users if they query them and helping moderators to preemptively take action. They often "act" as users, appearing with a username and "speaking" on the channel. Just as important, bots are independent bits of code that act with a kind of quasi autonomy. The presence of the moderator or streamer is not required, and bots continue to operate on a channel even if no live broadcast is occurring.

Almost from the get-go of the platform, users worked on bots developed specifically for Twitch. With names such as Nightbot, Xanbot, and Moobot, these bits of code monitor chat, checking against prohibited speech, filtering, answering simple questions, and providing regular information (for instance, when the streamer is next scheduled to broadcast). They are non-human community managers and regular members of moderation teams. Bots operate with autonomy on channels, but are regularly tweaked and extended by human moderators to better function based on the specific context of a channel. Word lists that the bot uses to watch for prohibited speech will be extended and modified, often on the spot, to deal with emerging channel behavior. The fact that bot behavior is malleable and subject to moderator input highlights that while they may at times act autonomously, what they do is deeply tied to both developer and moderator notions of what should be fostered or prohibited in chat.

Over the years, both Twitch software developers and third parties have continued to push tool development to better keep up with the practices of streamers and audience members. Lo (2018) offers a detailed account of the rich work that moderators do to create an assemblage of systems to facilitate their management of communities. From bots to tools like Logviewer, which allows mods to keep records of specific users' chats across multiple channels, she highlights the ways backstage labor has been adept at leveraging technology to manage broadcasts. Often it is working well beyond the given parameters of the platform. This is perhaps not surprising to anyone who follows the extensive ways that users reconfigure and modify game spaces. Moderators certainly bring that sensibility to their community management work.

One of the biggest challenges with these systems, however, is that it requires the broadcaster to know that these tools exist, understand how they work and which ones to use, and install and administer them. While web pages (including at Twitch) and forums are filled with advice about how to do this, it is a hurdle not everyone can get over. One of the most important developments in how the platform has tackled the issue of technology and community management occurred in December 2016 with the release of AutoMod, a pretrained, off-the-shelf piece of machine language software that was tweaked for Twitch. By simply going to your broadcast settings page you could configure different levels of protection akin to the work that third-party bots had been doing. If a streamer elected to use the tool, they could move a slider to set threshold levels for moderation. The system has been refined a bit since launch, and at the time of this writing breaks down into four categories: identity/language referring to "race, religion, gender orientation, disability, or similar"; sexually explicit language covering "sexual acts, sexual content, and body parts"; aggressive language dealing with "hostility towards other people, often associated with bullying"; and finally, profanity that includes "expletives, curse words, things you wouldn't say to grandma."

As the user slides the marker over, more category moderation kicks in. You cannot actually invoke the highest level of filtering for categories independently. For example, setting the slider to "more moderation" provides "more filtering" of the first three areas (indicated by three tiny shields) but none on profanity. The only way to achieve "most filtering" on aggressive language is to set the entire system to "most moderation" (which in turn triggers "more filtering" to the other categories). Aspects of the categorization and filter tiers are a bit unclear, and while experienced users of other bots might find the black box design of this system a bit limiting, it was certainly a crucial move in putting moderation tools into the hands of less experienced users.

Two additional factors make the tool notable: the disclosure that it leverages machine learning and natural language processing algorithms, and the way it shapes the experience of chat. While details about how machine learning and natural language processing are being used within the system were not specified at the time of release, and it is unclear how things have developed on that side of the technology since launch, one article noted that it may be one place where Amazon's purchase of Twitch is paying engineering dividends through the possible use of Amazon's AWS machine learning platform along with techniques that are coming to fruition in devices like the Echo (Orland 2016). Given the flexibility of chat communities in their attempts to constantly try and foil current bot systems, and the ongoing work that moderators have to do to keep up, a system that can "learn" and adapt would be game changing. Ultimately it is still unclear how that component will fare. As we've seen with a number of high-profile machine learning missteps (for example, Microsoft's artificial intelligence named Tay, which ended up spouting conspiracy, Nazi, and generally abusive speech it "learned" via online training), serious challenges remain to this approach.

A second aspect of AutoMod, and to my mind one of the most significant, is the way that the system will hold messages in a queue awaiting moderator action. Up until this tool, the state of moderated chat was one in which the sidebar of a stream could be a huge list of "<message deleted>" lines. Though the offending speech was removed (even quickly), its *presence* remained. These ghostly echoes of deleted text helped create a feeling that harassing things were going on in the channel even if you couldn't see the specifics. A viewer would sense the vibe was lousy and that it wasn't a great place to be.

The AutoMod system not only holds messages in a queue but also, if they not approved, does not show them, or any indication that they existed at all, in the chat. This is an incisive way to disrupt the affective power of visibly deleted messages, the lingering sense of harassment produced when traces of abusive speech remain. As one streamer put in a Kotaku article on the subject, "Don't give the attention to the people that are causing these problems, and nobody else gets the idea to jump on that bandwagon" (D'Anastasio 2016). AutoMod addresses the way that speech has a social presence and how an interface can facilitate that position. One of the least satisfying responses to harassment is telling a victim to simply ignore, block, or otherwise hide the speech. That approach completely misunderstands the act as both personal *and* social. Tools that remove harassing speech from the collective space and don't allow their echoes to linger via "<message deleted>" notifications are much more attuned to the social impact of harassment.

Compared to bots, DDOS attacks are a crude, simple form of technical intervention, but debilitating to a network when carried out at scale. Through a repeated "knocking at the door" of the target computer, they can disable a system by requesting that it respond to queries. DDOSing has been deployed for a variety of purposes, including political protest and, within the framework of this discussion, harassment.[6] DDOS vulnerabilities have not only come through Twitch itself but via the use of other programs, such as Skype, which exposes a user's IP address to those on their friend list. There is an unfortunate irony in the fact that the use of third-party tools to facilitate connecting to others can get turned against users in this way. By distributing the IP address to multiple attackers, the target's network system is overloaded, paralyzing it and shutting down the possibilities for communication and participation. It is not uncommon for popular streamers who regularly use Skype (and other IP-exposing programs) to pay for a proxy service to try to protect themselves. They may also filter those who they let into their "Skype circle" to only the most trusted and relegate others to alternate communication methods. The possibility of attack is enough to alter streaming practices. DDOSing has become such a ubiquitous part of networked life that it is simply taken as an everyday nuisance to be accounted for and hopefully prevented.

As we can see through the above examples, the work of community management and policing (even if in the negative) is regularly delegated out to nonhuman actors, many of whom can do the work of moderating, regulating, and disciplining communities well beyond what any single person can do. They come to act alongside the human moderators to do tremendous work in the overall governance of streaming spaces: from formally handling chat to socializing participants via their speech and actions. While we often only think of regulation at the level of policy or law, which I will now turn to, it is important to keep in mind a broader definition that encompasses disciplining and socializing at the interpersonal as well as community level, and that is carried out through humans and technologies that work together.

Policy

If community management speaks to the more micro level of regulation, policy is a middle layer between it and law. Though from its earliest days many invoked the rhetoric of an open and free network, the internet has in fact long had layers of governance, policy, and bureaucracy operating.[7] Given the multitude of organizations and interests involved, it is hard to imagine that it could be otherwise. While communities do a huge amount of work to govern themselves, most companies are not content to leave it solely in their hands. Policies arise, and in the case of live streaming, these include those coming from game developers, teams or agencies, sponsors, and the platform itself. Like other forms of governance, there are often skirmishes, many of which morph and adjust in relation to community practices.

Nearly all online services as well as game companies typically sketch out the boundaries of appropriate use of their platforms or content via documents like terms of use/service/conduct and end user license agreements, which users typically, though not always, have to agree to before use. The oft-remarked irony of these is that people generally do not read them in detail given that they tend to be pages long and filled with legal jargon. These agreements also regularly outline terms that can go against normal use practices, such as account sharing.[8]

In the case of Twitch, a number of issues have played a central role in their terms of use: the company's own intentions for the platform and its intended use, their need to maintain amicable relationships with game developers, the centrality of advertising to the financial model and subsequent reliance on audience, and navigating legal terrain around intellectual property. When I first began researching the site in 2012, Twitch was still very much in its early days of policy formulation. At that time, it hosted forums that were filled with discussions between streamers and a couple of official moderators. Those moderators fielded a wide range of questions from users, including what was permissible on the site. Posts with names like "How is racism handled?" "Emulators/ROMs, is it OK to stream?" and "What's the policy on listening to music while you game?" filled the conversation. During this period, the official forums hosted at Twitch.tv were an important community space for streamers to figure out what exactly they were allowed to do on the platform.

One moderator, Russell "Horror" Laksh, who was the site's lead administrator early on, did an enormous amount of work trying to explain policies to users. As he replied to a query asking if people were even allowed to *discuss* pirated games in a channel's chat, "We don't support piracy in any way, and I suggest you don't encourage piracy on your stream. There is nothing cool about theft" (Laksh 2011a). A big part of the work that these forum moderators undertook was focused on educating people not simply about how to do live streaming but also about the boundaries of UGC.

This period of Twitch policy development, and the direct conversations between Laksh and users, highlights a distinct moment in the site's history where those managing the service and those using it were still trying to figure out what, exactly, was appropriate. Although there were some clear lines in the sand (no streaming unreleased games or outright porn games, for example), much of the forum was filled with back-and-forth discussions. While formal moderators assumed a voice of authority, they encouraged users to be in ongoing conversation with them and ask about specific cases if they had any questions. Broadcasters themselves frequently weighed in, offering their thoughts on what was legitimate to pursue on the platform. Context and nuance were framed as central in navigating what was permissible, and pointed to a richer understanding of live streams as potentially complex visual and cultural products.

As the site grew, the official forum seemed to become a less tenable place to handle queries. Trying to officially keep up with fielding a mountain of specific content questions on the forums simply did not scale. Jared Rea, the community manager who was head of policy and moderation (including the volunteer mod team) during this early period, was instrumental in not only creating early terms of service that would provide guidelines for streamers but wording them in ways so as to make them accessible to average users. This approach set the tone that Twitch continued to take for many years whereby it adopted a more informal communication style to convey policy alongside the typical legal language being utilized. It was an effective rhetorical move given how iterative the policies were, morphing and changing in relation to developments on the site, external relations, and user practices. Given that Twitch regularly positions the platform itself as a community, with a passionate "family" of users, it navigates a balancing act as that framework is juxtaposed to formal and often-legal policies.

ADULT CONTENT

Despite Twitch trying to ground its policies and language in a colloquial tone that's in step with user practice, it has at times seemed to have to square a circle, and some decisions have been contentious. Aside from intellectual property issues (something I'll look at in more detail in the next section), the issue of not only adult content but also overall scrutiny around embodiment on the platform has caused many debates over the years.

One of the first threads on the early forum that really caught my attention was about pornography. Laksh had authored a post clarifying that Twitch didn't allow porn (including pornographic games) on the site and that it held a "ban first, ask questions later" approach. He went on to note, however, that "not all nudity is pornography. Specifically, I am talking about nudity within video games. If you are streaming a video game that is **not a porn based game,** as in, the fact that it has nudity [that] is not one of its main featured attractions, you will not be asked to stop, and you will not be punished." He said the title should be marked as "mature," and added, "If you ever have a question of wether [*sic*] or not you can stream a certain game, **please ask first!** It is better to be safe than sorry, as we cannot allow pornographic content on the site" (Laksh 2011b).

A poster then asked a follow-up question about if it was OK to stream *Second Life,* a sandbox virtual world fundamentally built around UGC that allowed people to create a wide range of customized avatars and spaces. Laksh (2011b) replied,

> For *second life* [*sic*] I am going to say no. *Second Life* is not itself a porn game, but a vast majority of the games user created items are porn related, to an unavoidable degree. The game does indeed have areas intended for teenagers, or general non-adult related content, but these areas are the prime target for trolls and others alike to just post the worst of their porn related collections! There isn't really a safe spot you could stream in that game without the risk of accidentally showing something we would not approve of. Because of all of this, I think the safest bet is to not allow this game in general, just to keep people out of trouble.

Second Life did certainly have areas where adult content and sexual behavior was the norm but it also hosted classroom spaces, gamelike zones, and even quasi-business hubs. Though reading Laksh's post gave me a chuckle—the danger of *Second Life*!—it did point to the way that the platform tries to navigate encouraging broadcasters to dive in and create compelling content for others but within "PG" bounds. Twitch's list of prohibited games, which includes titles that "violate our Community Guidelines as it applies to hate speech, sex, nudity, gratuitous gore, or extreme violence," also includes those with an Entertainment Software Rating Board classification of "Adults Only."

While many of the games listed certainly sound like they shouldn't be on the platform (or any, to be frank, with titles like *Battle Rape* or *The Maiden Rape Assault*), others have sparked broader conversation not just around adult-themed games, even with sexuality, but also about what it means to have such a popular media platform block particular subject areas or new cultural products wholesale. At a moment when more and more designers are pushing games to speak to serious, meaningful, emotionally mature, or nuanced issues, it should not be surprising if creators turn to the platform with content that pushes its boundaries.

One of the more nuanced discussions on this topic has centered on the games of indie designer Robert Yang, who has had several titles banned from the platform due to "sexually explicit acts or conduct" and issues around nudity. Yang (2015), whose work has taken up gay identity and sexuality in his games, has pointed out the strangeness of a policy that he characterizes as "as long as it's not important, it's OK." He maintains that Twitch's policies are opaque and unevenly applied, saying, "Their goal is to remain vague and hazy, so that they can randomly decide what 'too much sex' or the 'wrong kind of sex' is, while carving out special exceptions for large companies or business partners. I'm sure this is good for business, but it's very bad for creative culture" (Yang 2016). Developers like Yang who are doing deeply original, creative work on themes not regularly tackled in the mainstream game industry are put as a serious disadvantage.

A significant part of Yang's (2015) pushback on Twitch's policy is that it doesn't take into account context, or the ways that his games actually "focus heavily on ideas of consent, boundaries, bodies, and respect." Though many mainstream games may indeed not have as much nudity or sexuality as his, we should pause to think about how sexual threat and violence is regularly, even mundanely, deployed in popular titles. Many have certainly pointed out over the years how US media is all too casual about the ways that it broadcasts violence of all sorts, while panicking about nonexploitative nudity or sexuality. In this regard, Twitch's policies are not all that far off from its traditional broadcast television contemporaries, though we should keep in mind that cable at least provides an outlet for content not deemed suitable for a general viewer. On Twitch, there is as of yet no such bypass mechanism.

While the issue of adult content, including its definition and prohibition, is certainly a familiar one for many traditional media outlets, how it has played out on Twitch can't be reduced to quite the same framework. There are deeper underlying issues on the platform about what sorts of images, content, and modes of presentation it sees as core to its identity as well as what it wants to foster. Though it has expanded to allow a range of shows from games to people making cosplay outfits, and often signals that it values a wide range of creators and interests, it does at times revert back to narrower formulations.

DRESS CODES AND "FAKE GAMER GIRLS"

One of the most debated policies has been around the regulation of streamer attire. In many ways it goes to the heart of tensions that exist both on Twitch *and* within game culture more broadly regarding gender and participation. It taps into how the platform frames what counts as legitimate content and presence, and how that model at times runs up against actual user practices and desires. Though Twitch has continued to expand what it allows beyond straightforward video gaming—you can now see people engage in "social eating," music production, and any number of other creative endeavors— there remain boundaries that are articulated and enforced by the company, and policed by some of the community.

In October 2014, Twitch released a revised Rules of Conduct (eventually renamed Community Guidelines), setting off widespread coverage, heated discussion, and op-eds across a variety of sites. In it, Twitch specified the following guidelines regarding streamer attire on the platform:

> DRESS . . . APPROPRIATELY
> Nerds are sexy, and you're all magnificent, beautiful creatures, but let's try and keep this about the games, shall we? Wearing no clothing or sexually suggestive clothing—including lingerie, swimsuits, pasties, and undergarments—is prohibited, as well as any full nude torsos*, [sic] which applies to both male and female broadcasters. You may have a great six-pack, but that's better shared on the beach during a 2-on-2 volleyball game blasting "Playing with the Boys." We sell t-shirts, and those are always acceptable. #Kappa

* If it's unbearably hot where you are, and you happen to have your shirt off (guys) or a bikini top (grills) [a misspelling of "girls" as a linguistic meme], then just crop the webcam to your face. Problem solved. (Twitch 2014)

That day, popular streamer Meg Turney tweeted out a message that she'd received from Twitch informing her that an image in the profile panel on the site was deemed inappropriate and "not suitable for Twitch in any capacity," noting that it had to be removed within a week or the channel would be suspended. Dressed in lacy shorts and a bikini top, holding a game controller, and standing in what appears to be a living room decorated with a variety of game artifacts, the stylized professional-looking photo struck many as a poor choice for Twitch to target. Numerous commentators found the policy at odds with other material that was regularly broadcast on the platform, while some saw it as dovetailing with an ongoing set of attacks directed at women in game culture. Although Turney's original tweet expressed real outrage, she later commented to the *Huffington Post* that "it's not really slut-shaming, it's more like body policing. Or enforcing a stricter dress code. . . . I just think the whole situation is silly" (quoted in Beres 2014).

On the content front, many noted the irony of trying to regulate streamers' attire amid games that clearly violated the standards being imposed. As noted above, while Twitch prohibited explicitly pornographic games, the platform was filled with titles that regularly showed women in not only revealing clothes but also in scenes of sexual violence and harm— motifs that some genres routinely traffic in. Mitchell (2014b) turned his attention to this dissonance, observing, "If Twitch is trying to make it to the big leagues and be taken seriously, then at some point it's going to have to acknowledge the obvious contradiction built into its new policy: the games themselves display a lot more sexually suggestive themes than most streams." He went on to argue that it was not only within game content that the limits of this kind of policy were apparent. Twitch's own forays into supporting live music on the site had run aground when DJ and electronic dance music producer Borgore showcased a live event from his home but had to end the feed because it included women in bikinis hanging out poolside (Mitchell 2015).

Other critiques honed in on how the policy synched up all too well with broader battles around gender and sexism. Game critic Matt Albrecht, in a piece republished at the online popular culture fan site The Mary Sue, wrote about how the policy, while formally addressed to both men and women, was playing into larger panics about "fake gamer girls" and fears of women utilizing their sexuality for advantage within an entertainment context. He asserted that

> when a woman barters her sexuality for a competitive viewership advantage with no promise of actual sexual favors or bearing of offspring, those who are oblivious to the patriarchal systems that even lead to this sexual bartering system to begin with raise up their pitchforks and cry foul. . . . Never mind the implied criticism that these women streamers might all be those dreaded "fake gamer girls"; the truth is that women merely having female bodies, regardless of how conservatively they dress, will be perceived as sexually inviting and exploitative. Merely owning boobs is considered enough provocation for conservative critics and for harassers to feel justified. For women, there is never a sweet spot for their sexuality. (Albrecht 2014)

Albrecht's contention, harking back to Turney's comment that the very subjectivity and embodiment of women was being policed, was insightful giving the timing of it all. Twitch repeatedly tried to clarify that this wasn't a change but instead merely a restatement and clarification of a long-existing policy. Yet it occurred at a time when just a few months earlier, in August 2014, a faction known as GamerGate launched. That timing provided a particular tone and context that the statement got read within.

Trying to pass itself off as a movement about "ethics in gaming" while in practice acting as repudiations of feminism and the increasing heterogeneity of gamers within the culture, GamerGate became a black box term that contained a multitude of often vile and harmful impulses and practices.[9] While GamerGate could be devastatingly and dangerously focused, as when it came to women like game developer Zoë Quinn or cultural critic Anita Sarkeesian, it also served as a larger cultural ethos whose attention turned to whatever might slip into view. Challenges, whether from academics or popular press authors, to hegemonic ideas about games and gamers, or the costs of toxic masculinity, were met with virulent, frequently pinpointed attacks (typically coordinated in a handful of outlets like IRC, 4Chan, and Reddit).

During 2014 and 2015, a number of people became targets for those upset that game culture was, they felt, being disrupted by participants who might hold different sets of values and approaches. "Social justice warriors" were seen as interjecting too many "political" or "feminist" issues into game content and culture. Perhaps almost more powerful was the way that identity itself became an uneasy variable for so many of these reactionary stances.

Over and over again, GamerGate participants tried to argue that it wasn't that they didn't want women, people of color, or LGBTQIA folks in gaming but rather that those people shouldn't "drag their identities" into it. Anyone was welcome *as long as* they could fit into the forms of identity, embodiment, and engagement that already easily occupied gaming.

There has long been a painful irony at work in game culture. It has a history as a space for outsiders or the marginalized, for geeky women or forms of masculinity that didn't fit a hegemonic model. But it has also policed its boundaries in complex ways, and I am not alone in noting the dissonance of what was originally outsider culture becoming so intensely harsh a judge of *other* outsiders. The gauntlet for entry into game culture can be vicious, and its "rules" hard to pin down. Inhabiting a subjectivity that is permitted in it can seem like threading a needle.

One variable remarked on over the last several years, subject to heightened scrutiny, is femininity, whether embodied in men or women.[10] As a woman who is older, is known by initials, and doesn't dress in particularly feminine ways, I've long been struck by how little I've been targeted despite doing publicly feminist work. One of my longtime informants crystallized this for me one day when he said, trying to clarify his own frustration with "social justice warriors," that he didn't mind "people like me" who didn't "push their gender on everyone." As he commented, my name was gender neutral, and even my Twitter handle ("ybika") wasn't clearly gendered. Perhaps left unspoken was how my age also factored in. My own gendered identity performance was fine with him, and he said that if others were like that, he'd have no problems. It was the ones who make it "a thing" that cause problems. I hypothesized back that it was only because my gender performance didn't upset his mental schema for who was a legitimate participant in game culture that he had no problems with it. Other women in the space have remarked on this, observing that as long as they dressed "like a tomboy," or took up language conventions or other mannerisms of the men they gamed with, they had few problems.[11]

On Twitch, this has played out as tirades against what some see as "cleavage cams" and a strange fear that men are being manipulated by women's bodies.[12] Posts on the Twitch subreddit "alerting" the community to what they identify as a "cam girl" (sometimes "cam whore" or "titty streamer") regularly appear. As one poster, ellis0896, wrote on November 30, 2014, "There's a *League Of Legends* streamer right now who literally has the biggest breasts I've ever seen in my life but she has them hanging out of her top so is this still allowed? I don't want [to] ruin her income and whatnot but it should be about the game, not her incredibly large breasts." Another, HeartofTractors, cut to the chase more quickly on January 13, 2015, asking, "Why do so many of you put on make up and all this other beauty crap just to play games?" Over and over again, judgments and policing around femininity, sexuality, embodiment, and women's presence have come up. And while many took pains to point out that the policy was formally addressed to men as well (no bare chests allowed), simply put, their bodies were not under constant scrutiny like women's were. Rhetoric of evenhandedness completely sidestepped the reality and context in which the policy circulated.

A handful of women streamers jumped into the discussion, talking about the extent that they are harassed for just being who they are and articulating their frustration with the strange ways that the policy is out of step with everyday life. One, hmet11, responding on January 21, 2015, to a thread titled "When will Twitch take action against Female Streamers who clearly are using the streaming service as a platform to ask for money," wrote,

> Female streamer here. I'll try and say my piece without sounding defensive, although I'm pretty offended by this post. I've been streaming for about 8 months now. I do it because I love the community, have been playing games my whole life, and overall love it. But you know why else? I do it to make money. I work my ass off to get donations, grow my numbers, and hopefully one day get partnered, because i'd [*sic*] so much rather be a full time streamer than work some shitty 9–5 job. I feel pressured to never even wear low cut shirts, shirts I would wear in public to the supermarket as they're that acceptable, because punk asses like you come in my chat and automatically tell me I'm abusing the system to get money. So instead I feel the need to cover up.

There is, of course, an absurdity in accusing these women of using the service for financial benefit given how central that very ability has become for aspiring professional streamers. But over and over again, women—cis and trans, white and of color, gay and straight—have been targeted when their bodies, performances, or identities don't correspond to an imagined ideal of what a streamer should look like or be doing. The policy unfortunately seemed to legitimize, and indeed deputize, people who were keen on calling out women for not using the platform "right."

This occurred within a much larger trend both on the site and off to target anyone who wasn't deemed a legitimate occupier of game culture. Leslie (2015b) highlighted this long-standing pattern in an article about "Forsen Army," a group of trolls centered on the popular streamer Forsen that has been particularly vicious in finding women, LGBTQIA folks, and people of color who are streaming, and then "raiding" their channels to post hateful and harassing comments. The practice of channel raiding for harassment (versus surprising a small streamer with positive attention—another common practice) has a long history, and unfortunately the policy statement only ended up adding fuel to an already-burning fire within game culture.[13]

While Twitch as a whole certainly didn't traffic in this approach or endorse any of the harassment, in the context of the particular moment when GamerGate was on the rise and becoming a powerful cultural force, it was hard to not read a statement that encouraged streamers to "keep this about the games" as syncing all too well with a broader regressive turn in the overall policing of entree into game culture with an often-vicious hand. It didn't help that the statement even used the term "grills" instead of "girls." Though intended as a familiar "joke," the word has become persistently ugly shorthand that floods channels when a woman is on the stream, washing out any specificity that they have as a person and simply referring to them by their gender (much how the trihard emote gets spammed when a person of color is on-screen). Although several people inside the company confided in me that they were troubled by this "policy" and how it had all been handled, noting that internal discussions had at times been quite strong, the public face of the company remained unified.

In November 2015, bundled into a mix of many other updates, Twitch revised its policy again. This time the blog post announcing the changes was quite different in tone. No jokes, no mention of grills or sexy attire, but instead a simple bullet point amid others noting the update. The new policy succinctly stated (and continues to be so at the time of this writing), "Nudity and conduct involving overtly sexual behavior and/or attire are prohibited." The change was little remarked by the community; indeed, it was only a post on the subreddit several months after the fact that even alerted me to it. As with many of the other topics, dealing with everything from intellectual property to scams, the informal, insider lingo had been removed, and in its place, fairly black box rules remain—ones that the community continues, albeit less heatedly, to debate and police.

Law

The earliest days of Twitch's forums were filled with people asking not only about how to stream or what kinds of titles were allowed, but also fundamental questions about whether it was even *legal* to broadcast games at all without developer permission. Time and again, these questions went un-answered by official moderators, even when they replied to other queries. Other users would sometimes chime in to help, reassuring people that it was all covered by fair use "like on YouTube," but also routinely stating that they were unclear how Twitch as a company was navigating this issue. In the earliest days of the forums, the absence of a well-articulated statement from Twitch on the very legality of streaming—especially amid so many other content guideline answers—was notable.

There is a provocative intersection at work in our culture. The tremen-dous growth of digital gaming among youths and adults alike exists along-side as well as within regulatory and governance regimes, from everyday practices to software and law. Play does not exist outside these systems but rather navigates and makes meaning within as well as around them; it lives within a DMCA world. I have long been drawn to exploring this relationship as it is negotiated in the area of intellectual property and terms of service/use policies. In those moments of conflict, compromise, and control, we are afforded the opportunity to peer a bit more closely at systems of meaning and practice that are otherwise naturalized or hidden.

One of the most powerful things that the qualitative study of digital gam-ing has afforded us is a deep look at how players encounter software systems, and rather than only simply accepting them as given, take them and make something else. It is key to recognize this as a sociological account and not an individualistic one. While any single player may not tweak or alter their own individual play/game, the overall pattern is one of *transformation*. Game communities are avid, dynamic interlocutors with the systems that they engage. It could not be otherwise; this is fundamentally what culture does.

The work of culture also involves a constant dance around control and order. Regulation can take place at a variety of levels. It can operate top down, bottom up, or laterally across peers. It can be found in everything from code to social practices. Currently one key site for the governance of digital spaces is through the use of corporate policies (terms of service and end user license agreements), software, and intellectual property regimes. Underpinning this approach to regulation tends to be a basic assertion of ownership residing with developers and publishers; this is the frame that argues gamers make use of these digital artifacts essentially at their pleasure.

Yet it is unavoidable that cultural actors will always take up the objects and systems that they encounter and remake them for their own purposes. Games do not live outside culture but *within it*. They are objects *of* cul-ture, and as such are accountable to it. They are *at play* within culture. This formulation, of course, is itself still not quite right because there is no single "culture"; there are many. They overlap, diverge, and exist within their own ordering, tensions, and struggles with each other. As individuals, we move through and inhabit a range of them. It is a beautiful mess that poses both methodological and analytic challenges. But one thing we can be certain of is that there is no system that is somehow magically immune from the work of culture. This provocative entanglement is the norm.

Our current moment, however, is not evenly weighted in terms of power. As legal scholar Rebecca Tushnet (2010, 892) remarks,

> Copyright law's expansion tends to restrict individual freedoms more than those of specific represented industries. Even when exceptions or limits are preserved, they are often complex to the point of near-unintelligibility, so that only a well-advised institutional player can confidently take advantage of them. This is a deeply unhealthy system, guaranteeing that citizens attempting to express themselves and participate in cultural and political dialogue can find themselves unexpectedly threatened or silenced by copyright claims.

Equitable pushes, pulls, and scuffles are not what we find in digital gaming. Instead, we frequently see players struggle to use games within systems that are not always adapting to emergent practice. And far too often when new uses are acknowledged and addressed, it is within a framework that continues to uphold a flawed understanding of ownership. Companies, when they do "allow" unanticipated uses, never fundamentally reckon with the generative work that players do and deep investments that they can develop.

In addition to the larger organizational skirmishes such as the Spectate-Faker case that I recounted earlier, over the years I've seen players themselves struggle with this tension. On the one hand, they typically recognize, acknowledge, and value the work of developers, giving them tremendous praise and credit for games. At the same time, they can struggle with how to articulate their own sense that somehow something *more* is created through their interaction with systems that in turn make it also *theirs*. As one streamer insightfully put it,

> So when you stream and you add any elements of customization beyond the game itself, when you start creating your own content, when you start adding humor, and you start doing different things, I think it takes it to a new level that is outside of the black or white of saying it's owned by the game creator. It becomes something of your own and it's part of

the subculture of the internet as well. . . . The internet doesn't like the concept of people holding, withholding, valuable information or valuable resources from the community at large, especially to make money. That's not what we're about. That's not what the internet is about.

Legal scholar Julie Cohen contends that there has been a misguided understanding of creativity unpinning intellectual property regulation—one that has overly dichotomized author and reader/user. She writes that "what is needed is not a better definition of authorship, nor an airtight conception of usership that is distinct from authorship, but rather a good understanding of the complicated interrelationship between authorship and usership, and the ways in which that interrelationship plays out in the cultural environments where creative practice occurs" (Cohen 2012, 69). I develop this line one step further by taking the processes and words of live streamers to heart; I argue for conceptualizing play as *transformative work*, and as such, posing challenges to how we think about participation and ownership in a digital age.[14]

FAIR USE AND FAN PRODUCTION

Professionals and amateurs alike are constantly taking up materials produced by others and working with them. An important component of the US intellectual property regime is the designation of fair use (a component of the 1976 Copyright Act), which affords creators various kinds of protection when working with someone else's intellectual property. The Organization for Transformative Works (2015) notes that "fair use is the right to make some use of copyrighted material without getting permission or paying. It is a basic limit on copyright law that protects free expression. 'Fair use' is an American phrase, although all copyright laws have some limits that keep copyright from being private censorship." Generally speaking, there are a number of factors considered when a fair use claim is made:

- the purpose and character of the use
- the nature of the copyrighted work
- the amount and substantiality of the portion taken
- the effect of the use on the potential market[15]

These make up what is commonly referred to as the "four-factor" test, though they are not a test in any conventional sense; they are tied to juridical interpretation, and have posed tremendous confusion and frustration for professional and amateur creators alike.[16] Of particular interest for the argument here are the components of the test relating to the purpose and character of a work along with its market effects.

The purpose and character of new creative work is critical in understanding its legal position. Fair use offers a protective foothold for creative endeavors that utilize someone else's intellectual property and *transform* it through "adding new expression or meaning," and producing value "by creating new information, new aesthetics, new insights, and understandings." Transformative work generates a meaningfully new cultural artifact.

Amateur creators seeking fair use protection have done a great service in publicizing and animating conversations on the subject. Fan-driven sites like Fiction Alley and FanFiction.net as well as predecessor nodes on Usenet, mailing lists, and forums offered creators an opportunity to not only share their work but also discuss the climate of production and legal challenges. Sites such as Lumen (formerly known as ChillingEffects.org) or the Organization for Transformative Works have not only raised attention to legal issues around fan production but worked to provide resources and information to help people navigate this fraught terrain too.[17]

One of the central moves in educating fan producers about their legal footing has been in explaining fair use along with helping amateur creators utilize legal and rhetorical arguments to frame their activities. In practice, this has tended to mean that there has been an emphasis on noncommercial uses as well as situating fan activity as primarily driven by passion, love, and a kind of purity of intent free of monetary self-interest. The focus has emphasized a creative, community-oriented activity. This rhetorical strategy is particularly well captured in the Organization for Transformative Works's (2013) membership drive:

> Why do you participate in fandom? For many of us, the answer to that question is love—love of a favorite TV show, video game, or band; love of fannish communities and the friends we make there; or love of the creative process involved in transforming canon to create something new. Fans put in long hours making and consuming fanworks, traveling to conventions, moderating communities, and chatting about their latest fannish passions—not out of obligation, not for pay, but because it brings us joy.

This is an entirely understandable, even accurate representation for many amateur producers. It captures much of the pleasure, relationality, and commitment that develop for all creators. It speaks to a kind of serious leisure that helps us understand the level of commitment and investment that a fan might have (Stebbins 2004).

The problem, however, is that when this approach is framed as the dominant orientation, it leaves us critically and analytically unprepared to explore the commercial intent of amateur or fan producers. It can truncate our full understanding of how such endeavors can be forms of labor and work. It doesn't help us in navigating the skirmishes, battles, or tensions within emerging production models. While a compelling rhetorical shift to help fans reclaim some legal footing—and indeed perhaps a needed one at a particular historical moment—I am concerned it closes off too much both critically and analytically.

Within gaming we have long been faced with a much messier picture of fan and user production that has involved commercial or professional aspirations, and complex assemblages of actors and intents where notions of work, grind, and even pain are woven in. The standard rhetoric about fair use and fandom do not help us fully get at the range of creative activities that we see. Gamers often push the line of "noncommercial love" well past the point of breaking. In my previous work on massively multiplayer online games, I recounted the struggles between players and game developers/ publishers around the ownership of digital goods (Taylor 2006b). Whether it was trying to sell your account on eBay or trading digital items for "real-world" currency, there has long been a tradition in game spaces whereby fan and players have attempted to make money from their play.[18] There has also been a robust history in digital gaming of modding, add-on creation, and mapmaking by someone other than the formal game developer.[19] Sometimes these initiatives are noncommercial in orientation, but we have also seen developers—at times a fan/player of the game, and in other instances a more professional outfit—seek financial support for their work.

The second critical component to specifically pay attention to in fair use arguments is how the new creation impacts the preexisting work. Courts are particularly attuned to whether work "deprives the copyright owner of income or undermines a new or potential market for the copyrighted work." This is part of the reason that most people believe fair use is fundamentally about noncommercialism and that if they don't make money on something, it is automatically protected under fair use. That isn't actually the case, and the courts may rule you don't have a fair use claim even if you are giving something away for free.

Perhaps surprising to many, though, is the fact that some works that would fall under fair use protection may indeed negatively impact the existing market. It has been noted regarding parody, for instance, that

> it's possible that a parody may diminish or even destroy the market value of the original work. That is, the parody may be so good that the public can never take the original work seriously again. Although this may cause a loss of income, it's not the same type of loss as when an infringer merely appropriates the work. As one judge explained, "The economic effect of a parody with which we are concerned is not its potential to destroy or diminish the market for the original—any bad review can have that effect—but whether it fulfills the demand for the original." (Fisher v. Dees, 794 F.2d 432 [9th Cir. 1986]; Stim 2016, 276)

The economic side of a fair use assertion, while often tilting toward more highly valuing the noncommercial, is messier than at first glance. It is not at all clear, based on empirical evidence, that live streams as a wholesale category fulfill any original demand that we might attribute to a game. Indeed, part of what has made them such a vibrant new media space is that they regularly transform private play into public entertainment; they are often entirely new products. Given that fair use is oriented to "protect[ing the] freedom of expression and the capacity of a culture to develop" along with, as I will describe below, the power of transformative works, we can fruitfully probe the issue of commercialism (Aufderheide and Jaszi 2011, 26).

The growth of video production and distribution centered around games has also led to an explosion of creative activity that while using games as a digital playing field, exceeds the bounds of "just" playing. From the earliest productions that utilized game engines for movie making to the YouTube content producers who built an innovative new media scene by providing game-focused entertainment for others, we can see a long tradition of players taking up game artifacts and making something more—something often with commercial aspirations.[20] That many of these innovations and moves have involved the desire for monetization should not be simply dismissed. It speaks to a core issue that we would be remiss to overlook: the easy boundaries between commercial and noncommercial, amateur and paid, and fan and professional simply do not hold. The robust history of scholarship around participatory culture and media (including games) suggests that we need a fundamental reorientation of how we understand the work of play—one that explores its transformative nature.

PLAY AS TRANSFORMATIVE WORK

Over the course of researching gamers across multiple projects (from massively multiplayer online games to professional gaming to live streaming), I've come to see that they frequently hold much more nuanced approaches to understanding the productive and co-creative nature of their play. Game scholar Hanna Wirman (2009, section 2.3) argues that there are at least five forms of player productivity, ranging from the expressive to the instrumental, and they should "be understood as a precondition for the game as a cultural text." Sal Humphreys (2005), in her work on massively multiplayer online games, contends that linear notions of authorship and subsequent understandings of copyright are disrupted when accounting for a notion of "productive players." She and fellow game researcher John Banks have examined the power of users to reconfigure institutions and markets by their activities. They assert that this is most interestingly seen in the "hybrid configurations and the entities that emerge, which are an uneasy and at times messy mix of the commercial and non-commercial, markets and non-markets, the proprietary and the non-proprietary" (Humphreys and Banks 2008, 406).[21] These early game studies findings continue to express themselves in the work of live streaming producers as they try to situate—culturally, structurally, and legally—their creative engagements.

A large part of what broadcasters themselves are contending with is that, as one expressed it, "technology moves at a million miles an hour, and laws move like the opposite direction." One streamer I spoke with, thinking through the relationship between the game and his productions, said,

> What is it that keeps people watching my cast? Is it me as a person, or is it just that I'm playing the games that they want to see? I definitely think it's a mixture of both. I definitely have my core fan base of people who definitely watch my cast for me as a person, and those are the repeats. Those are the viewers who keep coming back, but there's definitely a percentage of viewers every night who just sort of pop in because they see me playing a certain game. . . . I really do believe you can watch two different people broadcast the same game and have totally different experiences and totally different stories.

The sense that a person's unique engagement with the system—the *particular* circuit between them and a game—is central to broadcasting animates many of the conversations that I find myself in with live streamers. There is typically a strong sense of the performative nature of gameplay: that the game provides a field on and through which individual play unfolds.[22]

The performative aspect and ownership stakes in this formulation were clearly articulated by one streamer I interviewed when he sought to find a good analogy to explain to me how he thought about his work. He likened what he does to a comedian or musician who, though using a club's venue, still creates something that is unique. Even though they are using the space, "the person who's up there performing, that's their act. That's theirs. So when I'm playing a game and I'm sitting there, I'm on stream, everything. And what is mine is anything, any content I create whenever I turn on my stream. That is my content. That is me. This is mine."

Another sought to point out the distinctiveness of this form of media, saying, "I totally get the legality of not sharing or streaming music and movies or books because those art forms, those mediums, they are very much set. When you watch a film, it is the same film beginning to end every time. Yeah, you can copyright that. For me, the act of watching somebody play a game, you are not experiencing a game."[23] Instead, he argued, you are watching a specific entertainment product—one produced through the streamer's unique actions assembled for a broadcast.

The live streamers I spoke with consistently drew out how their productions are transformative; that their work produced new forms of expression, aesthetics, and cultural products. It should perhaps not be surprising, then, when they also say, as one did, "If I could take my live stream and turn it into a brand that people want, and I can take that brand and turn it into a business, then that would be amazing." Another framed how he approached monetization as connected with both his passion for the work and pragmatic concerns:

> I want to make it clear that I make money so that I can stream. I don't stream to make money. . . . Nobody's just going live and play[ing] games and not think[ing] about providing for their kids or knowing what insurance you have, hospital bills, having money to pay for the car when it breaks down. It's an aspect of this that is inevitable that you have to think about. It's all hand in hand. It goes along with the territory. I'm going to approach the business side of this with the same intensity that I'm going to approach the gaming side of this. Because to me, it's all synonymous. It's all the same thing.

While much of what has been written around UGC and gaming has focused on its noncommercial side, over and over again, the live streamers I spoke with had woven together their creative and commercial aspirations. They also felt themselves bumping up against legal structures and understandings of game artifacts as narrowly construed intellectual properties. Yet their transformative work was always in the foreground of their stories.

VERNACULAR LAW

This gap between how they experience their work and creative outputs, and the legal structures that in turn regulate them, is worth lingering on. Perhaps one of the most interesting threads within recent legal scholarship has been an increasing turn toward the empirical along with the role of "vernacular law." Much in the same way that Burgess's helpful concept of "vernacular creativity" (2006, 2007) captures the ways that "everyday creative practices" are important and can thrive outside high culture or commercialized paths, legal scholars have sought to understand how creative professionals actually think about their process and the meanings around ownership in their daily lives.

While there is a powerful myth surrounding the necessity of avidly protecting intellectual property to maintain "monetary incentives and wealth maximization," as legal scholar Jessica Silbey (2015, 6) documents through her interviews with various kinds of creators, intellectual property holds "diverse functions and sporadic manifestations in the lives and work of artists, scientists and their business partners and managers."[24] Her story is one in which people who are commonly accorded intellectual property rights actually have a more nuanced understanding than the law typically does of its function and role in, and limits to, creative activity. Tushnet's examination of the ability of specific creative communities to sensibly evaluate fair use claims also speaks to the thoughtfulness that producers bring to the issue. As she argues, "While copyright owners' interests must not be ignored, and wholesale, commercial copying is extremely unlikely to constitute fair use, creative communities recognize these principles and are capable of respecting copyright's legitimate scope while preserving space for transformation" (2008, 104).

This is resonant with the flip side claims that user producers (such as live streamers) make when reflecting on their formal legal versus experiential standing. While often stating that they have no meaningful legal protections or rights, they simultaneously talk about a profound feeling that they have real stakes as creative producers—ones that should be acknowledged and formally recognized. The broadcasters I've spoken with over the years actually understand that the rhetoric around intellectual property does not line up with everyday practices and does a disservice to the complexities of cultural production. A much broader range of actors, and frequently in much messier ways than contemporary regulatory regimes acknowledge, produce innovation, cultural activity, and transformative works.

Legal scholars Burns Westen and David Bollier (2013) maintain that vernacular law—the rules and forms of moral legitimacy as well as the authority that can arise socially within everyday life—can offer a powerful "corrective to formal, organized legal systems" that may be deemed unjust, unresponsive, or dysfunctional. Communications scholar Olivia Conti (2013, n.p.) in exploring the emergence of UGC, suggests that "YouTube and other UGC platforms represent a fraught layer of mediation between institutional and vernacular."

These everyday conversations along with the lay theorizing around property claims and moral rights, or the desire for monetization by user producers, can be found in comment threads, subreddits, and ethnographic fieldwork. They consistently point to a more complex understanding of cultural production than we typically find constituted in the law. While claims about fair use offer "the assertion of creator agency against unfair copyright law, vernacular discourse represents the assertion of a localised [*sic*] community within a world dominated by institutional discourses" (ibid.). The arguments that live streamers regularly make about their productions represent a powerful form of vernacular interventions on legal frameworks—ones that at their heart, present a much more expansive rendering of creative action and production with commercial products. They highlight a deeply cocreative model of culture, echoing legal scholar Rosemary Coombs' (1998, 270) understanding that the "use of commercial media to make meaning is often a constitutive and transformative activity, not merely a referential or descriptive one."

As a company, Twitch certainly recognizes the protective power that a designation of transformative work holds for its broadcaster's content. The company's annual convention, TwitchCon, routinely hosts panels on the subject of intellectual property, offers partner- and affiliate-only discussions to directly answer general questions, and on a number of occasions, I've heard staff members encourage streamers to think about transformative aspects that they can add to their shows. Broadcasters are encouraged to become educated about what is legally permitted (no small feat given the overall legal limbo that much of this form of content creation lingers in). Plainly the company's interests are in broadcasters not running afoul of game developers or publishers, and it strives to have streamers engage in good faith practices.

That said, as a company it does not offer legal representation to its streamers, and situates them as independent producers who are encouraged to be educated about the issues and, ultimately, solely responsible for what they produce. As I was in the final stages of preparing this book, I learned that the company had, in partnership with the California Lawyers for the Arts and Legal.io (a legal services platform), launched a new site (at legal .io) to assist streamers with a variety of legal issues. It offers a number of guides, from licenses with Creative Commons to fair use and DMCA. Users can also find attorneys through the site, and get more info about creating limited liability companies or trademarks. On the one hand, it is great to see such resources being offered to broadcasters, who are frequently desperate for help and guidance. On the other, as labor scholar Jamie Woodcock more critically remarked to me, this type of setup has been a way that "gig economy" platforms have sidestepped meaningful accountability to their workers. Though these companies rest on the labor of nonemployees, they expect them to function as independent operators who bear the risk. Given how much the playing field is tipped against smaller content creators with our current intellectual property regimes, and how much precarity overall streamers face, I am concerned about the position this puts many of them in.

The desire of many live streamers to profit from their work, to live within what are admittedly turbulent commercial systems built on platforms that they don't own, must be better reckoned with. Such desires cannot be written off as simply co-opted fandom or exploitation, or simply tolerated monetization at the discretion of the "real" intellectual property holders. The activities of players, which might otherwise be understood as simply enacting a game as given, can be a form of productive, creative engagement and transformative work, warranting both cultural recognition and legal protection.

AUTOMATED ENFORCEMENT

Though we can push to think more expansively about the transformative work streamers do, when technology gets enlisted to embody legal structures, things can be painfully reduced. Earlier in the chapter, I discussed the varying ways that sociotechnical actors were enlisted, from bots to DDOSing. Given the abundance of UGC hosted on platforms, many companies have taken up technical solutions to try to deal with everything from child pornography to intellectual property infringement. Though human review and the manual handling of data still play significant roles in content management, increasingly software is being deployed to catch and remove problematic content. Technical interventions have similarly been deployed to help govern policy on Twitch. While some policies are oriented toward enforcing a brand identity, others serve a role in legal protection for the service itself.

Content distribution platforms like YouTube and Twitch seek legal safety against copyright infringement claims via the safe harbor provision of the DMCA. As legal scholar Joshua Fairfield (2009, 1031) notes in his review of how the law originally sought to address the potential risks that online services faced, they "would be protected from claims of vicarious and contributory infringement if they exercised their ability to control on behalf of third-party owners of intellectual property. . . . These safe harbors permit ISPs to take action to limit infringers, while avoiding liability for acting to control the content, if certain standards are met."[25] Under the safe harbor provision, providers must "acts expeditiously to remove, or disable access to, the material" that is the subject of a notice of infringement. It must also have a policy for terminating the accounts of repeat infringer[s]." Safe harbor can be revoked when a provider has knowledge of specific infringing activity and does nothing, or when it has a "financial benefit directly attributable to" the infringement (17 U.S. Code § 512).[26]

In practice, this provision has led platform companies to put mechanisms in place for copyright holders to easily make claims against infringing content, which is then removed from the service. Some of these claims go through human mediators, but increasingly they are handled by automated systems. For example, YouTube's (2013) ContentID works by having "rights holders deliver YouTube reference files (audio-only or video) of content they own, metadata describing that content, and policies on what they want YouTube to do when we find a match. We compare videos uploaded to YouTube against those reference files. Our technology automatically identifies your content and applies your preferred policy: monetize, track, or block." Systems such as this (often called "digital fingerprinting") are especially good at catching a wide variety of recorded video and audio.

In the case of live content, however, the challenges are significant. Patterns of identification may not be known in advance. Permissible use mashed together with creative content may confound the system. Indeed, early attempts at automatically catching and shutting down live streamed content resulted in a number of bungled efforts, including the wrongful flagging of Michelle Obama's 2012 Democratic National Convention speech that was live streamed on YouTube and the 2012 Hugo Awards broadcast over Ustream. In both cases, the platforms apologized for the error, but as *Wired* writer Geeta Dayal (2012) observed, "Copyright bots are being wired into that infrastructure, programmed as stern and unyielding censors with one hand ever poised at the off switch. What happens if the bot detects snippets of a copyrighted song or movie clip in the background? Say a ringtone from a phone not shut off at a PTA meeting? Or a short YouTube clip shown by a convention speaker to illustrate a funny point? Will the future of livestreaming be so fragile as to be unusable?"

In August 2014, Twitch announced that it would be using software from the company Audible Magic to catch and mute infringing audio in recorded video of streams. On rollout, however, some expressed annoyance with the technology, which mistakenly muted large sections of videos. Game music composer Danny Baranowsky, for instance, was surprised to find videos of a game that he was working on being hit by the software and having chunks muted, despite his not requesting such policing (Kollar 2014). Others found their content silenced merely due to game sounds included in the video. Twitch's own weekly show was itself briefly targeted and muted by the software. The launch coincided with rumors that Google was planning to buy Twitch; many who were already frustrated with YouTube's content management system saw this as a dire path for the platform. Others expressed broader concerns about how the widespread practice of having your favorite music play in the background while you streamed was going to be quashed in a way that undermined the vibrancy of broadcasts.[27] Given many had demonstrated an interest in being able to use music legally, perhaps via some payment system, the implementation was met with significant pushback.

Streamers perhaps had both less and more to worry about than this first brush with automated content regulation suggested. On the one hand, live content is some of the most difficult to handle through automated systems. Beyond basic issues about permissible content (such as with the Hugo Awards or via fair use claims), in the case of a Twitch broadcast there are multiple layers of audio as well as video content that would have to be pulled apart and parsed. As I described in chapter 3, raw gameplay content makes up only a portion of any given broadcast. Given the technical challenges, broadcasters could take some solace in the fact that software was unlikely to be able to fully regulate their content immediately. On the other hand, automated regulation of live content is becoming increasingly important to a variety of media stakeholders, especially as even traditional content like sports starts being distributed online. Given the potential revenue possibilities for strong software to enter the automated regulatory regime, it is likely just a matter of time.

Co-creative Culture

Ultimately, game live streaming has come to be another domain in which we can see the active, engaged participation of users working with, building on, and extending commercially available platforms. Their innovations, undertaken in concert with sites like Twitch, reveal the transformative work of play and shine a light on the co-creative mode at the heart of gaming. Rather than frame users and systems as oppositional, we might look to the ways that they iterate each other, shaping practices and meanings in an ongoing dance of cultural production. As game scholar Seth Giddings (2008, 160) has argued, "We are no longer looking at just a 'technology' and its 'users' but the event of their relationships, of their reciprocal configuration." The interrelation is key. From game artifacts to platforms like Twitch, users are constantly working over and transforming the systems that they encounter.

But even co-creative models have forms of control and regulation with them. At times those come from users themselves who seek to police boundaries and innovations, constraining for both good and ill the engagements of others. At other times, it is the work of moderation systems that put up guardrails to direct the participation of users. Whether through the work of human moderators or technology delegated to do so, formal community management is also influencing what is happening online.

Policy is typically where we see the institutional principles come into sharpest relief. Formalized structures—articulated in terms of use and community guidelines—highlight what companies see as permissible or legitimate behavior; those in turn both shape and constrain what users do in these systems. Far from being simple neutral platforms, companies like Twitch are invested in honing what happens at their site for a variety of reasons.

Finally, at the most macro level, we can see the ways that an understanding of intellectual property comes into direct conversation with work broadcasters are doing in these spaces. Perhaps one of the most striking things that you hear from streamers is how much thought they put into the transformative work that they do and how deeply aware they are of the ways that our current intellectual property regimes are not only out of step with their practice but also threaten creativity. And rather than simply seeing themselves as just freely appropriating the intellectual property of developers, they express a more nuanced understanding of how cultural products are *always* co-creative in nature.

In this and previous chapters, I have sought to show how game live streaming is made up of a complex assemblage of human and nonhuman actors, as well as organizations and platforms, that enact their vision via practices and policies. Anthropologist Paul Rabinow (2003, 56) has written of assemblages that "they are not yet an experimental system in which controlled variation can be produced, measured, and observed. They are comparatively effervescent, disappearing in years or decades rather than centuries." We can extend this framework to think about the assemblage of regulatory mechanisms that are at work interacting with, shaping, amplifying, and restricting the engagements of users. This circuit is always iterating, shifting in relation to human practices, social development, and technologies. Ultimately, cultural production is a system of co-creativity, and we must continue to push for institutions and law that recognize that foundational truth.

6

Live Streaming as Media

While the winter weather of early 2017 had been less severe than usual, the weekend of March 11–12 proved frigid. This did not, however, deter tens of thousands from making their way to the Boston Convention Center to attend the annual PAX East convention. I was back again myself, mostly to help staff a table for AnyKey in the Diversity Lounge, but also to see what Twitch might be up to. The schedule had a number of panels on it with titles like "Streaming 101: Starting Your Quest" or "How to Broadcast Safely as a POC/LGBTQIA/Female ID'd Streamer," revealing that live streaming was still a prime topic for gamers. I anticipated spending some time at the Twitch booth as well given that it was usually a great place to meet up with folks and get a big-picture view of how the site was situating itself broadly within game culture.

Even before I got on the expo floor, where various companies demonstrated games and hardware, I spotted something called the Twitch Prime Lounge. A couple of greeters welcomed in those of us passing by, noting that there were drinks in back and encouraging us to relax. The large purple-hued room was outfitted with screens broadcasting live gameplay, including coverage of the expo floor. Sofas, tables, and much-coveted electric outlets made the space a welcome stopover from the hectic convention. I spotted people playing board games, checking social media, chatting with each other, and watching the broadcasts. Perhaps the most interesting thing about the room was its focus on the nonstreamer. This wasn't the usual VIP-streamers-only area but instead a free space for the rest of us. It signaled a turn toward paying more attention to the mass of viewers and occasional broadcasters that the site garnered.

A small station was set up at the front of the room dedicated to teaching people how to stream. That little "how-to" area was a tip-off to the ongoing need that Twitch has to not only grow its audience but also bring new people into the content production process. The long tail made up of small channels matters for sustainability. While one of them might become the next big hit, they mostly generate the continual blips of activity that the platform needs. As Postigo (2014, 15) puts it regarding YouTube and other UGC platforms, they are

> not unlike a bettor at a roulette table who is in the happy position of betting on all the numbers, where the payout *in aggregate* outweighs what appears to be an otherwise wild investment. Some numbers don't pay, others pay a little, and some pay a lot. Some content types may thrive and then fade into obscurity, some commentators may be successful and then burn out, and some videos may go viral and others remain unknown. In aggregate, however, no matter what the scenario, YouTube the bettor always wins.

While large broadcasters and big esports tournaments draw impressive numbers that look good in press releases, the site banks on up-and-coming talent to keep it vital and buffer against the churn of content providers who taper off production.

The lounge also represented the clearest signal that Twitch was, indeed, an Amazon-owned company. Amazon Prime subscribers get Twitch Prime for free on linking their accounts, which gives them a variety of perks—ones that hopefully keep them coming back to the platform. Linking accounts ties users into an infrastructure that facilitates purchasing even more games and, likely almost as valuable, fosters data collection too. Even before I made it down to the expo floor, I began to see what appeared to be the next phase in Twitch's development.

As I headed down the escalators, I knew what to look for: the glowing purple booth. I spotted it quickly, sitting up front and off to the side of the massive hall. Though the purple hue remained, it was offset this year by light wood and white accents, a bit more muted in overall effect. As I got to the space, it quickly became apparent that "booth" was entirely the wrong word for it. Instead what I found were, essentially, two separate structures. The space was huge, and I couldn't quite tell in one glance where it began and ended. It wrapped around, with one of the sections housing the main broadcast and viewing spaces, an autograph-signing area, smaller "Streamer Zone" broadcast booths for partners to go live from the convention, glassed-in meeting rooms, and small info tables. The other section—a raised platform with a huge interior area dubbed the Partner Lounge—was the VIP area where select people could meet and mingle, all on display. It was a far cry from the first small booth that I encountered back in 2013. It embodied not only Twitch's growth but also its centrality in game culture and the multiple stakeholders—audiences and fans, content producers, game developers/publishers, advertisers, and sponsors—it had to juggle simultaneously. Like all PAX East's events, it was a fantastic opportunity to catch up with many streamers and get a feel for the current conversations happening around broadcasting.

A day later, I found myself sitting on my living room sofa with my partner as we watched Twitch on our television via one of our game consoles. It was 11 p.m., and we had tuned in to a special broadcast happening live from South by Southwest in Austin. We usually don't watch Twitch together, but we are both comedy fans, and one of our recent favorite shows, *HarmonQuest*, was going to do a live version on Twitch. *HarmonQuest* is an animated series that builds off Dan Harmon's podcast, *HarmonTown* (which had also been the subject of a 2014 documentary). Harmon is best known for creating the television show *Community*, but he has been a longtime podcaster as well. The podcast had a regular segment where people played a tabletop role-playing game together—definitely an interesting audio experiment in and of itself. That slice was picked up to be made into a partially animated show on Seeso, a now-defunct paid service only available online from Comcast/NBCUniversal. The media twists and turns in *HarmonQuest* alone are fascinating: podcast to documentary to television production, all with one foot in major media and another in the geeky indie sphere. Paired up with being broadcast on Twitch, it was hard to resist watching this quirky mix of media productions coming together for a bit of an experiment.

The show broadcast that night on Twitch was awkward and even painful at times, though the pathos of Harmon and the wit of his guests kept it moving. It was bookended by Koebel, a popular Twitch streamer who does his own live tabletop role-playing game productions on the site, interviewing *HarmonQuest*'s own game master, Spencer Crittenden. It was a strange collision, both in the broadcast and Twitch chat. Although *HarmonQuest* comes out of the podcast and indie comedy scene, the experience and reputation of the performers was something quite different than what you usually see on Twitch. This wasn't a broadcast in which the performers knew or even really cared about what might be happening in chat. The connection between performer and audience, so central to many Twitch productions, just wasn't there. This was, despite not being a mainstream media product, much more like a traditional show than a typical Twitch one.

The chat itself echoed the strange and not entirely successful marriage at work in this venture. Serious Harmon fans who had swung by to watch were confused by and even disdainful of the Twitch wrapping. On the other side, some Twitch fans who knew little about *HarmonQuest* found *it* unfunny, and with Harmon's increasing level of drunkenness (which he is widely known for), even worrying, and perhaps behavior that broke the terms of service for the site. It was as if two subcultures colliding on a strange internet outpost didn't quite know what to make of each other and didn't entirely like being in one another's company. The *HarmonQuest* cast didn't even seem to know what Twitch was, and that was spun off into its own comedic riff. Twitch regulars satirically groused in the chat that *HarmonQuest* would never get "partnered."

The *Los Angeles Times*, musing about the growing popularity of watching tabletop role-playing game campaigns online, unknowingly anticipated this tension when commenting on the length of *HarmonQuest* compared to some other shows such as *Critical Role* or, I'd add, one of Koebel's own entertaining live role-playing game shows on Twitch. The author remarked that *HarmonQuest* "makes its ventures a lot less time-consuming and ups the watchability quotient by throwing in animated segments in digestible half-hour episodes. Gamemaster Spencer Crittenden approaches the show as just that—a show." As Crittenden put it, "We specifically thought about the way things might get edited" (quoted in Phillips 2017).

Yet the multihour broadcasts that you find on Twitch, their lack of editing, the interaction and familiarity between audience and broadcaster, and fact that it is sometimes exactly *not* "digestible" but instead composed of long stretches of affective, engaged performance and spectating goes to the heart of what distinguishes something like *HarmonQuest* from its Twitch peers. Live streaming programs, while riffing on the televisual, have developed their own unique set of conventions, practices, and pleasures. They have their own sets of celebrities, their own histories and forms of interaction with their audiences. Though the broadcast of a raw, unanimated version of *HarmonQuest* might have on the surface seemed perfectly suited to Twitch, it missed the mark at least in part because it was out of tune with the specific conventions and pleasures of the platform.

Perhaps due to the fact that I'd just come off the PAX weekend and was now watching this strange mix of media forms, I also began to think about how the site was not entirely the same one that I had begun studying in 2012. Part of what happened in the intervening years is that experiments in the medium have grown to become conventions that themselves stand as unique televisual genres. Other instances of user-driven innovations have been pulled back into the very structure of the platform itself. Take, for example, the way donation systems went from being something that broadcasters created to support their endeavors to Twitch formalizing the Bits system, which while allowing audiences to donate money to a streamer, also gives the company a way to take a cut. And while it has certainly been the case that live streams offered tremendous grassroots marketing opportunities, the announced Amazon-linked "buy now" button to be embedded on channel pages sent a strong signal about the corporate commercial work they are made to do.

Even though variety streamers and esports production companies alike have been finding ways to broadcast gaming content to a global audience, the platform has begun to engage with more mainstream media forms, be it feel-good rebroadcasts of Bob Ross's painting show, Julia Child's cooking lessons, massive electronic dance music events, or as is happening as I write this, a *Power Rangers* marathon. I do not want to pitch a simplistic commercialization critique. Nor do I want to suggest that Twitch is trending toward just another mainstream media form. Indeed, part of what I have always found fascinating at the site were the ways that UGC producers have sought out revenue and professionalization, and would be thrilled to be considered an impactful personality alongside traditional media figures. And while there remain terrific vibrant forms of expression and production at work on the site, I do pause at the future of the platform as a space for expansive cultural expression. If Twitch simply becomes more and more of a marketing tool, or merely another branch of mainstream media distribution, and less a space of true transformative work, much will have been lost. Engagement that undertakes innovative performances, serious critique, challenging content, or modes that might not find a home elsewhere due to their unconventionality are critical for not only the vibrancy of the site but also its role in our culture.

Changing Media Industries

Over the decades there have been various prognostications about the "death of television," particularly in the face of "interactive" entertainment. All seem to fall by the wayside as the years go by. Miller (2010, 19) argues that it is silly to see the Internet in opposition to television; each is one more way of sending and receiving the other. The fact is that television has become *more* popular, not less. It is here to stay, whether we like it or not. I suspect that we are witnessing a transformation of TV, rather than its demise. What started in most countries as a *broadcast, national* medium, dominated by the state, is being transformed into a *cable, satellite, Internet*, and *international* medium dominated by commerce—but still called 'television.'"

One of my interviewees early on said to me that, "television in its current form is thirty years from being totally extinct." That phrase "in its current form" perhaps signals that they understood something many don't. While the devices and conventions may change, the televisual is going as strong as ever. As another frankly put it, "I know for a fact I'm going to be watching this shit when I'm fifty years old. I know a lot of people who are in their late twenties that will completely agree with that statement."

Of course, it would be a mistake to overlook the ways that these platforms and productions enact pushback and change on traditional media systems. With the rise of sites like Twitch as well as gaming more broadly, media tastes and forms of production are without a doubt shifting. UGC has become a critical component in our overall media world, and users are increasingly willing to consume these products much like any others. Alongside changes in traditional media consumption (from time shifting to "binge" watching) has been the rise of long-form and at times mundane game live streams in which viewers interact with broadcasters and each other. The line between audience and these (micro) celebrities gets breeched across a range of platforms, from Twitch to Twitter.

A more productive way of thinking about media transformations in light of the rise of gaming, UGC, and new production and distribution platforms is to see that there are circuits between traditional and new media spheres. People are still watching television and consuming traditional content *alongside* user-produced YouTube videos and Twitch's game live streaming channels. The media mix is the key. Content, producers, and audiences flow across a range of devices, platforms, and genres.

Some mainstream media outlets are picking up on this. For example, ELEAGUE has a home on both cable and satellite television as well as Twitch, and ESPN has broadcast several esports tournaments. Twitch, working in the reverse, has also begun more experiments in pulling traditional media content back onto the platform, such as its broadcasts of popular anime series. Some traditional media and sports stars have experimented with their own live streaming broadcasts, and Adam Silver, the head of the NBA, remarked that he'd like to see its games look more like Twitch (Kafka 2017).[1] And while we haven't yet seen any Twitch personalities make a big breakthrough to traditional media, perhaps that is to come. No matter what flows we find between content in these spheres, what is critical is that audiences seem to have adapted without too many problems to cobbling together their viewing across sites, devices, and various types of products. For many, the shift to producing content for other people—whether it is just friends and family or a larger audience—is increasingly common and not a big leap. The circuit is not just about viewing traditional or new media but moving between consumer and producer too. As one of the original funders of Justin.tv commented about live streaming platforms, "If this doesn't scare the shit out of TV networks, it's only because they don't understand it yet" (quoted in Rice 2012).

The Politics of Participation

This emergent flow is central to understanding our contemporary media space, and as Burgess and Green (2009, 79) put it, "Quietly bubbling away under the surface are the kinds of activities that might be recognized by feminist scholars of popular culture as the practices of cultural citizenship—mundane but engaging activities that create spaces for engagement and community-formation."[2] Yet as I hope I have demonstrated with my discussion of things like harassment or regulation, game live streaming should not be seen as an unencumbered or utopic story of the triumph of grassroots engagement. Serious challenges to open participation as well as broader structural considerations around ownership and forms of labor remain.

Cultural studies scholar Graeme Turner, a critic of overly optimistic theories of media transformation, argues that any democratizing potential found within these new media forms is "an occasional and accidental consequence of the 'entertainment' part, and its least systemic component." He writes that "the media industries still remain in control of the symbolic economy, and that they still strive to operate this economy in the service of their own interests," which are decidedly commercial (Turner 2010, 16). As he and others contend, there is no "necessary connection" between these new forms and democratic frameworks (Andrejevic 2009a).[3] While we may find much to be hopeful about in the practices that are arising on UGC sites, the critique is important to wrangle with.

Even proponents of participatory culture who see vibrant opportunities for everyday users to become active stakeholders caution against simplistic valorization of our contemporary moment. Jenkins (2009, 124), often seen as one of the strongest proponents of the growth of participatory culture, cautions in his reflections on YouTube that its

> utopian possibilities must be read against the dystopian realities of a world where people have uneven access to the means of participation and where many are discouraged from even trying. If YouTube creates value around amateur content, it doesn't distribute value equally. Some forms of cultural production are embraced within the mainstream tastes of site visitors and the commercial interests of the site owners. Other forms of cultural production are pushed to the margins as falling outside dominant tastes and interests.

The "participation gap" that he identifies is a serious one. As we have seen in the case of game live streaming, profound issues remain regarding who is able to meaningfully create and thrive on the platform, much less participate in a broader esports media environment.

It is also the case, as I explored with regard to the transformative work of play in live streaming, that serious concerns remain in terms of the labor of new producers and engagements of fans. From the earliest moments of UGC and user activity in shaping the internet, critics have alerted us to thinking about the potential exploitation and appropriation that occurs within these spaces.[4] They have cautioned us about the agility of commercial, commodified systems to inequitably trade on as well as regulate the passions and dedication of user producers, fans, and enthusiasts.[5] Being attuned to the labor situation that these media producers face is critical.

I take this critique seriously and see many ways in which game live streamers precariously navigate between self-determination, creative expression, and meaningful interaction and structures always at work to capture as well as regulate their endeavors. In my conversations with them (as with many gamers over the years), I have found them to be acutely aware of this tension. Indeed, they are frequently insightful theorists of their own experience, identifying the ways that they dance between their own desires and legal or economic structures that are always one moment away from tossing them out of the system. They knowingly, and often with great pleasure, engage in forms of affective and performative labor on platforms that they recognize are never fully theirs to control. The challenge for us as researchers and scholars is to honor their experience as active meaning-making agents who undertake complex navigations in everyday life, but not lose sight of serious forms of structural inequality and precariousness—ones that may also keep some from full participation in this space.

The Work of Play

One of the aspects worth lingering on a bit more weaves together these considerations of commercial media systems with the nature of gaming itself. Scholars Daniel Kreiss, Megan Finn, and Fred Turner (2011, 250) raise questions about how these new forms of production and engagement may have deeper corrosive effects, arguing,

> Peer production in particular may undermine our private autonomy by extending our professional lives into formerly private arenas. Thus digital collaboration may tend to privilege commercial actors. Just as peer production makes it easy for individuals to bring together their private and public selves, it also turns formerly private pleasures such as playing games into forms of labor and allows work to enter into intimate domains.

They look to sociologist Max Weber's concerns about the effects of bureaucracy as having new salience for our modern participatory—yet commercialized—culture.

Though not game scholars, their concern is resonant with those who fear that the world of work, rationalization, or instrumentality threatens what is good about play. I am sympathetic. There are real ways in which digital gaming and live streaming is interwoven with fraught systems that may at times encroach on our agency and participation. We must certainly be mindful and critically reflective about the structures—from commercialization to legal regulations—in which our play and leisure are increasingly seated. This is something that I've tried to tackle throughout all my studies of gaming.

But at its extreme, this is an old argument in the study of play, going back to theorist Roger Caillois's 1961 work *Man, Play, and Games*, and it has profoundly negative effects both methodologically and theoretically. Caillois (2001, 45) writes about the "contamination" of play by reality, obligation, and professionalism, asserting that "what used to be a pleasure becomes an obsession. What was an escape becomes an obligation, and what was a pastime is now a passion, compulsion, and course of anxiety. The principle of play has become corrupted. It is now necessary to take precautions against cheats and professional players, a unique product of the contagion of reality." Scholar Tom Brock (2017, 322), picking up Caillois's suspicion that professionalization corrupts pure play, looks at esports and maintains that the "perversion of agôn [competition] is a consequence of blurring work with play." Within this model, game live streamers would surely sit in the same penalty box that Caillois has tossed so many others.

I have now explored over several projects the instrumentality of particular kinds of play, the work that players do, and the modifications that they make to systems to foster even more rationalized play.[6] And while I share concern and caution regarding the ways that our gaming might be colonized and our agency limited, I am also accountable to situating player practices within participants' own descriptions of the pleasure, creativity, social connection, aspirations, and authentic experience that so often accompanies the work of play. While one response to these data might be to theorize the respondents as dupes or unreflective about their own lives, or have the conceit that we as analysts are the only ones to see a bigger picture, I go another way.

I would actually turn *back* to Weber's approach to understanding human action. As he writes, "We are *cultural beings*, endowed with the capacity and the will to take a deliberate attitude towards the world and lend it *significance*" (Weber 1949, 81). One of the most profound components of Weber's method and theory is that he understood the power of context, standpoint, and meaning making by individuals and groups. He saw the complexity between those and structural issues. Though one might argue that today's gamers and live streamers are, like the Calvinists Weber so powerfully described, doomed to an iron cage of their own making, I am less convinced.

The work of play is often deeply transformative. It can be filled with difficult pleasures, enjoyable instrumentality, and complex negotiations between system, self, and others. It can modulate in complicated ways between freedom and constraint, self-direction and obligation to oneself or a community. And indeed when gamers do identify the pleasures of play as slipping away, feel that things have become too straining, or decide to convert back into hobbyists, it is typically tied to a range of factors all coming to a head, not a discrete designation based on a single property of idealized play.

Sociological studies of digital gaming highlight how simplistic, individualistic, and dichotomous in their handling of the world some of our older theories of play have been. If we leaned more on anthropologists of play like Linda Hughes (2006), who in the 1980s was already doing these valuable studies, or Phillips Stevens (1978), or scholars of serious leisure like Robert Stebbins (1982, 2004), who all offer richer accounts that avoid dichotomous formulations, we would discover interpretive frames that help us think about the complexity of meaning and experience in play and games.[7] Though our games exist in specific contexts, and we are ourselves a product of particular moments, through our individual and collective action, we also create authentic meaning, make social connections, and can enact real transformations.

A move to interrogate simple work/play dichotomies through the lens of live streaming might have the side benefit of prompting a more meaningful consideration of our labor and leisure writ large. Looking at how people are creating experiences and content for their own fulfillment *and* the pleasure of others and their communities can provide insight into the complexities with which we navigate commercialized platforms. That we are doing this online, in networked environments, suggests we still have much to explore in our emerging media ecology.

NOTES

Chapter 1. Broadcasting Ourselves

1. Lembo (2000) uses the language of mindful versus habitual viewing to signal just a couple of the varying interior orientations one might take to television.

2. Over the years I've come to see that this image can be troubling to some, and I certainly critically appraise offerings much more than I did as a kid. But overall, television was frequently a powerful positive force in my life.

3. To name just a few, see Gray 1995; Hendershot 2016; Lembo 2000; McCarthy 2001; Mittell 2010; Morley 1992; Murray and Ouellette 2004; Spigel 1992; Spigel, and Curtin 1997.

4. Throughout this work, I use the term "platform" in ways that are generally in sync with Gillespie's (2018, 23) definition: "platforms are: online sites and services that a) host, organize, and circulate users' shared content or social interactions for them, b) without having produced or commissioned (the bulk of) that content, c) built on an infrastructure, beneath that circulation of information, for processing data for customer service, advertising, and profit. For the most part, platforms don't make the content; but they do make important choices about it." He adds that "d) platforms do, and must, moderate the content and activity of users, using some logistics of detection, review, and enforcement" (ibid., 25). My case offers some slight variations to his examples, however. Twitch has diverged in minor ways by creating its own content and also hands off the bulk of moderation to the community, both of which I will discuss more.

5. For additional insight on patterns across channels, see Deng et al. 2015.

6. Tarleton Gillespie (2018, 24) argues that "most social media companies have discovered that there is more revenue to be had by gathering and mining user data," and, though it has not happened yet, the Amazon purchase may be one way this comes to be a more powerful reality for Twitch, bringing it into line with non-gaming focused sites.

7. There have even been broadcasts of the classic game "mafia" (a variant on "werewolf") that involve a group of people with a secret assassin in their midst that they have to uncover simply by speculating, guessing, and in the case of the killer, bluffing.

8. Vlambeer has been particularly adept at leveraging new platforms for development processes. Their use of Valve's "Early Access" Steam program as well as YouTube to foster feedback and iteration has garnered interest, and praise, from both developers and gamers alike. The integration of Twitch, which Ismail described as "Performative Game Development," was presented at the 2014 Game Developer's Conference (http://www.edge-online.com/news/why-vlambeer -is-turning-nuclear-thrones-development-into-a-performance/). The company has a notably open approach to providing anyone authorization to not only use their games for creating videos or live streaming but also monetize that content (see http://vlambeer.com/monetize/).

9. See, for example, Linda Hughes foundational research from the 1980s.

10. Julian Dibbell's (1998) book on the text-based world LambdaMOO in particular offered a deeply important entry for Lawrence Lessig's (1999) now nearly canonical book *Code Is Law*—a work that helped articulate to an audience well beyond science and technology studies the deep interrelation between the technical and political. See also Lastowka 2010; Lastowka and Hunter 2004.

11. See, for example, Giddings 2008; Jakobsson 2011; Postigo 2016.

12. See, for example, Copier 2007;Mortensen 2006; Nardi 2010; Pearce 2009; Steinkuehler 2006; Sundén 2003; Turkle 1995.

13. See, for example, Gray 2014; Jenson and de Cassell 2008; Kennedy 2006; Kocurek 2015; Kolko 2000; Ruberg, forthcoming; Shaw 2014.

14. See, for example, Kendall 2002; Nakamura 2002, 2009; Gray 2016.

15. See, for example, Lowood 2011; Postigo 2003, 2015; Sotamaa 2007b; Wirman 2009.

16. See, for example, Banks 2013; Banks and Humphreys 2008

17. See, for example, Kline, Dyer-Witheford, and de Peuter 2003; Dyer-Witheford and de Peuter 2009.

18. While the majority of my focus was on Twitch, I did spend some time on competitor sites, and had conversations with those involved with them, to give me a broader context and sense of comparison.

19. AnyKey is an initiative of Intel and the ESL. Intel funded it from 2015–17, while ESL provided administrative assistance (helping make travel arrangements for events, bookkeeping, etc.). I was not paid for any of my time, though some of the Intel money, via ESL, supported a graduate student in my department for two years during this period (after the bulk of the data collection for this book).

20. Some interviewees articulate a value in being publicly known or recognized, especially in work that becomes a historical document. Being legitimized in a publication can be compelling. In this project, for example, I had an extensive conversation with a broadcaster who initially wanted to be named. Though my own ethical code compels me to anonymize, we spent time talking through both of our perspectives, and ultimately I offered to think about other ways I might help with publicizing their endeavors when appropriate outside the scope of this book or scholarly publications. I found the conversation valuable for talking through the issues with a participant as well as thinking about interventions those of us doing work in UGC environments might start to creatively consider as we navigate ethics and publications. For another look at the handling of reciprocity and esports in research, see Taylor 2016a.

21. Though I do not spend time discussing the relationship between Twitch and YouTube content here, streamer Philipp "Moldran" Karbun (2015) wrote his bachelor's thesis on live streaming, and discusses how broadcasters can leverage back and forth between the platforms to build their brand.

Chapter 2. Networked Broadcasting

1. For more on the history of interactive television, see Carey 1997; Jenson 2008.

2. As one of the first people to tackle esports broadcasting put it to me, "Frankly I've always been live, you know. I'm not one of the YouTube guys. Like I don't really, I mean it's not like I don't care about my VODs, but for me the thrill of broadcasting always came because it was live. We gauge this all the way back to the early 2000s, when we were doing the live audio broadcasting, you know. At that point we didn't really have places to put our MP3s either. So it was like if you didn't hear it live, you probably missed out on it."

3. One important qualification: Graeme Turner (2009) notes that it is all too easy for scholars to overreach in their analysis and imagine that US television trajectories hold true globally (which they don't). My argument in the following is focused on the US context.

4. See also Ducheneaut et al. 2008; Hallvard, Poell, and van Dijck 2016; Wang 2015; Wilson 2016.

5. For a historical overview, see Lotz 2014.

6. This shift is also happening on radio. With the dramatic growth of podcasting, more and more audio content, often produced by amateurs, is being distributed and broadcast via nontraditional outlets. Apps such as TuneIn radio can also help producers even bypass places like the Apple Store and run 24-7 radio stations. These often focus not on music but rather talk shows covering everything from politics to UFOs.

7. For more on how digital and network technology is altering traditional broadcast TV, see Gripsrud 2010; Lotz 2014; Turner and Tay 2009.

8. For more on the reality television and labor angle, see Andrejevic 2004.

9. Jean Burgess and Joshua Green (2009, 109) also wisely prompt us to remember that "there is much that *is* new about YouTube but there is also much that is old. . . . [T]he emergence of participatory cultures of all kinds over the past several decades paved the way for the early embrace, quick adoption, and diverse use of such platforms."

10. For an overview of some infrastructure issues related to online broadcasting, see Sandvig 2015.

11. For a more extensive list of "life logging" activities that often included televisual content such as Steve Mann's early experiments with wearables and cameras, see Achilleos 2003.

12. Live streaming remains a popular technology in sex work and the porn industry. A visitor to some adult live streaming sites would immediately notice the similarities in technological affordances and user interface conventions between them and game live streaming platforms.

13. For another discussion of JenniCam, "cyborg subjectivity," and gender via an early cam project, see Jimroglou 1999.

14. Though Senft's (2008, 38) work predates it slightly, she astutely anticipates how Justin .tv's "'featured channels,' for example, shows how the site has managed to mix 'reality ideology,' micro-celebrity, and streaming video technology to create JenniCams for a new era."

15. Alice Marwick (2013) picks up on these themes of celebrity and branding on social media.

16. The original site and assets were sold (after bankruptcy) in 2001. The current site, while still doing online streaming at the time of this writing, is a far cry from the prior one.

17. Niche, that is, at least in the public imagination. Sites like Chatroulette, which randomly connects people by video, continue to draw users (Kreps 2010). More significantly, adult live cam websites like Chaturbate or MyFreeCams are estimated to have in the range of several million daily hits.

18. See, for example, Burgess and Green 2009; Jenkins 1992, 2006a, 2006b; Kavoori 2011; Lange 2007, 2010; Snickars and Vonderau 2009.

19. See Jenkins 1992, 2006a.

20. The concept of vernacular creativity originated in Burgess 2007.

21. For fascinating historical analyses of arcades as both cultural and technological sites, see Kocurek 2015; Guins 2014.

22. Trying to understand why people watch is where the bulk of research on game live streams has centered thus far. Gifford Cheung and Jeff Huang (2011), for example, used the game *StarCraft* to explore why people enjoy spectating games. They found a range similar to my own (identifying categories like "the curious" or "the pupil"). In one of the earliest papers to examine live streaming specifically, Mehdi Kaytoue and colleagues (2012) analyzed Twitch streams over a hundred days and sought to understand patterns of viewership, particularly around esports. Thomas Smith, Marianna Obrist, and Peter Wright (2013) looked at how motivations might differ for viewers around genres like speedrunning, Let's Play's, and esports, and offered provisional reflections on notions of reciprocity or learning from others. Somewhat similarly, William

Hamilton, Oliver Garretson, and Andruid Kerne (2014) tap into the power of "participatory communities" as a draw for viewers who value social and shared experiences. Enrico Gandolfi's (2016) study echoes many of these same themes, situating viewership among the gaming habits and identities of the audience as well as the culture of gaming writ large. Finally, Max Sjöblom and Juho Hamari (2016, 6) adopt a uses-and-gratifications approach to understanding viewership, and conclude that "on a general level, our results reveal that all five classes of gratification (cognitive, affective, social, tension release, and personal integrative) were significantly associated with the main outcome variables related to how many hours and how many streamers individual users watch." See also Sjöblom et al. 2017.

23. This is akin to longtime findings in television studies that the majority of people do other things while watching TV (Morley 1992).

24. It is actually possible to utilize a third-party program (like an IRC client) to tap into the chat directly. While moderators, streamers, and other high-end users will do this, average audience members are simply using the chat window off to the side within the channel itself.

25. For more on creative approaches to shared live streaming experiences (outside gaming) and collective annotation practices, see William Gordon Mangum's (2016) work on the Deep-Stream platform.

26. Amanda Lotz does a good job of showing how changes in distribution channels frequently upset traditional audience measurement techniques and how engagement has become a new currency in the postnetwork era. This chase after engagement, which is something more than simply watching but also involves demonstrating your participation as a viewer through things like sharing on social media, has become a rubric around which a number of platforms now offer metrics.

27. See also Brody 2004; Kosterich and Napoli 2016; Burroughs and Rugg 2014.

28. Marcella Szablewicz's fascinating research on esports in China gives a slightly different twist to the work of audiences in large events there. She asserts that the spectacle of these tournaments is not meant to serve spectatorship but instead is a "platform on which nationalism and ideology are displayed. It is in these public settings that domestic and international audiences encounter representations of Chinese ideal citizenship, technological development, and market principles" (Szablewicz 2016, 271).

29. For more on this concept, see Bourdieu 1984; Adkins 2011.

30. Kan and Seibel both went on to become partners at Y Combinator and founders of Socialcam, Shear became CEO of Twitch, and Vogt went on to start a company dedicated to autonomous driving that was purchased by General Motors.

31. All amounts in US dollars unless otherwise indicated.

32. It is worth noting that this is also an angle that is reasonably critiqued across the industry as sidelining potentially good talent who do not identify as a gamer (a category we know cuts differentially, especially across gender and age).

33. See, for example, Gillespie 2007; Postigo 2012.

34. For more on sports live streaming, see Birmingham and David 2011; Mellis 2008.

35. Unlike Justin.tv, a later platform, Aereo, which for a fee broadcast cable TV via its website, was not able to resist the serious pushback by the cable companies and closed after just two years in operation. For a brief overview, see https://en.wikipedia.org/wiki/Aereo.

36. See Joshua Braun's (2013) fascinating discussion of Hulu and Boxee as sociotechnical systems for more on how we might bring an inflected form of analysis about science and technology studies into conversation with considerations of media infrastructure engineering.

37. The economic issues at stake in live streaming are often invisible but critical. For example, Justin.tv's "first web-server bill was $40,000" (Rice 2012). If it hit the maximum number of streams for a particular country, viewers would only be able to access the content by paying

a $9.99/month subscription fee. The costs that these "free" platforms incur can be some of the most important economic challenges they have to navigate, especially early on.

38. Alongside the technical specifications and help, Twitch (2018) provides this brief note on aesthetics: "Design is subjective, so we do not dictate what 'good design' means on our platform. However, there are several best practices you should consider, to ensure that your extension is a good experience for your audience." It goes on to discuss things like branding, color, layout, and other design elements.

Chapter 3. Home Studios: Transforming Private Play into Public Entertainment

1. For a look at how some players new to game live streaming approach a broadcast, see Rainforest Scully-Blaker and colleagues' (2017) research introducing people to the platform.

2. This is a video production technique whereby the subject is filmed in front of a green background that allows a new image to be inserted in its place. In the case of live streaming, the effect is that the face of the broadcaster is layered in front of the video game or other image.

3. David Chamberlin's (2011) fascinating look at the interrelation between interfaces, metadata, and power within media is worth mentioning.

4. At the time of this writing, the biggest differences between partners and affiliates are not around basic revenue-generating mechanisms (though Twitch does cover the payout fees for partners) but instead features such as channel emotes, video delay settings and storage, priority support from the company, and access to the "partnership team."

5. Conversations about ad blocking regularly take on a moral quality where streamers appeal to their audiences on the grounds of support or appreciation—something I discuss more later.

6. Anthony Pellicone and June Ahn (2017) analyzed streaming forum threads, and identified several similar components: assembling technology, building community, and adopting a gameplay attitude.

7. The term "crowd work" comes from the realm of stand-up comedy, and describes the interaction between the comedian and audience. Not all stand-up comics see themselves as good at crowd work, distinguishing it as an improvisational skill.

8. He also helpfully links this stance with strategies of management, highlighting that not all broadcast platforms promote active engagement. Walker contrasts the active posture with modes that inculcate passivity, simply offering people a way to broadcast play. This is resonant with my discussion of transformative play in chapter 5.

9. As J. P. McDaniel (2015), a popular streamer, noted about shifting from esports to variety streaming, "I had to retrain my brain with how to act when the camera's on in front of me. And it was really weird to be able to think about that. I don't know if anyone saw that or had to do that. For me, I never even thought about that I actually had to retrain everything. I'm still deadpan but it's very monotone. I would have the 'Welcome to the stream, I'm J.P. McDaniel blah blah blah.' Now I'm just like 'Hey, what's up.' Very social when it comes to that."

10. The practice of "stream sniping"—taking advantage of watching a streamer's broadcast while you play against them—is something that has grown over the years. At least one developer, Bluehole, the maker of the *PlayerUnknown's Battlegrounds*, has banned players for it.

11. As Greg Seigworth and Melissa Gregg (2014, 14) write in their helpful collection of essays on the subject, "Affect is found in those intensities that pass body to body (human, nonhuman, part-body, and otherwise), in those resonances that circulate about, between, and sometimes stick to bodies and worlds, and in the very passages or variations between these intensities and resonances themselves." Affect theory actually offers much to game studies more broadly, especially for those of us who regularly wrangle with data that are rooted in embodied experience

and complex circuits of relation between human and nonhuman actors. I could certainly imagine going back to my own prior fieldwork, on both massively multiplayer online games and esports, and using the lens to reexplore certain domains.

12. It's actually not uncommon to hear traditional entertainers characterize themselves similarly. I recall reading Steve Martin's autobiography, and being struck by his own descriptions of himself as shy and reserved.

13. For more on her analysis of relational labor as it relates to musicians, see Baym 2015, 2018.

14. Kaelan Clare Doyle Myerscough (2017) observed that she has also noticed the term "nation" get used—something that "itself could spawn an entire essay." This has certainly been used in sports, such as "Red Sox Nation."

15. This comment is incredibly similar to one of the musicians Baym (2012, 294) quotes, who says, "'I don't like to call them fans,' said O'Donnell, 'Not anymore. They're more like friends, people that are interested in my music and what I'm doing. [I get] three or four [emails] a day, and I'll answer, and I have good conversations with people.'"

16. This reminds me a bit of Dibbell's (2006) work in which he found that gold farmers in *World of Warcraft* would often, at the end of their shift, change location and log back into the game to play it for leisure.

17. While not formally holding back, I did at times hear broadcasters who had built their reputations around a single title (typically within esports) say that they at times struggled with boredom. After many years playing a particular title, some can come to feel that they are ready to move on, but know that making a jump to a new title can potentially pose a risk of losing some of their audience and having to perhaps compete against streamers who have already established title dominance.

18. Domestic space as the prime live streaming location for individuals has evolved in just the past couple years. With the advent of streaming via cell phones, broadcasting is happening now at all times and in a wide range of spaces. It is also being used to tap into civic engagement, protest, and documentation—from the live streaming of the Ferguson protests to the powerful and devastating Facebook live stream of Philando Castile's shooting at the hands of Saint Paul, Minnesota, police.

19. I was fortunate to able to visit India during the course of this project and go to the largest game cafe in New Delhi as well as spend time with the folks working hard to build esports there. One of the ways that they were tackling the infrastructure issue was creating game cafes not only as a site of play but also as a place to produce live streams. The home studio model doesn't fit in everywhere, and it remains critical to pay attention to material details.

20. When his grandmother died, he shared the news and his grief with his community. The fact that many of his audience had known or seen her online in some way surely made her death impact differently than if they hadn't.

21. Broadcaster Ryoga Vee (2016), in talking about how he faced challenges even trying to find people of color to speak about these subjects publicly at TwitchCon, noted, "The people who I did reach out to turned me down for an interesting reason. They said, 'That sounds like a great panel, but I can't be a part of it.' I'm like why? 'I don't want to alienate my fan base.' They were absolutely terrified that if they spoke out about how racism makes them feel, about how the chat is, or just how the community is, that they would lose subscribers, that people wouldn't follow them anymore, that they would be labeled a social justice warrior." For more on how LGBTQIA gamers navigate complex relationships between their identity, games, and expectations around their tastes and preferences, see Shaw 2014.

22. Often in conversations about gender and live streaming, the popular broadcaster Kaceytron is brought up as a prime illustration of a failed system. Her streams, which can reach thousands watching her play games like *League of Legends*, also play host to a stream of misogynistic

comments by audience members in her chat. For some, she is an example of the awful ways that women are treated on the platform as they face on onslaught of sexist abuse and commentary. Others use her as an instance of the worst kind of "gurl gamer," a woman who trades on her sexuality in lieu of actual gaming expertise. I see Kaceytron as someone playing with the expectation game I've been describing, taking game culture's misogyny, the expectations around what a woman should bring to the platform, and turning it back on itself. She is, as I am not alone in musing, trolling the trolls. For a closer analysis of her channel, see Consalvo, forthcoming.

23. Jefferson (2014) recounts the history of the emote and how it has come to be linked with the trihard tagline in an Ask.FM answer: "Like 4 days later, a few Twitch Cops were lurking in my chat (which was a big deal because I was way smaller back then, like <300 viewer average), saw me going extra apeshit with the swag (because they were there) and asked 'why is he trying so hard?' The rest is history."

24. Earlier I leaned on Ahmed's (2004) notion of affective economies to talk about the social work that emotions do in building streaming communities along with connections between broadcaster and audience. But it's instructive to note that the majority of her argument in the article I cite actually deals with the powerful "binding" role that things like language can hold in constituting hatred and fear as both social and material.

25. For more information on what Twitch provides to people seeking partnership, see http://help.twitch.tv/customer/en/portal/articles/735127-tips-for-applying-to-the-partner-program.

26. For an extensive overview of advertising in the digital age, see Turow 2011.

27. It is worth mentioning that this means a broadcaster will not get a big revenue bump if a special ad campaign is sold at a higher than normal rate.

28. The challenges to advertising online are without a doubt part of a longer struggle around television advertising (including the advent of technologies like the remote control or DVRs). For more on this, see Lotz 2014; Meehan 2005.

29. At the time of this writing, the info page for advertisers lists the following regions that SureStream currently works in: the United States, Canada, Germany, France, Sweden, Belgium, Poland, Norway, Finland, Denmark, the Netherlands, Italy, Spain, Switzerland, Austria, Portugal, the United Kingdom, Australia, and New Zealand. I have been unable to confirm with Twitch if the old system, in which ad blockers remain effective, is still in use in the remaining locales.

30. They are not alone in their assessment. Journalist Doc Searls has also long been tracking signs that the online advertising bubble is about to pop. For a good overview, see http://blogs.harvard.edu/doc/2016/05/09/is-the-online-advertising-bubble-finally-starting-to-pop/.

31. Ethan Zuckerman (2014) has issued his own indictment of the advertising-centric model for the web, arguing against the broader corrosive effects that come from the data aggregation and manipulation: "I have come to believe that advertising is the original sin of the web. The fallen state of our Internet is a direct, if unintentional, consequence of choosing advertising as the default model to support online content and services."

32. Though such figures are certainly impressive, live streaming insider and former Twitch admin Moblord (2017) noted in his analysis of the stats that when you break down the numbers, the folks at the topmost end of the streaming pyramid are akin to that thin slice who makes it into the NFL.

33. For a helpful overview of its use at the Evolution Championship Series in 2016, see Demers 2016; Steiner 2016.

34. The affiliate program was not yet in existence when I undertook the bulk of my research so I do not have any substantial data on if that group feels the same. Anecdotally, it does seem as if gratitude comes into play for them as well.

35. Twitch's deployment of a brand identity meant to inspire a sense of belonging and loyalty is not dissimilar to Nickelodeon's strategy (Banet-Weiser 2007).

36. Sections 317 and 507 are notable. For additional information, see https://transition.fcc .gov/eb/broadcast/sponsid.html.

37. It is worth mentioning that this event dovetailed with the rise of the GamerGate movement, which was supposedly focused on ferreting out what it identified as ethical violations in games coverage. One prominent content creator, John "Total Biscuit" Bain, was a vocal spokesperson around payola in the industry and seen by many in the GamerGate movement as shining a light on questionable industry practices. In the United Kingdom (where Bain was from), the British Advertising authority had also weighed in on the matter of undisclosed endorsements—in that case, "after several U.K. YouTubers were paid to praise Oreos, but none of the videos were clearly labelled as an advertisement" (Hawkins 2014).

38. This ability is possible because of the OpenID API that Steam's trading system utilizes. For more details about how Valve handled the situation, see chapter 4.

39. For an in-depth analysis of the Steam platform with an eye toward labor and political economy, see Joseph 2017.

40. For an overview of Washington State's regulatory rulings and Valve's response, see Campbell 2016b.

41. One, Thomas "Syndicate" Cassell, is accused of not following FTC disclosure rules several times. See https://en.wikipedia.org/wiki/Tom_Cassell.

42. In fact, it appears as if MCNs have been in decline as a serious organizing structure, even on YouTube, despite being tremendously popular and powerful at one period. As a TechCrunch piece noted, "It isn't a YouTube-only world anymore. Now, of course, we have Facebook, Snapchat, Twitter, Amazon and a host of other behemoths that have significantly evolved into digital-first media companies themselves. These 'off YouTube' platforms are increasingly important to both creators and the former MCNs supporting them that want to distribute their content across as many platforms as possible (tailored to the specific DNA of each)" (Csathy 2016).

Chapter 4. Esports Broadcasting: Ditching the TV Dream

1. See, for example, the helpful collection from Wenner 1998.

2. For a detailed history of early esports, see Taylor 2012.

3. Both British Sky Broadcasting and Star TV were a part of Rupert Murdoch's NewsCorp.

4. For more on my visits to the CGS offices, attending its last championship, and an analysis of its fit in the scene at that time, see Taylor 2012.

5. One longtime broadcaster described how his sense of the power of live content had links back to his days listening to famed AM radio broadcaster Art Bell, who he considered a childhood hero: "I would listen to Art Bell all the time. I grew up listening to some other AM radio personalities. They were my inspiration for basically saying, 'I want to do a gaming show obviously, you know, not with aliens and ghosts, but I just liked how Art was himself. I like that he talked frankly. I liked that he called people out when he interviewed them. I just, I liked that guy.' AM radio was all live, right. I mean, occasionally you rebroadcast, but you're listening to it because it's like sort of an active listening and that's just, I feel like that's kind of the mentality that I was sort of raised on. So that's just kind of why I tend to lean toward the live versus the archive and VOD." In addition to doing more traditional commentating, he was one of the earliest people to do an esports talk show, complete with call-ins.

6. This is perhaps not dissimilar from the earliest days of computer game development birthed from the hobbyist community.

7. A notable exception was in South Korea, where broadcast television stepped in and had the infrastructure as well as money to make distribution possible.

8. The early history of arcade video captures is compellingly covered in the 2007 documentary *King of Kong*, directed by Seth Gordon.

9. For a glimpse into a proposed broadcast system at HLTV, see Otten 2001.

10. My field notes put this as 2004, but I defer to his date here.

11. It is worth noting that all continue to hold significant roles within the esports and game broadcasting industry.

12. Graham (ibid.) provides some fantastic historical tidbits in this post including insight into the earliest video broadcasting: "Another interesting fact is that at one point Nullsoft tried to create 'Nullsoft Video.' Before we broadcasted on Windows Media and Quicktime Broadcaster (and even before Stickam/Ustream/Twitch/etc) we attempted to stream our first major event using this technology, QuakeCon 2004, DOOM 3 1v1. The end result was a 320x240 presentation of Doom 3 that is absolutely LOL when you look at what is being done today (and how awesome the quality is)."

13. ATEM, despite seeming to be an acronym, is actually a name used by the Black Magic line of switchers. "M/E" does, however, stand for mix effects in this context.

14. For more on the concept of serious leisure, see Gillespie, Leffler, and Lerner 2002; Stebbins 2004.

15. I recall when Emma Witkowski and I did some research (2010) at the large LAN party DreamHack, and only cluing in late in the event that much of the multiplayer gaming was being organized not in person but rather online via several IRC channels.

16. There is yet another fascinating layer as well: the incredibly long shifts that these events require mean that people have to find time to squeeze in personal connection with family back home. Over the years I have seen backstage Skype chats with children and partners, Facebook windows open to connect with friends, and personal emails interleaved with work ones.

17. Fieldwork in these spaces was continually one of varying focuses and attentions, conscious and inadvertent over the course of several days. These are methodological and likely theoretical challenges when doing work on networked spaces. Where, exactly, is the field you are in? It is, quite literally, multisited (Marcus 1995). To actually be present is not only to attend to what is materially there but also how the production is made up of a range of distributed technologies and infrastructures. The technologies at work in broadcasting an event like this span from those we most immediately recognize to those who not only go unseen but are, quite intentionally, made hidden to most observers as well. This isn't only a research curiosity; it is a powerful reality for those who do production work.

18. There is also a tremendous amount of preproduction work that happens that can include everything from making tournament brackets to laying schematics for all aspects of the event.

19. One of the best peeks into some behind-the-scenes work in esports production can be found in the 2015 documentary *All Work, All Play*, directed by Patrick Creadon.

20. She did, however, note a broader range of frames across titles such that there was not an easy one-to-one correspondence with traditional sports. She additionally found that the ways that casters handle narrating pro players performances involves considerations of gender.

21. None of this is dissimilar from contemporary sports. Stadiums regularly have screens up showing closer views of the play, broadcasting for people standing waiting for food or going to the bathroom. We could also think of the attendee tuned into radio coverage while simultaneously watching (something I found myself doing at one event where the announcers couldn't be heard well in the audience).

22. The training component of moderation is still fairly uneven. As one lead esports moderator put it to me, "[The guidelines are] common sense, really. I think over time, Twitch chat has just kind of like started to moderate themselves, like OK, no spamming, links, no all caps. And a

lot of that can also be really just by bots. You have a bot watching the channel like, 'Oh, this guy's typing in all caps for the past five minutes. I think we should ban him.'"

23. See Dosh 2016; "Major League" 2013; Thompson 2014.

24. In addition, 2008 was when the "official Blizzard fansite WoW Radio broadcast live audio via SHOUTcast" (http://central.gutenberg.org/articles/eng/BlizzCon).

25. As Demers (2016) mentions in his analysis of crowdfunding, "Due to advocacy by him (and according to other accounts), this eventually was rectified for James and other talent. American talent reportedly received different contracts with a base. Russian talent did not know their base fee until they were paid." The uneven handling of this is worrying. As a side note, it is probably worth mentioning that Gabe Newell, cofounder of Valve, ended up publicly berating Harding for issues related to his performance.

26. For more on this, see Taylor 2012. See also some of the white papers on AnyKey.org, an initiative focused on diversity in esports.

27. We might also extend this to say that with a few exceptions, the model is racialized and it is white men in particular who are the imagined audience.

28. For an excellent overview of serious critical issues around this form of data, see boyd and Crawford 2012.

29. For more on this, see Ang 1991; Morley 1992; Silverstone 1994.

30. For more on how gender and age are often mistakenly conflated in game demographic analysis, see Yee 2008.

31. Similarly, I would not want to ground equity in esports around a case about science, technology, engineering, and mathematics training, education, or "pipelines"; access to esports should be seen as a basic human right like any other.

32. See, for example, Bleier 1986; Fausto-Sterling 1985, 2000; Laqueur 1990; Longino 1990; Tarvis 1992.

33. This also included women's participation more broadly: "It's not just viewership, but engagement. Fantasy football participation grew to include 6.4 million women in 2013, a 10 percent single-year jump from the 5.8 million who played in 2012" (Chemi 2014).

34. "Pink jerseys" epitomize a poor intervention and tend to be the shorthand for simplistic attempts. For more on the oversimplification of addressing women in the MLB audience, see Angi 2014.

35. For more on this, see Angus 2013.

36. For more along this line, see Applebaum 2014.

37. Frankly things are not much better for older men, not to mention women, either. As a 2014 *New York Times* article put it, "Working, in America, is in decline. The share of prime-age men—those 25 to 54 years old—who are not working has more than tripled since the late 1960s, to 16 percent. More recently, since the turn of the century, the share of women without paying jobs has been rising, too. The United States, which had one of the highest employment rates among developed nations as recently as 2000, has fallen toward the bottom of the list" (Applebaum 2014).

38. For more on this argument, see Taylor 2008.

39. This competition extends to hiring. Given the industry's community and enthusiast roots (even within formal companies), it is perhaps not surprising that it has been a small world so far. While many begin their esports careers with scrappy grassroots start-ups, ultimately there are a handful of viable companies you can work for if you really want to build a long professional life in the scene. In much the same way that top players may move from team to team, business talent itself is a valuable commodity, and over the last few years it has been fascinating to watch people move across competing companies.

40. It is also rumored that informal nonpoaching agreements for employees have been utilized and at times broken.

41. For more on DreamHack, see Taylor and Witkowski 2010.

42. WME is the product of a 2009 merger between the William Morris Agency (which dated back to 1898) and Endeavor Talent Agency. Both agencies had a notable impact on the entertainment industry, from films to music. In 2013, WME acquired IMG, which is actively involved in multiple levels of sports talent and media deals.

43. Notably, other onetime television events have continued since the CGS. In 2015 alone, both the BBC and ESPN ventured into broadcasting major tournaments.

44. Astute readers will catch that this occurred about five months before the MLG purchase.

45. Interestingly, third-party companies are also getting into licensing scuffles with each other. In January 2017, ESL filed suit against Azubu for $1.5 million for breach of contract. ESL had sold Azubu the rights to stream its content and alleged that it had never been paid. In late March 2018 it was reported that the suit was settled in December 2017, though the terms were not disclosed (Brautigam 2017, 2018).

Chapter 5. Regulating the Networked Broadcasting Frontier

1. See Lingle 2016.

2. This is a thread explored by game studies over a number of years. See, for example, some of my prior work on governance and control (Taylor 2006a, 2006b, 2012).

3. Though in online systems this is a difficult status to truly enforce as users can (if not IP banned) simply create a new account and come back onto the channel.

4. For a consideration of how pranking and trolling also cycle into live streaming performances, see Karhulahti 2016.

5. There is another form of bot (though not related to chat) worth briefly mentioning here: the viewbot. Viewbots are artificial "viewers" that inflate audience numbers, helping boost channel visibility and notoriety. Viewbots are cheap to buy online as a service via a website, and are regularly the subject of skirmishes, accusations, and rebuttals. People will accuse a streamer of using viewbots, and sometimes streamers will claim that someone has sent viewbots to their channel in an attempt to disrupt them. There are also countertools, such as the third-party "Twitch Bot Detector" that tries to identify channels that are utilizing bots and publicly tweets the information out (@botdetectorbot).

6. For more on the protest uses of DDOS, see Sauter 2014.

7. For the classic example of a call for net libertarianism, see Barlow 1996.

8. For more on this, see Taylor 2006b.

9. For more on GamerGate, see Chess and Shaw 2015; Dewey 2014; Hathaway 2014; Massanari 2017; Parkin 2014.

10. For more on this, see Uszkoreit, forthcoming; Witkowski, forthcoming.

11. Maddy Myers (2014) tackles some of these issues.

12. At times this even takes on a "think about the children quality," as in the poster, Why_the_Flame, who wrote on May 22, 2015, that "Twitch has created an environment where it pays to be sexually suggestive (one prominent 'cam girl' has even unashamedly boasted about this on live stream chat with Twitch admins present), on a site that isn't age gated to prevent hormonal youngsters from being suckered in by their actions."

13. There are even YouTube videos documenting and celebrating these raids on women streamers.

14. The notion of transformation in play appears in several works: the transformational component of play particularly around learning (see, for example, Sasha Barab, Melissa Gresalfi, and Adam Ingram-Goble's [2010] overview of this approach), child's play as transformative (see

TWC Editor 2009), Katie Salen and Eric Zimmerman (2003), on transformation in play, and Olli Sotamaa's (2007a) consideration of malleable rule structures. See also Esther MacCallum-Stewart's (2014) overview of this concept within game studies relating to fan producers. The formulation that I am using here—transformative work—leverages a slightly different valence (both in terms of a legal conversation and the *work* of play), though it is certainly resonant with these other uses.

15. The fair use guidelines from the Stanford University Libraries (2015) helpfully relate that there is a "fifth [unspoken] fair use factor" to be aware of: "Fair use involves subjective judgments and are often affected by factors such as a judge or jury's personal sense of right or wrong. Despite the fact that the Supreme Court has indicated that offensiveness is not a fair use factor, you should be aware that a morally offended judge or jury may rationalize its decision against fair use."

16. The Stanford University Libraries (2015) site observes that "determining what is transformative—and the degree of transformation—is often challenging. For example, the creation of a Harry Potter encyclopedia was determined to be 'slightly transformative' (because it made the Harry Potter terms and lexicons available in one volume), but this transformative quality was not enough to justify a fair use defense in light of the extensive verbatim use of text from the Harry Potter books. (Warner Bros. Entertainment, Inc. v. RDR Books, 575 F. Supp. 2d 513 (S.D. N.Y. 2008)." See also http://www.nolo.com/legal-encyclopedia/fair-use-what-transformative.html for more examples.

17. For a helpful listing of notable cease-and-desist orders that have hit fan communities over the years, see http://fanlore.org/wiki/Cease_%26_Desist.

18. See Castronova 2005; Dibbell 2006.

19. See Postigo 2003; Sotamaa 2007b; Taylor 2006a.

20. See Lowood and Nitsche 2011; MacCallum-Stewart 2014; Postigo 2015, 2016.

21. For more on this issue, see Banks 2013.

22. I found a similar argument articulated when I researched massively multiplayer online spaces where players spoke of emergence in a virtual world (Taylor 2006a, 2006b) and among professional esports competitors, who regularly identified their gameplay as highly skilled, virtuoso performances on a digital playing field, akin to professional athletes (Taylor 2012). For more on the complexity of performance and the law, see Tushnet 2013.

23. This is akin to Espen Aarseth's (1997) notion of the ergodic and the unique properties of what he terms "cybertexts."

24. Her book is a powerful answer to Cohen's (2012, 66) call to pay attention to actual experience, such as when she observes, "The copyright system's account of cultural development is relatively incurious about users and their behavior. . . . But if creative practice arises out of the interactions between authors and cultural environments—if authors are users first—failure to explore the place of the user in copyright law is a critical omission."

25. Though the provision originated as a discussion around internet service providers, Fairfield (2009, 1038) observes that it is one invoked by companies beyond that scope (he was particularly concerned with how game companies might need to deal with it), and indeed clarifies that "companies that carry data without interfering or selecting the content are rewarded and protected under a net neutrality paradigm; companies that interfere with data distribution open themselves to risk." He argues that regarding potential risks, game companies need to evaluate "if game gods merely repost or edit third-party content, then there is no liability. But if the game gods editorialize or recontextualize the content, then liability may result" (ibid., 1044).

26. For more on how platforms are approaching issues around content moderation and the safe harbor provision, see Gillespie 2018.

27. Twitch provides its users with a selection of royalty-free tracks through its Music Library service, but most people seem to prefer to listen to their own favorite music while they stream.

Chapter 6. Live Streaming as Media

1. As this manuscript was in the last moments of being edited, the NBA in fact announced its own esports league built around the NBA2K game, thus bridging the traditional and electronic version of the sport.

2. See also Kylie Jarrett's (2009) discussion of the "hybrid discourses" of podcasting for a related conversation on the possibilities for public debate within new media.

3. As Turner (2011, 686) bitingly notes elsewhere, "I do not think anyone denies that the convergence of media and communications technologies is actually happening. Convergence culture, on the other hand, looks to me to be about 20 percent fact and 80 percent speculative fiction. The claims made for its significance are as dramatic as they are unconvincing."

4. See, for example, Terranova 2000; Andrejevic 2009b.

5. Both Matt Hills (2002) and Jarrett (2008a) have written convincingly on this point.

6. See Taylor 2006a, 2006b, 2012.

7. See Henricks 2015.

BIBLIOGRAPHY

Aarseth, Espen. 1997. *Cybertext: Perspectives on Ergodic Literature*. Baltimore: Johns Hopkins University Press.

Achilleos, Kyriacos. 2003. "Evolution of Lifelogging." Paper presented at the 4th Annual Multimedia Systems, Electronics, and Computer Science Conference, University of Southampton, Southampton, UK.

Adkins, Lisa. 2011. "Cultural intermediaries." In *Encyclopedia of Consumer Culture*. 1st ed. Thousand Oaks, CA: Sage.

Ahmed, Sara. 2004. "Affective Economies." *Social Text* 22 (2): 117–39.

Albrecht, Matt. 2014. "Twitch's New 'Dress Appropriately' Policy Is Founded on Obliviousness." *Fireside*, October 28. http://fireside.gamejolt.com/post/twitch-s-new-dress-appropriately -policy-is-founded-on-obliviousness-i8xbwpty.

Andrejevic, Mark. 2004. *Reality TV*. Lanham, MD: Rowman and Littlefield Publishers.

———. 2009a. "Critical Media Studies 2.0: An Interactive Upgrade." *Interactions: Studies in Communication and Culture* 1 (1): 35–51.

———. 2009b. "Exploiting YouTube: Contradictions of User-Generated Labor." In *The YouTube Reader*, edited by Pelle Snickars and Patrick Vonderau, 406–23. Stockholm: National Library of Sweden.

———. 2009c. "The Twenty-First Century Telescreen." In *Television Studies after TV*, edited by Graeme Turner and Jinna Tay, 31–40. London: Routledge.

Ang, Ien. 1991. *Desperately Seeking the Audience*. London: Routledge.

Angi, Cee. 2014. "Baseball Still Doesn't Understand Women." *SBNation*, June 17. http://www .sbnation.com/mlb/2014/6/17/5816758/baseball-promotions-fields-of-fashion-marketing -to-women.

Angus, Kelly. 2013. "Female Sports Fans: An Untapped Sports Marketing Demographic." AskingSmarterQuestions. http://www.askingsmarterquestions.com/female-sports-fans-an -untapped-sports-marketing-demographic/.

Applebaum, Binyamin. 2014. "The Vanishing Male Worker: How America Fell Behind." *New York Times*, December 11. https://www.nytimes.com/2014/12/12/upshot/unemployment -the-vanishing-male-worker-how-america-fell-behind.html.

Aufderheide, Patricia, and Peter Jaszi. 2011. *Reclaiming Fair Use*. Chicago: University of Chicago Press.

Banet-Weiser, Sarah. 2007. "The Nickelodeon Brand: Buying and Selling the Audience." In *Cable Visions: Television beyond Broadcasting*, edited by Sarah Banet-Weiser, Cynthia Chris, and Anthony Freitas, 234–52. New York: NYU Press.

Banks, John. 2013. *Co-Creating Videogames*. London: Bloomsbury.

Banks, John, and Sal Humphreys. 2008. "The Labor of User Co-Creators." *Convergence* 14 (4): 401–18.

Barab, Sasha A., Melissa Gresalfi, and Adam Ingram-Goble. 2010. "Transformational Play: Using Games to Position Person, Content, and Context." *Educational Researcher* 39 (7): 525–36.

Barlow, John Perry. 1996. "A Declaration of Independence in Cyberspace." Electronic Frontier Foundation. https://www.eff.org/cyberspace-independence.

Barrett, Brian. 2016. "Netflix's Grand, Daring, Maybe Crazy Plan to Conquer the World." *Wired*. March 27. https://www.wired.com/2016/03/netflixs-grand-maybe-crazy-plan-conquer-world/.

Batchelor, James. 2015. "Twitch Creates VP of Game Developer Success Role." MCV, November 16. https://www.mcvuk.com/development/twitch-creates-vp-of-game-developer-success-role.

Baym, Nancy. 2012. "Fans or Friends? Seeing Social Media Audiences as Musicians Do." *Participations* 9 (2): 286–316.

———. 2013. "Data Not Seen: The Uses and Shortcomings of Social Media Metrics." *First Monday* 18 (10). http://firstmonday.org/ojs/index.php/fm/article/view/4873/3752.

———. 2015. "Connect with Your Audience! The Relational Labor of Connection." *Communication Review* 18 (1): 14–22.

———. 2018. *Playing to the Crowd*. New York: NYU Press.

"Before and after Title IX: Women in Sports." 2012. *New York Times*, June 17. http://www.nytimes.com/interactive/2012/06/17/opinion/sunday/sundayreview-titleix-timeline.html#.

Beres, Damon. 2014. "Twitch Insists Gamers Keep Their Clothes On." *Huffington Post*, October 28. http://huff.to/1tfxcDD.

Berg, Madeline. 2016. "The Highest-Paid YouTube Stars 2016." *Forbes*, December 5. http://www.forbes.com/sites/maddieberg/2016/12/05/the-highest-paid-youtube-stars-2016-pewdiepie-remains-no-1-with-15-million/#614b51aa6b0f.

Birmingham, Jack, and Matthew David. 2011. "Live-Streaming: Will Football Fans Continue to Be More Law Abiding than Music Fans?" *Sport in Society* 14 (1): 69–80.

Blackmon, Samantha. 2015. "TL;DL: On the Need for Diversity in Twitch Streams and Let's Plays." Not Your Mama's Gamer, March 27. http://www.samanthablackmon.net/notyourmamasgamer/?p=7075.

Bleier, Ruth. 1986. "Sex Differences Research: Science or Belief?" In *Feminist Approaches to Science*, edited by Ruth Bleier, 147–64. New York: Pergamon Press.

Bourdieu, Pierre. 1984. *Distinction: A Cultural Critique of the Judgement of Taste*. Translated by Richard Nice. London: Routledge.

Bowker, Geoffrey C., and Susan Leigh Star. 1999. *Sorting Things Out: Classification and Its Consequences*. Cambridge, MA: MIT Press.

boyd, danah, and Kate Crawford. 2012. "Critical Questions for Big Data." *Information, Communication, and Society* 15 (5): 662–79.

Bratich, Jack Z. 2008. "Activating the Multitude: Audience Powers and Cultural Studies." In *New Directions in American Reception Study*, edited by Philip Goldstein and James Machor, 33–56. Oxford: Oxford University Press.

Braun, Joshua. 2013. "Going over the Top: Online Television Distribution as Sociotechnical System." *Communication, Culture, and Critique* 6:432–58.

Brautigam, Thiemo. 2017. "ESL Sues Azubu, Claims a Minimum of $1.5 Million." *Daily Dot*, September 3. https://dotesports.com/business/news/esl-sues-azubu-for-one-and-a-half-million-17063.

———. 2018. "Lawsuit Over $1.5M between ESL and Azubu Settled." *Esports Observer*, March 30. https://esportsobserver.com/esl-azubu-lawsuit-settled/.

Breslau, Rod "Slasher". 2012. "MLG CEO Enters the Arena." *GameSpot*, July 24. https://www.gamespot.com/videos/sundance-digiovanni-interview/2300-6356131/.

Brock, Tom. 2017. "Roger Caillois and E-Sports: On the Problems of Treating Play as Work." *Games and Culture* 12 (4): 321–39.

Brody, William. 2004. "Interactive Television and Advertising Form in Contemporary U.S. Television." In *Television after TV*, edited by Lynn Spiegel and Jan Olsson, 113–32. Durham, NC: Duke University Press.

Bruns, Axel. 2006. "Towards Produsage: Futures for User-Led Content Production." In *Proceedings Cultural Attitudes towards Communication and Technology 2006*, edited by Fay Sudweeks, Herbert Hrachovec, and Charles Ess, 275–84. Tartu, Estonia.

———. 2009. "The User-Led Disruption: Self-(Re)Broadcasting at Justin.Tv and Elsewhere." Paper presented at EuroITV'09, Leuven, Belgium, June 3–5.

Brustein, Joshua, and Eben Novy-Williams. 2016. "Virtual Weapons Are Turning Teen Gamers into Serious Gamblers." *Bloomberg.* https://www.bloomberg.com/features/2016-virtual-guns-counterstrike-gambling/.

Burgess, Jean. 2006. "Hearing Ordinary Voices: Cultural Studies, Vernacular Creativity, and Digital Storytelling." *Continuum: Journal of Media and Cultural Studies* 2 (20): 201–14.

———. 2007. "Vernacular Creativity and New Media." PhD diss., Queensland University of Technology.

Burgess, Jean, and Joshua Green. 2009. *YouTube: Online Video and Participatory Culture.* Cambridge, UK: Polity.

Burroughs, Benjamin, and Adam Rugg. 2014. "Extending the Broadcast: Streaming Culture and the Problems of Digital Geographies." *Journal of Broadcasting and Electronic Media* 58 (3): 365–80.

Caillois, Roger. 2001. *Man, Play, and Games.* Translated by Meyer Barash. Urbana: University of Illinois Press. First published 1961.

Caldwell, John. 2004. "Convergence Television." In *Television after TV*, edited by Lynn Spigel and Jan Olsson, 41–74. Durham, NC: Duke University Press.

Campbell, Colin. 2016a. "Racism, Hearthstone, and Twitch," Polygon, May 12. http://www.polygon.com/features/2016/5/12/11658440/twitch-abuse-hearthstone.

———. 2016b. "Valve Fires Back at Washington State Gambling Commission over CS:GO Betting." Polygon, October 18. http://www.polygon.com/2016/10/18/13318326/valve-fires-back-at-washington-state-gambling-commission-over-cs-go-betting.

Carey, John. 1997. "Interactive Television Trials and Marketplace Experiences." *Multimedia Tools and Applications* 5:207–16.

Castronova, Edward. 2005. *Synthetic Worlds.* Chicago: University of Chicago Press.

Chaloner, Paul. 2015. Talking Esports: A Guide to Becoming a World-Class Esports Broadcaster. http://redeyehd.co.uk/talking-esports-a-free-book-on-esports-broadcasting/.

———. 2016. "Monte's Claims Outline Deeper Debate in Caster Pay." Slingshot, September 27. https://slingshotesports.com/2016/09/27/paul-redeye-chaloner-montecristo-caster-pay-league-of-legends/.

Chamberlin, David. 2011. "Scripted Spaces." In *Television as Digital Media*, edited by James Bennett and Niki Strange, 230–54. Durham, NC: Duke University Press.

Champlin, Alexander. 2016. "Risky Play: Swatting Streamers, or Now You're Playing with (Police) Power." *Media Fields Journal* 11:1–11.

Chemi, Eric. 2014. "The NFL Is Only Growing because of Women." *Bloomberg*, September 26. http://www.bloomberg.com/news/articles/2014-09-26/the-nfl-is-growing-only-because-of-female-fans.

Chess, Shira, and Adrianne Shaw. 2015. "A Conspiracy of Fishes, or, How We Learned to Stop Worrying about #GamerGate and Embrace Hegemonic Masculinity." *Journal of Broadcasting and Electronic Media* 59 (1): 208–20.

Cheung, Gifford, and Jeff Huang. 2011. "Starcraft from the Stands: Understanding the Game Spectator." Paper presented at CHI 2011, Vancouver, BC, May 7–12.

Citron, Danielle Keats. 2014. *Hate Crimes in Cyberspace*. Cambridge, MA: Harvard University Press.

Clark, Taylor. 2017. "How to Get Rich Playing Video Games Online." *New Yorker*, November 20.

Cohen, Julie. 2012. *Configuring the Networked Self: Law, Code, and the Play of Everyday Practice*. New Haven, CT: Yale University Press.

Consalvo, Mia. Forthcoming. "Kaceytron and Transgressive Play on Twitch." In *Transgressions in Games and Play*, edited by Kristine Jørgensen and Faltin Karlsen. Cambridge, MA: MIT Press.

Constine, Josh. 2016a. "Facebook Live Attacks Twitch with Game Streaming." TechCrunch, June 6. https://techcrunch.com/2016/06/06/facetwitch/.

———. 2016b. "Heads Up Twitch, Facebook Just Hired Gamer Snoopeh for Its E-Sports Division." TechCrunch, June 16. https://techcrunch.com/2016/06/16/boom-face-shot/.

Conti, Olivia. 2013. "Disciplining the Vernacular: Fair Use, YouTube, and Remixer Agency," *M/C Journal* 16 (4). http://www.journal.media-culture.org.au/index.php/mcjournal/article/view/685.

Coombs, Rosemary J. 1998. *The Cultural Life of Intellectual Properties: Authorship, Appropriation, and the Law*. Durham, NC: Duke University Press.

Copier, Marinka. 2007. "Beyond the Magic Circle." PhD diss., Utrecht University.

Csathy, Peter. 2016. "Whatever Happened to MCNs?" Tech Crunch, June 10. https://techcrunch.com/2016/06/10/whatever-happened-to-mcns/.

D'Anastasio, Cecilia. 2016. "Twitch's AutoMod Is Already a Game-Changer, Streamers Say." Kotaku Australia, December 15. http://www.kotaku.com.au/2016/12/twitchs-automod-is-already-a-game-changer-streamers-say/.

Dave, Paresh. 2016. "Riot Games Closes in on Landmark Streaming Deal for E-Sports with Mlb Advanced Media." *Los Angeles Times*, November 22. http://www.latimes.com/business/technology/la-fi-tn-la-tech-20161122-story.html.

Davis, Wendy. 2012. "Justin.tv, UFC Settle Copyright Lawsuit." Mediapost, April 20. http://www.mediapost.com/publications/article/172946/justintv-ufc-settle-copyright-lawsuit.html?edition=.

Dayal, Geeta. 2012. "The Algorithmic Copyright Cops: Streaming Video's Robotic Overlords." *Wired*, September 6. https://www.wired.com/2012/09/streaming-videos-robotic-overlords-algorithmic-copyright-cops/all/.

Demers, Matt. 2016. "Thoughts on Twitch Cheering Post-Evo 2016." MattDemers.com, July 19. http://mattdemers.com/thoughts-on-twitch-cheering-post-evo-2016/.

Deng, Jie, Felix Cuadrado, Gareth Tyson, and Steve Uhlig. 2015. "Behind the Game: Exploring the Twitch Streaming Platform." *NetGames: IEEE 14th International Workshop on Network and Systems Support for Games*. Zagreb, Croatia, December 3–4.

Dewey, Caitlin. 2014. "The Only Guide to Gamergate You Will Ever Need to Read." *Washington Post*, October 14. https://www.washingtonpost.com/news/the-intersect/wp/2014/10/14/the-only-guide-to-gamergate-you-will-ever-need-to-read/?utm_term=.d6b3e716787a.

Dibbell, Julian. 1998. *My Tiny Life*. New York: Holt.

———. 2006. *Play Money*. New York: Basic Books.

Distortednet. 2014. "Does Anyone Else Feel 'Weird' When They Witness Stuff Like This?" Reddit, November 18. https://www.reddit.com/r/Twitch/comments/2mo6k6/does_anyone_else_feel_weird_when_they_witness/cm61rjm.

Domise, Andray. 2017. "Black Streamers Are Here to Save the Gaming Community." Fanbros, November. http://fanbros.com/black-streamers-save-gaming/.

Dosh, Kristi. 2016. "The Evolution of Marketing to Female Sports Fans." *Forbes*, February 22. https://www.forbes.com/sites/kristidosh/2016/02/22/the-evolution-of-marketing-to-female-sports-fans/#2b4155bf7fc3.

Dovey, Jon, and Helen Kennedy. 2006. *Game Cultures: Computer Games as New Media*. New York: Open University Press.

Ducheneaut, Nicolas, Robert J. Moore, Lora Oehlberg, James D. Thornton, and Eric Nickell. 2008. "SocialTV: Designing for Distributed, Sociable Television Viewing." *International Journal of Human-Computer Interaction* 24 (2): 136–54.

Dyer-Witheford, Nick, and Greig de Peuter. 2009. *Games of Empire*. Minneapolis: University of Minnesota Press.

Ellohime. 2015. "From Private Play to Public Entertainment: Live-streaming and the Growth of Online Broadcast." Panel at the MIT Game Lab, March 5. http://gamelab.mit.edu/event/from-private-play-to-public-entertainment-live-streaming-and-the-growth-of-online-broadcast/.

Fairfield, Joshua A. T. 2009. "The God Paradox." *Boston University Law Review* 89:1017–68.

Fausto-Sterling, Anne.1985. *Myths of Gender*. New York: Basic Books, 1985

———. 2000. *Sexing the Body: Gender Politics and the Construction of Sexuality*. New York: Basic Books.

Federal Trade Commission. 2000. "Advertising and Marketing on the Internet: Rules of the Road." https://www.ftc.gov/tips-advice/business-center/guidance/advertising-marketing-internet-rules-road.

Filewich, Carling "Toastthebadger". 2016. "'Enough Is Enough': Confessions of a Twitch Chat Moderator." GosuGamers. https://www.gosugamers.net/hearthstone/features/39013-enough-is-enough-confessions-of-a-twitch-chat-moderator.

Fisher, Eran. 2015. "'You Media': Audiencing as Marketing in Social Media." *Media, Culture, and Society* 37 (1): 50–67.

Fitzgerald, Drew, and Daisuke Wakabayashi. 2014. "Apple Quietly Builds New Networks." *Wall Street Journal*, February 4, section B1.

Ford, Colin, Dan Gardner, Leah Elaine Horgan, Calvin Liu, a. m. tsaasan, Bonnie Nardi, and Jordan Rickman. 2017. "Chat Speed OP Pogchamp: Practices of Coherence in Massive Twitch Chat." *CHI 2017*, 858–69. Denver, CO, May 6–11.

Freitas, Evan. 2016. "Presenting the Twitch 2016 Year in Review." Twitch, February 16. https://blog.twitch.tv/presenting-the-twitch-2016-year-in-review-b2e0cdc72f18.

Gandolfi, Enrico. 2016. "To Watch or to Play, It Is in the Game: The Game Culture on Twitch.tv among Performers, Plays, and Audiences." *Journal of Gaming and Virtual Worlds* 8 (1): 63–82.

Gannes, Liz. 2009. "Copyright Meets a New Worthy Foe: The Real-Time Web." Gigaom, May 21. https://gigaom.com/2009/05/21/copyright-meets-a-new-worthy-foe-the-real-time-web/.

Giddings, Seth. 2008. "Playing with Nonhumans: Digital Games as Technocultural Form." In *Worlds in Play: International Perspectives on Digital Games Research*, edited by Suzanne de Castell, and Jen Jenson, 115–28. New York: Peter Lang.

Gillespie, Dair L., Ann Leffler, and Elinor Lerner. 2002. "If It Weren't for My Hobby, I'd Have a Life: Dog Sports, Serious Leisure, and Boundary Negotiations." *Leisure Studies* 21:285–304.

Gillespie, Tarleton. 2007. *Wired Shut*. Cambridge, MA: MIT Press.

———. 2010. "The Politics of Platforms." *New Media and Society* 12 (3): 347–64.

———. 2018. *Custodians of the Internet*. New Haven, CT: Yale University Press.

Google. 2018. "Multi-Channel Network (MCN) Overview for YouTube Creators." April 8. https://support.google.com/youtube/answer/2737059?hl=en.

Graham, Marcus. 2011. "Why Is It Called Shoutcasting?" Reddit, November 20. https://www .reddit.com/r/starcraft/comments/mioko/why_is_it_called_shoutcasting/.

Gray, Herman. 1995. *Watching Race*. Minneapolis: University of Minnesota Press.

Gray, Kishonna. 2014. *Race, Gender, and Deviance in Xbox Live*. Oxford: Elsevier.

———. 2016. "They're Just Too Urban: Black Gamers Streaming on Twitch." In *Digital Sociologies*, edited by Jessie Daniels, Karen Gregory, and Tressie McMillan Cottom, 355–68. Bristol, UK: Policy Press.

Gregg, Melissa. 2011. *Work's Intimacy*. Malden, MA: Polity Press.

Gripsrud, Jostein. 2010. *Relocating Television: Television in the Digital Context*. London: Routledge.

Guins, Raiford. 2014. *Game After: A Cultural Study of Video Game Afterlife*. Cambridge, MA: MIT Press.

Hall, Stuart. 1980. "Encoding/Decoding." In *Culture, Media, Language*, edited by Stuart Hall, Dorothy Hobson, Andrew Lowe, and Paul Willis, 117–27. London: Hutchinson.

Hallvard, Moe, Thomas Poell, and José van Dijck. 2016. "Rearticulating Audience Engagement: Social Media and Television." *Television and New Media* 17 (2): 99–107.

Hamilton, William A., Oliver Garretson, and Andruid Kerne. 2014. "Streaming on Twitch: Fostering Participatory Communities of Play within Live Mixed Media." *CHI 2014*, 1315–24. Toronto, ON, April 26–May 1.

Harry, Drew. 2012. "Designing Complementary Communication Systems." PhD diss., Massachusetts Institute of Technology.

Hathaway, Jay. 2014. "What Is Gamergate, and Why? An Explainer for Non-geeks." Gawker, October 10. http://gawker.com/what-is-gamergate-and-why-an-explainer-for-non-geeks -1642909080.

Hawkins, Zoe. 2014. "British Ad Authority Clamping Down on YouTube Payola." Critical Hit, November 27. http://www.criticalhit.net/gaming/british-ad-authority-clamping-down-on -youtube-payola/.

Hendershot, Heather. 2016. *Open to Debate*. New York: Broadside Books.

Henricks, Thomas S. 2015. *Play and the Human Condition*. Urbana: University of Illinois Press.

Hernandez, Patricia. 2015. "Competitive *Call of Duty* Player Says Leaving Twitch Is His 'Biggest Regret.'" Kotaku, October 19. https://kotaku.com/competitive-call-of-duty-star-says -leaving-twitch-is-hi-1737337557.

Hicks, Antonio. 2017. "Streamlabs Live Streaming Report Q2'17—53% Growth, $100M+, Twitch and YouTube Crushing It." Streamlabs, August 2. https://blog.streamlabs.com/streamlabs -live-streaming-report-q217-53-growth-100m-twitch-youtube-crushing-it-1b9048efb4e2.

Hillis, Ken. 2009. *Online a Lot of the Time*. Durham, NC: Duke University Press.

Hills, Matt. 2002. *Fan Cultures*. London: Routledge.

Hughes, Kit. 2014. "'Work/Place' Media: Locating Laboring Audiences." *Media, Culture, and Society* 36 (5): 644–60.

Hughes, Linda. 2006. "Beyond the Rules of the Game: Why Are Rooie Rules Nice?" In *The Game Design Reader*, edited by Katie Salen and Eric Zimmerman, 504–17. Cambridge, MA: MIT Press. First published 1983.

Humphreys, Sal. 2005. "Productive Players: Online Computer Games' Challenge to Conventional Media Forms." *Journal of Communication and Critical/Cultural Studies* 2 (1): 36–50.

Hwang, Tim, and Adi Kandar. 2013. "The Theory of Peak Advertising and the Future of the Web." PeakAds. http://peakads.org/images/Peak_Ads.pdf.

Jakobsson, Mikael. 2011. "The Achievement Machine." *Game Studies* 11 (1). http://gamestudies .org/1101/articles/jakobsson.

Jarrett, Kylie. 2008a. "Beyond Broadcast Yourself: The Future of YouTube." *Media International Australia* 126 (1): 132–44.

———. 2008b. "Interactivity Is Evil! A Critical Investigation of Web 2.0." *First Monday* 13 (3). http://firstmonday.org/ojs/index.php/fm/article/view/2140/1947.

———. 2009. "Private Talk in the Public Sphere: Podcasting as Broadcast Talk." *Communication, Politics, and Culture* 42 (2): 116–35.

Jefferson, Mychal "Trihex." 2014. "How Does It Actually Feel Beeing [*sic*] an Emoticon on Twitch?" Ask.FM, October 24. https://ask.fm/trihex/answers/119066915888.

Jenkins, Henry. 1992. *Textual Poachers*. New York: Routledge.

———. 2006a. *Convergence Culture*. New York: NYU Press.

———. 2006b. *Fans, Bloggers, and Gamers*. New York: NYU Press.

———. 2009. "What Happened before YouTube." In *YouTube: Online Video and Participatory Culture*, edited by Jean Burgess and Joshua Green, 109–25. Cambridge, UK: Polity.

Jensen, Jens F. 2008. "Interactive Television: A Brief Media History." In *6th European Conference: EuroITV 2008*, edited by Manfred Tscheligi, Marianna Obrist, and Artur Lugmayr, 1–10. Salzburg, Austria, July 3–4.

Jenson, Jen, and Suzanne de Cassell. 2008. "Theorizing Gender and Digital Gameplay." *Eludamos* 2 (1): 15–25.

Jhally, Sut, and Bill Livant. 1986. "Working as Watching: The Valorization of Audience Consciousness." *Journal of Communication* (Summer): 124–43.

Jimroglou, Krissi M. 1999. "A Camera with a View." *Communication and Society* 2 (4): 439–53.

Johnson, Mark, and Jaime Woodcock. 2017. "'It's Like the Gold Rush': The Lives and Careers of Professionally Video Game Streamers on Twitch.tv." *Information, Communication, and Society*. http://eprints.lse.ac.uk/86374/.

Jones, Jeffrey. 2015. "As Industry Grows, Percentage of U.S. Sports Fans Steady." Gallup, June 17. http://www.gallup.com/poll/183689/industry-grows-percentage-sports-fans-steady.aspx.

Joseph, Daniel. 2017. "Distributing Productive Play." PhD diss., Ryerson University.

Kafka, Peter. 2017. "The Head of the NBA Wants His Games to Look More Like Twitch." *Recode*, September 13. https://www.recode.net/2017/9/13/16304278/nba-twitch-adam-silver-tv-ratings-facebook-amazon.

Kane, Mary Jo. 1995. "Resistance/Transformation of the Oppositional Binary: Exposing Sport as a Continuum." *Journal of Sport and Social Issues* 19:191–218.

Karbun, Philipp. 2015. "An Overview of Technical, Financial, and Community Aspects of YouTube Video Production and Gaming Live Streams." Master's thesis, Vienna University of Economics and Business.

Karhulahti, Veli-Matti. 2016. "Prank, Troll, Gross, and Gore: Performance Issues in Esport Live-Streaming." Paper presented at the First International Joint Conference of DiGRA and FDG, Abertay University, Scotland, August 1–6.

Kavoori, Anandam. 2011. *Reading YouTube: The Critical Viewers Guide*. New York: Peter Lang.

Kaytoue, Mehdi, Arlei Silva, Loïc Cern, Wagner Meira Jr., and Chedy Raïssi. 2012. "Watch Me Playing, I Am a Professional: A First Study on Video Game Live Streaming." *WWW 2012 Companion*, 1181–88. Lyon, France, April 16–20.

Kendall, Lori. 2002. *Hanging Out in the Virtual Pub*. Berkeley: University of California Press.

Kennedy, Helen W. 2006. "Illegitimate, Monstrous, and Out There: Female 'Quake' Players and Inappropriate Pleasures." In *Feminism in Popular Culture*, edited by Joanne Hollows and Rachel Moseley, 183–201. Oxford: Berg.

Kline, Stephen, Nick Dyer-Witheford, and Greig de Peuter. 2003. *Digital Play*. Montreal: McGill-Queen's University Press.

Kocurek, Carly. A. 2015. *Coin-Operated Americans*. Minneapolis: University of Minnesota Press.

Koebel, Adam. 2016. "Dire Straights: How LGBT+ Streamers Survive and Thrive." Panel at TwitchCon, San Diego, CA, September 30–October 2.

Kolko, Beth E. 2000. "Erasing @race: Going White in the (Inter)Face." In *Race in Cyberspace*, edited by Beth E. Kolko, Lisa Nakamura, and Gilbert B. Rodman, 213–32. New York: Routledge.

Kollar, Phillip. 2014. "Twitch Audio Copyright Changes Are Terrible, Poorly Implemented, and Absolutely Necessary." Polygon, August 8. http://www.polygon.com/2014/8/8/5982043 /twitch-audio-copyright-necrodancer-changes-shitty-poorly-implemented-necessary -content-id-youtube.

Kosterich, Allie, and Philip M. Napoli. 2016. "Reconfiguring the Audience Commodity: The Institutionalization of Social TV Analytics as Market Information Regime." *Television and New Media* 17 (3): 254–71.

Kreiss, Daniel, Megan Finn, and Fred Turner. 2011. "The Limits of Peer Production: Some Reminders from Max Weber for the Network Society." *New Media and Society* 13 (2): 243–59.

Kreps, David. 2010. "Foucault, Exhibitionism, and Voyeurism on Chatroulette." *Cultural Attitudes towards Communication and Technology Conference*, 207–16. Murdoch University, Australia.

Laskh, Russell. 2011a. "Policy on discussing piracy?" Twitch.tv Support Forum. December.

———. 2011b. "Game Nudity!" Twitch.tv Support Forum. September.

Lange, Patricia. 2007. "The Vulnerable Video Blogger: Promoting Social Change through Intimacy." *Scholar and Feminist Online* 5.2 (Spring). http://sfonline.barnard.edu/blogs /printpla.htm.

———. 2008. "Publicly Private and Privately Public: Social Networking on YouTube." *Journal of Computer-Mediated Communication* 13:361–80.

———. 2010. "Achieving Creative Integrity on YouTube: Reciprocities and Tensions." *Enculturation* 8. http://enculturation.net/achieving-creative-integrity.

Langenscheidt, Leonard. 2017. "How Intellectual Property Rights Are Hurting Esports Teams." *Esports Observer*, February 22. http://esportsobserver.com/how-ip-rights-are-hurting -esports-teams/.

Laqueur, Thomas. *Making Sex: Body and Gender from the Greeks to Freud*. Cambridge, MA: Harvard University Press, 1990.

Lastowka, Gregory F. 2010. *Virtual Justice*. New Haven, CT: Yale University Press.

Lastowka, Gregory F., and Dan Hunter. 2004. "Laws of the Virtual Worlds." *California Law Review* 92 (1): 1–73.

Le, Mike. 2017. "Monetization and Livestreaming: 2015 and 2016." Streamlabs, January 24. https://blog.streamlabs.com/monetization-in-livestreaming-2015-2016-c08835ca2331.

Lembo, Ron. 2000. *Thinking through Television*. Cambridge: Cambridge University Press.

Leslie, Callum. 2015a. "The Biggest Esports Business Moves of 2015." *Daily Dot*, December 16. http://www.dailydot.com/esports/biggest-esports-business-moves-2015/.

———. 2015b. "Meet the Forsen Army, the Vanguard of Twitch's Dark Side." *Daily Dot*, February 11. https://dotesports.com/hearthstone/forsen-army-harassment-twitch-katy-coe-1385.

———. 2016. "The CS:Go Gambling Scandal: Everything You Need to Know." *Daily Dot*, July 26. http://www.dailydot.com/esports/csgo-gambling-scandal-explained/.

Lessig, Lawrence. 1999. *Code Is Law*. New York: Basic Books.

Lin, Kevin. 2012. "TwitchTV Knowledge Bomb No. 1: Advertising." Team Liquid, January 5. http://www.teamliquid.net/forum/starcraft-2/300563-twitchtv-knowledge-bomb-no-1 -advertising.

Lingle, Sam. 2016. "Riot Makes Billions from LOL, but Its President Blames Team Owners for Not Investing More into the Scene." *Daily Dot*, August 23. https://dotesports.com/league-of -legends/reginald-marc-merrill-riot-games-3744.

Lo, Claudia. 2017. "Models of Moderation." Unpublished manuscript.

Longino, Helen E. 1990. *Science as Social Knowledge: Values and Objectivity in Scientific Inquiry.* Princeton, NJ: Princeton University Press.

Lotz, Amanda. 2014. *The Television Will Be Revolutionized.* 2nd ed. New York: NYU Press.

Lowood, Henry. 2011. "Video Capture." *The Machinima Reader*, edited by Henry Lowood and Michael Nitsche, 7–22. Cambridge, MA: MIT Press.

Lowood, Henry, and Michael Nitsche, eds. 2011. *The Machinima Reader.* Cambridge, MA: MIT Press.

MacCallum-Stewart, Esther. 2014. *Online Games, Social Narratives.* New York: Routledge.

"Major League: Gay and Lesbian Internet Users Are Avid Sports Fans." 2013. Nielsen, June 26. http://www.nielsen.com/us/en/insights/news/2013/major-league--gay-and-lesbian-internet-users-are-avid-sports-fan.html.

Mangum, William Gordon. 2016. "DeepStream.tv: Designing Informative and Engaging Live Streaming Video Experiences." Master's thesis, Massachusetts Institute of Technology.

Marcus, George. 1995. "Ethnography in/of the World System." *Annual Review of Anthropology* 24:95–117.

Marwick, Alice. 2013. *Status Update.* New Haven, CT: Yale University Press.

Massanari, Adrienne. 2017. "#Gamergate and the Fappening." *New Media and Society* 19 (3) 329–46.

McCarthy, Anna. 2001. *Ambient Television.* Durham, NC: Duke University Press.

McDaniel, J. P. 2015. "From Private Play to Public Entertainment Panel: Live-streaming and the Growth of Online Broadcast." Panel at the MIT Game Lab, March 5. http://gamelab.mit.edu/event/from-private-play-to-public-entertainment-live-streaming-and-the-growth-of-online-broadcast/."

Meehan, Eileen R. 2005. *Why TV Is Not Our Fault.* Lanham, MD: Rowan and Littlefield.

Mellis, Michael J. 2008. "Internet Piracy of Live Sports Telecasts." *Marquette Sports Law Review* 18 (2): 259–84.

Merrill, Marc. 2015a. "I'm the Admin of SpectateFaker." Reddit, February 21. https://www.reddit.com/r/leagueoflegends/comments/2woxph/im_the_admin_of_spectatefaker_after_reading/cotgdum/.

———. 2015b. "SpectateFaker: What We Learned and What We'll Do." *League of Legends*, February 27. http://na.leagueoflegends.com/en/news/riot-games/announcements/spectatefaker-what-we-learned-and-what-well-do.

Miller, Toby. 2009. "Approach With Caution And Proceed With Care." In *Television Studies After Television*, edited by Graeme Turner and Jinna Tay, 75–82. London: Routledge.

———. 2010. *Television Studies.* London: Routledge.

Mitchell, Ferguson. 2014a. "Dota 2 Is the Richest of the Big Esports, but Its Players Are the Poorest." *Daily Dot*, August 13. http://www.dailydot.com/esports/dota-2-prize-distribution-players/.

———. 2014b. "Twitch Wants to Be Your Moral Police, and That's a Problem." *Daily Dot*, October 30. https://dotesports.com/general/twitch-dress-code-unfair-845.

———. 2015. "Twitch's Harsh Rules of Conduct Are Holding It Back." *Daily Dot*, March 18. https://dotesports.com/esports/twitch-borgore-music-explicit-content/.

Mittell, Jason. 2010. *Television and American Culture.* Oxford: Oxford University Press.

MMAJunkie Staff. 2011. "Ufc Owners File Suit against Justin.Tv for Copyright and Trademark Infringement." January 21. http://mmajunkie.com/2011/01/ufc-owners-file-suit-against-justin-tv-for-copyright-and-trademark-infringement.

Moblord. 2017. "Partner Football." *Streamer News*, August 4. http://streamernews.tv/2017/08/04/partner-football/.

Morley, David. 1992. *Television, Audiences, and Cultural Studies.* London: Routledge.

Mortensen, Torrill. 2006. "WoW Is the New MUD." *Games and Culture* 1 (4): 397–413.

Mulligan, Jessica. 2003. *Developing Online Games*. San Francisco: New Riders.

Murphy, Sheila C. 2011. *How Television Invented New Media*. New Brunswick, NJ: Rutgers University Press.

Murray, Susan, and Laurie Ouellette. 2004. *Reality TV*. New York: NYU Press.

Myers, Maddy. 2014. "Hyper Mode: How to Be Visibly Femme in the Games Industry." *Paste*. March 13. https://www.pastemagazine.com/articles/2014/03/hyper-mode-gdc-fashion.html.

Myerscough, Kaelan Clare Doyle. 2017. Personal communication.

Nairn, Vince. 2016. "LCS Owners Send Letter to Riot Games about Concerns regarding Relegation, Financial Stability, and Charter Membership." Slingshot, November 12. https:// slingshotesports.com/2016/11/12/riot-games-lett-lcs-owners-league-of-legends-concerns -relegation-financial-stability/.

Nakamura, Lisa. 2002. *Cybertypes*. New York: Routledge.

———. 2009. "Don't Hate the Player, Hate the Game." *Critical Studies in Media Communication* 26 (2): 128–44.

Nakandala, Supun, Giovanni Luca Ciampaglia, Norman Makoto Su, and Yong-Yeol Ahn. 2016. "Gendered Conversation in a Social Game-Streaming Platform." Unpublished manuscript. https://arxiv.org/abs/1611.06459.

Nardi, Bonnie. 2010. *My Life as a Night Elf Priest*. Ann Arbor: University of Michigan Press.

Neff, Gina. 2012. *Venture Labor*. Cambridge, MA: MIT Press.

Newbury, Elizabeth. 2017. "The Case of Competitive Video Gaming and Its Fandom." PhD diss., Cornell University.

Newman, James. 2002. "In Search of the Videogame Player." *New Media and Society* 2 (3): 405–22.

Nissenbaum, Helen. 2010. *Privacy in Context*. Stanford, CA: Stanford Law Books.

Nixon, Sarah. 2015. "The Female Streamers Dilemma." Not Your Mama's Gamer, April 26. http:// www.nymgamer.com/?p=7965.

Nixon, Sean, and Paul du Gay. 2002. "Who Needs Cultural Intermediaries?" *Cultural Studies* 16 (4): 495–500.

OGNCasters. 2016. "MSI." Nexus, March 23. https://nexus.vert.gg/msi-30f7f6cdd946.

Organization for Transformative Works. 2013. "Fandom Is Love: OTW April Membership Drive." http://transformativeworks.tumblr.com/post/47040420151/fandom-is-love-otw -april-membership-drive.

———. 2015. "F.A.Q." November 30. http://transformativeworks.org/faq#t456n22.

Orland, Kyle. 2016. "Twitch Rolls out Automated Tool to Stem Wave of Chat Harassment." *Ars Technica*, December 12. http://arstechnica.com/gaming/2016/12/twitch-rolls-out -automated-tool-to-stem-wave-of-chat-harassment/.

Otten, Martin. 2001. "Broadcasting Virtual Games in the Internet." Unpublished manuscript.

Parker, Trey. 2016. "Felix Kjellberg (a.k.a. PewDiePie)." *Time*. http://time.com/4302406/felix -kjellberg-pewdiepie-2016-time-100/.

Parkin, Simon. 2014. "Zoe Quinn's Depression Quest." *New Yorker*, September 9. http://www .newyorker.com/tech/elements/zoe-quinns-depression-quest.

Parks, Lisa. 2004. "Flexible Microcasting: Gender, Generation, and Television-Internet Convergence." In *Television after TV*, edited by Lynn Spiegel and Jan Olsson, 133–56. Durham, NC: Duke University Press.

Partin, William. 2017. "Greed Is Good! Political Economy of Crowdfunding in DoTA 2." *Medium*, August 20. https://medium.com/@willpartin/greed-is-good-political-economy-of -crowdfunding-in-dota-2-7cecdfe78343.

Pearce, Celia. 2009. *Communities of Play*. Cambridge, MA: MIT Press.

Pellicone, Anthony, and June Ahn. 2017. "The Game of Performing Play." Paper presented at CHI 2017, Denver, CO, May 6–11.

Phillips, Jevon. 2017. "'Critical Role' and 'Harmonquest' Prove Watching Role-Playing Games Can Be Fun, but 4 Hours?" *Los Angeles Times*, February 22. http://www.latimes.com/entertainment/tv/la-et-st-role-playing-online-games-20170222-story.html.

"The Playboy Interview: Roone Arledge." 1976. *Playboy*, October, 63–86.

Postigo, Hector. 2003. "From Pong to Planet Quake: Post-Industrial Transitions from Leisure to Work." *Information, Communication, and Society* 6 (4): 593–607.

———. 2012. *The Digital Rights Movement: The Role of Technology in Subverting Digital Copyright*. Cambridge, MA: MIT Press.

———. 2014. "The Socio-Technical Architecture of Digital Labor: Converting Play into YouTube Money." *New Media and Society* 18 (2): 332–49.

———. 2015. "Playing for Work." In *Media Independence: Working with Freedom or Working for Free*, edited by James Bennett and Niki Strange, 202–22. New York: Routledge.

Rabinow, Paul. 2003. *Anthropos Today: Reflections on Modern Equipment*. Princeton, NJ: Princeton University Press.

Rice, Andrew. 2012. "The Many Pivots of Justin.Tv: How a Livecam Show Became Home to Video Gaming Superstars." Fast Company, June 15. https://www.fastcompany.com/1839300/many-pivots-justintv-how-livecam-show-became-home-video-gaming-superstars.

Roettgers, Jako. 2009. "House Committee Takes on Live-Streaming Piracy." Gigaom, December 15. https://gigaom.com/2009/12/15/house-committee-takes-on-live-streaming-piracy/.

Ruberg, Bonnie. Forthcoming. *Playing Queer*. New York: NYU Press.

Salen, Katie, and Eric Zimmerman. 2003. *Rules of Play: Game Design Fundamentals*. Cambridge, MA: MIT Press.

Sandvig, Christian. 2015. "The Internet as the Anti-Television." In *Signal Traffic*, edited by Lisa Parks and Nicole Starosielski, 225–45. Urbana: University of Illinois Press.

Sattler, Michael. 1995. *Internet TV with CU-SeeMe*. Indianapolis: Sams Publishing.

Sauter, Molly. 2014. *The Coming Swarm*. New York: Bloomsbury.

Schiefer, Johannes. 2015. "Modern Times Group to Make Major Investment in ESL." *ESL-Gaming*, January 7. https://www.eslgaming.com/article/modern-times-group-make-major-investment-esl-2121.

Scott, Mark. 2015. "Study of Ad-Blocking Software Suggests Wide Use." *New York Times*, August 10. http://bits.blogs.nytimes.com/2015/08/10/study-of-ad-blocking-software-suggests-wide-use/?_r=0.

Scully-Blaker, Rainforest, Jason Begy, Mia Consalvo, and Sarah Ganzon. 2017. "Playing along and Playing for on Twitch." *Proceedings of the 50th Hawaii International Conference on Systems Sciences*, Kona, January 4–7.

Seibel, Michael. 2009. "Testimony for the Hearing on 'Piracy of Live Sports Broadcasting over the Internet.'" Committee on the Judiciary, US House of Representatives, December 16.

Seigworth, Greg, and Melissa Gregg. 2010. *The Affect Theory Reader*. Durham, NC: Duke University Press.

Sell, Jesee. 2015. "E-Sports Broadcasting." Master's thesis, Massachusetts Institute of Technology.

Senft, Theresa M. 2008. *Camgirls: Celebrity and Community in the Age of Social Networks*. New York: Peter Lang.

Shaw, Adrienne. 2014. *Gaming at the Edge*. Minneapolis: University of Minnesota Press.

Shear, Emmett. 2013. "Hi I'm Emmett Shear, Founder and CEO of Twitch, the World's Leading Video Platform and Community for Gamers. Ask Me Anything!" Reddit, May 23. https://www.reddit.com/r/IAmA/comments/1exa2k/hi_im_emmett_shear_founder_and_ceo_of_twitch_the/.

Sherr, Ian. 2014. "Xbox Endorsements on YouTube Cause Flap." *Wall Street Journal*, January 21. http://blogs.wsj.com/digits/2014/01/21/xbox-endorsements-on-youtube-cause-flap/.

Shimpach, Shawn. 2005. "Working Watching: The Creative and Cultural Labor of the Media Audience." *Social Semiotics* 15 (3): 343–60.

Silbey, Jessica. 2015. *The Eureka Myth*. Palo Alto, CA: Stanford University Press.

Silverstone, Roger. 1994. *Television and Everyday Life*. London: Routledge.

Sjöblom, Max, and Juho Hamari. 2016. "Why Do People Watch Others Play Video Games? An Empirical Study of the Motivations of Twitch Users." *Computers in Human Behavior* 75:985–96.

Sjöblom, Max, Maria Törhönen, Juho Hamari, and Joseph Macey. 2017. Content Structure Is King." *Computers in Human Behavior* 73:161–71.

SK Telecom T1. 2015. "Notice." Facebook, February 23. https://www.facebook.com/SKsports.T1/posts/1618205308413628.

Smith, Thomas P. B., Marianna Obrist, and Peter Wright. 2013. "Live-Streaming Changes the (Video) Game." *EuroITV'13*, 131–38. Como, Italy, June 24–26.

Snickars, Pelle, and Patrick Vonderau, eds. 2009. *The YouTube Reader*. Stockholm: National Library of Sweden.

Sotamaa, Olli. 2007a. "Let Me Take You to the Movies: Productive Players, Commodification, and Transformative Play." *Convergence* 13 (4): 383–401.

———. 2007b. "On Modder Labour, Commodification of Play, and Mod Competitions." *First Monday* 12 (9). http://firstmonday.org/article/view/2006/1881.

Spangler, Todd. 2015. "Turner, WME/IMG Form E-Sports League, with TBS to Air Live Events." *Variety*, September 23. http://variety.com/2015/tv/news/turner-wme-img-esports-league-tbs-1201600921/.

Spigel, Lynn. 1992. *Make Room For TV*. Chicago: University of Chicago Press.

Spigel, Lynn, and Michael Curtin. 1997. *The Revolution Wasn't Televised*. New York: Routledge.

Stanford University Libraries. 2015. "Measuring Fair Use: The Four Factors." October 10. http://fairuse.stanford.edu/overview/fair-use/four-factors/.

StarLordLucian. 2015a. "I Was the Dude Running SpectateFaker." Reddit, February 12. https://redd.it/2vmrfs.

———. 2015b. "SpectateFaker Admin Here: Here's My Final Decision regarding the Stream." Reddit, February 23. http://redd.it/2wtetm.

Stebbins, Robert A. 1982. "Serious Leisure: A Conceptual Statement." *Pacific Sociological Review* 25:251–72.

———. 2004. *Between Work and Leisure: The Common Ground of Two Separate Worlds*. New Brunswick, NJ: Transaction Publishers.

Steiner, Dustin. 2016. "EVO Is Giving Their Twitch Cheer Money to the Players." PvP Live, July 15. https://pvplive.net/c/evo-is-giving-their-share-of-cheer-money-to-the-pl.

Steinkeuhler, Constance. 2006. "The Mangle of Play." *Games and Culture* 1 (3): 199–213.

Stenhouse, Henry. 2016. "What It Takes to Be a Counter-Strike: Global Offensive Observer." PC Gamer, February 7. http://www.pcgamer.com/what-it-takes-to-be-a-counter-strike-global-offensive-observer/.

Sterne, Jonathan. 2012. "What If Interactivity Is the New Passivity?" *Flow* (April 9). *https://www.flowjournal.org/2012/04/the-new-passivity/*.

Stevens, Phillips, Jr. 1978. "Play and Work: A False Dichotomy." *Association for the Anthropological Study of Play Newsletter* 5 (2): 17–22.

Stim, Richard. 2016. *Getting Permission: How to License and Clear Copyrighted Materials Online and Off*. 6th ed. Berkeley, CA: Nolo.

Stuart, Tess. 2013. "Rage against the Machinima." *Village Voice*, January 9. http://www.villagevoice.com/news/rage-against-the-machinima-6437191.

Sundén, Jenny. 2003. *Material Virtualities*. New York: Peter Lang.

Szablewicz, Marcella. 2016. "A Realm of Mere Representation? 'Live' E-Sports Spectacles and the Crafting of China's Digital Gaming Image." *Games and Culture* 11 (3): 256–74.

Tarvis, Carol. 1992. *The Mismeasure of Woman*. New York: Simon and Schuster.

Taylor, Nicholas Thiel. 2016. "Now You're Playing with Audience Power." *Critical Studies in Media Communication* 33 (4): 293–307.

Taylor, T. L. 1999. "Life in Virtual Worlds: Plural Existence, Multimodalities, and Other Online Research Challenges." *American Behavioral Scientist* 43 (3): 436–49.

———. 2006a. "Does WoW Change Everything? How a PvP Server, Multinational Playerbase, and Surveillance Mod Scene Caused Me Pause." *Games and Culture* 1 (4): 1–20.

———. 2006b. *Play between Worlds: Exploring Online Game Culture*. Cambridge, MA: MIT Press.

———. 2008. "Becoming a Player: Networks, Structures, and Imagined Futures." In *Beyond Barbie and Mortal Kombat: New Perspectives on Gender and Gaming*, edited by Yasmin Kafai, Carrie Heeter, Jill Denner, and Jennifer Y. Sun, 50–65. Cambridge, MA: MIT Press.

———. 2009. "The Assemblage of Play." *Games and Culture* 4 (4): 331–39.

———. 2012. *Raising the Stakes: E-Sports and the Professionalization of Computer Gaming*. Cambridge, MA: MIT Press.

Taylor, T. L., and Emma Witkowski. 2010. "This Is How We Play It: What a Mega-LAN Can Teach Us about Games." *Foundations of Digital Games Conference Proceedings*, Monterey, CA, June 19–21.

Terranova, Tiziana. 2000. "Free Labor: Producing Culture for the Digital Economy." *Social Text* 18 (2): 33–58.

TitleIX.info. 2016. "History of Title IX." http://titleix.info/History/History-Overview.aspx.

Thomas, Luke. 2012. "Justin.Tv Wins Partials Dismissal of UFC Lawsuit, Case Still Ongoing." MMAFighting, March 22. http://www.mmafighting.com/news/2012/3/22/2891833/justin-tv-dismissal-zuffa-ufc-lawsuit-trademark-copyright-mma-news.

Thompson, Derek. 2014. "Which Sports Have the Whitest/Richest/Oldest Fans?" *Atlantic*, February 10. https://www.theatlantic.com/business/archive/2014/02/which-sports-have-the-whitest-richest-oldest-fans/283626/.

———. 2015. "The Economy Is Still Terrible for Young People." *Atlantic*, May 19. https://www.theatlantic.com/business/archive/2015/05/the-new-normal-for-young-workers/393560/.

Toal, Drew. 2012. "The TV Show Will Fire Back!" Gameological Society. http://gameological.com/2012/04/the-tv-show-will-fire-back/.

Toner, Ruth. 2017. "Toxicity and Moderation." Paper presented at the Game UX Summit, Toronto, ON, October 4–6.

Turkle, Sherry. 1995. *Life on the Screen*. New York: Simon and Schuster.

Turkle, Sherry, and Seymour Papert. 1990. "Epistemological Pluralism." *Signs* 16 (1): 128–57.

Turner, Graeme. 2009. "Television and the Nation." In *Television Studies after TV*, edited by Graeme Turner and Jinna Tay, 54–64. London: Routledge.

———. 2010. *Ordinary People and the Media*. Los Angeles: Sage.

———. 2011. "Surrendering the Space." *Cultural Studies* 25 (4–5): 685–99.

Turner, Graeme, and Jinna Tay, eds. 2009. *Television Studies after TV*. London: Routledge.

Turow, Joseph. 2011. *The Daily You*. New Haven, CT: Yale University Press.

Tushnet, Rebecca. 2008. "User-Generated Discontent: Transformation in Progress." Georgetown University Law Center Working Paper. http://scholarship.law.georgetown.edu/fwps_papers/66.

———. 2010. "I Put You There: User-Generated Content and Anticircumvention." *Vanderbilt Journal of Entertainment and Technology Law* 12 (4): 889–946.

———. 2013. "Performance Anxiety." *Journal of the Copyright Society of the U.S.A.* 60:209–48.

TWC Editor. 2009. "Diane E. Levin: Child's Play as Transformative Work." *Transformative Works and Cultures* 2. http://journal.transformativeworks.org/index.php/twc/article/view/105/80.

Twitch. 2014. "Twitch Rules of Content." October 27. http://help.twitch.tv/customer/portal/articles/983016-twitch-rules-of-conduct.

———. 2016a. "How to Use AutoMod." December 12. https://help.twitch.tv/customer/portal/articles/2662186-how-to-use-automod.

———. 2016b. "Introducing SureStream." November 2. https://blog.twitch.tv/introducing-surestream-for-a-better-video-ad-experience-on-twitch-3ca5ce3287c.

———. 2016c. "Seasonal Trends in Advertising and Revenue." June 1. https://help.twitch.tv/customer/portal/articles/880219-seasonal-trends-in-advertising-and-revenue.

———. 2016d. "Twitch and Third-Party Terms of Service and User Agreements." July 13. https://blog.twitch.tv/twitch-and-third-party-terms-of-service-and-user-agreements-b9827599e0fc#.9qbdvv2tg.

———. 2017a. "IRL FAQ." January 18. https://help.twitch.tv/customer/portal/articles/2672652-irl-faq.

———. 2017b. "Twitch Overview." Unpublished, personal communication.

———. 2017c. "TwitchCon 2017 Keynote Celebrates Creators, Announces Upcoming Features, and Shares Latest Milestones." *Business Wire*, October 20. http://www.businesswire.com/news/home/20171020005247/en/TwitchCon-2017-Keynote-Celebrates-Creators-Announces-Upcoming.

———. 2018. "Extensions Guide." https://dev.twitch.tv/docs/extensions/guide/.

UFC. 2011. "Zuffa Files Suit against Justin.tv." January 21. http://www.ufc.com/news/zuffa-sues-justin-tv-copyright-infringement?id=.

Uricchio, William. 2004. "Televisions's Next Generation." In *Television after TV: Essays on a Medium in Transition*, edited by Lynn Spigel and Jan Olsson, 163–82. Durham, NC: Duke University Press.

———. 2008. "Television's First Seventy-Five Years: The Interpretive Flexibility of a Medium in Transition." In *The Oxford Handbook of Film and Media Studies*, edited by Robert Kolker, 286–305. Oxford: Oxford University Press.

Uszkoreit, Lena. Forthcoming. "Girl Playing <3: Video Game Live Streaming and the Perception of Female Online Gamers." Unpublished manuscript.

Vee, Ryoga, Chinemere Iwuanyanwu, D'Juan Irvin, and Terrance Miller. 2016. "Diversify Twitch." Panel at TwitchCon, San Diego, CA, September 30–October 2.

Walker, Austin. 2014. "Watching Us Play: Postures and Platforms of Live Streaming." *Surveillance and Society* 12 (3): 437–42.

Wang, Jing. 2015. "TV, Digital, and Social: A Debate." *Media Industries Journal* 1 (3). http://quod.lib.umich.edu/m/mij/15031809.0001.311?view=text;rgn=main.

Weber, Max. 1949. *The Methodology of the Social Sciences*. Translated and edited by Edward A. Shils and Henry A Finch. New York: Free Press.

Weber, Rachel. 2015. "Twitch Appoints VP of Game Developer Success." Gamesindustry.biz, November 16. https://www.gamesindustry.biz/articles/2015-11-16-twitch-appoints-vp-of-game-developer-success.

Wenner, Lawrence, ed. 1998. *MediaSport*. London: Routledge.

Westen, Burns H., and David Bollier. 2013. "The Importance of Vernacular Law in Solving Ecological Problems." CSWire Talkback, December 13. http://www.csrwire.com/blog/posts/1147-the-importance-of-vernacular-law-in-solving-ecological-problems.

White, Michelle. 2006. *The Body and the Screen*. Cambridge, MA: MIT Press.

Wilson, Sherryl. 2016. "In the Living Room: Second Screens and TV Audiences." *Television and New Media* 17 (2): 174–91.

Wirman, Hanna. 2009. "On Productivity and Game Fandom." *Transformative Works and Cultures* 3. http://journal.transformativeworks.org/index.php/twc/article/view/145/115.

Witkowski, Emma. Forthcoming. "Doing/Undoing Gender with the Girl Gamer in High Performance Play."

"Workshop #1 White Paper: Women in Esports." 2015. AnyKey. http://www.anykey.org/wp-content/uploads/AnyKey_Workshop_1-White_Paper-20October2015.pdf.

Yang, Robert. 2015. "On My Games Being Twice Banned by Twitch." September 24. https://www.blog.radiator.debacle.us/2015/09/on-my-games-being-twice-banned-by-twitch.html.

Yang, Robert. 2016. "Why I Am One of the Most Banned Developers on Twitch." Polygon, July 14. https://www.polygon.com/2016/7/14/12187898/banned-on-twitch.

Yee, Nick. 2008. "Maps of Digital Desires: Exploring the Topography of Gender and Play in Online Games." In *Beyond Barbie and Mortal Kombat: New Perspectives on Gender and Gaming*, edited by Yasmin Kafai, Carrie Heeter, Jill Denner, and Jennifer Y. Sun, 83–96. Cambridge, MA: MIT Press.

YouTube. 2013. "Content ID." http://www.youtube.com/t/contentid.

———. 2017. "Statistics." https://www.youtube.com/yt/press/en-GB/statistics.html.

Zuckerman, Ethan. 2014. "The Internet's Original Sin." *Atlantic*, August 14. https://www.theatlantic.com/technology/archive/2014/08/advertising-is-the-internets-original-sin/376041/.

INDEX

Aarseth, Espen, 274n23
advertising (and ad revenue), 10, 116–19.
  See also under home studio broadcasters;
  Twitch
Aereo, 266n35
affect theory, 86, 267n11
Ahmed, Sara, 89, 269n24
Albrecht, Matt, 232–33
Alejandre, Christina, 205
Amazon.com, 4, 25, 38, 60, 119, 120, 142,
  179, 225, 253; Mechanical Turk program,
  125
Andrejevic, Mark, 190
AnneMunition, 91–92, 107–8, 109–10, 113–14
AnyKey Organization, 16, 172, 252, 264n19
Aoki, Steve, 64, 125
API (application programming interface),
  60, 130, 179
arcades, 4, 37, 145, 271n8
Arledge, Roone, 152, 169, 208
Astromoff, Kathy, 60–61
audiences. *See* networked audience;
  spectatorship
AutoMod, 224–26
avatars, 103, 229
Azubu, 212–16, 273n45

Bain, John "Total Biscuit," 270n37
BAMTech, 177, 216
Banks, John, 243
Baranowsky, Danny, 249
Baym, Nancy, 89–90, 133, 135, 189
Bell, Art, 270n5
Bertino, Phil "inFeZa," 165
Blackmon, Samantha, 108–9
Blizzard, 3, 177, 180–81, 199–200, 206–7,
  209
BlizzCon, 178, 180–81
Bollier, David, 246
Bornstein, Steve, 206–7
"boundary objects," 15

Bowker, Geoffrey, 15
Bratich, Jack, 46
Breslau, Rod "Slasher," 180
British Premier League, 56
Brock, Tom, 260–61
Bruns, Axel, 33, 55
Burgess, Jean, 33–34, 245, 258, 265n9,
  274n24
Burks, Mike, 139
Burroughs, Benjamin, 55–56

Caillois, Roger, 260–61
Call of Duty, 201–2, 206, 210
cam culture, 29–32, 53; "cam girls," 31;
  "social cam" websites, 3
Campbell, Colin, 172
Cassell, Thomas "Syndicate," 129, 270n41
Chaloner, Paul "Redeye," 139, 148–49,
  166–67
Chamberlain, David, 267n3
Championship Gaming Series (CGS),
  139–40
Champions League, 209
Champlin, Alexander, 222
chat windows, 1, 6, 15, 42–44, 67–68, 75, 81,
  88–90, 141, 144, 266n24; bots and, 223;
  "crowdspeak" in, 42; in esports, 171–75;
  moderators and, 219–20
Citron, Danielle, 171
Cohen, Julie, 239
ComicCon, 137–39
community management, 20, 21, 62, 69, 94,
  115, 173–75, 218–27
Conti, Olivia, 246
Coombs, Rosemary, 246
cosplay, 6, 48, 64, 137, 217, 231
Counter-Strike Go (*CSGO*), 128–29, 170, 180,
  205, 206, 210–11
Critical Role, 255
Crittenden, Spencer, 254–55
CU-SeeMe, 29–31

A NOTE ON THE TYPE

This book has been composed in Adobe Text and Gotham.
Adobe Text, designed by Robert Slimbach for Adobe,
bridges the gap between fifteenth- and sixteenth-century
calligraphic and eighteenth-century Modern styles.
Gotham, inspired by New York street signs, was designed
by Tobias Frere-Jones for Hoefler & Co.